THE PSYCHOLOGY OF ECONOMIC DECISIONS

Centre for Economic Policy Research

The Centre for Economic Policy Research is a network of over 530 Research Fellows and Affiliates, based primarily in European universities. The Centre coordinates the research activities of its Fellows and Affiliates and communicates the results to the public and private sectors. CEPR is an entrepreneur, developing research initiatives with the producers, consumers, and sponsors of research. Established in 1983, CEPR is a European economics research organization with uniquely wide-ranging scope and activities.

CEPR is a registered educational charity. Institutional (core) finance for the Centre is provided by major grants from the Economic and Social Research Council, under which an ESRC Resource Centre operates within CEPR; the Esmée Fairbairn Charitable Trust; and the Bank of England. The Centre is also supported by the European Central Bank; the Bank for International Settlements; 22 national central banks; and 45 companies. None of these organizations gives prior review to the Centre's publications, nor do they necessarily endorse the views expressed therein.

The Centre is pluralist and non-partisan, bringing economic research to bear on the analysis of medium- and long-run policy questions. CEPR research may include views on policy, but the Executive Committee of the Centre does not give prior review to its publications, and the Centre takes no institutional policy positions. The opinions expressed in this report are those of the authors and not those of the Centre for Economic Policy Research.

Centre for Economic Policy Research
90–98 Goswell Road
London EC1V 7RR
UK

Tel: (44 20) 7878 2900   Fax: (44 20) 7878 2999
Email: cepr@cepr.org   Website: www.cepr.org

The Psychology of Economic Decisions

VOLUME I

RATIONALITY AND WELL-BEING

Edited by
ISABELLE BROCAS
and
JUAN D. CARRILLO

OXFORD
UNIVERSITY PRESS

*This book has been printed digitally and produced in a standard specification
in order to ensure its continuing availability*

OXFORD
UNIVERSITY PRESS

Great Clarendon Street, Oxford OX2 6DP

Oxford University Press is a department of the University of Oxford.
It furthers the University's objective of excellence in research, scholarship,
and education by publishing worldwide in

Oxford New York

Auckland   Cape Town Dar es Salaam Hong Kong Karachi
Kuala Lumpur Madrid Melbourne Mexico City Nairobi
New Delhi Shanghai Taipei Toronto
With offices in
Argentina Austria Brazil Chile Czech Republic France Greece
Guatemala Hungary Italy Japan South Korea Poland Portugal
Singapore Switzerland Thailand Turkey Ukraine Vietnam

Oxford is a registered trade mark of Oxford University Press
in the UK and in certain other countries

Published in the United States
by Oxford University Press Inc., New York

© CEPR 2003, excepting contributions by Kahneman and Hilton

The moral rights of the author have been asserted

Database right Oxford University Press (maker)

Reprinted 2008

ISBN 978-0-19-925108-7

To my parents

I. B.

To my father

J. D. C.

Acknowledgement

The papers in this volume were presented at a CEPR/ECARES conference on Psychology and Economics, held in Brussels on June 8th–10th 2001, and organized as part of CEPR'S Public Policy research programme. We gratefully acknowledge financial assistance for this meeting from the European Commission through its Euroconference programme (contract number HPCF-CT-1999-00175).

Contents

Contents

List of Figures

List of Tables

Introduction

ISABELLE BROCAS AND JUAN D. CARRILLO

The main reason for organizing a conference and editing a book that collects the views of both psychologists and behavioral economists is our intimate conviction that researchers in these two fields can and must work together. First, they can work together because both want to address the same kind of issues. Highlighting the connections between the different contributions is fairly easy, and part of this introduction is devoted to this task. The links are not exhaustive. Instead, it is just an indication of this potential for cooperation. Second, they must work together because, also as witnessed by the contributions in this book, similar questions are tackled from very different angles. There is indeed a strong complementarity between the two approaches that needs to be exploited, and cooperation seems the natural way to achieve this.

If the benefits of collaboration are so prominent, why do we observe some reluctance from both sides to join forces? In our opinion, the researchers are worried about the tools and methodologies employed in the other field. Naturally, there is no full agreement within each field, but still it is a mainstream view. Sometimes these concerns are well grounded, sometimes they are due to the development of research habits and the idea that a different perspective is necessarily less adequate. In any case, they constitute an important obstacle for debates and interactions. We would like to list a (incomplete) series of concerns that researchers in each field have for the practices of their counterparts. These have been gathered through informal discussions, mainly during the conference in which the papers collected in this book were presented. Obviously, the objections that can be made to any overgeneralization apply to our exercise. The reader should view this outline merely as an indication of some general attitudes and worries. Besides, the absence of input from a psychologist in writing this introduction increases the likelihood that we may have misinterpreted some arguments.[1]

One of the main concerns of some psychologists when looking at the behavioral Economics literature is what they consider an excessive degree of formalism. It is true that a certain amount of mathematical training is often necessary in order to understand theoretical contributions (and this may need some investment). However, the economists would argue that mathematical formulations are used exclusively as a communication language, whose advantages are clarity and precision. Second, the psychologists are also quite skeptical about the

---

[1] Needless to say that they also represent general views, which are not shared by every single researcher in the field.

'as if' approach of Economics where, provided that the models explain the facts, it does not matter whether the axioms are an accurate representation of the intrinsic features of individuals. The economists would claim that human decision-making is, for sure, governed by processes of a different nature than the underlying processes defined by economic models. However, this does not imply that the latter are not a good and dual representation of the former. Third, the economists are also criticized for their excessively simplistic view of the world and, in particular, of human nature. Obviously, the models are just caricatures of reality so, by definition, they only capture a tiny aspect of it. A blind belief in the prescriptions of a model is just as absurd as a straight rejection of its conclusions based on their simplicity. Fourth, there has been a tradition in Economics to believe that individual deviations from the standard rational behavior do not deserve special attention, because the market forces alone will eventually correct these mistakes and/or displace these agents. Although this view is now challenged within the field, it has contributed to raise the suspicion of the psychologists about the economists' approach to human behavior.

How about the general concerns of economists about the practices in Psychology? Probably, the main criticism is the absence of a general framework in which all the contributions can be embodied. The economists like to think of papers as the pieces of a grand puzzle, which is in continuous construction, evolution, and even destruction. Furthermore, this general framework is supposed to provide a benchmark for comparison and a reference to be challenged by new theories and hypotheses. Naturally, a general approach to human behavior requires important simplifications and therefore goes against the desire of psychologists to provide an exhaustive treatment of every specific situation (see the third concern expressed above). For this reason, the psychology literature is more prone to adopt a case by case approach. Overall, there is an obvious tradeoff between accuracy and the generality of explanations. Another concern (which in fact is the opposite of the fourth issue raised in the previous paragraph) is the tendency in Psychology to extrapolate individual anomalies to the aggregate level. The economists argue that, even if deviants survive when the whole economy is taken into account, they are nevertheless likely to play a less important role. Naturally, the importance of this issue depends on whether the goal is to explain an anomaly or to quantify its consequences.

The absence of a unified vocabulary is another obstacle to inter-field debates, although this is probably somewhat easier to surpass. Notions like 'rationality', 'utility', 'preferences', 'emotion', 'cognition', 'esteem', etc. have different connotations for different people and this may result in severe misunderstandings. Ideally, in order to obtain a fruitful collaboration, people should share the way of formalizing problems. If this cannot be achieved, there should at least be a common language to define them.

Where do we go next? As Caplin and Leahy point out, the most productive alliances lie where strength meets strength. Probably, the main comparative advantage of the psychologists is their deep understanding of the behaviors, feelings, and motivations of individuals, together with some well-developed experimental skills to test the competing hypothesis about human nature. The economists excel at developing normative frameworks, which can be used as a benchmark to conduct welfare analyses and obtain policy implications. By joining forces in this way, Economics and Psychology could confront the two major objections that each field has encountered separately. These are, respectively, an unrealistic degree of sophistication or rationality of individuals, and a lack of prescriptions to improve future behavior and increase welfare.

We will now present a synopsis of each contribution, placing a special emphasis on the links between the different papers, both in terms of the issues addressed and the methodologies employed. We hope that it will serve as a guide for readers interested in specific topics, but also that it will trigger their curiosity for other questions. However, first we would like to say a few words about the issues of rationality and irrationality. Probably, one of the most controversial debates concerning human behavior is to determine whether individuals maximize their expected utility or if they sometimes pursue self-defeating goals. In other words, how rational humans are. The fact that almost all the papers in this volume treat this problem, in one way or another, is a clear symptom of its importance. Nevertheless, the objective of this book is not to provide a straight answer to this question. Instead, each paper suggests some resolved or unresolved puzzles that should encourage further thinking.

I. THE CAUSES AND CONSEQUENCES OF 'IRRATIONAL' CONDUCTS

Since understanding the rationality or irrationality of choices is at the heart of the debates between social psychologists and behavioral economists, it seems natural to start this book with the contributions that address most directly this question. We might wonder whether it is important to know if a specific conduct can be termed as rational or not. Although each author has his own views about rationality, one can deduce from the papers that they are not so much concerned with the label itself. In fact, this issue is very much left to the reader's judgment, and we sympathize with this attitude. What really interests the authors are the reasons and repercussions of any kind of self-defeating behavior. The three approaches to this question collected in the book are introduced in the next paragraphs.

According to Baumeister (Chapter 1), three main reasons may push individuals to undertake self-defeating activities: deliberate self-harm, harmful decisions as an inevitable by-product of some beneficial actions (and whose cost outweighs the benefits), and choices directed to obtain benefits but undertaken in a way that they produce the opposite effect. The author argues the existence of evidence only for the last two types of self-defeating behavior, and explores some theories to explain the circumstances under which people make such irrational choices. First, under emotional distress individuals are both less able to correctly evaluate the consequences of their choices, and less likely to think carefully about the relative advantages of the different alternatives. This provides a rationale for the typical 'think twice before you act' maxim. Second, social considerations are also a cause of self-defeating actions. People with high self-esteem are concerned with the impressions made on others. When their ego is threatened, they are likely to make foolish choices. Similarly, feeling rejected partly inhibits the willingness to take care of oneself.[2] Last, Baumeister argues that people need some kind of energy in order to think correctly and that, as for any muscle, this resource depletes when it is used. Hence, forcing individuals to address a number of important issues may impair their subsequent ability for self-regulation.

Some theories about the cost of thinking have already emphasized the idea that humans cannot always evaluate all the alternatives before making their choices (see also the framing problem in Chapter 9). Baumeister takes a further step by arguing that the cost of thinking for each decision increases, as more and more choices have to be made. Moreover, if thinking refers to past events, this also provides support for the optimality of memory management, a theory that is carefully analyzed in Chapter 8. Pursuing this concept of self-regulation capacity as a muscle or form of energy, one may argue that the aptitude for self-regulation can be developed through its exercise. Therefore, if this conjecture is correct, self-regulation would then be costly in the short term but highly beneficial in the long term. We would also like to mention the striking ability of Baumeister (and, in fact, of all the authors in the experimental contributions of this book) to alter the moods and emotions of subjects for the purpose of their experiments, without raising suspicion.[3] For economic theorists like us, noting this capacity to create affective conditions is extremely reassuring.

Probably the most special contribution from the point of view of the economists and the behavioral psychologists is the paper by Berridge (Chapter 2), which looks at rationality from the perspective of a neuroscientist. The author starts with a specific definition of irrational behavior that builds on the distinction between liking and wanting: a choice is considered irrational if the individual chooses what he does not expect to like (or, equivalently, when the alternative selected is wanted disproportionately to its expectation of being liked).[4] Berridge argues that such a form of irrationality does exist. For example, a series of experiments on consumer behavior shows that the subliminal presentations of happy (resp. angry) faces, even though not consciously perceived, increase (resp. decrease) the rating and willingness to pay for a consumption commodity. The key issue is that the experimental subjects do not experience any change in their affective state. Hence, the decision utility or manifested choice of

---

[2] The key of Baumeister's argument is that choices under emotional shocks or ego threats are different from those under normal circumstances and yield a systematically lower utility.

[3] Chapter 13 deals in great detail with the issue of suspicion in experiments by the psychologists and the economists.

[4] Note the importance of the term 'expectation' since, in a world of uncertainty, it can be perfectly rational to (ex-post) regret and make (ex-ante) an optimal choice.

an individual can be altered by subliminal stimuli without affecting his predicted utility or expected liking for the commodity in the future (see Chapter 10 for a further analysis of the distinction between decision and predicted utility).

A natural issue for an affective neuroscientist is, then, to explore which brain mechanisms underlie aspects of decision and predicted utility. One well-known hypothesis is that the mesolimbic dopamine system mediates pleasure. However, this notion of pleasure refers indistinguishably to what the subject 'wants' and what it 'likes'. If, as Berridge's theory suggests, wanting a reward and liking a reward are two separate things, it may be that different brain systems activate these two psychological processes. This would in turn explain the mechanism behind the irrational conduct of wanting something more than it is expected to be liked. This hypothesis is tested in another set of experiments developed by the author. The main conclusion is that the dopamine activation affects decision utility (how much a reward is wanted) but not predicted utility (how much it is liked).

This theory has important policy implications. It is commonly argued that people consume addictive substances because they underestimate the probability of getting hooked. Once the individual is at this stage, a drug therapy that includes subliminal messages will not affect how drugs are perceived or liked, but it will decrease the incentives to consume them. This, in turn, will diminish the physical addiction component and therefore have long-lasting effects. Another interesting conjecture is that in stressful situations, predicted and decision utilities tend to diverge. Is it because stress also activates different brain systems? Note that this point is related to Baumeister's description of the set of situations in which individuals are likely to undertake self-defeating activities (Chapter 1).

Schooler et al. (Chapter 3) analyze the impact on actual happiness of both monitoring and pursuing happiness. In a first experiment, subjects are asked to listen to music for a period of time. The authors show that checking and reporting the moment-to-moment pleasure derived from the activity decreases its benefit. Similarly, attempting to maximize happiness leads to frustration that undermines the ability to feel the pursued pleasure. The overall conclusion is that monitoring and pursuing happiness are both self-defeating. A second natural experiment focuses on the ex-post assessment of happiness derived from a special event like New Year's Eve 2000. The conclusions are quite consistent with the previous experiment. They suggest that high prospects of a hedonistic experience result in disenchantment. Moreover, the likelihood of feeling disappointed is proportional to the time and effort spent in the preparation of the event.

The paper is in line with previous research about the role of introspection in the ability to derive pleasure. As in this literature, introspection modifies the assessment of a hedonistic experience. Besides, the self-defeating result is quite robust; it holds both for the pursuit and the monitoring of happiness, given a moment-to-moment and an ex-post evaluation of pleasure, and in a natural and a laboratory experimental context.

In our view, the results of the second experiment are far more striking than those of the first one. After all, thinking about one's feelings is costly (see

Chapters 1, 8, and 9 for ideas along this line). It may then be natural that the necessity to constantly provide a report diminishes the individual's capacity to experience pleasure. Instead, in the New Year's Eve case, the fact that only one report is requested implies that, according to the standard rational framework, the assessment should not be systematically modified. Indeed, there is a fundamental difference between reporting the pleasure of a past event (which measures remembered utility) and reporting moment-to-moment pleasure (which measures experienced utility).[5] Similarly, forcing individuals to pursue happiness (as in the first experiment) is also effort consuming, and therefore may decrease the total utility. By contrast, in the second experiment, subjects freely choose their level of investment in the pleasurable activity. Hence, those who decide to incur high costs should not be necessarily more disappointed than the others. This systematic bias in the expectations of hedonistic experiences are closely related to the tendency of individuals to overestimate the likely duration of happiness following a positive event, a result obtained by Wilson, Gilbert, and Centerbar, which is carefully explained in Chapter 11.

II. IMPERFECT SELF-KNOWLEDGE AND THE ROLE OF INFORMATION

The two obvious limitations of the traditional economic analyses of human behavior are the assumptions that individuals have an accurate knowledge of their own preferences and that their utility is not affected by the anticipation of future events. These are clearly unrealistic. For instance, the joy of future parenthood, the stress preceding a serious medical operation, or the tolerance to an addictive substance are not only hard to evaluate before actually experiencing them, they also influence current well-being. But the lack of a precedent is not the only reason for inaccurate self-knowledge. The temporal evolution of preferences and unpredictable changes in mood imply that a repeated exposure to the same situation does not guarantee a convergence to complete self-knowledge and optimal behavior. Furthermore, as argued by Wilson et al. (Chapter 11), individuals are endowed with several self-regulatory mechanisms that systematically bias self-perception and therefore block the learning process. The papers presented in Part II study three different aspects of the strategic value of transmitting information, when either the current utility is affected by the anticipation of future events (Chapter 4) or self-preferences are imperfectly known (Chapters 5 and 6).

Caplin and Leahy (Chapter 4) argue that the anticipation of future events stimulates some emotions such as joy, excitement, fear, stress, apprehension, etc. These sensations have a direct impact on the current utility of individuals. Under these circumstances, obtaining news about the likelihood of future occurrences not only affects future welfare (through the standard effect of acting

---

[5] For the interested reader, Kahneman's contribution (Chapter 10) is fully devoted to this distinction.

under better information) but also current welfare, as uncertainty is a key factor that determines the intensity of the above mentioned emotions. When news is expected to stimulate negative emotions, avoiding information can be profitable.

The authors illustrate the effect of anticipatory feelings with the anxiety provoked by an upcoming surgical procedure. According to several studies reported in their paper, accurate information about the risks of an operation can, other things equal, either increase or decrease the anxiety of patients depending on the nature of the operation and the personality of the patient. Naturally, there are many other less dramatic situations in our everyday life where individuals have a strict preference for either early or late uncertainty resolution: the sex of a child before his/her birth, the weather forecast in the destination for the holidays, the physical aspect of a blind date, etc.

According to this theory, the beliefs of individuals about future events affect their current utility in a similar way to memories of past episodes. However, one important difference is the type of devices employed by individuals to increase their welfare. In the case of anticipatory feelings, Caplin and Leahy (Chapter 4) highlight the importance of information gathering and information avoidance. As we will see in Part III, in the case of bounded memory and imperfect recall, Benabou and Tirole (Chapter 8) and Gilboa and Gilboa-Schechtman (Chapter 7) develop theories centered around the strategic value of memory management and mental accounting, respectively.

Overall, in Caplin and Leahy, beliefs enter the utility function directly via the emotional predisposition. Given that information about the likelihood of future events affects not only future decision-making but also current payoffs, the anticipatory feelings raise the welfare issue of optimal provision of information. For example, should a doctor accurately inform his patient about the dangers of the upcoming operation? If the patient absorbs information at its face value, then the optimal strategy would probably consist of providing only stress-reducing news. However, patients are likely to anticipate the strategic provision of information by the doctor, that is to interpret the absence of evidence as stress-inducing news. Under these circumstances, the doctors might benefit from developing strict rules of behavior. All these welfare effects are important, especially if we take into account that moods also have a direct impact on the post-operation pace of recovery.[6]

Another natural situation where information can be detrimental, is the case of an individual with self-conflicting goals. Brocas and Carrillo (Chapter 5) study the optimal acquisition of information by an agent with imperfect self-knowledge, who discounts events in the near future relatively more heavily than events in the distant future. This type of temporal preference—also known as hyperbolic discounting or present-biased preferences—has recently received a great deal of

---

[6] Note that situations where uncertainty per se affects utility are pervasive. For example, many people declare that they do not enjoy watching a recorded sports game, even if they do not know the final score.

attention (see e.g., the references in Chapters 5 and 8 of this book). Probably, the main reason for the success of hyperbolic discounting is its greater predictive power of individual behavior than traditional time-consistent exponential discounting. Obviously, such discounting is not suitable for every single situation; Trope and Liberman (Chapter 12) for example, develop a radically different theory of time-inconsistent choices.

Under the above mentioned conflict of preferences, Brocas and Carrillo show that an individual may optimally decide to avoid information, even if the news is freely available. As usual, being better informed allows him to improve his current decision-making. However, every piece of information is automatically shared with the future incarnations, who also take better decisions from their future perspective. Because of the intrapersonal conflict, these future optimal choices do not necessarily coincide with the first-best ones from the current viewpoint.[7]

The paper analyzes a wide range of situations in which the individual might be willing to remain strategically ignorant. It provides testable predictions concerning the aggregate effects of rational ignorance on observed behavior. If the activity involves current benefits and negative internalities (i.e. costs on future welfare), the individual will hold pessimistic prospects about the expected payoff of undertaking the activity. By contrast, if the activity yields current costs and positive internalities (i.e. benefits on future welfare) he will remain deliberately optimistic. An illustration of this idea is the case of smoking (a pleasurable activity with negative internalities). The fear of overconsuming cigarettes due to hyperbolic discounting, may induce an agent with negative current beliefs about the effects of tobacco on his health not to collect extra information and quit. Conversely, an individual facing difficult research projects (that require substantial effort but provide positive internalities) will hold positive beliefs on his capacity to succeed in order to avoid inefficient procrastination.

One interesting alley for future research would be to combine the preferences over beliefs motive for information avoidance (Chapter 4) with the intrapersonal conflict motive (Chapter 5). In particular, one may wonder in which direction the inclusion of anticipatory feelings on the incentives of an agent with present-biased preferences to acquire information is likely to have an affect.

The paper by Bodner and Prelec (Chapter 6) also deals with the issue of imperfect self-knowledge. The authors study optimal decision-making by an individual with different levels of conscience. According to their theory, when an individual undertakes an action, he signals his preferences not only to the outside world but also to himself. For example, a dieter unable to resist the temptation of an extra piece of cheese cake reveals to himself a lack of willpower, an individual who starts an extramarital relation draws inferences about the true love for his partner, a night spent in a casino signals to a gambler his propensity to this vice (this last example is studied in detail in the paper), etc.

---

[7] Benabou and Tirole (Chapter 8) include imperfect memory in this same framework. As a result, every piece of information is not necessarily shared.

Naturally, a necessary condition for actions to be a diagnosis of preferences is that the information possessed by the agent when making decisions must be greater than when interpreting the effects of such decisions. In Bodner and Prelec's words: 'the gut knows [...], but the mind does not'. Hence, in this context, the reason for the agent's willingness to manipulate information is not the existence of an intrapersonal conflict of preferences (as in Brocas and Carrillo) but rather the possibility of drawing inferences about oneself from the selected actions.

One of the most important issues of this self-signaling approach is the degree of sophistication (or rationality) of the individual. Does the decision-maker take the action anticipating the diagnostic effects of his choices, that is the impact of the decision on his future self-perception and utility? The first possibility is to assume that the decision-maker only maximizes his utility. Choices are then interpreted at their 'face value' and inferences are just a by-product. One example is the dieter who refrains from having dessert depending on the strength of the temptation, and happily concludes that he possesses a great willpower whenever he succeeds in controlling his desires. A second possibility is to assume that the individual integrates the effects of his actions in the revision of beliefs. Under this approach, the same dieter knows that he might have resisted the temptation, precisely to convince himself that he has a great willpower. Although closer to individual rationality, this alternative is nevertheless paradoxical: how can someone draw a conclusion from an action whose goal is precisely to achieve this inference?

We would like to conclude by mentioning some considerations that could be of interest for further investigation in a self-signaling framework. First, the individual may decide to seek or avoid the type of situations in which the unknown trait is likely to be revealed, depending on the anticipation of his reaction. For example, the willpower of a dieter will be especially threatened at family dinners (this point is addressed by Benabou and Tirole (Chapter 8) in a context of the hyperbolic discounting of future payoffs). Second, the importance of the diagnosis effect of choices is endogenous. The value of learning about self-preferences is given by the likelihood of facing a similar situation in the future, but this probability itself affects the current behavior. Last, two (Bayesian) individuals with the same expected beliefs may exhibit radically different attitudes if these beliefs are drawn from different distributions: an uncompromising individual (who interprets any relapse as evidence of a complete lack of willpower) will adopt a more rigid attitude than a more self-indulgent person. Including some of these possibilities would increase the number of insights that can be gained with this novel approach to human reasoning.

III. IMPERFECT MEMORY AND LIMITED CAPACITY TO PROCESS INFORMATION

We have emphasized in Part II the role played by the anticipation of future feelings and actions on current decision-making. The memories of past events have a mirror image effect on behavior. Surprisingly, except for some notable exceptions, economic analyses have largely neglected the natural tendency to recall imperfectly past information and decisions. One standard reason for not incorporating this human weakness, is to argue that individuals will keep track of past news or behaviors if these are sufficiently important. For most everyday situations, it seems clear that recording activities is not an easy task, as witnessed, for example, by the popularity of complicated electronic memory devices such as the Palm Pilots. The three contributions introduced here study the different aspects of an imperfect ability to analyze information. A distinction is made between imperfect recall (Chapters 7 and 8) and imperfect information processing capacity (Chapter 9).

The starting point of Gilboa and Gilboa-Schechtman (Chapter 7) is the observation that, in some circumstances, individuals take current decisions as if they create a precedent for future conduct. Naturally, under free will, the application of this Kantian's categorical imperative to oneself constitutes a cognitive mistake. The paper argues that an individual with imperfect recall may not be able to remember all the contingencies that led to his past decisions. If this is the case, then a simple rule of behavior expected to be blindly imitated by every future incarnation may in fact be the optimal strategy. The authors illustrate this idea with several examples of such rules: 'buying an expensive sweater only for my birthday', 'taking two glasses of wine only in family dinners', etc. These behaviors allow some extravagant purchases and some indulgence of vices, but they are not dangerous for the financial and health states, respectively.

One should notice that the type of situations analyzed above belong to a broad class of phenomena termed in the psychology literature as 'mental accounting'. According to this theory, any decision can entail a psychological side effect that cannot be ignored by the individual, but which may or may not operate depending on the circumstances (following the previous example, a person might not feel guilty when buying an expensive sweater, if and only if it occurs under an exceptional occasion). Usually, the mental accounting literature takes for granted this psychological reasoning, and limits the attention to analyze its costs and benefits for the individual as well as its effects on decision-making. The strength of the paper by Gilboa and Gilboa-Schechtman is to show that this heuristic 'overgeneralization' conduct may, in fact, be the result of an optimization process under the constraint of imperfect recall.

Although it is a theory based on imperfect memory, one can notice the intimate relation of Chapter 7 with the papers by Bodner and Prelec (Chapter 6) and Brocas and Carrillo (Chapter 5). As in the first one, the individual uses his own actions to convey information to himself (useful because of bounded memory rather than because of an incomplete information with oneself). As in the second one, the individual achieves some self-discipline (through the self-imposed rule rather than through strategic ignorance), which is beneficial for his long-term payoffs. Last, the paper raises a number of puzzling questions that could be the object of further study. Of particular interest would be to investigate the mental processes that determine in which directions the overgeneralization is formed.

Benabou and Tirole (Chapter 8) explore further aspects of imperfect recall. Their theory adds imperfect recall, to three other aspects that are non-standard in traditional economic models. Two of them, imperfect self-knowledge and the hyperbolic discounting of payoffs, have already been discussed. The third one, introduced to account for selective memories, is the ability to influence the probability of remembering past events. However, it is noted that individuals cannot fool themselves, that is, they cannot decide which information is retained and which one is forgotten. The paper reviews a surprisingly rich set of predictions obtained with a combination of these elements.

One particularly interesting result is that individuals may exhibit either over- or under-regulation of their behavior. While deficient self-restraint has been often emphasized as the result of a hyperbolic discounting of future payoffs, these type of preferences have long been criticized for their inability to explain compulsive, excessive self-restraint behavior (like greediness or workaholism). Benabou and Tirole show that such conducts are just 'two sides of the same coin' and that, depending on the initial beliefs about one's capacity to resist temptations, individuals may exhibit one attitude or the other. When memory repression is costly but recall is costless, the authors show that the incentives for memory manipulation are higher the degree of time-inconsistency and the lower the cost of repression. Last, Benabou and Tirole also analyze (in a different context and without issues of imperfect memory) some problems related to social interactions. They consider relations like parents/children and teachers/students. The former have some private information that is important for the decision-making of the latter and may decide whether to offer explicit incentive schemes, to reward performance. The paper argues that, in some circumstances, such schemes may be weak positive reinforcers. Furthermore, such rewards become negative reinforcers once they are withdrawn.

In our view, one of the strengths of the memory management theory developed in the paper is that it endogenizes the individual's level of recall within the traditional Bayesian framework.[8] The authors highlight the fact that the hyperbolic discounting agents are more willing to repress memories than their exponential discounting peers. However, if recall is also costly, the marginal benefits of remembering past episodes is sometimes smaller for the former than for the latter. Overall, our intuition is that predictions about which type of agent is going to exhibit the highest degree of recall will not always go in the same direction. Another important point is that, as the paper argues, affecting the probability of remembering some episodes might not have the expected impact on behavior and welfare. Trying to forget may well be an attempt to escape what cannot be escaped. Psychoanalysts and psychotherapists base their therapies on the fact that individuals never forget important (positive or negative) episodes of life;

---

[8] Obviously, one should not take this approach too literally: individuals do not decide on how much to recall. However, the probability of not forgetting can be increased (memory exercise, written notes, etc.) or decreased (attention management, drinking, etc.).

memories can be repressed in the unconscious, but they still affect behavior. It would be interesting to find some support in the neuroscience literature, for this self-regulatory ability of individuals to affect their capacity to recall events.

More generally, Chapters 7 and 8 raise important questions about how the mind (and specially the memory) works. For instance, our ability to memorize episodes is likely to depend on the episodes themselves. In particular, there is some evidence that each episode of our life is stored in a particular area of our brain where other similar events are also stored, and all are consciously remembered in the same proportion. Is there one kind of memory or many? Where is memory stored? How is memory organized? Are there different kinds of storage processes that serve the maintenance of different types of information in memory? These questions are still open.

Gabaix and Laibson (Chapter 9) offer a different approach to the issue of an imperfect capacity to process information. They argue that, in complex problems, even a superpowerful computer cannot determine the payoff of all the different alternatives. As a result, humans employ some heuristic simplifications of the problems, in order to come as close as possible to the optimal solution. Their goal is, then, to understand which are the main tricks or rules of thumb that lie behind human inferences.

To explore this simplification process, the authors assume that attention and cognition are scarce resources (a point also made in Chapter 1) that have to be allocated as efficiently as possible. Then, they build a model based on the premise that the option of continuing the analysis declines when cognitive analysis yields little new insights, and when one particular choice gains a large edge over the other alternatives.[9] Once these theoretical option value postulates are established, it is possible to determine the optimal choice given this specific simplifying rule to reduce the complexity of the problem. The authors test their model by comparing the realized choices of experimental subjects in complex settings with the predictions of (i) their 'directed cognition' model, (ii) the rational choice model (in which the exact payoff of all the alternatives can be computed), and (iii) some other variants of the rational choice model (in which, for example, all the information in the distant future is disregarded). Interestingly, Gabaix and Laibson's model outperforms the rational choice model and (at least) breaks even with its variants in predicting the behavior of individuals.

This paper can be viewed as a first step towards a better understanding of the heuristics employed by individuals to think both quickly and effectively. Naturally, the next question is to determine how robust is its predictive power, when we introduce some modifications in the problem under scrutiny. For example, in the experiment considered in the paper, subjects choose between several decision trees each of them with different intermediate payoffs, but of the same order of magnitude. One may wonder how the predictive power of the model would be

---

[9] Stated differently, thinking is more valuable when there is a lot of information to be learned, and when there is much more information to be learned in one alternative than in the others.

modified if one alternative were substantially better than the others, but the way to reach it remained uncertain. The authors also argue that a major benefit of understanding which are the most common simplification tricks is that this would help to determine the circumstances where humans are likely to commit systematic judgment errors. Naturally, the prescriptions to avoid such mistakes would then be tremendously helpful. Last, in many cases it is not even possible to determine ex-ante, which are the relevant alternatives, and instead these are discovered when some intermediate decisions are already made. It would be interesting to determine whether a similar type of model would be a good predictor of the agents' behavior in this alternative setting.

IV. TIME AND UTILITY

As we saw in Part II, the temporal dimension can affect the assessment of utility if the individual has anticipatory feelings (Chapter 4) or an intrapersonal conflict of preferences over time (Chapter 5). However, time and utility are connected in many other subtle ways, through the mental representation of future events and memories of past episodes. The papers presented here offer three new theories about these interactions.

Kahneman (Chapter 10) proposes a new way of evaluating the utility of individuals over a period of time that is the starting point for the conception of an objective measure of happiness. The author starts from Bentham's notion of experienced utility (the idea that utility refers to past experiences that in turn determine the optimal future decisions to be made) and extends the concept to an intertemporal setting. He claims that a 'memory-based approach' that depends on a retrospective assessment of the whole experience is often a bad way to assess the individual's overall experienced utility. For example, in the case of a painful experience with a varying intensity, the total remembered utility depends mostly on the highest level of pain and the intensity of pain suffered at the end (the peak/end rule). In particular, duration has only a mild effect in the evaluation of utility. Kahneman argues that, under some conditions, a 'moment-based approach' in which total utility results from summing all the instantaneous moment-utilities is the best measure of the overall experienced utility. Besides, the moment-based approach is also suitable for constructing a measure of objective happiness. This measure has the important advantage over standard subjective well-being criteria that it does not require the individuals to report their memories of past experiences.

The paper raises a number of important questions and policy implications, some of which are partly addressed in his discussion. One issue of interest is to understand the causes and consequences of distorted memories about past utilities. It may be that adverse past experiences have a negative impact on current and future pleasure, so that the distortion is just a self-regulatory mechanism that helps people to overcome such experiences. A consequence is that it induces individuals to repeatedly incur the same mistakes in their decision-making (naturally, from a moment-based point of view !).[10] A second point of interest is to compare the essence of moment-based and memory-based utilities. As Kahneman points out, the present experiences are the only real ones. This suggests that the moment-based approach captures the aggregation of real experiences. On the other hand, what determines our current feelings and moods are the memories of the past and the anticipations of the future. These are best captured with the memory-based approach.

The theory certainly has many possible applications. Consider for instance the following provocative example. The main goal of imprisonment is not to make the convicts suffer but rather to deter them (ex-ante) from committing a crime and (ex-post) to relapse.[11] Applying the previous terminology, the optimal policy is then to maximize the (negative) remembered utility and minimize the (negative) total utility. These two goals can jointly be achieved by inflicting short punishments with an intensive painful peak. Furthermore, a measure like probation, which is basically a soft and prolonged punishment, should be entirely avoided.

We would like to conclude the review of this paper by noting that using the difference between remembered and total utility to design policies, raises serious ethical concerns. In particular, as the author shows, it is fairly easy to manipulate people's decisions by making experiences intensively painful or pleasurable at some points in time. It is also unclear how to propose welfare prescriptions. Indeed, even if they are manipulated the people feel happy—in which case manipulation could be viewed as improving welfare—nevertheless these individuals have their will restricted. Furthermore, it is not clear which utility criterion (total or remembered utility) is the most adequate to measure welfare.

The experienced utility may not only reflect the evaluation of past events but also the beliefs about the evaluation of future events, in which case it is termed as a predicted utility. The objective of the work by Wilson et al. (Chapter 11) is very much related to this notion of predicted utility. The authors study the ability of individuals to forecast their future affective state. The authors show that individuals are quite accurate in predicting the valence and the intensity of their emotional reactions. However, they suffer from a durability bias, that is a systematic overestimation of the duration of their future feelings after an affective shock. This bias occurs independently of whether the emotion is positive (winning a large sum of money in the lottery) or negative (death of a loved person).

Wilson and his colleagues show that the main reason for such an emotional evanescence is a human innate tendency to 'reduce [ex-post] uncertainty about the world by finding meaning in it'. According to this theory, the notion of durability bias is then intimately related to that of hindsight bias, which is the

---

[10] Note also that, in order to address this matter, one should first determine whether such distortions depend on the valence of the experience.

[11] Some people argue that it is also a way of putting them aside in society. We will not discuss this point.

tendency to find ex-post predictable, the realization of an ex-ante uncertain event. In other words, the rationalization of an occurrence decreases its emotional content, because being more predictable also means being less extraordinary.

The paper takes a further step by arguing that emotional evanescence can also be functional. As in the case of food, there is an optimal degree of happiness. In order to maintain the emotional state within some bounds, a self-regulatory mechanism is automatically triggered-off whenever it reaches an excessively low or excessively high level. Last, individuals may increase the permanence of pleasure by inhibiting the process of making novel events that look ordinary. As shown in some experiments reported in the paper, the emotional state of individuals is most durable when they are most uncertain about the reasons for the occurrence of a positive event.

To sum up, this paper explores in detail some reasons for the durability of happiness. It is therefore complementary to the contributions on the pursuit (Chapter 3) and the evaluation (Chapter 10) of happiness. It also raises some questions about the accuracy in the evaluations of future emotional states. One might argue that some individuals deliberately misreport their affective forecasts. This can occur either because of social norms (people would probably doubt my feelings as a parent if I state that life would go on even if my child dies) or as a self-justification of current choices (working excessively to get a particular job is justified only if I think that it is going to change my life afterwards). Last, it would be interesting to explore in more detail the costs of the durability bias. The authors insist on this cost for negative events. However, even for a positive event, overestimating the duration of happiness can also be extremely harmful. For example, an individual may undertake an ex-ante costly investment decision with the anticipation of an immense expected benefit. Such a decision can be foolish if the pleasure ends up being mild.

The paper by Trope and Liberman (Chapter 12) adds a third perspective to the evaluation of events at different points in time, and their effect on utility. The starting point of their 'temporal construal theory' is the idea that the representation of a given activity depends on its temporal distance. In particular, when the distance from a future event is important, its representation is more likely to contain essential features (high-level construals) and less likely to contain superficial features (low-level construals) than when the distance is small. Hence, when the high-level construal of an activity is positive (resp. negative) and its low-level construal is negative (resp. positive), then it is more likely to be desirable than another activity with a neutral high and low construal as the distance for the realization of the activities increases (resp. decreases). One should notice that the most fundamental difference in the traditional theories of time-inconsistent choices (such as the hyperbolic discounting theory presented in Chapters 5 and 8 or the valence theory) is that the temporal construal theory builds on changes over time in the *mental* representation of events, rather than on the mechanical changes in the relative discounting of consecutive periods.

The authors provide several experiments to support their theory. In one of them, some subjects were asked to indicate their interest in performing an interesting main task (i.e. with a high and positive construal) together with a boring filler one (i.e. with a low and negative construal). The other subjects had to indicate their interest in performing a boring main task with an interesting filler one. Not surprisingly, the individuals showed a greater interest for the first combination of tasks than for the second one. More important, the difference in the attractiveness of the two combinations was greater when the subjects were supposed to perform the tasks in the distant future than when they were supposed to perform them in the near future.

Overall, the main prediction of the temporal construal theory is that the distant future choices are mainly influenced by the central, superordinate, abstract (high construal) characteristics, whereas the near future choices are mainly regulated by the peripheral, subordinate, concrete (low construal) features. However, one should realize that the same activity can be *perceived* by the individual as having a high or a low level of construal depending on how it is presented to him, that is it can be manipulated to some extent. This has important implications. For example, working in an organization often implies performing a job that has both an easy, simple paperwork component and a difficult, innovative thinking component. Trope and Liberman's theory predicts that, if the task has to be completed in the near future the employer should motivate the individual to work hard on it by emphasizing ease. In contrast, if it has to be completed in the distant future, then motivation is best achieved by emphasizing its challenging aspect.

V. EXPERIMENTAL PRACTICES IN PSYCHOLOGY, ECONOMICS, AND FINANCE

Performing a controlled experiment is probably one of the most natural and direct ways to improve the understanding of human conduct. The psychologists have known this for a long time. Nowadays, the research papers published in leading behavior Psychology journals, where theories are not supported by some empirical or experimental evidence hardly exist. Surprisingly, this practice is much less common in Economics. Certainly, experimental Economics is a well-developed field, whose relative importance is constantly rising. However, there still exists a significant fraction of researchers (which includes the authors of this introduction) who devote their effort to present new theories (based on intro-spection, casual observation, previous empirical or experimental research, etc.), analyze their implications, and provide some policy prescriptions but do not offer any new test of their arguments. As a well-known behavioral psychologist not familiar with the practices in Economics put it: 'Many economists tell a nice story, provide an elegant model and draw convincing conclusions... but where is the data?' Some people may argue that a basic comparative advantage argument pushes towards specialization in either theory or experiments. However, it is pretty obvious that sometimes the only way to fully understand a problem is by addressing both the issues simultaneously. The papers collected in Part V offer three different perspectives on experiments in Psychology, Economics, and Finance.

Hertwig and Ortmann (Chapter 13) compare the experimental practices in behavioral Economics and behavioral Psychology. They argue the existence of four main differences in the design of experiments. First, the economists provide a precise set of actions among which the subjects of the experiment have to choose; the psychologists often do not. Second, the economists systematically repeat experimental trials; the psychologists do not. Third, the economists almost invariably provide monetary incentives based on performance; the psychologists do not. Last, the economists rarely deceive the participants in their experiments; the psychologists often do.

Their analysis focuses on the last two issues. It shows that, performance-based rewards are often important for inducing participants to incur the cognitive effort necessary to avoid errors in judgment. In other words, under monetary incentives, the behavior of individuals is closer to the predictions of normative models and the variability of data is reduced considerably. Concerning deception, the authors argue that anticipating the possibility of being deceived raises the suspicion and the second-guessing of the participants. This, in turn, distorts their motivation and ultimate behavior.

The main counterargument exposed by psychologists for the suitability of avoiding monetary payments is that the goal of many experiments is, precisely, to test the motivations of individuals to undertake certain actions. Strong monetary incentives crowd out other intrinsic motivations, and therefore bias the results. As for deception, there are two main reasons in favor of its use. First, when the study concerns issues like prejudice or social conduct, an open statement of the purpose of the study will induce subjects to act strategically and conform to what they believe is socially acceptable conduct. Second, it is sometimes necessary to artificially create some conditions, which are otherwise unlikely to occur, in order to perform a controlled experiment. An extreme example is to produce an emergency situation in order to analyze decision-making under stress.

Overall, the authors argue that it is obviously impossible to include monetary payments and to avoid deception when non-monetary rewards and deception are precisely the object of the study. However, they also claim that experimenters should avoid these two practices whenever the goal of the study points towards a completely different direction. In other words, they advocate an empirical approach to the evaluation and selection of variables in experimental designs. In our view, there are a couple of points that deserve a more in-depth treatment. One is that 'monetary' and 'performance-based' payments are often different issues. First, because flat participation fees with no (or small) bonuses if results are good can be considered as monetary incentives, but they are not (or weakly) correlated with performance. And second, because it is possible to offer rewards that are contingent on performance without necessarily implying money transfers (high grades, granting the participation in a more important study, etc.). The other is that it is sometimes difficult to determine whether suspicion affects behavior or not: when the authors report a study in which suspicious participants have a less conformist attitude than their non-suspicious peers, it may well reflect the existence of a correlation between the two characteristics rather than a causality.

Hilton (Chapter 14) reviews the psychological traits, biases, and judgment errors that are likely to play an important role in financial contexts. The paper starts with a description of individual actions and judgments that can be labeled as 'irrational' according to the traditional definition of the homo-economicus, as well as some experiments that support the existence of such a departure. The behaviors include illusion of control, overconfidence, a false interpretation of evidence, loss aversion, framing effects, and the underuse of information. The author then analyzes some social conducts that are also hard to reconcile with the traditional utility maximization paradigm: irrational herd behavior, over- and under-reaction to news, communication and inefficient aggregation of information, and the effects of accountability on decision-making. Last, the paper provides some potential applications of some well-known findings in psychology to the marketing of financial products and the management of human resources. In particular, it discusses how the design and presentation of financial products affects the decisions of non-professional investors, and how an efficient training of traders directed to correct their biases in judgments can increase their performance.

Hilton's contribution is a clear example of the potential benefits of a tight collaboration in the fields of Psychology and Finance. In recent years, there has been a growing tendency in the field of behavioral finance to rediscover the propensity of individuals to make systematic errors in judgment and decision-making. A more efficient research strategy would be to rely on the rich tradition that psychologists have in analyzing these patterns of behavior. Using the already existing conclusions, it is then possible to draw the inferences that are most relevant for the field and to provide policy prescriptions that improve the efficiency of institutions. However, one of the biggest dangers of adopting this strategy is the possibility of losing the rigorous and critical approach that economists have always displayed when analyzing human behavior. In other words, before invoking a non-standard argument to explain a given behavior, it might be useful to clearly understand whether and why the traditional theories do not provide satisfactory explanations to the issue under study.

One interesting alley for future research, not discussed in the paper, is to study the circumstances under which an irrational individual behavior is likely to survive in the long run. The social value of individual irrationality has been recognized for a long time. An example borrowed from the finance literature: an individual who completely disregards public evidence in favor of his own criterion reveals by the means of his actions his private information to the entire population. The private value of irrationality has also received some support. For instance, there is always one 'crazy' individual in every group or tribe. This person usually gets the best deals in simple bargaining situations, independent of his/her true level of insanity. However, it would be interesting to provide a systematic analysis of the type of situations in which irrationality is likely to improve outcomes either for the individual himself or for the society as a whole.

The relation between irrational behavior at the individual and at the aggregate level is at the heart of the last contribution in Part V, namely the one by Fehr and Tyran (Chapter 15). As the authors argue, one of the main differences between the researchers in Psychology and in Economics or Finance is the following. On one side, the psychologists analyze individual anomalies and then extrapolate for the aggregate behavior. On the opposite side, economists overestimate the likelihood that competitive market forces correct individual anomalies.

The paper analyzes the problem of individual and aggregate irrational behavior in the case of 'money illusion'. This theory roughly says that illusion-free individuals should react to changes in real prices but not to changes in nominal prices (in other words, I should feel equally happy if both inflation and my wage increase by 4 percent than if both remain constant). The authors propose a market experiment in which individuals post prices and obtain benefits, depending on the prices set by other individuals. The game is characterized by strategic complementarities (the optimal reaction to a price increase by the opponents is to increase own prices) and a nominal shock, that is a change in the quantity of money, which does not affect profits if all the individuals change their nominal prices in the same percentage. The paper shows that, not surprisingly, individuals exhibit more inertia in their price adjustment to shocks when prices are posted in nominal rather than real terms. More importantly, the adjustments are also slower when individuals play against other individuals than when they play against computers. The overall conclusion is that the severe nominal inertia is not so much due to individual irrationality but rather to the uncertainty of individuals on whether they are facing other rational individuals.

Although the paper is concerned with a very specific issue (of interest mainly for economists), its implications are much more general. In fact, taking a close look at the general experimental setting, one can realize that the results are indeed special instances of two widely recognized theories in psychology: the importance of framing effects (i.e. how different presentations of the same situation lead to different individual responses) and the role of beliefs about others' beliefs (just like in the famous 'beauty contest' example). It would be interesting to explore the interactions between these two phenomena in other contexts.

SOME CONCLUDING REMARKS

The main goal of this introductory chapter has been to provide some flavor of the fifteen contributions collected in the book. We have tried to emphasize the similarities in the questions addressed by the different authors and, at the same time, the diversity in their approaches. In particular, as we have discussed, there are several marked differences between the methodologies employed by the economists and the psychologists. In our view, there is a tremendous potential for cooperation between researchers in the two fields due, precisely, to this combination of common interests and different perspectives.

We have grouped the papers according to some general themes such as irrationality, self-knowledge, memory, etc. However, there are so many similarities in the issues addressed by the authors, that it would have been equally possible to propose totally different topics, like time-discounting theories, happiness, emotions, etc. We also hope that the questions raised in the brief review of each chapter and the suggestions for further investigation will stimulate the intellectual curiosity of the readers.

PART I

THE CAUSES AND CONSEQUENCES OF 'IRRATIONAL' CONDUCTS

1

The Psychology of Irrationality: Why People Make Foolish, Self-Defeating Choices

ROY F. BAUMEISTER

Self-destructive or self-defeating behavior has been an enduring fascination in psychology. One reason for this fascination is that it shows the limits of the model of the human being as a rational decision-maker. A rational being should by definition pursue enlightened self-interest. Self-defeating behavior constitutes a failure to pursue enlightened self-interest. Such patterns suggest dark psychological motivations or at least troubling, costly failures of human reason.

Plenty of human behavior does produce results that are harmful or costly to the self. People commit suicide, engage in unsafe sexual practices, smoke cigarettes, procrastinate, hurt and alienate people they love, waste their money, neglect to take their medicine or wear their seat belts, and perform many other destructive acts that could seemingly be avoided. Self-defeating behavior is quite real; the only question is why people do it.

There are several possible answers. These can be sorted into three broad categories, based on how much the person intends or chooses the harm to self.

The first is deliberate self-harm. Freud eventually concluded that people have an innate drive to bring about their own suffering, failure, and death. Other theorists have also written about having a death wish or a self-destructive impulse. The essence of this view is that people sometimes want to bring misfortune on themselves, such as to punish themselves when they feel guilty.

A second category involves tradeoffs. In this category, the person does not want to experience suffering or harm and instead wants something good. Unfortunately, the good outcome is linked to something bad. The essence is that the person accepts the bad in order to get the good. Of course, nearly all choices involve some kind of tradeoff, insofar as one must sacrifice some positive options in order to get others. A self-defeating tradeoff is best defined by the fact that, at least in the long run, the costs outweigh the benefits.

The final category consists of counterproductive strategies. The person is pursuing some positive outcome, but the person chooses some way of getting it that does not work and in fact produces a negative, undesirable outcome. In other words, it consists of a goal-directed behavior that backfires and produces the opposite of the intended result.

Systematic reviews of research literature on normal, adult human behavior has found little or no evidence of the first category of deliberate self-harm, but ample evidence of patterns that fit the second and third categories (see Baumeister, 1997; Baumeister and Scher, 1988; Berglas and Baumeister, 1993). The failure of research to support the first category casts severe doubt on the view that people have death wishes or self-destructive motivations. Even people who feel quite guilty do not generally seek out punishment or suffering—on the contrary, they may try to avoid punishment even though they acknowledge their guilt. At the extreme, suicide appears to be sought more commonly as an escape from suffering than as the fulfillment of self-destructive wishes, and in that respect it resembles a tradeoff more than any primacy of self-destructive wishes (see Baumeister, 1990).

Based on these conclusions, we think the effort to understand self-destructive actions should emphasize tradeoffs and counterproductive strategies. A survey of the evidence about each type can yield some general patterns and conclusions.

1. TRADEOFFS

The essence of a self-defeating tradeoff is that the person (or group) pursues some positive benefit or gain that is linked to some cost or risk. Self-defeat is accomplished when the eventual cost outweighs the gain.

Examples of self-defeating tradeoffs can be listed as follows. Several unhealthy behaviors arise because of the pursuit of pleasures such as good taste, intoxication, or chemically based euphoria. Self-handicapping involves creating external barriers to one's own success in order to have a good excuse for anticipated failure; for example, a poor performance is discounted if the person did not study or prepare adequately. Shy people may withdraw from social interactions in order to avoid possible rejection, but in the process they prevent themselves from having the opportunity to form the interpersonal attachments they desire. People fail to take their medicine or comply with health care instructions, especially when those procedures involve feeling bad or looking foolish.

Two patterns are commonly found with self-defeating tradeoffs. First, many tradeoffs involve short-term gains but long-term costs. Hence, the people take the immediate pleasure and seem to discount the eventual risks or harm. Second, in many tradeoffs the benefits seem certain but the costs seem only possible. In both these cases, it is possible to see how the eventual costs can outweigh the gains. A person oriented toward the here and now, for example, might choose the immediate gain even though the long-term cost will eventually outweigh it.

To illustrate these with cigarette smoking: Smoking is often self-destructive in a very literal sense, because the smoke causes lung cancer and death. People do not smoke in order to die from lung cancer, however, but rather they smoke for the pleasure and satisfaction that come from tobacco. The pleasure is thus traded off against the disease and death. It is self-defeating because dying of lung cancer is generally regarded, in the long run, as outweighing the pleasure: One loses more than one gains. But the gains are immediate and the costs are delayed, insofar as the pleasure of smoking comes at once whereas the disease does not materialize for decades. Moreover, the pleasure is reliably predictable (almost certain) whereas the costs are uncertain: Many smokers do not die from lung cancer.

Procrastination also illustrates these patterns. Many people procrastinate and some even claim that it is a good strategy, because they do their best work under the pressure of a deadline. We did a longitudinal study of procrastination among students in a class, and we measured both their performance in the class and their health. We found that procrastinators enjoyed better health than people who got their work done ahead of time. The procrastinators got poorer grades, however, suggesting that procrastination is costly in terms of work. There was one question about the health results, however: We had measured health early in the semester, when the deadline was far away. In a second study, we measured health both early and late. We replicated the finding that procrastinators were healthier early in the semester. We found however that they were much sicker at the end of the semester, when the deadline was close. In fact, they were so much sicker then that they ended up being sicker overall, despite their better health early in the semester (Tice and Baumeister, 1997).

To be sure, one may debate on whether the health outcomes add up to a self-defeating pattern. The sum of total illnesses was greater for the procrastinators, and they were also the most intensely sick (given that their greater illness was packed into a shorter period). On the other hand, one could argue that some people might prefer to have all their illnesses concentrated in a short time rather than spread out over the semester, so in that view the procrastination period was an adaptive and rational way of scheduling the illnesses (although scheduling illnesses just when one is supposed to be preparing for exams hardly seems ideal). In our view, the net increase in total illness qualifies this pattern as self-defeating, but the main reason to regard procrastination as self-defeating is its deleterious effect on performance.

Procrastination is thus clearly self-defeating. It takes the short-term benefit of low stress and good health when the deadline is far away, but it pays a high price in terms of delayed stress and illness, which in the long run causes them to be worse off overall. Most important, procrastination seems to lead to poorer performance: The procrastinators got lower grades on all assignments.

2. COUNTERPRODUCTIVE STRATEGIES

Many instances of self-defeating behavior involve counterproductive strategies. The essence of this is that the person is pursuing a desirable outcome but chooses a strategy or approach that backfires and produces the opposite of the desired result. Thus, the person is pursuing a positive goal, but the person's method of pursuing it thwarts the efforts to achieve it.

There are several patterns that contribute to these failures. One is faulty knowledge. The person may have a false understanding of what behaviors will produce what results (i.e., a false understanding of contingencies). For example, some people drink alcohol when they are depressed because they think alcohol will cheer them up—but in fact drinking when depressed often makes the depression worse, because alcohol is in fact a depressant. Likewise, performers may respond to the pressure for success by focusing attention on their internal processes so as to monitor themselves more effectively, but this monitoring disrupts the automatic execution of skills and thus causes poor performance, commonly called 'choking under pressure.' Another is excessive persistence: The person encounters initial failure but refuses to give up. In American culture, people are taught from early childhood that persistence will lead to success eventually, but sometimes this is plainly false, and misguided persistence—'throwing good money after bad'—ends up wasting a significant amount of resources.

Another pattern arises when the person knows what to do but fails to implement it. Faulty knowledge may contribute to overconfidence so that the person does not recognize the need to be careful and thorough.

3. CAUSES OF SELF-DEFEATING CHOICES

We now consider why people make these self-defeating or self-destructive choices. Our laboratory work has examined a series of hypotheses and theories. Let me report on the ones that have worked out reasonably well.

3.1. Emotional Distress

There is a long history of assuming that people who are emotional become irrational and make bad decisions. Yet, the research has not provided a clear or consistent support for the view that emotion leads to impaired thinking or other negative effects. In fact, some studies find that emotion causes people to think more carefully and thoroughly, possibly more accurately, and sometimes more creatively. Clearly, emotion can benefit the thought process.

When we looked at the research findings about self-defeating behaviors, however, it was apparent that emotion seemed to be involved in many of them, especially aversive emotional states. Hence, we thought there must be a link between emotional distress and self-defeating behavior. But what kind of link? Freudians suggested that when people feel guilty, they want to suffer or be punished, but we did not find any evidence of that, and indeed the whole idea of wanting to suffer was not supported. Hence, we needed a different theory.

We then began to look at risk-taking. The idea was that people who were upset would take stupid risks, and these would therefore sometimes lead to destructive outcomes. An upset person might drive too fast in traffic, and sometimes this would lead to a crash. An angry person might get into an argument or fight with someone and get hurt as a result. Of course, sometimes taking risks might lead to positive outcomes, or at least non-negative ones. The reckless driver may sometimes arrive at the destination faster than the safe driver, with neither a crash nor a speeding ticket to detract from the positive outcome. But overall, taking more foolish risks will increase the frequency of bad outcomes, and so risk-taking could well mediate between emotional distress and self-defeating outcomes.

A crucial distinction must be made between rational and irrational risks. After all, it is almost impossible to avoid all risks, and many risks are worth taking in order to secure positive outcomes. To pursue the traffic example, it is risky to drive in a car at all, because sometimes even safe drivers are killed (such as if other drivers run into them). The risk-taking only qualifies as self-defeating if the costs outweigh the benefits in some objective sense. It may be safer to walk to work than drive, but only slightly, and driving may save many hours off the trip every day, so it becomes rational to drive. In contrast, driving recklessly may at best save only a couple of minutes, whereas it increases the danger substantially, and so reckless high-speed driving may not be rational.

Our research therefore had to emphasize not only taking risks but taking stupid risks. The theory was that emotionally upset people would be more inclined than others to take ill-advised risks, in which the downside outweighed the potential for gain in some objective sense.

To test this theory, we set up experiments in which people had to choose between two lotteries. One of them involved playing it safe: The person was told he would have a 70 percent chance of winning $2, which our students do appreciate, but it is clearly not very much money. The other lottery was a long shot: A 2 percent chance of winning $25, which is quite a bit more money. In both cases, if they lost, they would be subjected to stressful noise. If you calculate the expected gain (which involves both the value of the possible outcomes and their likelihood), the two-dollar lottery was the correct, rational choice, with an expected gain of $1.40 as compared with only a 50 cent expected gain for the long shot. The noise would make that difference even bigger. Thus, choosing the long-shot risky lottery was objectively, statistically an irrational choice, because it was likely to produce a poorer outcome than the play-it-safe lottery.

We put people into various emotional states, using a variety of strong procedures (see Leith and Baumeister, 1996). We found, repeatedly, that most people would make the correct choice of the two-dollar lottery. This was especially common among people in neutral and in good moods. But people who were upset strongly tended to make the foolish, risky choice of the long shot. Thus, emotional distress produced a tendency to take stupid risks.

Why? We had two theories about that. One was that when you already feel bad, you have more to gain and less to lose. This was based on the framing theory and a change in the subjective utility of various outcomes. Isen, Nygren, and Ashby (1988) have argued that when people feel good, they rationally become risk-averse, because they have more to lose and less to gain. Yet, we failed to find any evidence that emotional distress changed the way people appraised the outcome.

Roy F. Baumeister

Our second theory was that people who were upset simply failed to think through the implications and consequences. They would just see the $25 option and grab for it, without thinking through the odds and other outcomes.

In a crucial experiment, we tested these two theories against each other. We made people angry and then brought them to the lottery choice procedure. In one condition, however, we insisted that they spend about a minute listing the advantages and disadvantages of each lottery. The first theory would predict an even stronger tendency to choose the long shot, because the extra reflection would make the change in subjective utility that much clearer: You already feel bad, so you have more to gain and less to lose by taking a risk.

In contrast, the second theory would predict that the effect would disappear. If the stupid risk-taking depends on not thinking through the options, then forcing people to think them through should eliminate the stupid choices. This is what we found: People who were required to list the advantages and disadvantages did not make the foolish, risky choice of the long-shot, even though they were just as angry as the other people.

Another possible explanation for these findings was that thinking about the outcomes altered people's emotional state. However, ratings of people's moods suggested that this did not happen. The angry people were still (equally) angry, regardless of whether they had made their decision rapidly or had been instructed to stop and think before making their choice. In this study, the time people spent in the 'stop and think' condition was typically less than one minute, so it did not have much opportunity to cause them to calm down. Hence, it looks like the main fact of considering the various outcomes and probabilities was the decisive factor.

Yet another possible theory would be that people who are upset somehow desire to fail, and so they deliberately chose the outcome most likely to produce a bad result. This suggestion is contradicted by the 'stop and think' procedure, however, for if they wanted a bad outcome, they would have chosen it all the more reliably when they could effectively calculate the odds and outcomes. Another experiment (unpublished) was also relevant. Instead of making the risky outcome the bad one, we changed the matrix of outcomes so that the risky outcome had the better expected gain (and hence was the rational, optimal choice). This made no difference. Emotionally distraught people preferred the risky option then too, whereas happy and emotionally neutral participants favored the safer outcome. Thus, the emotionally upset people were not looking for a bad outcome.

3.2. Threatened Egotism

A second idea was that people's concern with their self-esteem and with making a good impression on other people could cloud their judgment and produce bad, costly choices. There were several signs of this in the previous literature. For example, self-handicapping is done to avoid the loss of face that accompanies failure, because the handicap eliminates most of the disgrace over failure. Like-wise, self-destructive patterns of seeking revenge, binge eating, alcohol abuse, wasteful persistence, and choking under pressure have been linked to threats to esteem.

We conducted some studies to examine directly the effects of threats to egotism (Baumeister et al. 1993). Again we used a gambling procedure. This time, people were invited to bet money on their own performance. Specifically, we had them practice a video game until they were somewhat proficient, and then they performed ten trials, recording the score on every trial. Then the experimenter said that actually the person had been performing against a criterion, without knowing it, and had earned U.S. $3. This allowed us to give each person U.S. $3 in coins. We said this was because the person had surpassed the criterion score on three of the ten trials. We told the person the criterion score was some round number between his third best and fourth best score. (For nearly all participants, the scores clustered together according to a normal distribution, with a slight trend toward improvement with continued practice.)

Then the experimenter said there would be one more trial, with the same criterion score. On this one, the person was invited to bet any part of the U.S. $3 on being able to surpass it. If the person beat the criterion, he would receive triple the amount that was bet. In contrast, if the person failed to surpass it, he would lose whatever he bet. (Similar results were found with females in another study.) Thus, the bet was approximately fair: The person had about a one-third chance of tripling his money. There was no strong rational pull either to bet or not bet.

The main thing we measured was how much money the person possessed at the end of the study. This depended both on the bet and the performance. In an important sense, you had to know how well you would be able to perform in order to bet effectively. The person could do well by just keeping the money and not making any bet. The person could do really well by making a large bet and then performing well. Making a large bet and not performing well brought the bad outcome, however.

Just before the person made the bet, the experimenter brought in results from a creativity test the person had taken earlier. By random assignment, half the people were told they did really well and were quite creative. The others were told they had done very poorly, in fact the worst score the experimenter had seen. The experimenter invited the participant to make an excuse (such as a lack of sleep) for doing so badly, and then said that the excuse was not valid because it was shown that a lack of sleep had no effect on performance. This was done to compound the embarrassing or humiliating nature of the failure. Furthermore, the participants were all students in a psychology course, and the professor was the experimenter, so the poor performance seemed to be quite important.

The results depended on the level of self-esteem. When people were told that they had done well on the creativity test, the people with a high self-esteem ended up with more money than people with a low self-esteem. Thus, they made a low bet if they were not going to perform well, or they made large bets if they were going to do well. This fits the evidence that people with a high self-esteem know themselves better and can manage themselves better than people with a low self-esteem.

But the good performance of people with a high self-esteem vanished when they received a blow to their pride in the form of being told that they had done poorly on the creativity test. These people seemed eager to wipe out the loss of face by winning a large bet. Sure enough, they made larger bets than in any other condition, but they did not perform well enough to justify these bets, and so they ended up losing most of their money. They finished the experiment with less money than people with a low self-esteem.

Thus, people who think highly of themselves are often quite concerned with looking good and making a good impression. When this favorable view of self is threatened by criticism or embarrassing failure, they become irrational and make foolish, costly choices.

Was this self-defeating? One might propose that the people with a high self-esteem who had received the bad feedback felt they had much to gain and little to lose by making a large bet. It could even be suggested that they might feel proud about making the large bet, even if they lost, because they might view their large bet as a heroic gesture. Yet, these suggestions are contradicted by people's ratings. The people who lost the bet felt bad about it afterwards, and there was no difference between a high and low self-esteem on that score. They were sorry they had bet all their money and lost it.

3.3. Self-Regulation Failure

Self-regulation refers to how the human psyche manages and controls itself, including altering its inner states, overriding initial responses, and keeping itself on track toward goals. When this system fails, a broad variety of maladaptive and self-defeating behavior can arise. Put another way, the rational pursuit of enlightened self-interest often requires you to do something other than what you most feel like doing at the moment, and so self-regulation is required.

Let me return to the experiments I already described on emotional distress and self-defeating behaviors (i.e., with the lottery choice). The finding was that people who were upset would choose the foolish, long-shot lottery instead of the objectively better play-it-safe lottery. When we required them to stop and think before deciding, specifically to list the advantages and disadvantages of both options, they no longer made bad choices. The implication is that people who are upset make self-defeating choices because they fail to consider the options fully. This finding suggests an important role for self-regulation. When people are upset, they feel like just making an impulsive decision based on whatever grabs their attention or seems desirable. To avoid making foolish, risky decisions, they ought to consider the risks and costs more carefully. Self-regulation is needed to make oneself consider all facets of the decision options. Apparently, then, emotional distress impairs people's willingness to self-regulate their decision process and to think things through.

More generally, self-defeating behavior is often based on pursuing a short-term gain that carries a long-term risk or cost. This, too, is often an issue of self-regulation. In fact, there is some reason to think that the capacity for self-regulation evolved precisely for this reason: In other words, it was highly adaptive for human beings to be able to resist temptations to do something with an immediate payoff but a long-term cost. Eating one's seed corn, for example, would be very tempting to any hungry animal, including early humans, but it is self-defeating in the long run because there is nothing left to plant in the spring.

Research on the delay of gratification (e.g., Mischel, 1974, 1996) also illustrates the adaptive importance of self-regulation, and indeed I regard this work as highly important, pioneering work that helped lead to the modern understanding of self-regulation. The typical procedure involves a choice between an immediate, small reward or a delayed, larger reward. The delayed reward is the logical, rational choice, yet people have difficulty resisting the temptation to take the immediate reward. Self-regulation constitutes the ability to resist that immediate temptation and do what is best in the long run.

Our research has uncovered a surprising fact about this capacity for self-regulation: It seems to depend on a very limited energy resource. It operates like a muscle or strength, or a form of energy. The essence of this is that when it is used, it gets 'tired' or depleted, and for a while afterward the self cannot function so effectively.

We have conducted many experimental tests of this (see Baumeister, Bratslavsky, Muraven, and Tice, 1998; Muraven, Tice, and Baumeister, 1998), but let me provide one example. We asked participants in this study to avoid eating anything for three hours before their scheduled session, which generally meant that they had to skip lunch. To tempt them, we prepared a delicious tray of chocolates and cookies. In fact, we baked some of these in the laboratory before they arrived, and the aroma of freshly baked chocolate cookies was very strong. Each participant was then seated at a table where there was a tray of cookies and chocolates, and this must have seemed very appealing to them. Unfortunately for them, we told them that they had been assigned to another condition in the experiment, and their task would be to eat radishes, and sure enough there was a bowl of radishes on the table as well. We left them alone for five minutes with the instruction to eat as many radishes as possible and nothing else. The point was to require them to resist temptation: They really wanted the chocolates and cookies, but they had to forego any such treats and eat radishes instead. For comparison purposes, another group of participants was allowed to eat the cookies and chocolates, and a third group had no food at all.

Then we got rid of all the food and gave them problems to solve. These involved tracing geometric figures without re-tracing any lines or lifting one's pen from the paper. We wanted to see how long they would keep trying before giving up. In reality the problems were not solvable, and so it was quite frustrating and discouraging to work on them, and we assumed that the people would have to use self-regulation to make themselves do that. We timed how long they kept trying until they gave up. (We also counted how many attempts they made on each puzzle.)

The results showed a very strong effect, indicating that the self's resources were depleted. That is, people in the 'radish condition' quit much faster on the puzzles, as compared to people who ate chocolate, or people who had had no food. Resisting the temptation to eat chocolate had used up some crucial energy or strength, which was therefore not available to help them keep trying at the difficult problems.

Naturally, the social scientists will have many questions about such an experiment, and we conducted many others to rule out possible alternative explanations. One might wonder whether the participants were angry with the experimenter for not letting them have the chocolates, or were simply reluctant to do any more work for the experimenter. We have measured people's feelings and attitudes after the first task, and typically there is no difference, so the mood and attitude do not explain the effects. (In fact, in one study, depleted people spent a longer time enduring a boring film, so they were not thinking 'I've already done enough and should leave as soon as possible.') One might also object that quitting rapidly on an impossible task is actually adaptive rather than self-defeating. Hence, we conducted another study with solvable anagrams, and there too we found that the depleted people performed worse (see Baumeister et al., 1998; also Muraven et al., 1998).

The analogy to a muscle goes beyond the pattern of getting 'tired' after exertion. In other studies, we have found that the capacity for regulating oneself can be strengthened over time. That is, people who performed minor exercises in self-control for two weeks, such as trying to improve their posture (i.e., stand and sit straight), showed improvements in self-control on laboratory tasks relative to people who did not exercise (Muraven et al. 1999). Thus, just as a muscle becomes tired when exercised but eventually becomes stronger, the capacity for self-control becomes depleted in the short run but may be strengthened in the long run if it is used regularly.

So, why do people give up prematurely or fail to regulate themselves properly? One reason is that it takes some inner resource to do so, and sometimes that resource is depleted. More familiar signs of this pattern are found when people's resources are depleted by coping with stress. What happens then? They channel all their resources into meeting the deadline or handling whatever the main stress involves. As a result, their self-control breaks down in other spheres. They may resume smoking cigarettes, or eat too much, or drink too much. They may become irritable and obnoxious, which often involves a failure of affect regulation (emotional control). They may do other impulsive things, like becoming aggressive.

3.4. Decision Fatigue

The findings on depletion of the self's inner resources extend beyond self-regulation. Our research suggests that all acts of volition—including, crucially, making choices and decisions—also draw on that same resource. In other words, making decisions consumes one of the self's important inner resources. This is probably one reason people are creatures of habit: Habit, routine, and automatic processes avoid having to expend resources by making choices.

We have several findings that point to this conclusion. In one study, we had people make one big important decision. Specifically, we asked them to agree to make a speech contrary to their own personal beliefs, a procedure that many psychology experiments on attitude change have used. Other people were simply told that they would have to make that speech, without being told that it was ultimately their decision (Baumeister et al., 1998).

The next part of the procedure was exactly the same as in the radish and chocolate experiment: We measured how long it took before they gave up trying to solve some difficult puzzles. The people who had simply been instructed to make the speech persisted just as long as the control group. In contrast, the people who had had to make a personal decision to make that speech gave up much faster. Making that decision used up some inner resource.

Recently, we followed up that finding with several more experiments that caused 'decision fatigue' by having people make a series of small choices (Twenge et al. 2000). We pretended to be doing consumer research, and we asked each participant to make a series of binary choices between products. Thus, would you rather have a red or a green t-shirt? A lemon scented or a vanilla scented candle? Blue or yellow socks? We told them that they would actually receive one of the products they had chosen, at the end of the experiment. For comparison purposes, a control group was asked to rate how often they had used each of these products in the past six months, and they too were told they would receive one of the products.

Later, we measured their capacity for self-regulation by asking them to drink as much as they could of an unpleasant, bitter tasting beverage. We told them it was good for them (it contained vinegar), and so this corresponded to the common need to do something unpleasant but which was good for you, like taking medicine. We also offered to pay them five cents for each ounce they could drink.

These studies showed that making many decisions depletes the self. The people who made choices between products later were less able to make themselves drink much of the aversive beverage. This was true even if there were different experimenters for the two parts of the experiment (i.e., the choices and the drinking)—so any feelings toward the first experimenter would not be likely to carry over toward the second experimenter in an ostensibly unrelated study. Meanwhile, the people who simply rated the products, without making decisions, consumed significantly more of the bitter beverage.

Thus, the act of making decisions drains some important resource out of the self. The result is a temporary impairment of the person's ability to function. Some people have described the feeling to us that 'I don't want to make any decisions tonight.' They feel specifically unable to make choices and decisions.

This feeling fits well with the results of these experiments, because making choices is hard work that depletes an inner resource that seems quite limited. People can only really make a few serious choices at a time, and then the capacity for choosing has to recover and replenish before they are fully effective again.

3.5. Rejection and Belongingness

Our current work has turned up another important cause of self-defeating behavior: Rejection and the threat of being alone. We don't fully understand why it has this effect, but the effect is consistent and quite strong.

The basis for this line of work is the idea that people have a powerful and fundamental 'need to belong.' In fact, we think that the drive to form and maintain connections with at least some other human beings is nearly universal and more powerful (and more fundamental) than the desire for self-esteem and many other common motives (see Baumeister and Leary, 1995, for a review).

In a series of studies, we have exposed people to a blow that thwarts their need to belong. We do this in two ways. In one procedure, a group of people meet and spend some time getting to know each other, and then they are put into separate rooms. We tell them they are going to pair off for the next part and they should all list the persons with whom they want to work. Half the participants, by random assignment, are told that they were selected by everybody in the group, but because this creates a procedural obstacle, they will have to work alone. The others are told that nobody chose them, and so they too will have to work alone. Thus, everybody ends up working alone, but for half of the group it was because nobody wanted them, whereas the others were accepted by everybody.

The other procedure involves giving a psychological test and then telling them that their statistical profile indicates that they will probably end up alone in life. Others are told they will end up well connected with others or, in a 'bad control' condition, that they will be accident prone and suffer many broken bones and minor injuries.

Then we measure the self-defeating behavior. We have consistently found that the rejection manipulation makes people engage in self-defeating behavior. The accepted ones, and even the accident-prone ones, tend to behave rationally, but the rejection somehow eliminates the will to take care of oneself. We have measured this in multiple ways. In one study, people made fewer healthy and more unhealthy choices. In another, they ate more fattening foods. In another, we used the lottery choice procedure, and the rejected ones made more foolish, high-risk choices. In yet another, we used the drinking vinegar procedure, and they were less effective at making themselves drink. We have also found that this social rejection impairs people's performance on IQ (intelligence) tests, makes people more aggressive, and makes them less willing to help someone who asks for help. This last is especially surprising, because one would think that a social rejection would cause the person to want to make new friends, and lending help is a good way to do this. But they did the opposite.

Nor were these effects due to emotional distress. We measured their emotional state. Not surprisingly, the rejected ones felt the worst. But these feelings did not predict their self-defeating choices.

Apparently, a major rejection strikes at some core feeling or motivation, and the effect is like getting hit on the head with a block of wood. People become incapable of regulating their own behavior, and they engage in an assortment of self-destructive and antisocial responses.

4. CONCLUSION

The human capacity for rational, enlightened action is certainly a tremendous advantage. Why then do people sometimes fail to use it? Why do they perform acts that bring risks and costs to themselves? Why do they make bad decisions that depart from rational self-interest?

Our research has outlined several answers.

1. Under emotional distress, people shift toward favoring high-risk, high-payoff options, even if these are objectively poor choices. This appears based on a failure to think things through, caused by the emotional distress.
2. When self-esteem is threatened, people become upset and lose their capacity to regulate themselves. In particular, people who hold a high opinion of themselves often get quite upset in response to a blow to their pride, and the rush to prove something great about themselves overrides their normal and rational way of dealing with life.
3. Self-regulation is required for many forms of self-interested behavior. When self-regulation fails, people may become self-defeating in various ways, such as taking immediate pleasures instead of delayed rewards. Self-regulation appears to depend on a limited resources that operates like strength or energy, and so people can only regulate themselves to a limited extent.
4. Making choices and decisions depletes this same resource. Once the resource is depleted, such as after making a series of important decisions, the self becomes tired and depleted, and its subsequent decisions may well be costly or foolish.
5. The need to belong is a central feature of human motivation, and when this need is thwarted such as by interpersonal rejection, the human being somehow ceases to function properly. Irrational and self-defeating acts become more common in the wake of rejection.

Again, we have never found much evidence that people ever develop an actual desire to suffer or to fail. There is no basic motivation for self-destruction. Instead, self-defeating behavior arises by means of tradeoffs and counterproductive strategies. These are greatly increased by the five factors we just outlined.

These, then, are some of the keys to human irrationality. Given how prevalent and powerful they can be, we should perhaps be surprised at how often people do manage to make intelligent, prudent, wise decisions, rather than being dismayed at how often they make foolish and costly ones!

REFERENCES

Baumeister, R.F. (1990). Suicide as escape from self. *Psychological Review, 97,* 90–113.

—— (1997). Esteem threat, self-regulatory breakdown, and emotional distress as factors in self-defeating behavior. *Review of General Psychology, 1,* 145–74.

—— Bratslavsky, E., Muraven, M., and Tice, D.M. (1998). Ego depletion: Is the active self a limited resource? *Journal of Personality and Social Psychology, 74,* 1252–65.

—— and Leary, M.R. (1995). The need to belong: Desire for interpersonal attachments as a fundamental human motivation. *Psychological Bulletin, 117,* 497–529.

—— Heatherton, T.F., and Tice, D.M. (1993). When ego threats lead to self-regulation failure: Negative consequences of high self-esteem. *Journal of Personality and Social Psychology, 64,* 141–56.

—— and Scher, S.J. (1988). Self-defeating behavior patterns among normal individuals: Review and analysis of common self-destructive tendencies. *Psychological Bulletin, 104,* 3–22.

Berglas, S.C. and Baumeister, R.F. (1993). *Your own worst enemy: Understanding the paradox of self-defeating behavior.* New York: Basic Books.

Isen, A.M., Nygren, T.E., and Ashby, F.G. (1988). Influence of positive affect on the subjective utility of gains and losses. It is just not worth the risk. *Journal of Personality and Social Psychology, 55,* 710–17.

Leith, K.P. and Baumeister, R.F. (1996). Why do bad moods increase self-defeating behavior? Emotion, risk-taking, and self-regulation. *Journal of Personality and Social Psychology, 71,* 1250–67.

Mischel, W. (1974). Processes in delay of gratification. In L. Berkowitz (Ed.), *Advances in experimental social psychology* (Vol. 7, pp. 249–92). San Diego, CA: Academic Press.

—— (1996). From good intentions to willpower. In P. Gollwitzer and J. Bargh (Eds.), *The psychology of action* (pp. 197–218). New York: Guilford.

Muraven, M., Tice, D.M., and Baumeister, R.F. (1998). Self-control as limited resource: Regulatory depletion patterns. *Journal of Personality and Social Psychology, 74,* 774–89.

—— Baumeister, R.F., and Tice, D.M. (1999). Longitudinal improvement of self-regulation through practice: Building self-control through repeated exercise. *Journal of Social Psychology, 139,* 446–57.

Tice, D.M. and Baumeister, R.F. (1997). Longitudinal study of procrastination, performance, stress, and health: The costs and benefits of dawdling. *Psychological Science, 8,* 454–8.

Twenge, J.M., Baumeister, R.F., Tice, D.M., and Schmeichel, B. (2000). *Decision fatigue: Making multiple personal decisions depletes the self's resources.* Manuscript submitted for publication, Case Western Reserve University, Cleveland, OH.

2

Irrational Pursuits: Hyper-Incentives from a Visceral Brain

KENT C. BERRIDGE

The purpose of this chapter is to consider the possibility that people make choices that are *irrational*—in a strong sense of the term. I acknowledge at the outset that many readers might object to a strong notion of irrational choice, either on the grounds that it is a contradiction in terms, or because it seems a mere admission of ignorance about someone else's private hedonic world. Yet, I will argue that irrational choice may be both plausible and in some cases demonstrable.

The notion of irrational choice may seem to be self-contradictory when viewed from the perspective that people always choose what has the most value or decision utility to them. If one defines 'having the most value' as 'what one chooses', then by definition one always chooses the most valued outcome. However, as documented by a number of authors in this volume, people may sometimes choose an outcome whose eventual *hedonic value* does not *justify* their choice (see Chapters 1, 3, 10, and 11).

Or a pronouncement of irrational choice might seem to imply nothing more than our ignorance about another's private hedonic priorities. After all, if *de gustibus non disputandum est*, then individual tastes are not a matter for dispute, nor can they be deemed either rational or irrational. What you like is the legitimate basis for your own choice. An outsider may not share or understand the basis of a particular choice, but it is presumptuous for that reason alone to call it irrational (it is an interesting and legitimate question for psychology to ask why one likes the things one does, and to identify causes of liking—but that is a separate issue).

Still, irrational choices may yet be possible, even when private expectations and likings are known, and even from the point of view of the individual who has them. What I want to consider here is whether there are degrees of irrationality regarding choice, and whether there are real-life examples of irrational choice.

I thank Richard D. Gonzalez for discussion of these ideas and for suggesting the Latin quotation about tastes. I also thank Juan Carrillo and Cindy Wyvell for their thoughtful comments on an earlier version of the manuscript. Finally, I thank Andrew Caplin (who suggested the home-shopping scenario) and Daniel Kahneman for helpful conversations at the Brussels conference in June 2000.

Let's grant at the outset that the rationality or irrationality of your choice has nothing to do with why you like it, or with whether anyone else likes it too. The question of rationality hinges only on whether your choice consistently follows your expectations of hedonic likes. A truly *irrational choice* would be to choose what you *expect not to like*.

If an outcome is much liked, then by the rational criteria of hedonic decision making, it should also be much wanted (Gilbert and Wilson, 2000). The outcome should be wanted exactly to the degree that it is expected to be liked. *Expected* to be liked is the crucial phrase here. Human expectations of what will be liked can often be in error, but being wrong has nothing to do with rationality. Expectations may be wrong because of ignorance of the outcome or because of cognitive distortions. For example, Gilbert and Wilson and colleagues have shown that when people predict their future hedonic well being in the face of an adverse future outcome they tend to underestimate their emotional resiliency, and to underestimate also the compensating influence of other positive future outcomes (Gilbert and Wilson, 2000; Gilbert et al., 1998; Wilson et al., 2000).

Perhaps a closer approach to irrationality comes from demonstrations by Kahneman and colleagues of the systematic 'violations of logic' in people's choices that are based upon the systematic distortions of hedonic memory (Kahneman, 2000). A person's prediction of hedonic impact can be wrong even for the next occurrence of an already familiar outcome (Kahneman et al., 1993; Kahneman and Snell, 1992; Redelmeier and Kahneman, 1996). Kahneman argues that people base their memory of a hedonic event on a few prototype moments that occurred during that event, even when those moments do not reflect the full hedonic impact of the event as a whole (Kahneman, 2000). For example, people may thus be induced to choose a longer pain over a shorter one that gives less total pain, due to an end-decrement that creates the memory illusion that the longer pain was less intense (Kahneman et al., 1990, 1993; Redelmeier and Kahneman, 1996). These cases distort choice by distorting the cognitive expectations of future hedonic impact. To the degree that wanting for an outcome is based on expected liking, any distortion of hedonic expectations will rationally result in a misguided choice. The wrong choice will be based on a false expectation.

Making the wrong choice on the basis of false hedonic expectations is misguided but not strictly irrational. A misguided choice remains rational as long as it corresponds to a maximized expectation of liking. If I believe that I will like an outcome very much, then I am rational to want it, to choose it over others, to work hard for it exactly to the degree that I expect to like it—even if I turn out not to like the outcome after all. Rationality cannot be held responsible for the accuracy of my expectations, only for the consistency with which I act upon them. (One could argue that once one knows distortions of expectation may occur, then rationality demands the application of new strategies to avoid being fooled by distortions again. But such a high-level degree of rationality is beyond our current scope. Here we are interested, simply, in whether there are choices that fail to meet even the *ordinary* criteria for rationality.)

1. STRONG IRRATIONALITY

So what would be needed, in addition, to make a choice truly irrational? I wish to focus here on the *intrinsic rationality of a given decision*, rather than on properties such as transitivity that are assessed over a series of decisions. Irrational choice is something more than the mere mistaken belief about future liking. It is choice that diverges from the expectations of future liking (presuming the choice is not constrained by non-hedonic criteria). To aid the discussion, I will adopt here the utility terminology of Kahneman (Kahneman, 1999; Kahneman et al., 1997) to distinguish between *experienced utility* (actual liking for an outcome), *remembered utility* (memory of liking in the past), *predicted utility* (expected liking for the outcome in the future), and *decision utility* (manifest choice of the outcome).

For the purposes of this chapter, *I define a choice to be rational* so long as *Decision Utility = Predicted Utility*, and the choice maximizes both the decision and predicted utility (regardless of whether the prediction of future experienced utility proves to be correct). By contrast *irrational choice is defined to be possible only when Decision Utility > Predicted Utility*, such that a choice that maximizes the decision utility results in suboptimal predicted utility. In other words, an outcome is irrationally chosen only when it is wanted disproportionately to its expectation of being liked.

If truly irrational wanting is wanting what one does not like and does not expect to like, this may seem so bizarre and unlikely that economists and psychologists could safely dismiss the possibility. Why consider a phenomenon that cannot exist? But irrational wanting may indeed exist. There are several phenomena that approach irrational wanting, at least by incorporating increasing degrees of divergence of the decision utilities from the predicted utility. Further, there is evidence to suggest that, within strictly limited circumstances, irrational wanting may be quite a powerful control of choice and pursuit behavior. Irrational wanting may be a phenomenon that needs to be reckoned with.

2. EXPERIMENTAL APPROACHES: MANIPULATION OF DECISION UTILITY BY IRRELEVANT (UNCONSCIOUS) CAUSE

In some instances, a person may be entirely unaware of the occurrence of an event that influences their wanting for an outcome (Nisbett and Wilson, 1978; Wilson and Schooler, 1991; Winkielman et al., 2000; Zajonc, 1980). The most striking examples come from the work of Zajonc and colleagues on the subliminal (unconscious) presentation of a manipulation that changes preference for a later event (Murphy and Zajonc, 1993; Winkielman et al., 1997; Zajonc, 1980, 1998). For instance, the subliminal presentation of a happy or angry emotional facial expression, even though not consciously perceived, nonetheless alters the preference ratings of aesthetic value for a subsequent item that is consciously evaluated, such as the aesthetic value of a Chinese ideogram (Kunst-Wilson and

Zajonc, 1980; Winkielman et al., 1997). It seems plausible to presume that, irrelevant causes do not act by changing explicit expectations about the utility of the ideogram because the causal manipulations work at an unconscious level.

The subliminal shifts of decision utility apply not only to verbal or pencil and paper ratings, but also to real consumption behavior. This was recently demonstrated in a study conducted by Piotr Winkielman at the University of Denver, his student Julie Wilbarger, and me (Winkielman et al., 2000). Winkielman and colleagues found that the subliminal emotional expressions altered people's actual consumption and their willingness to pay for a fruit drink in ways that diverged somewhat from rationality.

Relevant to the degree that such subliminal effects on consumption behavior might be regarded as operating outside the bounds of rationality, we wanted to clarify the degree to which subliminal affective priming is truly unconscious. Are people simply unaware of the causal facial expression that produces an emotional response in them, but able to consciously experience the hedonic emotion itself in an ordinary way? If so, a case could be made that a conscious hedonic shift in mood could operate in a rational manner, by changing the hedonic value of choices considered after the shift in mood. Or are people actually unconscious of their own emotional reaction (in addition to being unaware of the subliminal facial expression that caused it)? An unconscious emotional reaction is more difficult to construe in rational terms.

Winkielman et al. assessed the conscious emotional reactions by asking subjects to rate online their subjective mood immediately after subliminal exposure to emotional facial expressions, and then measured their actual consumption behavior, in the form of how much beverage they subsequently poured for themselves and how much they drank (Winkielman et al., 2000). The subliminal stimuli were happy, neutral, or angry facial expressions, which lasted for only 1/60th of a second, and were followed immediately by a second 'masking' photograph of a face with a neutral expression, which stayed on the screen long enough to be seen consciously. The subjective experience of this procedure is that one is aware only of the neutral face that follows the subliminal emotional expression. Participants were told that their task was to guess the gender of the neutral face they saw. All the participants later denied having seen any emotional expressions, and were unable to recognize them, confirming that the emotional stimuli were indeed subliminal.

In another experiment, other subjects were given a single sip of the beverage after seeing the faces, and asked to rate how much they liked the drink, how much they wanted to consume, and how much they would be willing to pay for a can of the beverage.

The results showed that a subliminal exposure to *happy* facial expressions caused thirsty participants to choose to take more of the fruit-flavored drink when they poured their own glass than if they had seen only neutral facial expressions (Winkielman et al., 2000). They also consumed or swallowed more of what they poured after seeing happy expressions than after neutral expressions.

Their consumption behavior was increased by the happy expression, even though they had no conscious awareness of the expression or of any change in their mood.

By contrast, participants who had been subliminally flashed *angry* facial expressions did exactly the opposite. They took less of the drink when pouring than after neutral expressions, and they swallowed less of the drink from their glass. Thus, the effect on the objective decision utility of the drink was bivalent. Consumption behavior could be driven either up or down by the subliminal stimuli. Again, subjects whose consumption behavior was decreased experienced no corresponding decrease in their intervening ratings of a subjective hedonic mood, which could have explained their behavior (Winkielman et al., 2000).

When ratings of the drink itself were assessed after a sip, the same subliminal stimuli altered the ratings of wanting for the drink and of monetary value (Winkielman et al., 2000). The thirsty participants gave higher ratings after subliminal happy expressions than after angry expressions in answer to the question 'How much would you pay for this drink in a store?'. *They were willing to pay more than twice as much* (over 40 cents per can, U.S.$) *after seeing subliminal happy expressions* compared to after seeing subliminal angry expressions (less than 20 cents per can). They also gave higher ratings to the question 'How much do you want this drink' after the happy versus angry subliminal stimulus. These changes in the subjective decision utility of the drink again were not accompanied by changes in the subjective hedonic mood (Winkielman et al., 2000).

Thus, happy subliminal faces did not make drinkers feel better in general, nor did subliminal angry faces make them feel worse. Instead the subliminal stimuli rather directly altered the decision utility of the next affectively-laden event they encountered: in this case, the flavored drink.

Given that we are presently interested in irrational pursuits, I want to focus on the *increases* in decision utility caused by the subliminal exposure to a happy facial expression. The decision utility of the fruit-drink was increased by several measures: thirsty subjects took more of the fruit-drink when they could control the amount poured into their glass, they drank more after taking it, rated their wanting for it higher after a sip, and increased their stated willingness to pay money for the fruit-drink. By all of these indices, the subliminal emotional expressions increased the subjects' wanting for the drink (Winkielman et al., 2000).

But is a subliminal want irrational? The answer is not entirely clear. Certainly, the cause of the increased pursuit is unrelated to the outcome pursued (for the sake of argument, let us count the pouring behavior as a pursuit). Further, there is no a priori reason to suspect that the subliminal presentations altered explicit beliefs about the hedonic value of the drink. The people have no reason to change their assessment of a drink's potential pleasure after a subliminal exposure to an emotional expression they do not consciously see, which induces an implicit emotional reaction they do not consciously feel. However, Winkielman et al. did not explicitly ask subjects about their expectations so this remains only a conjecture. The question remains open.

Unconsciously magnified pursuit might well be called unreasonable—in the sense that no good reason could be given for the magnification. But the lack of a good reason is not quite enough to call it irrational by our definition of irrational given above—namely, acting in contradiction to the expectation of pleasure. An irrelevant cause is not necessarily an irrational pursuit, not even if the irrelevant cause is unconscious. Subliminal wants may not be the stuff of strongly irrational pursuits. Perhaps we should look elsewhere for a truly irrational pursuit.

3. THE BRAIN MECHANISMS OF EXPERIENCED UTILITY AND DECISION UTILITY

A better understanding of the irrational forms of pursuit may come from considering the brain mechanisms that underlie aspects of decision utility. Let us start by considering where in the brain the utility value of rewards might be mediated. The answer to this question depends on whether by utility of a reward we mean its instantaneous experienced utility (hedonic impact of a reward at the moment it is experienced, or reward liking), remembered utility (declarative memory of hedonic impact, or reward memory), predicted utility (declarative expectation of future hedonic impact, or reward expectation), or decision utility (choice value—corresponding to predicted utility but also involving other factors, or reward wanting).

There are quite a number of structures and neural systems in the brain that are activated by rewards and are candidates to mediate utility (Berridge, 2002; LeDoux, 1996; Panksepp, 1998; Rolls, 1999; Shizgal, 1999). These include several regions of the neocortex, such as the prefrontal cortex at the front of the brain (especially the orbitofrontal part, which is closest to the eyes), the cingulate cortex (at the top of the brain, near the middle between the two hemispheres), and the two amygdala (nestled within the temporal lobes at either side of the brain). The brain reward systems also include several structures and neural circuits beneath the cortex, such as the mesolimbic dopamine system that projects from the midbrain up to the nucleus accumbens and other targets, the nucleus accumbens itself (immediately underneath the neocortex at the front of the brain), and the ventral pallidum and lateral hypothalamus (at the base of the forebrain), which receive outputs from the accumbens.

There is reason to think that the orbitofrontal and cingulate cortex may mediate the cognitive aspects of declarative predicted and declarative remembered utilities—conscious expectations and memories (Balleine and Dickinson, 1998a; Damasio, 1999; Rolls, 1999). The nucleus accumbens, ventral pallidum and lateral hypothalamus are likely to mediate basic aspects of experienced utility or hedonic impact (Berridge, 1999; Panksepp, 1998; Peciña and Berridge, 2000; Shizgal, 1999). For a specific aspect of *decision utility*, however, especially relevant to the possibility of irrational pursuit of rewards, we should turn to the subcortical mesolimbic dopamine system that projects from the midbrain up to the accumbens (Figure 2.1) (Berridge and Robinson, 1998).

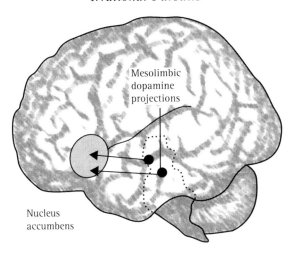

Figure 2.1. *The brain mesolimbic dopamine system. Dopamine neurons project from the midbrain up to the nucleus accumbens*

4. THE MESOLIMBIC DOPAMINE SYSTEM FOR REWARD UTILITY

The mesolimbic dopamine system is famous as a brain substrate of reward utility. There are ample reasons for that fame. The dopamine neurons are turned on by many naturally pleasurable events, at least under some circumstances, such as eating a delicious new food or encountering a sex partner (Ahn and Phillips, 1999; Fiorino et al., 1997; Mark et al., 1994). The dopamine neurons are also activated by most artificial rewards, such as drugs like cocaine, amphetamine, heroin, ecstasy, etc. (Wise, 1998). And many of the brain sites at which direct electrical stimulation is rewarding tend to activate the dopamine neurons or the targets of dopamine neurons (Flores et al., 1997; Hoebel et al., 1999; Panksepp, 1998; Shizgal, 1997, 1999; Yeomans, 1989). Finally, drugs that block the dopamine receptors, disrupting the system, cause animals to stop working in many situations—as though food, sex, cocaine, heroin, brain stimulation reward, etc., lose their reward properties after the suppression of dopamine neurotransmission (Wise, 1982).

Many hypotheses have been offered for the precise role of the mesolimbic dopamine systems in reward (Berridge and Robinson, 1998; Panksepp, 1998; Salamone et al., 1997; Schultz, 1998; Servan-Schreiber et al., 1998; Wise, 1982). Most famous has probably been the *hedonic hypothesis* that dopamine is the brain's 'pleasure neurotransmitter' that mediates hedonic impact at the moment of the actual reward (Gardner, 1997; Volkow et al., 1999; Wise, 1982; Wise and Bozarth, 1985).

Pleasure or hedonic impact is most closely related to instantaneous or experienced utility. Most neuroscientists have not used the utility terminology to describe the dopamine system, but one who has is Peter Shizgal, a leading affective neuroscientist. Shizgal has pondered which type of utility (among instantaneous and predicted decision utilities) might be activated by a rewarding brain electrode that stimulates the medial forebrain bundle, and so it is worth noting his opinion here. Shizgal explicitly chooses experienced or instantaneous utility as the type turned on by brain stimulation, positing that 'rewarding stimulation achieves its grip over ongoing behavior by simulating the real-time effect of a natural reward on the evaluative system, that is, *by driving instantaneous utility to positive values*' (Shizal, 1999, p. 503, italics added). Defining what he means by instantaneous utility, Shizgal writes, 'instant utility is experienced along an opponent hedonic dimension ('good/bad') while biasing the individual to continue or terminate the current course of action. States and stimuli that produce *positive values of instant utility are experienced as pleasurable...*' (Shizgal, 1999, p. 502, italics added). Thus, Shizgal essentially affirms the hedonic hypothesis that a neural basis for pleasure consists of high rates of firing of mesolimbic and related neurons, caused by a rewarding hypothalamic electrode.

The hypothesis that the mesolimbic dopamine mediates pleasure is based on hundreds of affective neuroscience experiments, all interpreted on the assumption that changes in the degree to which rewards are *wanted* by an animal reflects changes in the degree to which the rewards are *liked*. The assumption that wanting reflects liking is both plausible and no doubt often true—but perhaps not *always* true (Berridge and Robinson, 1998). The assumption may not be true in particular when applied to the brain mesolimbic dopamine systems (Berridge and Robinson, 1998; Robinson and Berridge, 2000).

5. THE BRAIN SYSTEMS FOR REWARD 'LIKING': MEASURING HEDONIC IMPACT OR INSTANTANEOUS EXPERIENCED UTILITY

I shared the belief that the mesolimbic dopamine neurotransmission was probably a mechanism for pleasurable reactions until about 10 years ago. But I no longer believe that dopamine mediates positive hedonic 'liking' for rewards, and this change of opinion is directly relevant to the possibility and mechanisms of irrational pursuit. My opinion changed as the result of surprising results in a series of experiments in our laboratory, which attempted to more directly expose the role of the mesolimbic dopamine systems (e.g., Berridge and Robinson, 1998). We asked simply whether dopamine mediates the *basic hedonic impact caused by a simple reward such as a sweet taste*. The experiments were part of our larger effort to identify the crucial brain mechanisms that cause positive affective reactions (i.e., that generate a positive affect) to pleasurable rewards. In a sense, we have sought to directly identify the neural bases of the instantaneous experienced utility.

Our search for pleasure in the brain has used an approach that looks for brain manipulations able to cause changes in an immediate reflection of the degree of hedonic 'liking' impact produced by a reward—namely, changes in *natural affective reactions that are normally elicited by tasty food* (Berridge, 2000). Natural affective reactions are probably most familiar to readers in the form of facial expressions of pleasure and displeasure. To give the reader an idea of how we proceed, for example, a sweet taste elicits from a human infant a positive affective facial reaction: a pattern of tongue protrusions, lip sucking, facial relaxation, and the occasional smile (Steiner, 1979; Steiner et al., 2001). A bitter taste, by contrast, elicits a completely different aversive pattern of gapes, nose wrinkling, head shaking, etc. Of course, we would never use a human infant in an affective neuroscience experiment. However, humans are not alone in their capacity for affective reactions to tasty food. Chimpanzees, orangutans or gorillas, our closest primate relatives, have facial positive and negative affective reactions to tastes that are highly similar to those of the human babies (Steiner et al., 2001). Old world monkeys (primate relations that evolved in Africa and Asia), and New world monkeys (more distant relations that evolved in South America), also have behavioral affective reactions to sweet or bitter tastes, and even rodents such as rats show taste elicited affective reactions that are homologous to those of primates (Figure 2.2). Sweet tastes, for example, elicit tongue protrusions from all, whereas bitter tastes elicit gapes and headshakes. The measurement of these affective reactions by animals after neural manipulations allows us to make an affective neuroscience study of how brain systems mediate the basic hedonic impact of a tasty reward (Berridge, 2000).

Affective reactions to taste
Basic measure of 'liking'
Positive to sweet

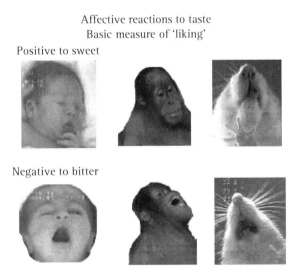

Negative to bitter

Figure 2.2. *The basic hedonic impact or experienced utility reflected in natural affective reactions. The affective reactions of a human infant, a young orangutan, and a rat, elicited by sweet and bitter tastes (Berridge, 2000a)*

Using the technique of measuring affective reactions elicited directly by the hedonic impact of a sweet taste, we have identified several brain systems that mediate the hedonic 'liking' for tastes. For example, neural circuits in the nucleus accumbens that use morphine-like opioid neurotransmitters, circuits in the ventral pallidum and lateral hypothalamus, and GABA-receptor circuits in the brainstem's parabrachial nucleus, all appear crucial to mediate the positive hedonic impact of tasty rewards (Cromwell and Berridge, 1993; Peciña and Berridge, 2000; Söderpalm and Berridge, 2000). Activating these neural systems in the brain of rats causes increases in the positive hedonic reactions that reflect the hedonic impact of a sweet reward. These are brain mechanisms capable of causing increased positive values of experienced utility or 'liking' for such a reward.

6. 'WANTING' REWARD VERSUS 'LIKING' REWARD: INCENTIVE SALIENCE HYPOTHESIS OF DOPAMINE FUNCTION

My colleagues and I expected the mesolimbic dopamine systems to mediate the taste pleasure too. We were wrong—and at first very surprised—to find in a series of studies that the dopamine manipulations had no effect on the positive affective reactions to natural taste pleasures. We tried drugs that suppressed the dopamine systems (Peciña et al., 1997; Treit and Berridge, 1990), drugs that activated the dopamine systems (Treit and Berridge, 1990; Wyvell and Berridge, 2000), an electrical stimulation similar to Shizgal's of the lateral hypothalamus and of the medial forebrain bundle (Berridge and Valenstein, 1991), and chemically-induced brain lesions that selectively destroyed virtually all the dopamine neurons while sparing other circuits (Berridge and Robinson, 1998; Berridge et al., 1989). None of those manipulations of the mesolimbic dopamine altered our measures of the basic hedonic impact or the experienced utility (although they dramatically altered other traditional aspects of food reward more related to decision utility, such as whether food was pursued or eaten).

What psychological process can masquerade as pleasure in so many psychological tests yet not be pleasure? What psychological process is normally activated when a reward is 'liked'—in addition to the 'liking' itself? Rewards are usually conceived as things that are both liked and wanted. They are wanted just to the degree that they are liked—and vice versa. After all, that is rational. Liking and wanting are often viewed as nearly synonymous (indeed, an element of wanting is found even in the definitions of experienced utility used by Kahneman (Kahneman et al., 1997) and Shizgal (1999), namely persistence in goal-directed action; however, it is possible to view this element instead as a part of the decision utility). The solution we found ourselves pushed to adopt was to split the usual notion of reward into two parts and to stress the difference between the erstwhile synonyms.

What if liking and wanting are separable psychological processes, mediated by separate brain systems? And what if the mesolimbic dopamine systems mediate wanting for rewards specifically—and not a liking for rewards at all? A version of that hypothesis has helped resolve our paradox of brain manipulations that changed so many measures of how much a reward was wanted, without changing a measure of how much it was liked.

My colleagues and I have coined the phrase *incentive salience* for the form of 'wanting' we think is mediated by the brain dopamine systems. We believe that the brain dopamine systems attribute the representations of rewards with incentive salience whenever a cue for the reward is encountered. The incentive salience causes the cue and its reward, in our view, to become momentarily more intensely attractive and sought. We often use the term 'wanting' to refer to incentive salience—putting the words in quotation marks as a caveat to denote that this particular type of decision utility is somewhat different from what is meant ordinarily by the word wanting. For one thing, 'wanting' in the incentive salience sense is different in that it need not have a conscious goal or declarative target of predicted utility for it to control choice and pursuit—quite unlike the ordinary conscious wanting, which always has a declarative target (namely, an explicit expectation of predicted hedonic utility).

Wanting and 'wanting' thus differ, both psychologically and in their brain substrates (Berridge, 2001; Berridge and Robinson, 1998; Dickinson et al., 2000). Wanting is a conscious desire that depends on the cortical systems. 'Wanting' is cue-triggered incentive salience, leading to the pursuit of the cued reward, which need not be consciously experienced in order to control behavior, and which depends on the mesolimbic dopamine systems.

7. WANTING (CONSCIOUS DESIRE FOR A DECLARATIVE GOAL) VERSUS 'WANTING' (CUED ATTRACTION TO SALIENT INCENTIVE)

Wanting in the ordinary sense means a conscious desire for a cognitively-represented outcome, essentially a form of decision utility that corresponds directly to predicted utility. But the more basic incentive salience form of 'wanting' has actually been a topic of study for decades in animal studies of the psychology and behavioral neuroscience of reward and conditioned incentive motivation (albeit not couched quite in the terms or concepts I will use) (Berridge, 2001; Bindra, 1978; Dickinson and Balleine, 1994; Dickinson et al., 2000; Rescorla, 1988; Toates, 1986, 1994). Conditioned incentive motivation is controlled by processes that have more in common with the associative learning mechanisms known as Pavlovian conditioning rather than with the declarative, consciously-accessible, and logical mechanisms of goal-directed cognition. The literature on conditioned incentive motivation is very large (for reviews see Berridge, 2001; Bindra, 1978; Dickinson and Balleine, 1994; Toates, 1986). Here, I will only mention the most relevant features.

Reward cues are logically valued for the pleasures they predict—that is, future states of experienced utility, which will occur after the cued reward is obtained.

A core of the incentive salience notion is that reward cues also often become 'wanted' themselves. This process is not strictly logical (and sometimes it has consequences that are downright illogical, costly, or even pathological—but nonetheless it is lawful and quite powerful). In traditional psychological parlance, the reward cues become conditioned incentive stimuli. There are many instances known in both human and animal psychology, but the process has probably been studied most in laboratories of animal learning theory and affective neuroscience. Animals quickly come to approach, seek out, and even attempt to consume conditioned incentives under certain circumstances. Conditioned incentive cues also have priming effects on the pursuit of their cued rewards—they have the power to evoke a strong 'wanting' for their associated hedonic rewards, and to potentiate behavior aimed at obtaining these rewards (Berridge, 2001; Bindra, 1978; Toates, 1986).

8. AFFECTIVE NEUROSCIENCE: ACTIVATING 'WANTING' AS A FORM OF DECISION UTILITY

A door may be opened to a truly irrational pursuit by considering the conditioned incentive salience or 'wanting' process that we believe are mediated by the brain mesolimbic dopamine systems. Recent experiments in our laboratory on this system appear to have produced a moderate but true form of irrational pursuit (Wyvell and Berridge, 2000), in which 'wanting' for a cued incentive outstrips both the actual hedonic impact and the expectations of future hedonic impact.

It is possible to tweak the brain rather selectively in affective neuroscience studies conducted in animals, by the use of experimental techniques such as the microinjection of drugs. If a microinjection of a tiny droplet of amphetamine is made directly into the nucleus accumbens, it causes the mesolimbic neurons to release their synaptic stores of dopamine and related neurotransmitters. This specifically activates the accumbens neuronal receptors. A microinjection is painless because it is made through a previously implanted cannulae, placed into a selected brain structure weeks earlier when the animal was totally anesthetized. Brain tweaks of this sort are not limited to animal studies of course (major brain tweaks also happen to humans who suffer from certain pathological conditions, or who take many types of drugs). Much smaller brain tweaks happen to us all every minute of every day, as natural events cause the mesolimbic dopamine activity to rise or fall. The affective neuroscience studies of animals simply allow us to focus, intensify, and control such rises in neural activation to better identify their psychological consequences.

9. ARE ANIMALS CAPABLE OF IRRATIONAL PURSUIT?

We have defined irrational pursuit as the pursuit of an outcome that is not jus-tified by the cognitive expectations of the hedonic value of that outcome. A shift to incorporate animal studies in this context may therefore strike the reader as problematic. Irrational pursuit requires, first, that animals be capable of cognitive expectations of an outcome's hedonic value (predictive utility or wanting in the ordinary sense), second that we be able to assess these expectations of hedonic value, and third that we be able to detect when pursuit deviates from those expectations. Before we can consider a possible instance of irrational pursuit from animal affective neuroscience studies, we had better make a brief detour into the psychology of animal learning to see if this is feasible.

How can one estimate an animal's expectation of hedonic value? A possible solution to this difficulty has been suggested by a leading psychologist of animal learning, Prof. Anthony Dickinson of Cambridge University in England (Dickinson and Balleine, 1994; Dickinson et al., 2000). Dickinson, together with Bernard Balleine and other colleagues, has developed a clever way to ask a mere rat about its cognitive expectations of reward value, and to detect changes in these expectations. Dickinson and colleagues ask rats about their expectations of the value of a food or drink reward, in part by testing their willingness to work for the rewards when they must be guided principally by these expectations alone. The rats are first trained to work for the real rewards, which come only every so often, so the rat has to persist in working if it wishes to earn its corresponding reward. Then the rats are tested for their willingness to work for these rewards later under so-called *extinction conditions*, when the rewards no longer come at all. Since there are no longer real rewards, the rats have only their expectations of reward to guide them (along with any non-expectational forms of learning that can support their learned response; for more discussion on these issues, see Berridge, 2001).

Naturally, without real rewards to sustain efforts, performance in the extinction test gradually falls off. But since the rats originally learned that perseverance pays off, they persist for quite some time in working based largely on their expectation of reward. Even a single experience of a new value of the reward is sufficient to shift this expectation-guided performance in extinction, if its experienced utility value is altered—but that single experience of a new experienced utility value is essential. Dickinson and Balleine conclude that a taste of the altered experienced utility of a reward, henceforth, essentially alters its remembered utility. The new hedonic memory in turn alters the reward's predicted utility, and thus its decision utility or degree to which it is cognitively wanted—all in a rational manner (Dickinson and Balleine, 1994; Dickinson et al., 2000). Alteration in cue-triggered 'wanting' based on incentive salience, by contrast, acts in a more direct manner that circumvents the rational chain of experience-remember-predict-and-choose, and needs no explicit new experience with the altered experienced utility in order to alter behavior (Balleine and Dickinson, 1998*a,b*; Dickinson and Balleine, 1994; Dickinson et al., 2000).

The issues involved in using a Dickinson-style approach to tease apart cognitive wanting from cue-triggered 'wanting' are rather complex. I have discussed them at greater length elsewhere (Berridge, 2001), and the interested reader is referred also to Dickinson's articles mentioned above. For our purpose it is enough to say that these techniques of assessing animals' cognitive expectations of hedonic value can be of great use in detecting transient instances when the decision utility suddenly diverges from the predicted utility after the brain is viscerally tweaked. They allow an affective neuroscience of irrational pursuit.

10. IRRATIONAL PURSUIT: VISCERAL MESOLIMBIC ACTIVATION OF 'WANTING' FOR A CUED HYPER-INCENTIVE

We can now approach the possibility of observing an irrational level of a high decision utility for a hedonic outcome by combining brain tweaks in the form of amphetamine microinjections, which activate the mesolimbic dopamine systems, with Dickinson's techniques for assessing predicted utility and conditioned incentive motivation. Cindy Wyvell, a doctoral student in our laboratory at the University of Michigan, has done just that (Wyvell and Berridge, 2000). Wyvell has examined the effect of the mesolimbic activation, caused by the amphetamine microinjection in the nucleus accumbens, on decision utility grounded either in the predicted utility of a sugar reward or in its conditioned incentive salience. She found dopamine activation to cause a transient but intense form of irrational pursuit linked to incentive salience. The irrational level of pursuit has two sources that restrict its occurrence and duration: a visceral brain factor (mesolimbic activation) and a psychological factor (the presence of a reward cue). When both factors are present simultaneously, Wyvell finds that reward pursuit is driven to an irrational level, which is more than four times its normal value (Wyvell and Berridge, 2000).

In this experiment, Wyvell first trained rats to work on some days instrumentally for occasional sugar pellet rewards by pressing a lever (a second lever was also present, but pressing on the second earned nothing, and merely measured the rats' general tendency to move around and do things). On different days, the rats learned a reward cue (CS+) for the sugar pellets, by being exposed to Pavlovian pairings in which sugar was preceded by either the illumination of a small light in the lever (for some rats) or by a sound (for other rats). In these cue-learning sessions, the rats did not have to work for sugar rewards—instead rewards came automatically after each cue. All the rats were implanted with a microinjection cannulae so that a droplet of amphetamine or of a drug-free vehicle solution could be infused into their nucleus accumbens. Finally, the rats were tested for work using the Dickinson extinction procedure after they had received either the amphetamine or vehicle microinjections. During this test, their performance could be guided only by the predicted utility of sugar because they received no real sugar rewards (no experienced utility or response reinforcement). And while they pursued their expected reward, their reward cue (light or sound for 30 s) was occasionally presented to them over the course of the half-hour session. In a related experiment, Wyvell tested the effect of amphetamine microinjections on the experienced utility or hedonic impact of real sugar, by measuring the positive hedonic patterns of the affective reactions of rats as they received an infusion of sugar solution directly into their mouths (Wyvell and Berridge, 2000). What would be enhanced by the mesolimbic dopamine activation: experienced utility, predicted utility, decision utility, or all three? The answer turns out to be *decision utility* alone, and *only a piece of it* at that.

Remember that in this experiment the experienced utility of a sugar reward is measured by the hedonic reactions to its taste, while the decision utility of sugar is measured by how hard the rat works for the expected sugar. But there are *two types* of decision utility to be assessed here. One type is *ordinary wanting*, when the rat works guided primarily by its expectation or the predicted utility of sugar (measured by the baseline performance on the lever). Another type of decision utility adds '*wanting*' (conditioned incentive salience attributed by the meso-limbic systems to the representation of sugar reward that is activated by the cue) to ordinary wanting, during the brief 30 s presentations of the reward cue. Wyvell found that the activation of the dopamine neurotransmission in the accumbens, caused by the microinjections of amphetamine directly into that brain structure, did not substantially change the baseline lever pressing in the absence of the reward cue, indicating no effect of the amphetamine on the predicted utility of the sugar reward, or on the ordinary wanting or the decision utility of sugar based on the cognitive expectations of predicted utility (Wyvell and Berridge, 2000). Similarly, amphetamine did not increase the positive hedonic affective reactions elicited by the taste of real sugar, indicating that the amphetamine did not increase the hedonic impact or the experienced utility of the sugar reward. However, the amphetamine microinjection still enhanced decision utility of the sugar reward in the 'wanting' sense of cue-triggered pursuit.

The amphetamine in the accumbens caused the sugar cue to trigger a relative frenzy of pursuit for the reward, 400 percent higher than the normal level without mesolimbic activation, whenever the cue was presented (Wyvell and Berridge, 2000). This relatively intense level of work for the sugar reward was transient, and decayed within minutes—only to be triggered again by the next reward cue. It is unlikely that the mesolimbic activation altered any stable cognitive representa-tion of the predicted utility of the sugar reward, because the amphetamine was present in the nucleus accumbens throughout the entire session, but the intense enhancement of pursuit lasted only while the cue stimulus was actually present. Thus, it seems implausible that the intensely high pursuit was rational (i.e., matched by an intense increase in the predicted utility). If the cue-triggered intense pursuit was not rationally matched by an elevated expectation of pre-dicted utility, then we must conclude that the cue triggered a momentary divergence of the decision utility from the predicted utility. In other words, the mesolimbic activation caused the reward cue to become a hyper-incentive, triggering an irrationally high (albeit temporary) level of 'wanting' for the sugar reward. The high level of 'wanting' decision utility was irrational because it was not justified by a matching increase for the same reward in either the experienced utility (i.e., no increase in affective reactions to the taste of sugar) or predicted

Kent C. Berridge

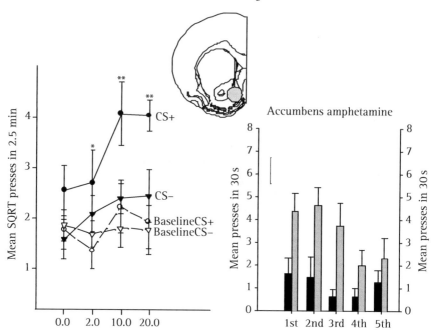

Figure 2.3. *The hyper-incentive effects of a reward cue gated by the visceral mesolimbic activation. The amphetamine microinjection in the nucleus accumbens magnifies the decision utility of the sugar reward in the presence of the reward cue (CS+), but has little effect on lever pressing for sugar in the absence of a cue (baseline, reflecting predicted utility) or during an irrelevant cue (CS−) (left). Decision utility amplification comes and goes with the cue during a single session after an amphetamine microinjection (right). The black bars denote work in the absence of the reward cue, the grey bars show the elevation when the cue was present. Modified from Wyvell and Berridge (2000)*

utility (i.e., no increase in the baseline effort for sugar in the absence of a reward cue) (Figure 2.3).

Cue-triggered 'hyper-wanting' is irrational and transient. It is repeatedly reversible, even over the short span of a 30 min test session, in which irrational 'wanting' was triggered and then decayed several times (Wyvell and Berridge, 2000). It is triggered by the encounter with reward cues, and at that moment it exerts its irrational effect, disproportionate to the cognitively expected hedonic value of the reward. One moment the dopamine-activated brain of the rat simply wants sugar in the ordinary sense. The next moment, when the cue comes, the dopamine-activated brain both wants sugar and 'wants' sugar to an exaggerated degree. A few moments later it has returned to its rational level of wanting appropriate to its expectation of reward. Moments later still, the cue is encountered again, and excessive and irrational 'wanting' again takes control.

For the brain in a state of mesolimbic activation, the conditioned reward cue becomes a hyper-incentive cue, able to trigger an irrational degree of pursuit for the sugar reward. During the mesolimbic brain excitation, the cue confers a momentary decision utility upon the outcome, beyond what its actual (or predicted) hedonic value can justify.

11. COMPARISON TO VISCERAL FACTORS

This view of hyper-incentive cue prompting irrational pursuit by a viscerally-activated brain, seems consistent with the theory of Loewenstein and colleagues regarding *visceral factors* as an influence on decision making (Loewenstein, 1996, 1999; Loewenstein and Schkade, 1999). Regarding irrational wanting in particular, cue-triggered hyper-incentive motivation caused during the brain meso-limbic activation dovetails with Loewenstein's suggestion that 'there are certain types of influences or incentives that operate independently of, and overwhelm, individual deliberation and volition' (Loewenstein, 1996, p. 276). For Loewenstein, the visceral factors include states of hunger, sexual arousal, and drug addiction. All of these states interact with the brain dopamine systems. For example, the mesolimbic dopamine systems are most highly activated by a taste of food when animals are hungry (Wilson et al., 1995). The visceral states can also be triggered by incentive cues (Loewenstein, 1996), and may be more highly aroused by freshly potent stimuli, such as a fresh course in a meal or a new sexual partner (Loewenstein, 1996). Accordingly, Phillips and colleagues have shown that the mesolimbic dopamine systems are most activated in animals when the palatable food is fresh (Ahn and Phillips, 1999), or when a fresh sexual partner is encountered (Fiorino et al., 1997).

Loewenstein views the visceral states as having a negative hedonic tone themselves (Loewenstein, 1996), which is slightly different from the view of incentive salience that I have presented here. Hunger states and other 'drives' may facilitate the mesolimbic activation, but their negative affective tone (if any) is not essential to the resulting increase in cue-triggered 'wanting' (Berridge, 2001; Toates, 1994). Positive motivational states may equally suffice, so long as they activate the brain mesolimbic systems. For example, in Wyvell's experiment on irrational cue-triggered 'wanting' for the sugar reward, the mesolimbic dopamine activation was caused directly by a microinjection of amphetamine into the brain's nucleus accumbens (Wyvell and Berridge, 2000). Similar brain amphetamine microinjections trigger the relapse of heroin pursuit in previously addicted rats (Stewart and Vezina, 1988), relevant to the incentive-sensitization that may underlie addiction (Robinson and Berridge, 2000). But such micro-injections are unlikely to induce an aversive drive state. The accumbens amphetamine microinjections are preferred and chosen by animals, rather than avoided (Carr and White, 1986; Phillips et al., 1994). However, for many predictions the hedonic valence of the visceral states is not a source of serious difference between Loewenstein's view and incentive salience. In general, the incentive salience hypothesis and the relevant experimental results are fully supportive of Loewenstein's visceral factors theory (Loewenstein, 1996, 1999), and provide one specific mechanism by which visceral factors might actually overwhelm volition to produce irrational choices.

12. RELEVANCE OF HUMAN DECISION MAKING TO PSYCHOLOGISTS AND BEHAVIORAL ECONOMISTS

I am not so rash as to propose that the type of irrational choice sketched here is a model to be simply applied to human decision making. Rats are not humans; associatively-established conditioned stimuli for rewards do not replicate the full range of imagery and representation cues that impinge on human choices; a lever box with one reward is not an adequate model of human choice; and the brain microinjections are an artificial manipulation of the decision utility. My purpose here is simply to suggest truly irrational pursuit as a phenomenon for consideration, and to raise some relevant issues regarding the affective neuroscience of goal pursuit and human choice that may prove useful to psychologists and behavioral economists.

13. HYPER-INCENTIVES FOR NORMAL HUMANS

What are the human implications if this interpretation of irrational 'wanting' is correct? While admittedly humans are not rats, humans have brain dopamine systems that can be expected to respond similarly to reward cues and to influence the decision utility of associated rewards (Childress et al., 1999; Sell et al., 1999; Servan-Schreiber et al., 1998). Beyond this, it is possible that for human minds the cognitive representations of rewards might serve to interact with dopamine systems in some circumstances, instead of the associative cues that are useful in animal studies. Could the vivid imagery of an outcome, evoked or spontaneous, interact with the human brain in a state of high-but-normal mesolimbic activation to create an irrational hyper-incentive for a human? This is an open question for the future.

14. HYPER-INCENTIVES IN ADDICTION

Humans do not have microinjection cannulae in their brains, but human drug addicts routinely activate their brain dopamine systems in pharmacological ways. Further, there is considerable evidence to suggest that drug addicts may undergo potentially permanent incremental changes in their brain dopamine systems, known as neural sensitization (Robinson et al., 1998). Neural sensitization may increase the cue-triggered activity of mesolimbic systems in a way that parallels the effect of the amphetamine microinjection, creating hyper-incentive drug cues that trigger the compulsive pursuit of drug rewards (Robinson and Berridge, 1993, 2000). Incentive-sensitization is an explanation of addiction based on irrational choice.

Neural sensitization means that the dopamine neurons become hyper-excitable and physically altered (Badiani et al., 1997; Robinson et al., 1998; Robinson and

Kolb, 1999). The sensitized neural systems are not always in a hyper-excited state, but once sensitized they can be triggered into a hyper-excited state if the drug is taken again, and their triggering into hyper-excitation is strongly gated by reward cues. My colleague Terry Robinson and I have suggested that neural sensitization in the brains of human drug addicts may be responsible for the development of addictive and compulsive drug taking (Robinson and Berridge, 1993, 2000). This explanation for addiction is especially useful for understanding relapse (often triggered by the encounter with drug cues) in addicts who have been abstinent for some time. Relapse by abstinent addicts is one of the most powerful aspects of addiction, and one of the most difficult features to explain rationally. After all, first time users may over-estimate their ability to resist addiction, or over-estimate the pleasure of the drug, or under-estimate the costs they will pay if they become addicts (Herrnstein and Prelec, 1991). All of those expectations may be wrong, but if the novice user holds them, then drug use is not irrational. But for the experienced addict, who knows these beliefs to be incorrect, to take the drug means the predictable loss of control. If the addict wishes to quit, and has decided that drug pleasures are not worth the costs, then to take the drug again is irrational. Yet, addicts do frequently relapse and do take the drug again, especially when they encounter drug cues. And they do so even when they do not feel the specific symptoms of withdrawal. Hyper-incentive cues, able to provoke the irrational decision utility from a sensitized brain, may be a mechanism for the irrational pursuit of drugs. If drug cues trigger the activation of sensitized mesolimbic dopamine systems, then an addict may be moved to take drugs again by hyper-incentive 'wanting'. Such an excessive 'wanting' may sometimes be irrational, but need be no less potent for that.

15. APPLICATIONS TO ORDINARY LIFE

Are the choices of ordinary humans ever tipped by cues and imagery in an irrational sense? Does the decision utility of outcomes we consider in our lives ever fluctuate independent of the predicted utility under the influence of vivid cues?

Consider one final scenario. Imagine that a consumer watching a television home shopping channel is more likely to choose to buy an item shown at a particular moment, than to get in the car later that day and drive to the store for the physical purchase of the same item. If so, the image on television is a cue-like influence on choice. Immediacy of arrival of the actually-bought item itself seems not very relevant to this choice. The item itself is delayed, whether one buys through the shopping channel and waits days for delivery or one waits to go to the store oneself. It may even be faster to drive to the store for the item than to wait days for delivery. The power of the shopping channel may come from the immediacy of the image and its influence on the momentary decision to buy— not from any home shopping advantage regarding the item itself (let us assume the home shopper drives to pick up the item, which equalizes transaction efforts).

But although the item itself arrives no sooner for the home shopper, the cue and image of the item are immediate and prompt a decision to buy.

To the degree that vivid imagery and cues induce shoppers to choose what they would not have chosen in the absence of those cues, the mesolimbic dopamine and incentive salience 'wanting' may play a role, and sometimes operate outside the bounds of declarative conscious awareness. To the degree that choices based on 'wanting' diverge from the expectations of future hedonic consequences, an irrational choice has been made.

If an irrational choice occurs at all in normal human life, the situations that will produce it will be relatively rare. By the mechanism considered here, it would require a high excitability in the mesolimbic brain 'wanting' systems and a simultaneous immediate encounter with the reward cues. Whether these situations occur at all, and if so, how frequently, are questions for the future. But the evidence discussed above suggests that, under the right conditions, irrational choice may be a powerful phenomenon.

One may 'want' more than one wants. Decision utility may transiently detach and soar above predicted utility, as well as above eventual experienced utility. If so, the outcomes will be pursued to a degree disproportionate both to their actual liking and to their current expectation of being liked. That is just irrational.

REFERENCES

Ahn, S. and Phillips, A.G. (1999). Dopaminergic correlates of sensory-specific satiety in the medial prefrontal cortex and nucleus accumbens of the rat. *Journal of Neuroscience, 19*(19), B1–6.

Badiani, A., Camp, D.M., and Robinson, T.E. (1997). Enduring enhancement of amphetamine sensitization by drug-associated environmental stimuli. *Journal of Pharmacology and Experimental Therapeutics, 282*(2), 787–94.

Balleine, B.W. and Dickinson, A. (1998a). Goal-directed instrumental action: contingency and incentive learning and their cortical substrates. *Neuropharmacology, 37*(4–5), 407–19.

—— and ——(1998b). The role of incentive learning in instrumental outcome revaluation by sensory-specific satiety. *Animal Learning and Behavior, 26*(1), 46–59.

Berridge, K.C. (1999). Pleasure, pain, desire, and dread: Hidden core processes of emotion. In D. Kahneman, E. Diener, and N. Schwarz (Eds.), *Well-being: The foundations of hedonic psychology* (pp. 525–57). New York: Russell Sage Foundation.

—— (2000). Measuring hedonic impact in animals and infants: microstructure of affective taste reactivity patterns. *Neuroscience and Biobehavioral Reviews, 24*(2), 173–98.

—— (2001). Reward learning: Reinforcement, incentives, and expectations. In D. L. Medin (Ed.), *The Psychology of Learning and Motivation* (Vol. 40, pp. 223–78). New York: Academic Press.

—— (2002). Comparing the emotional brain of humans to other animals. In R. J. Davidson, H.H. Goldsmith, and K. Scherer (Eds.), *Handbook of Affective Sciences* (chapter 7). Oxford: Oxford University Press.

—— and Robinson, T.E. (1998). What is the role of dopamine in reward: hedonic impact, reward learning, or incentive salience? *Brain Research—Brain Research Reviews, 28*(3), 309–69.

—— and Valenstein, E.S. (1991). What psychological process mediates feeding evoked by electrical stimulation of the lateral hypothalamus? *Behavioral Neuroscience, 105*(1), 3–14.

—— Venier, I.L., and Robinson, T.E. (1989). Taste reactivity analysis of 6-hydroxydopamine-induced aphagia: Implications for arousal and anhedonia hypotheses of dopamine function. *Behavioral Neuroscience, 103*(1), 36–45.

Bindra, D. (1978). How adaptive behavior is produced: a perceptual-motivation alternative to response reinforcement. *Behavioral and Brain Sciences, 1,* 41–91.

Carr, G.D. and White, N.M. (1986). Anatomical disassociation of amphetamine's rewarding and aversive effects: an intracranial microinjection study. *Psychopharmacology (Berl), 89*(3), 340–6.

Childress, A.R., Mozley, P.D., McElgin, W., Fitzgerald, J., Reivich, M., and O'Brien, C.P. (1999). Limbic activation during cue-induced cocaine craving. *American Journal of Psychiatry, 156*(1), 11–18.

Cromwell, H.C. and Berridge, K.C. (1993). Where does damage lead to enhanced food aversion: the ventral pallidum/substantia innominata or lateral hypothalamus? *Brain Research, 624*(1–2), 1–10.

Damasio, A.R. (1999). *The feeling of what happens: body and emotion in the making of consciousness.* (1st ed.). New York: Harcourt Brace.

Dickinson, A. and Balleine, B. (1994). Motivational control of goal-directed action. *Animal Learning and Behavior, 22,* 1–18.

—— Smith, J., and Mirenowicz, J. (2000). Dissociation of Pavlovian and instrumental incentive learning under dopamine antagonists. *Behavioral Neuroscience, 114,* 468–83.

Fiorino, D.F., Coury, A., and Phillips, A.G. (1997). Dynamic changes in nucleus accumbens dopamine efflux during the Coolidge effect in male rats. *Journal of Neuroscience, 17*(12), 4849–55.

Flores, C., Arvanitogiannis, A., and Shizgal, P. (1997). Fos-like immunoreactivity in forebrain regions following self-stimulation of the lateral hypothalamus and the ventral tegmental area. *Behavioural Brain Research, 87*(2), 239–51.

Gardner, E.L. (1997). Brain reward mechanisms. In J.H. Lowinson, P. Ruiz, R.B. Millman, and J.G. Langrod (Eds.), *Substance Abuse: A Comprehensive Textbook* (3rd ed., pp. 51–85). Baltimore: Williams and Wilkin.

Gilbert, D.G. and Wilson, T.D. (2000). Miswanting: Some problems in forecasting future affective states. In Forgas (Ed.), *Feeling and thinking: the role of affect in social cognition.* Cambridge: Cambridge University Press.

Gilbert, D.T., Pinel, E.C., Wilson, T.D., Blumberg, S.J., and Wheatley, T.P. (1998). Immune neglect: A source of durability bias in affective forecasting. *Journal of Personality and Social Psychology, 75*(3), 617–38.

Herrnstein, R.J. and Prelec, D. (1991). Melioration—a Theory of Distributed Choice. *Journal of Economic Perspectives*, 5(3), 137–56.

Hoebel, B.G., Rada, P.V., Mark, G.P., and Pothos, E.N. (1999). Neural systems for reinforcement and inhibition of behavior: Relevance to eating, addiction, and depression. In *Well-being: The foundations of hedonic psychology* (pp. 558–572). New York: Russell Sage Foundation.

Kent C. Berridge

Kahneman, D. (1999). Objective happiness. In *Well-being: The foundations of hedonic psychology* (pp. 3–25). New York: Russell Sage Foundation.

—— (2000). Evaluation by moments: past and future. In D. Kahneman and A. Tversky (Eds.), *Choices, values, and frames* (pp. 651–79). Cambridge: Cambridge University Press.

—— Fredrickson, B.L., Schreiber, C.A., and Redelmeier, D.A. (1993). When more pain is preferred to less: adding a better end. *Psychological Science, 4*, 401–5.

—— Knetsch, J., and Thaler, R. (1990). Experimental tests of the endowment effect and the Coase theorem. *Journal of Political Economy, 98*, 1325–48.

—— and Snell, J. (1992). Predicting a changing taste. *Journal of Behavioral Decision Making, 5*, 187–200.

—— Wakker, P.P., and Sarin, R. (1997). Back to Bentham? Explorations of experienced utility. *The Quarterly Journal of Economics, 112*, 375–405.

Kunst-Wilson, W.R. and Zajonc, R.B. (1980). Affective discrimination of stimuli that cannot be recognized. *Science, 207*(4430), 557–8.

LeDoux, J. (1996). *The Emotional Brain: The Mysterious Underpinnings of Emotional Life.* New York: Simon and Schuster.

Loewenstein, G. (1996). Out of control: Visceral influences on behavior. *Organizational Behavior and Human Decision Processes, 65*(3), 272–92.

—— (1999). A visceral account of addiction. In J. Elster and O.J. Skog (Eds.), *Getting hooked: Rationality and addiction* (pp. 235–64). Cambridge: Cambridge University Press.

—— and Schkade, D. (1999). Wouldn't it be nice? Predicting future feelings. In *Well-being: The foundations of hedonic psychology* (pp. 85–105). New York: Russell Sage Foundation.

Mark, G.P., Smith, S.E., Rada, P.V., and Hoebel, B.G. (1994). An appetitively conditioned taste elicits a preferential increase in mesolimbic dopamine release. *Pharmacology Biochemistry and Behavior, 48*(3), 651–60.

Murphy, S.T. and Zajonc, R.B. (1993). Affect, cognition, and awareness: affective priming with optimal and suboptimal stimulus exposures. *Journal of Personality and Social Psychology, 64*(5), 723–39.

Nisbett, R.W. and Wilson, T.D. (1978). Telling more than we can know: verbal reports on mental processes. *Psychological Review, 84*, 231–59.

Panksepp, J. (1998). *Affective Neuroscience: the Foundations of Human and Animal Emotions.* Oxford: Oxford University Press.

Peciña, S. and Berridge, K.C. (2000). Opioid eating site in accumbens shell mediates food intake and hedonic liking: map based on microinjection Fos plumes. *Brain Research, 863*, 71–86.

Peciña, S., Berridge, K.C., and Parker, L.A. (1997). Pimozide does not shift palatability: Separation of anhedonia from sensorimotor suppression by taste reactivity. *Pharmacology Biochemistry and Behavior, 58*(3), 801–11.

Phillips, G.D., Robbins, T.W., and Everitt, B.J. (1994). Bilateral intra-accumbens self-administration of d-amphetamine: antagonism with intra-accumbens SCH-23390 and sulpiride. *Psychopharmacology (Berl), 114*(3), 477–85.

Redelmeier, D.A. and Kahneman, D. (1996). Patients memories of painful medical treatments: real-time and retrospective evaluations of two minimally invasive procedures. *Pain, 66*(1), 3–8.

Rescorla, R.A. (1988). Pavlovian conditioning. It's not what you think it is. *American Psychology, 43*(3), 151–60.

Robinson, T.E. and Berridge, K.C. (1993). The neural basis of drug craving: an incentive-sensitization theory of addiction. *Brain Research Reviews, 18*(3), 247–91.

—— and Berridge, K.C. (2000). The psychology and neurobiology of addiction: an incentive-sensitization view. *Addiction, 95*(8 (Suppl. 2)), S91–S117.

—— Browman, K.E., Crombag, H.S., and Badiani, A. (1998). Modulation of the induction or expression of psychostimulant sensitization by the circumstances surrounding drug administration. *Neuroscience and Biobehavioral Reviews, 22*(2), 347–54.

—— and Kolb, B. (1999). Alterations in the morphology of dendrites and dendritic spines in the nucleus accumbens and prefrontal cortex following repeated treatment with amphetamine or cocaine. *European Journal of Neuroscience, 11*(5), 1598–604.

Rolls, E.T. (1999). *The Brain and Emotion*. Oxford: Oxford University Press.

Salamone, J.D., Cousins, M.S., and Snyder, B.J. (1997). Behavioral functions of nucleus accumbens dopamine: empirical and conceptual problems with the anhedonia hypothesis. *Neuroscience and Biobehavioral Review, 21*(3), 341–59.

Schultz, W. (1998). Predictive reward signal of dopamine neurons. *Journal of Neurophysiology, 80*(1), 1–27.

Sell, L.A., Morris, J., Bearn, J., Frackowiak, R.S. J., Friston, K.J., and Dolan, R.J. (1999). Activation of reward circuitry in human opiate addicts. *European Journal of Neuroscience, 11*(3), 1042–8.

Servan-Schreiber, D., Bruno, R.M., Carter, C.S., and Cohen, J.D. (1998). Dopamine and the mechanisms of cognition: Part I. A neural network model predicting dopamine effects on selective attention. *Biological Psychiatry, 43*(10), 713–22.

Shizgal, P. (1997). Neural basis of utility estimation. *Current Opinion in Neurobiology, 7*, 198–208.

—— (1999). On the neural computation of utility: Implications from studies of brain stimulation reward. In *Well-being: The foundations of hedonic psychology* (pp. 500–24). New York: Russell Sage Foundation.

Söderpalm, A.H. V. and Berridge, K.C. (2000). The hedonic impact and intake of food are increased by midazolam microinjection in the parabrachial nucleus. *Brain Research, 877*(2), 288–97.

Steiner, J.E. (1979). Human facial expressions in response to taste and smell stimulation. *Advances in Child Development and Behavior, 13*, 257–95.

—— Glaser, D., Hawilo, M.E., and Berridge, K.C. (2001). Comparative expression of hedonic impact: Affective reactions to taste by human infants and other primates. *Neuroscience and Biobehavioral Reviews 25*(1), 53–74.

Stewart, J. and Vezina, P. (1988). A comparison of the effects of intra-accumbens injections of amphetamine and morphine on reinstatement of heroin intravenous self-administration behavior. *Brain Research, 457*(2), 287–94.

Toates, F. (1986). *Motivational Systems*. Cambridge: Cambridge University Press.

Toates, F.M. (1994). Comparing motivational systems—an incentive motivation perspective. In C.R. Legg and D.A. Booth (Eds.), *Appetite: Neural and Behavioural Bases* (pp. 305–27). New York: Oxford University Press.

Treit, D. and Berridge, K.C. (1990). A comparison of benzodiazepine, serotonin, and dopamine agents in the taste-reactivity paradigm. *Pharmacology Biochemistry and Behavior, 37*(3), 451–6.

Volkow, N.D., Wang, G.J., Fowler, J.S., Logan, J., Gatley, S.J., Wong, C., Hitzemann, R., and Pappas, N.R. (1999). Reinforcing effects of psychostimulants in humans are associated with increases in brain dopamine and occupancy of D-2 receptors. *Journal of Pharmacology and Experimental Therapeutics, 291*(1), 409–15.

Wilson, C., Nomikos, G.G., Collu, M., and Fibiger, H.C. (1995). Dopaminergic correlates of motivated behavior: importance of drive. *Journal of Neuroscience, 15*(7), 5169–78.

Wilson, T.D. and Schooler, J.W. (1991). Thinking too much: introspection can reduce the quality of preferences and decisions. *Journal of Personality and Social Psychology, 60*(2), 181–92.

—— Wheatley, T., Meyers, J.M., Gilbert, D.T., and Axsom, D. (2000). Focalism: A source of durability bias in affective forecasting. *Journal of Personality and Social Psychology, 78*(5), 821–36.

Winkielman, P., Berridge, K.C., and Wilbarger, J. (2000). Subliminal affective priming of hedonic value: Unconscious reactions to masked happy versus angry faces influence consumption behavior and drink evaluation. *Unpublished manuscript.*

—— Zajonc, R.B., and Schwarz, N. (1997). Subliminal affective priming resists attributional interventions. *Cognition and Emotion, 11*, 433–65.

Wise, R.A. (1982). Neuroleptics and operant behavior: the anhedonia hypothesis. *Behavioral and Brain Sciences, 5*, 39–87.

—— (1998). Drug-activation of brain reward pathways. *Drug & Alcohol Dependence, 51*(1–2), 13–22.

—— and Bozarth, M.A. (1985). Brain mechanisms of drug reward and euphoria. *Psychiatric Medicine, 3*(4), 445–60.

Wyvell, C.L. and Berridge, K.C. (2000). Intra-accumbens amphetamine increases the pure incentive salience of sucrose reward: Enhancement of reward 'wanting' without 'liking' or response reinforcement. *Journal of Neuroscience, 20*(20), 8122–30.

Yeomans, J.S. (1989). Two substrates for medial forebrain bundle self-stimulation: myelinated axons and dopamine axons. *Neuroscience and Biobehavioral Review, 13*(2–3), 91–8.

Zajonc, R.B. (1980). Feeling and thinking: preferences need no inferences. *American Psychologist, 35*, 151–75.

—— (1998). Emotions. In D.T. Gilbert, S.T. Fiske, and G. Lindzey (Eds.), *The handbook of social psychology* (4th ed., Vol. 2, pp. 591–632). Boston: McGraw-Hill.

3

The Pursuit and Assessment of Happiness can be Self-Defeating

JONATHAN W. SCHOOLER, DAN ARIELY,
AND GEORGE LOEWENSTEIN

> The only way to avoid being miserable is not to have enough leisure to wonder whether you're happy or not. (George Bernard Shaw)
>
> Happiness is as a butterfly, which, when pursued, is always beyond our grasp, but which, if you will sit down quietly, may alight upon you. (Nathaniel Hawthorne)

All sentient creatures presumably favor pleasure over pain. However, only humans, with their unique capacity for planning and self-reflection, have the capacity to deliberately attempt to conduct their lives so as to maximize their hedonic experience. The fact that we are able to consider the potential short- and long-term hedonic benefits of our actions, does not mean of course that it is necessarily advisable to attempt to deliberately maximize happiness. Nevertheless, a cornerstone of western thought is the assumption that the explicit pursuit of happiness is and should be a primary source of human motivation. The preeminence of this goal is exemplified in the US Declaration of Independence, which characterizes the pursuit of happiness as a 'self-evident' and 'inalienable right.' Consistent with this tradition, psychologists have observed that the explicit goal of maximizing happiness is a core motivation of many individuals, particularly those in western cultures (for reviews, see Kityama and Markus, 2000; Myers, 1992, 2000). For economists, the notion that individuals maximize utilities has long been considered a cornerstone of economic theory. However, conceptualizations of the relationship between maximizing utilities and the explicit pursuit of happiness have varied in response to evolving notions of utility.

Since the ascension of neoclassical economics at the end of the nineteenth century, the concept of utility has played a central role in economics. However, economists' interpretation of the term has evolved, and, because economists believe that people maximize utility, their understanding of human behavior has evolved in parallel. For Bentham, who invented the term, utility was

The writing of the manuscript was supported by a grant to the first author from the Center for Consciousness Studies.

commensurate with happiness. Hence, the early neoclassical economists, who adhered to the Benthamite interpretation, viewed behavior as a matter of maximizing happiness. Responding, in part, to the psychology of their time (Lewin, 1996), however, early neoclassical economists became skeptical of whether people were really maximizing, or even attempting to maximize, their own happiness. These doubts, along with the perennial problem that utility cannot be measured in an objective fashion, led to attempts to explain behavior in more psychologically neutral terms. These attempts culminated in the ordinal utility/ revealed preference perspective, according to which human behavior is simply a matter of taking actions designed to satisfy one's preferences (see Loewenstein, 1992; Stigler, 1965; for a discussion of these developments).

The ordinal utility revolution did not occur without dissent. I.M.D. Little (1957), for example, in his *Critique of Welfare Economics*, lamented that ordinal utility hobbled economists' ability to draw implications about the welfare effects of economic policies. Amartya Sen (1973) commented on the vacuousness of the revealed preference concept as well as the patent unrealism of the small number of testable predictions that it does make (e.g., stability, consistency, and convexity). Philosophers raised questions about what it means to satisfy one's preferences in a dynamic setting in which preferences and endowments change (Page, 1968). Even John Hicks, a member of the triad credited with the concept of ordinal utility, in his later writings, stated that 'the ordinal utility revolution, in which I played a role, was not nearly so much of an advance as I supposed' (Hicks, 1976).

These problems have led some, including most prominently Daniel Kahneman and his colleagues, to advocate a return to the Benthamite concept of utility (see, e.g., their paper titled *Back to Bentham?* (Kahneman et al., 1997)). As Kahneman points out, many of the most important questions for economics, such as whether people can successfully predict their own future utilities or whether people are successful in maximizing utility, are only meaningful under the older, Benthamite, interpretation of the term (Kahneman and Varey, 1991). It is also worth noting that many economists who publicly embrace ordinal preferences, often refer to utility in ways that betray a lingering hedonic interpretation of the concept.

While agreeing with Kahneman and the other critics of ordinal utility that Benthamite utility offers a richer and more promising foundation on which to build Economics, our goal is to highlight some problems with the Benthamite utility that have not received much attention from economists. We point to three specific problems that interfere with people's ability to optimize their own levels of utility.

First, people may have only a limited explicit access to the utilities that they derive from experiences. As many writers have commented, maximizing utility in the real world involves a hopelessly complex constrained optimization problem. But think of how much more difficult it is to solve such a problem if one lacks access to the criterion variable! Maximizing utility when one cannot assess one's own level of utility is as futile as the task of a firm that tries to maximize its profits without being able to measure them.

Second, when people do attempt to assess their own level of utility, such efforts may adversely affect their well-being—that is, undermine the utility they are attempting to measure. Like the Heisenberg uncertainty principle in physics, which says that one cannot measure the energy of a particle because the act of measurement affects the particle's energy level, introspection about happiness may be impossible because introspecting affects (and potentially undermines) happiness. Moreover, even if there were no measurement interferences, there might be a significant hedonic cost to doing so.

Third, happiness-seeking may be a self-defeating goal. A variety of lines of psychological research suggest that explicit efforts to maximize one's happiness can undermine the ability to achieve happiness. Like many other goals, such as not thinking about a problem (Wenzlaff and Wegner, 2000) or re-experiencing a mood (Wegner, Erber, and Zanakas, 1993) the pursuit of happiness may be self-defeating. Therefore, to the extent that economic agents do attempt to deliberately maximize happiness, they are unlikely to succeed.

We review research pertinent to these three points, then present the results from two studies—one laboratory experiment and one field study—that were designed to examine the impact on happiness of monitoring one's happiness and of trying to be happy. It should be noted at the outset that, while we raise problems with Benthamite utility, these comments should not be construed as a call for the perpetuation of ordinal utility. Ordinal utility suffers from its own set of problems, including several that are analogous to those we discuss here. Perhaps the conclusion that should be drawn is that utility maximization is an imperfect representation of human behavior, regardless of one's definition of utility.

1. THE LIMITS OF HEDONIC INTROSPECTION

Most researchers who study happiness or subjective well-being, while recognizing that there is some error in self-report measures, nevertheless take individuals' assessments of their happiness at face value. As Myers, one of the foremost purveyors of this research observes: 'By definition, the final judge of someone's subjective well-being is whomever lives inside that person's skin. "If you feel happy" noted Jonathan Freedman "you are happy—that's all we mean by the term"' (Myers, 2000, p. 57).

There are a number of reasons why many psychological researchers have been inclined to accept individuals' reports of their hedonic states. First, there is a certain definitional self-evidence to our ability to assess the utility that we derive from experiences. What, after all, could it mean for an individual to be happy if they were not aware of it? Second, research exploring individuals' self-reports of global subjective happiness has shown the construct to have relatively stable qualities of validity and reliability. For example, Lyubomirsky and Lepper (1999), in a recent analysis of 14 studies that used a simple four item global happiness scale, found that individuals' self-reports of their overall happiness tended to correlate reasonably well with the assessments made by friends and spouses, with correlations in the range 0.41–0.66. Test and re-test reliabilities were also reasonably high with a mean correlation of 0.72, and in the range 0.55–0.90.

Although individuals may have some global sense of their overall degree of well-being, there is also considerable evidence that reports of global happiness can be powerfully influenced by the situational context in which individuals are queried. A famous example of the difficulty of judging one's global happiness comes from the research of Strack, Martin, and Stepper (1998), who asked some college students how many times they had gone out on a date in the last month, then how happy they had been overall. Other students were asked the same questions but in the reverse order. For those asked about dates first, the correlation between the two items was 0.66; for those asked about happiness first, the correlation was close to zero. These results suggest that instead of recalling their hedonic state over the last month, the students seemed to be looking for more objective cues about whether their last month had been good or bad and attempted to judge their happiness based on those cues. When the information about dates was activated, it played a more prominent role in these evaluations. Additional studies have demonstrated that individuals' general assessment of their happiness can be similarly biased by a number of other situational factors including, the current weather (Schwarz and Clore, 1983), finding a dime (Schwarz, 1987), and the outcome of soccer games (Schwarz et al., 1987). We next describe a few more specific classes of evidence regarding peoples' difficulties in accessing their own utilities.

1.1. Distinguishing between Visceral Experience (Experiential Consciousness) and Reflective Appraisal (Meta-Consciousness)

One recourse to the difficulties associated with making global judgments about happiness and life satisfaction has been to argue that, while individuals may have difficulty summating their experiences over time, they are capable of providing snapshot assessments of their hedonic experience at any given moment (Kahneman, 1999, p. 5). Kahneman distinguishes between 'subjective happiness' measures in which respondents 'state how happy they are' and 'objective happiness' measures that are 'derived from a record of instant utility.' The assumption underlying this view is that individuals maintain a continuous and reportable hedonic experience, but errors occur when individuals attempt to recollect and average valenced moments over time. According to this view, these difficulties can be averted by asking individuals to make spontaneous moment by moment assessments, and the researchers rather than the respondents do the averaging over time. Although we concur with the claim that individuals experience a continuous and potentially measurable hedonic valence, we believe that great caution must be taken in assuming that individuals' moment to moment hedonic assessments reflect their underlying experience.

Our central claim is that an understanding of hedonic utility depends critically on an appreciation of the fundamental distinction between individuals' continuous hedonic experience and their intermittent reflective appraisal (alternately referred to as 'meta-awareness or meta-consciousness' (Schooler, 2001, 2002)) of that experience. We, like many other researchers, assume that every waking moment entails a *hedonic experience* that is subjectively registered as visceral feelings (Damasio, 1994; Loewenstein, 1996) accompanied by a host of physiological responses including changes in the cardio-vascular flow (Tomaka et al., 1997), eye blink response (Lang, 1995), and brain activation (e.g., Lane et al., 1997). However, we further assume that, although individuals' hedonic experience is continuous, their meta-awareness of this experience is only intermittent. The demands of life are such that it is simply not possible to continually monitor how we are feeling at every moment of the day. As a result one can *feel* happy or sad, without explicitly noticing this at the time. The three of us, and we expect many readers, have had the experience of having our spouse tell us that we were unhappy, which we had not realized until alerted of the undeniable truth. Similarly, research on 'flow states,' which occurs when individuals are deeply absorbed in challenging tasks, suggests that many of life's most positive experiences occur when individuals are not explicitly aware of the pleasure they are feeling at the time. As Csikszentmihalyi (1999, p. 825) puts it:

Strictly speaking, during the experience of [of flow] people are not necessarily happy because they are too involved in the task to have the luxury to reflect on their subjective states.... But afterwards, when the experience is over, people report having been in as positive a state as it is possible to feel.

If we often, if not typically, have hedonic experiences in the absence of meta-awareness of those experiences, then it should not be assumed that our hedonic experience and our explicit appraisals of experience are necessarily identical.

1.2. Inferring Hedonic Response on the Basis of One's Own Behavior

If people have difficulties accessing their own utilities, how do we make decisions about pleasure and pain? Our claim here is that because the translation from hedonic experience into an explicit appraisal is very difficult, if not impossible, people often rely on *inferences* to estimate their own utilities. Such inferences can draw on a variety of sources including self-observation, situational context, and our theories about how we think we should be feeling (for similar claims see Schwarz, 1987; Schwarz and Clore, 1983; Schwarz and Strack, 1999). *In short, we suggest that individuals' hedonic experiences are typically represented as visceral non-verbal feeling states. However, when compelled to make hedonic judgments, individuals draw on inferencing processes in order to translate these visceral states into an explicit hedonic appraisal.*[1]

---

[1] The present account represents somewhat of a compromise between the disparate positions of Zajonc (1984) who argued that preferences need no inferences and Lazarus (1984) who argued that all emotional appraisals are mediated by cognitive considerations. Like Zajonc, we argue that individuals can *experience* preferences without drawing on inferences. However, like Lazarus (1984), we argue that

In the following discussion we briefly review the evidence that individuals can lack meta-awareness of their underlying hedonic experience and therefore must draw on various external sources in order to infer how they must be feeling.

1.2.1. *Inferring Attitudes from One's Behavior*

The notion that individuals may lack a direct insight into their affective state, and therefore must infer their state based on a situational context, dates back at least as far as William James (1884), who suggested that individuals infer emotions by observing their actions. Accordingly, rather than running from a bear because one feels fear, James suggested that individuals run from a bear, and in observing this behavior, infer that they must be feeling fear. The view that we are promoting here is analogous to James' theory of emotion with one critical difference. In keeping with the suggestion that individuals maintain continuous hedonic experience, we argue that one does indeed 'feel' fear as soon as one sees the bear. However, one may not explicitly appraise the emotion as such until one reflects on one's behavior. Thus, from our perspective when one sees a bear one immed-iately *feels* fear, runs, and upon reflecting on the fact that one is running, becomes meta-conscious of the fact that one is experiencing fear.

The claim that individuals infer their responses to stimuli by observing their own behavior has its more recent exemplification in the self-perception theory of Daryl Bem. According to the Self-Perception Theory (Bem, 1967, 1972), indivi-duals infer their own attitudes and preferences in much the same way as they infer those of others. As Bem (1972, p. 2) put it, 'Individuals come to "know" their own attitudes, emotions and other internal states partially by inferring them from observation of their own overt behavior and/or the circumstances in which this behavior occurs.' The self-perception theory was originally articulated as an alternative to the Cognitive Dissonance Theory (Festinger, 1957), which hypo-thesized that individuals alter their attitudes in order to reduce the unpleasant internal conflict (dissonance) that can arise when attitudes and behavior are discrepant. For example, the notion of cognitive dissonance reduction was used to account for why individuals who agree to participate in an inherently boring task for $1 report liking it better than those who agree to participate for $20, (Festinger and Carlsmith, 1959). According to the cognitive dissonance account, individuals who agree to participate for $1 experience dissonance between the perceived modest compensatory value of a dollar, and the perceived aversiveness of participating in a routine task. They, therefore, alter their appraisal of the task in order to reduce dissonance. Bem, in contrast, argued that individuals do not feel any internal dissonance, but rather, lacking insight into their own hedonic response, infer their attitudes by observing their own behavior. Consistent with this view, Bem demonstrated that many attitude judgments previously ascribed to

---

individuals' explicit appraisals generally require cognitive inferences. Our claim is that the source of the disagreement in this debate stems from a failure to consider the distinction we draw here between visceral hedonic experience, which does not require inferences, and explicit hedonic appraisals, which typically, if not always, invoke inferencing processes.

dissonance reduction were mirrored by the *inferences* of observers who never actually participated in the experiments, but rather anticipated the attitudes of participants in the studies based on the scenarios alone. For example, when hearing the scenario of an individual volunteering to participate in an experiment for a dollar, the judges assumed that the task was more enjoyable than they did when they learned of participants agreeing to participate for $20.

Since Bem's original postulation of the self-perception account of cognitive dissonance, there has been some controversy regarding which mechanism, cognitive dissonance or self-perception, best accounts for the extant data. Although some disagreements still exist, most researchers now accept that both processes can come into play depending on the circumstances. When disparities between original attitudes and subsequent behavior are very large, the cognitive dissonance processes in all likelihood come into play; however, when the differences are more modest, self-perception alone may be the primary operator (see Fazio, 1987; for a review). Indeed, the self-perception theory has been used to account for many findings in the psychological literature. For example, the self-perception theory accounts for why individuals' assessment of the intrinsic interest of an activity is reduced when they receive a reward for engaging in it (Lepper et al., 1973). Accordingly, they infer that the receipt of the reward must be the reason they are doing it, and, thus, come to estimate their interest as being less. The self-perception theory can also account for the effects of supressing facial expressions. For example, Strack et al. (1998) had research participants view cartoons, while holding a pen in the mouth in a manner that either did or did not inhibit the muscles associated with smiling. Participants found the cartoons significantly less amusing when they held the pen in a manner that inhibited smiling. These and similar findings (e.g., Olson, 1990) illustrate how individuals' preferences can be based, at least in part, on inferences drawn from observing their own behavior. Critical, to the self-perception approach is the underlying premise *that individuals can and often do lack meta-awareness of their own internal states*, and thus must infer it in much the same way as others. As Bem put it: 'To the extent that internal cues are weak, ambiguous, or uninterpretable, the individual is functionally in the same position as an outside observer' (Bem, 1972, p. 2).

1.2.2. *Misattribution Theory*

Although observation of one's own behavior is an important source of inference regarding the state of one's hedonic response to an experience, it is not the only source. Research on misattribution suggests that individuals also infer their affective/hedonic responses on the basis of the situational context in which they find themselves. For example, in a classic study by Schachter and Singer (1962), participants were given either a norepinephrine or a placebo pill and then were exposed to a confederate who behaved either pleasantly or unpleasantly. The context of the confederate powerfully influenced the manner in which they evaluated the arousal resulting from the norepinephrine, such that relative to the placebo they reported feeling more elated when exposed to the pleasant confederate and more annoyed when exposed to the unpleasant one. Since this original study, a number of limitations to its scope and interpretation have arisen (e.g., Reisenzein, 1983). Nevertheless, the basic claim that individuals can misattribute the source of arousal and thereby alter their hedonic assessment, has remained intact. For example, arousal induced by exercise can be misattributed to anger (Zillman, 1978) and arousal induced by fear can be misattributed to sexual attraction (Dutton and Aaron, 1974).

A key assumption of the misattribution theory is that individuals do have an underlying subjective experience; however, this hedonic experience is ambiguous and therefore open to interpretation based on the context of the situation. This fact is important because it supports our basic contention that explicit hedonic appraisals represent the evaluation of a difficult-to-discern hedonic feeling that is interpreted in the light of inferences.

1.2.3. *Infering Value from Behavior (Anchoring Effects)*

The under-specificity of hedonic experience not only plays a role in self-reported hedonic evaluations, it can also affect economic decisions based on hedonic appraisals, including the price that individuals are willing to pay for an experience. This phenomenon is illustrated in a series of studies conducted by Ariely et al. (2000) that examine the anchoring effects in the valuation of hedonic experiences. In a typical experiment, subjects first experience an aversive tone over headphones. Next, they are asked whether, *hypothetically*, they would be willing to listen to the tone again for 30 s for either a small payment (10 cents) or a larger payment (90 cents). After answering the hypothetical question, respondents enter a real market in which they indicate the prices for which they are willing to listen to the tone, and if their prices are accepted by the market mechanism, they get the tone for the specified duration and the amount of money that is the outcome of the market mechanism. (The mechanisms used were all methods, such as the Becker–Degroot–Marschak procedure (1963), designed to give subjects an incentive to reveal their true value for an object.) The results revealed that subjects' valuations are powerfully affected by the initial response to the hypothetical question (the anchor) they are exposed to.

In an even more dramatic, albeit somewhat less tightly controlled study, the researchers asked one set of students if they would be willing to listen to their professor (Ariely) read 10 min of *Leaves of Grass* to them if they were paid $10. Others were asked if they would pay $10 for the same experience. The researchers then elicited prices (which could be positive or negative) from students for listening to *Leaves of Grass* for 1, 3, or 10 min. Again, students' values were powerfully influenced by the initial question. Those asked if they would pay were willing to pay to listen to the poetry, and those asked if they would listen if they were paid, needed to be paid to do it. But, whether they valued the experience positively or negatively, they named higher amounts of money for longer durations of poetry. Participants had no idea whether this was a positive or negative experience, but they knew that it was more positive or negative if it was longer. Whether they have sampled it (as in the case of the tone) or not, individuals seem to be limited in their ability to assess hedonic experiences—even in some cases whether the experience is positive or negative. They draw on any available cues, including the arbitrary anchor values, to resolve the ambiguity.

2. THE EFFECTS OF HEDONIC INTROSPECTION

The evidence we have reviewed so far suggests that when people attempt to assess their own hedonic state they not only access internal visceral feelings, but also use any available cues to help them infer their own likely feelings. In Section 2, however, the relative importance of these two inputs—internal feelings and inferences—seems to depend on the nature of the introspective process.

2.1. The Effects of Introspection on Hedonic Appraisals

Given the sizable body of research that relies on the hedonic appraisal of experience as a primary measure, surprisingly little research has examined the impact *per se* of monitoring hedonic experiences on the appraisal of such experiences. Ariely (1998) reports one of the very few studies that specifically examined the impact of on-line hedonic appraisals. Participants were presented with a series of painful stimuli of varying intensities, profiles (intensity changes over time), and durations. At the end of each painful experience, the participants provided overall retrospective appraisals of the amount of pain that they experienced during the trial. Half of the participants evaluated the experience only in retrospect (after it ended), while the other half were also asked to provide continuous evaluations of the intensity of the experience as it unfolded (also known as moment by moment or on-line evaluations). The comparison of these two groups (see also Ariely and Zauberman, 2000) showed that once respondents 'created' the moment by moment evaluations, their overall evaluation of the experience as a whole was influenced by the momentary responses they produced. Moreover, the results showed that the respondents were less influenced by the way the experience unfolded over time (e.g., they were less sensitive to the changes in intensity over time), suggesting that their hedonic experience was muffled. Ariely's findings are consistent with the general claim that introspection can produce inferences that can reduce individuals' sensitivity to their own hedonic experience. Accordingly, participants in the no on-line evaluation condition, may have been able to access subtle differences in their affective state that followed being subjected to sequences of painful experiences. In contrast, participants in the on-line condition, by simply relying on their mean reported response, may have lost access to their actual hedonic experience.

In addition to Ariely's demonstration that on-line hedonic introspection can reduce hedonic differences associated with the duration of aversive stimuli, other studies have provided evidence that introspective techniques that specifically encourage reflective inferencing can overshadow individuals' sensitivity to their underlying hedonic response.

2.1.1. Introspective Techniques that Minimize Sensitivity to Underlying Hedonic Experience

A number of studies suggest that, inducing decision-makers to verbally reflect upon their decision processes can increase their weighting of considerations that can be verbalized, and decrease their access to gut-level feelings. In a study by Wilson and Schooler (1991), participants sampled five different strawberry jams. In the reflection condition, participants were then asked to reflect on their evaluation, listing the reasons why they felt the way they did about each jam. All the participants were then asked to rate the five jams. The correlations between the participants' jam ratings and those of the experts (provided by *Consumer Reports*) were then assessed. Wilson and Schooler found that whereas control subjects provided ratings that were closely aligned with that of the experts ($r = 0.56$), the judgments of the participants who analyzed their reasons were completely unrelated ($r = 0.16$) to that of the experts. Within the current context, the findings of Wilson and Schooler can be interpreted as suggesting that reflection caused the participants to emphasize the inferences that they made about their experience and 'lose touch' with their actual hedonic feelings.

One possible concern with Wilson and Schooler's study is that it used the experts' opinions as the normative basis for assessing the quality of participants' hedonic judgments. Failing to agree with an expert does not necessarily mean that one's opinions are unreflective of the utility that one derives from an experience. The participants in the self-reflection condition might simply have had different hedonic experiences, which were well captured by their self-reports. A follow up study by Wilson et al. (1993), however, counters this interpretation. The participants examined various art posters. In the reflection condition, they analyzed why they felt the way they did about the posters and then rated them. In the control condition they simply rated the posters without reflection. Participants were then given the opportunity to select a poster and take it home. When Wilson et al. contacted the participants two weeks later, they found that those in the reflection condition were less satisfied with their choices (and less likely to have hung them up) than those in the control condition. The fact that participants who engaged in reflection were ultimately less satisfied with their selections, suggests that reflection did not simply change their perceived utilities. Rather, these findings suggest that reflection actually undermined people's ability to decipher the utilities that they had actually experienced, and which they re-experienced after the impact of self-reflection had worn off.

The above findings provide just a sampling of studies that indicate that self-reflection may impair people's ability to decipher the hedonic value of experience. Other studies have found similar effects of self-reflection on people's ability to judge the utility of courses (Wilson and Schooler, 1991), peanut butter (Schooler and Wilson, 1991), puzzles (Wilson et al., 1984), pens (Wilson, 1990), and even relationships (Wilson et al., 1984).

2.1.2. *Introspective Techniques that Maximize the Sensitivity to Hedonic Experience*

If encouraging verbal reflection diminishes individuals' access to their own visceral reactions, then one should expect that introspective techniques that decrease verbal reflection would lead to appraisals that are more in line with individuals' actual underlying visceral experience. Indeed, several studies have found that when self-reflection is minimized by forcing individuals to make very quick hedonic judgments, the hedonic assessments become realigned with the actual experience. For example, Wilson and Lindsey (as reported in Wilson et al., 2000) had participants evaluate the quality of their relationship with a significant other. Some participants engaged in self-reflection, analyzing the reasons for their evaluations. Others simply gave an overall rating. As in prior studies, they found that self-reflection reduced people's ability to adequately gauge the quality of their relationship, as revealed by the fact that those who analyzed their reasons were less able to predict the quality of their relationship at a later date relative to the control subjects who did not engage in self-reflection. However, Wilson and Lindsey included an additional condition in which, following self-reflection, participants made very quick (3 s) evaluations. In this condition, the correlations between participants' ratings of their relationship and their later reported ratings was as high as it was for participants who did not engage in self-reflection at all. Apparently, discouraging self-reflection by having people make rapid judgments restores their ability to access their own 'gut' level reactions.

In addition to quick judgments, other techniques may also encourage individuals to draw more on their hedonic experience by enabling them to be more keen observers of their own visceral responses. For example, a number of studies have found that when individuals engage in tasks with a mirror present, their hedonic appraisals tend to more closely correspond to their subsequent behaviors (e.g., Scheier and Carver, 1977). One possible interpretation of such findings is that the mirror gives the individuals a greater opportunity to observe and/or experience their own visceral hedonic response, and thus enables them to draw more accurately on this source of information.

In sum, it seems that hedonic appraisal may access internal visceral states depending on the manner in which individuals introspect. When individuals are encouraged to explicitly reflect on the basis for their attitudes and preferences, their hedonic appraisals rely more heavily on inferences. In contrast, when they are forced to make quick gut judgments (or have a mirror present), their hedonic appraisals seem to reflect better their actual hedonic experience.

2.2. The Impact of Introspection on Hedonic Experience

There are a number of reasons to think that engaging in hedonic appraisal might, in addition to altering how individuals appraise the situation, affect the hedonic experience itself. First, if, as seems likely, hedonic introspection increases the focus on the self, then such a reflection may detract from the amount of attention that is devoted to the activity itself, which may in turn detract from the experience. In addition, if, as we have suggested, individuals have difficulty explicitly deciphering the degree of enjoyment that they are deriving from an experience, then extensive self-reflection might cause the individuals to overlook subtle features of the experience, thereby missing out on the hedonic utility that they might have otherwise enjoyed. Finally, it is possible that engaging in hedonic appraisal might cause individuals to attend to elements of the experience that might have, could have, or should have been, and such comparisons may lead to disappointment and regret.

Although little research has specifically looked at the effects of experimentally manipulating the monitoring of hedonic experiences on the attainment of happiness, a variety of studies have reported correlational evidence that is consistent with the proposition that monitoring happiness undermines happiness. For example, numerous studies have examined the relationship between individuals' tendency to introspect and their overall reported happiness. The consistent finding in this research is that chronically happy people are less introspective (Lyubomirsky and Lepper, 1999; Veenhoven, 1988). Moreover, chronically unhappy people tend to show relatively high levels of self-consciousness, self-focused attention, and ruminative thinking (Ingram, 1990; Musson and Alloy, 1988). One potential interpretation of such findings is that, introspective individuals may be particularly apt to reflect on their reactions to experiences that may decrease their enjoyment (or exacerbate their displeasure) with the experiences themselves. However, there are a variety of alternative accounts of this relationship. For example, given the evidence that depressed individuals may (at least in some cases) be more realistic about their situations (Taylor and Brown, 1994), it may be that self-reflection simply undermines individuals' ability to view their lives through rose-colored glasses. Furthermore, because the relationship between reflection and happiness has largely been correlational, it is unclear whether introspection causes unhappiness or unhappiness causes introspection.

There have been some experimental studies that are also supportive of the disruptive effects of introspection on hedonic experience, although these studies are also open to alternative interpretations. For example, there is an extensive literature suggesting that self-awareness (e.g., being put in the presence of a mirror), can cause aversive experiences due to discrepancies that individuals detect between their personal aspirations and the attainment of those aspirations (Duval and Wicklund, 1972). Although it has also been noted that self-awareness can occasionally lead to a more positive contrast between aspirations and attainments (e.g., Wicklund 1975), the more common finding is that self-awareness leads to a disappointing assessment and thus produces aversive states.

There are of course some important differences between the self-awareness induced by a mirror and the more specific introspection about a particular hedonic experience. For example, assessing how one feels about a particular experience does not necessarily require an assessment of whether one is living up to one's goals. Nevertheless, the general finding that self-awareness can often be aversive is certainly consistent with the hypothesis that attending to the hedonic quality of a specific experience might undermine it.

Although relatively little research has examined experimentally the impact of hedonic introspection on the achievement of hedonic satisfaction *per se*, some studies have examined the related issue of how attending to one's perception of mirth influences the experience of humor. For example, Cupchik and Leventhal (1974) found that when individuals were asked to scrutinize their mirth response to humorous cartoons, they actually found them less funny. If one can ruin a joke by focusing too hard on how funny one finds it, it follows that hedonic introspection may similarly undermine other positive hedonic experiences. Clearly, what is needed are experimental studies that explicitly manipulate individuals' hedonic monitoring and then examine its impact on their hedonic experience. As will be discussed, we recently completed such an investigation. We will provide the preliminary evidence that hedonic assessment can, in fact, undermine hedonic experience. However, before considering this evidence we first introduce another central challenge to economic approaches that rely on the assumption that individuals attempt to maximize happiness, namely, that the pursuit of happiness may itself be self-defeating.

3. THE IMPACT OF THE PURSUIT OF HAPPINESS ON THE ATTAINMENT OF HAPPINESS

A central premise of much economic theory, and indeed a primary assumption of western culture as exemplified in the US Declaration of Independence, is the premise that the pursuit of happiness is a primary (and worthy) human goal. However, there are a number of reasons to suspect that the pursuit of happiness, at least when it is made the primary explicit motivation for behaviors, may actually be self-defeating. We will discuss three of them next.

3.1. Faulty Theories of Happiness

One reason why pursuing happiness can be self-defeating is that people simply have faulty theories about what is likely to give them happiness. For example, there is considerable evidence that people underestimate their own tendency to adapt hedonically to continuing experiences, both positive and negative (e.g., Gilbert et al., 1998; Loewenstein and Frederick, 1997). Such a tendency may cause people to over-select goals that produce lasting material changes, such as an increase in income or status, in the mistaken belief that such changes will produce enduring increases in happiness. Initially, such goals may indeed produce happiness. However, as individuals adapt to their improved state, they may reach an equilibrium whereby they no longer experience the gain (Brickman and Cambell, 1971). However, having previously experienced pleasure from material gains, individuals may develop a habit of pursuing this goal above all others, without recognizing the habituation and decreasing marginal utility associated with their further gains (for a formal model of this process, see Loewenstein et al., 2000). Consistent with this prediction, it has been found that individuals who see the accumulation of wealth as a primary goal are ultimately less happy than those who put less emphasis on material gains. For example, Kasser and Ryan (1993) gave participants a questionnaire that assessed the degree to which they (1) sought to accumulate wealth and (2) expected that they would significantly increase their wealth. Strikingly, participants who valued and/or expected increased wealth revealed markedly lower degrees of happiness as evidenced by a variety of measures including lower well-being and self-actualization and increased anxiety and depression. In a subsequent study that also included objectifiable consequences of global well-being, Kasser and Ryan (1996) found that individuals who focused on gaining wealth as a life goal showed more physical symptoms and lower daily affect relative to individuals who focused on the gaining of other goals, such as achieving psychological growth, having satisfying relationships with family and friends, and improving the world.

Of course, the fact that individuals who seek wealth tend to be less happy does not in itself prove that the explicit pursuit of happiness is the cause of their unhappiness. It might be that unhappy people are more motivated to change their state, and so they seek wealth as a way to improve their otherwise unhappy lives. And indeed there is some evidence that is consistent with such a contention. Specifically, Kasser and Ryan (1996) also found that individuals who have had troubled childhoods are more likely to view the explicit pursuit of wealth as a primary goal than individuals with a less problematic childhood.

3.2. Changing Goals

A second reason why the pursuit of happiness may be self-defeating is that it may cause people to treat activities not as ends in themselves, but rather as a means towards something else, namely the gaining of happiness. As previously noted, considerable research indicates that when individuals engage in activities for external reward (e.g., money) the activities lose their intrinsic appeal (for a review see Deci et al., 1999). Typically, in such studies the extrinsic reward is entirely distinct from the intrinsic hedonic value of the experience itself—for example, getting paid for a task that one would typically enjoy. Nevertheless, it seems plausible that if individuals view gaining happiness as something above and beyond the intrinsic appeal of the activity itself, such a motivation might simi-larly detract from the utility that is derived from an experience. For example, one might go to a concert with the primary motivation of genuinely wanting to listen to the music. Such a motivation would be unquestionably intrinsic and thus should lead to a positive experience. However, if a person goes to a concert with the explicit goal of gaining happiness, then the music itself is no longer the primary motivation for the task. In short, the hedonic value of an experience may be com-promised to the degree that one is engaging in a task with the goal of achieving happiness, rather than with the goal of genuinely valuing the activity itself.

3.3. Monitoring Happiness

A third, closely related reason for why engaging in activities with the primary goal of achieving happiness may be self-defeating, is that it may encourage one to regularly monitor whether this goal is being achieved. As already noted, there are several reasons why regular monitoring might be detrimental including, reducing the amount of attention devoted to the activity itself, impairing sensitivity to the subtle positive features of the experience, and inducing unfavorable comparisons to a never attained goal state.

Whereas, incorrect theories about the determinants of happiness can cause people to engage in the wrong kinds of activities to maximize happiness, the latter two causes (changing goals, and monitoring) can produce a negative relationship between trying to be happy and being happy based simply on one's mental attitude. Both causes point to a 'catch-22' type of situation in which happiness is undermined by simply having the mindset of explicitly trying to be happy. The best evidence for this proposition comes from studies that examine the relationship between happiness and selfishness. One marker of individuals' focus on the explicit goal of achieving happiness involves the relative degree to which individuals put themselves before others. As Myers (2000) observes: 'Selfish people are, by definition, those whose activities are devoted to bringing themselves happiness.' However, although selfish individuals are seemingly devoted to the explicit attainment of their own happiness, various sources of evidence suggest that, like the pursuit of materialistic gains, engaging in life's activities with an eye to benefiting oneself may defeat the very goals that such actions are presumably meant to attain.

Two studies empirically supported the self defeating aspects of perusing happiness: Using a questionnaire survey, Rimland (Myers, 2000) had participants list acquaintances and then rate them on a number of different dimensions including both selfishness and happiness. Rimland found that those individuals who were characterized as less selfish were also rated as happier than those who were characterized as more selfish. Of course, there are some problems with questionnaire studies of this sort, for example, participants might feel less positively towards their selfish acquaintances and so their low estimations of the happiness of their selfish peers might in effect reflect 'wishful thinking.' However, more controlled studies have led to similar conclusions. In a more controlled study, Konow (2000) had participants engage in a dictator game in which one participant is given the role of 'dictator' and is allowed to control the relative amount of resources allocated to himself and his teammates. Konow correlated participants' selfish behavior in this study with their self-reported happiness. Strikingly, individuals who devoted more resources to their teammates reported overall higher levels of happiness and life satisfaction relative to those who were more miserly in their allocations. This finding further supports the view that selfishness, although seemingly motivated by the explicit goal of putting one's own happiness above all else, is ineffective in leading to the attainment of this goal.

In sum, the initial findings are consistent with the proposition that the explicit pursuit of happiness can be self-defeating. There are, however, a number of theoretical and methodological issues that cloud exactly how we should interpret these findings. Most important, all of the studies that have examined the issue have been correlational in nature, demonstrating that people with particular proclivities, namely towards materialism and self-promotion, tend to be less happy. One interpretation of such findings is that the tendency to pursue happiness leads these individuals to be less happy. However, it is also possible that an initial tendency to be unhappy leads individuals to want to be happy and to select specific goals that, whether effective or ineffective, they believe will promote their own happiness. Clearly, additional studies are needed that more directly assess and manipulate the specific goal of maximizing happiness. In Section 4 we describe two such studies.

4. PRELIMINARY INVESTIGATIONS OF THE PURSUIT AND ASSESSMENT OF HAPPINESS ON THE ACHIEVEMENT OF HAPPINESS

In the last several sections we have argued that both the attempts at monitoring happiness and attempting to maximize happiness may be self-defeating. Although we believe we have made a reasonable case for both of these claims, at present they remain tenable conjectures. Fortunately, however, they are testable, and we have begun to develop an empirical line of investigation to test them. In the following section, we briefly review two preliminary studies that explored the possible roles of explicit monitoring and maximizing on individuals attainment of happiness. The first is an experimental investigation of the impact of monitoring and trying to be happy on the happiness that individuals derive from listening to music. The second is a field study in which we examined the relationship between individuals' efforts to be happy and their achievement of happiness in a real world situation that exemplifies the singular goal of maximizing happiness: New Year's Eve celebrations.

4.1. The Impact of Monitoring and Effort on the Hedonic Experience Associated with Listening to Music

As noted above, most of the studies suggesting that reflection and the pursuit of happiness can reduce happiness have been correlational. Thus, one critical step in demonstrating the relationship between these variables and happiness is to show that the experimental manipulations of effort towards and monitoring of happiness can alter individuals' achievement of happiness. Toward this end, we conducted a study (Experiment 1) in which participants listened to music, with either (1) no instructions, (2) instructions to try to be happy, (3) instructions to monitor their happiness, or (4) instructions to both try to be happy and monitor their happiness. We used Stravinsky's *Rites of Spring* as our musical selection because we expected its complexity and use of discordant tones to make listening to it hedonically ambiguous. Our reasoning was that individuals might find it more challenging to explicitly reflect on the quality of their hedonic experience when faced with a novel hedonically ambiguous sound. Accordingly, with hedonically ambiguous stimuli, individuals' theories, beliefs, and other factors unrelated to the experience itself may be particularly likely to color their assessments of their hedonic experience. Similarly, hedonically ambiguous music may be the most likely to frustrate individuals' direct attempts at making themselves happy. Thus, we reasoned that a hedonically ambiguous stimulus would be a sensible source to begin our search for reactive effects of efforts to monitor and maximize hedonic experience.

The participants first answered an elaborate series of questions that included a number of nine point likert scale mood measures. These included two critical questions: 'How happy do you feel right now?' and 'What is your mood right now?' In addition, the participants were shown a schematic face, that could be adjusted from frowning to smiling, and were asked to set the face to the level that reflected their current level of happiness. These various questions were embedded with a number of additional questions regarding their experience with and interest in music, to minimize the likelihood that the participants in the control group (no instruction condition) would infer that they were listening to the music to affect their mood. The participants then listened to the music. Those in the monitoring condition continually adjusted a movable scale (akin to those used in focus groups) to indicate their moment-to-moment happiness. Those in the try to be happy condition were asked to try to make themselves feel as happy as possible. The control subjects were simply asked to listen to the music. After listening to the music all the participants were once again given the various mood/happiness measures.

To assess the impact of our experimental manipulations on happiness, we examined the changes in individuals' responses to the critical happiness questions before and after listening to the music. The results of this investigation provide preliminary evidence that both monitoring and efforts to maximize happiness can actually impair the achievement of happiness. As can be seen in Figures 3.1 and 3.2, monitoring happiness significantly reduced happiness as indicated on both the numeric happiness scale and smile-face happiness measure. As can be seen in Figure 3.3, trying to be happy also reduced individuals' hedonic experience, albeit primarily by lowering the reported mood.

The results of this study are preliminary and need replications. Nevertheless, several cautionary conclusions seem appropriate. First the fact that monitoring happiness reduced individuals' ability to benefit from listening to music (as indicated by both the happiness and analogue face measures) suggests that vigilantly monitoring one's ongoing hedonic experience can undermine one's ability to actually gain happiness. Second, the fact that trying to be happy lowered the mood suggests that individuals' efforts to pursue happiness may have led to frustration, which undermined their ability to feel the pleasure that they

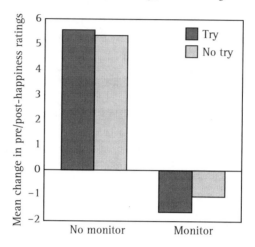

Figure 3.1. *The effects of trying and monitoring on changes in the reported happiness*

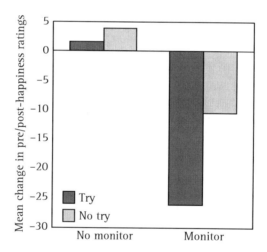

Figure 3.2. *The effects of trying and monitoring on changes in the reported happiness with an analogue face measure*

sought. Finally, the fact that the pattern of findings varied somewhat across the measures suggests that individuals' reports of their hedonic experience do not all derive from a single underlying experience. Rather, each term appears to induce a somewhat different calculus for assessing hedonic experience. Such a conclusion supports the contention that assessments of hedonic experience are filtered through the lens of reflective inferences, and therefore the context of the question may influence how hedonic experience is surmised and reported.

Of course, the suggestion that different measures might differentially tap hedonic experience and inference also highlights an important limitation of the

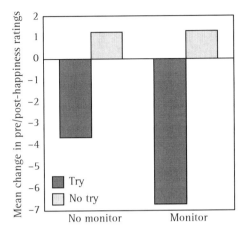

Figure 3.3. *The effects of trying and monitoring on changes in the reported mood*

present study. Although we have suggested that the monitoring of happiness undermines experienced happiness, it is also possible that monitoring happiness simply enabled the participants to derive a more accurate assessment of their actual hedonic experience. Accordingly, the difference in reported happiness between the monitoring and non-monitoring conditions might have been driven by the participants in the no monitoring condition who, when queried afterwards about their happiness, may have simply inferred that they should be happier since after all they had just listened to music. At present, it is not possible to determine whether monitoring happiness undermined individuals' happiness or enabled them to make a more realistic appraisal of their actual hedonic state. However, in either case, the net result was that individuals in the monitoring condition believed that they were less happy. Thus, whether monitoring reduces perceived happiness because it detracts from the experience, or because it forces individuals to make a more realistic appraisal of their hedonic state, its bottom line effect was to lower individuals appraisals of their own happiness.

Clearly, the above study provides a mere a glimpse of the interesting and potentially complex relationships that may exist between efforts to maximize and monitor happiness, and the ability to achieve it. Nevertheless, it supports our suggestion that attempts at maximizing and monitoring happiness can undermine the very happiness that people are attempting to discern and foster.

4.2. The Costs of Trying to have a Good Time: New Year's Eve, 2000

If, as we have been suggesting, deliberate attempts at maximizing happiness can undermine individuals' ability to achieve happiness, then occasions that are designed with the singular purpose of maximizing happiness, might often backfire. There are few occasions that are more likely to exemplify the singular goal of maximizing happiness than the New Year's Eve celebrations, particularly the millennium celebration of 2000 (the one starting on December 31st, 1999). The 2000 new year's celebration thus provided an excellent opportunity for us to explore the hypothesis that attempts to maximize happiness may be counter-productive. In the context of new year's celebration, we predicted that those individuals who devoted the greatest effort to having a good time, would actually have a less positive experience than those who were less singularly focused on maximizing their happiness.

To explore the hypothesized relationship between the pursuit and the achievement of happiness on New Year's Eve, we e-mailed friends, colleagues, and various list-serves, during the last week of December 1999, and asked them to visit our web site and answer a few questions about their plans for New Year's Eve. We asked them how large a celebration they were planning, how much they expected to enjoy New Year's Eve, and how much time and money they were expecting to spend on their New Year's Eve celebration.

About 475 people participated in our study. In the two months that followed, we e-mailed our participants again and asked them to answer the same questions about their actual experiences during New Year's Eve. For each individual, we took the difference between their response of how much they expected to enjoy New Year's Eve, and how much they reported to have enjoyed it after the fact. We used this difference measure as the basis for our analysis.

We first examined whether the magnitude of the celebration would influence the enjoyment of New Year's Eve compared with expectations. In our questions we asked participants whether they were expecting to have a small celebration, a bash, or to not celebrate at all. We analyzed the happiness difference as a function of these three categories. The results showed that in fact, most subjects (83 percent) were disappointed with their New Year's Eve celebration (mean disappointment 1.62 on a 10-point scale). More interestingly, the size of the planned celebration had an effect on the enjoyment difference ($F(2467) = 8.53$, $p < 0.001$). The effect of the planned celebration size was such that respondents who indicated they expected to have a bash were the most disappointed ($M = -2.43$), followed by participants who expected a small celebration ($M = -1.57$), followed by the participants who did not expect a celebration at all ($M = -0.9$).

Next, we regressed the difference in enjoyment from New Year's Eve celebra-tion on our respondents' anticipation of enjoyment, expected money spending, and expected time spending. The overall model was significant ($F(3265) = 99.48$, $p < 0.001$), and so were the coefficients for anticipation (coeff $= -0.82$, $t = 15.175$, $p < 0.001$), and expected time spent on preparations (coeff $= -0.27$, $t = 2.28$, $p = 0.023$). The coefficient for monetary expenses was not significant (coeff $= -0.13$, $t = 1.09$, $p = 0.28$).

The results of this field study suggest that high expectation can lead to dis-appointment, and that spending time and effort (and perhaps money) on an event can increase dissatisfaction. Although, like Experiment 1, this study is clearly in need of further replication and investigation, there are a number of preliminary implications that it suggests, particularly when it is considered in light of the findings of Experiment 1 and other recent psychological investigations. The observation that high expectations were associated with particular disappointment, supports a variety of recent studies indicating that individuals often have difficulty anticipating their future subjective states (Gilbert et al. 1998; Loewenstein and Schkade, 1999). Furthermore, although we cannot know for certain the relationship between high expectations and monitoring of the hedonic experience in the course of the celebration, it seems quite plausible that individuals with high expectations would, in fact, be more apt to monitor whether those expectations were being met. Thus, this study provides at least suggestive evidence that the spontaneous monitoring of hedonic experience (that is, outside the context of experimentally induced manipulations) also disrupts hedonic experience, and thus lends further credence to the conclusions of Experiment 1.

In addition to its potential implications for the disruptive effects of monitoring, the fact that those individuals who put the most energy into preparing their celebrations also reported the greatest disappointment complements the conclusion of Experiment 1, as it suggests that explicit efforts to achieve happiness can, at least in some situations, backfire. Moreover, because this study was conducted in the field without any experimental promptings, it suggests that the disruptive effects of pursuing happiness observed in Experiment 1 were not simply a byproduct of compelling individuals to pursue a goal that they themselves had not spontaneously initiated. Together, the findings of these two studies suggest that the explicit pursuit of happiness can be disruptive both when it is encouraged by an external agent (i.e., the experimenter) and when it is self-identified. These combined findings, thus, suggest that explicit attempts at maximizing happiness, at least under certain circumstances, may indeed represent an irrational approach for achieving this goal.

5. ECONOMIC AND PSYCHOLOGICAL IMPLICATIONS

We hope that the preceeding discussion has persuaded the reader that it is appropriate to entertain the likelihood that individuals can lack explicit awareness of the quality of their hedonic experience, and that efforts to monitor and maximize happiness can have deleterious consequences. Given the viability of these premises and the goals of this volume, it seems appropriate to consider their implications for both economics and psychology.

5.1. Implications for Economics

One of the reasons that the Benthamite utility was abandoned was that it could not be measured. As Jevons (1871) wrote, 'I hesitate to say that men will ever have the means of measuring directly the feelings of the human heart.... It is from the quantitative *effects* of the feelings that we must estimate their comparative amounts.' Economists wanted to predict behavior from the assumption that people wanted to maximize happiness. But, unable to measure happiness, they were forced to infer what people thought promoted happiness from observing their behavior. Eventually, economists came to recognize the circularity in inferring happiness from behavior and then using it to predict behavior. Happiness, they reasoned, was a superfluous intervening construct, and economists reinterpreted utility as an index of preference. If the Benthamite utility is to be useful as an explanatory construct, there has to be some way of measuring it.

As we have discussed, there are significant problems associated with measuring hedonic experience. While it may some day be possible to measure well-being physiologically, those days are not yet here, so the only possible methods involve subjective self-reports. One problem with self-reports of global happiness that has received considerable attention is that, existing methods are highly unreliable and subject to myriad biases and measurement artifacts (see Schwarz and Strack, 1999, for an overview of the problems). However, our focus is somewhat different. We argue, that people may not be able to introspect accurately about their own level of happiness, and that doing so—that is, introspecting—can actually undermine happiness.

If individuals' reflective inferences can influence even their on-line appraisals, then we must be cautious in assuming that momentary hedonic appraisals necessarily capture their underlying hedonic experience (cf. Kahneman, 1999). Thus, the present analysis suggests that calls to return to Benthamite utilities that rely on self-report measures must be tempered by the inherent limitations of subjective reports, and the inherent impact that collecting self-reports may have on underlying experience. It seems likely that, under many situations, individuals may be able to provide an explicit assessment of their hedonic state that provides a reasonably accurate and non-reactive appraisal of their actual hedonic experience. However, the present analysis suggests that at least sometimes, perhaps particularly when individuals are faced with novel and/or hedonically ambiguous experiences, an explicit hedonic appraisal may misrepresent and/or alter actual experience. Clearly, additional research is needed to determine more precisely the specific situations in which explicit hedonic appraisal influences or distorts a hedonic experience. Only after such research is conducted will we be able to assess the full ramifications of the present analysis, for economic approaches that rely on the subjective reporting of hedonic experience.

In addition to the challenges of measurement, the present analysis also suggests another potential challenge to economic perspectives that assume that individuals should always attempt to maximize utility; namely, that such efforts may actually be counter-productive. This conjecture is based in part on the observation that explicit instructions to maximize happiness in our experimental study reduced happiness. Admittedly however, there is another alternative account of this finding that does not challenge the utility maximization view of economics. Specifically, by encouraging our participants to maximize their happiness we may have encouraged them to engage in an effortful strategy that undermined their utility maximization strategy. However, it should also be noted that a comparable relationship between effort to maximize pleasure and actual achieved pleasure was also observed in our field study, in which we did not compel participants to engage in potentially non-optimal strategies. Thus, while it may well still be true that individuals can maximize utilities under some conditions, the present findings suggest that *deliberate* efforts to do so may lead individuals to engage in non-utility maximizing behaviors.

The above perspective thus suggests that there may be a cost to the adoption of economic models that encourage individuals to deliberately pursue their own self interest. Although economies may thrive when individuals act to maximize their self-interest, as Adam Smith argued, individuals who effortfully engage in such strategies may pay the price of a devaluation of the actual utilities that they derive from their gains. In short, whereas the productivity of economies may flourish when every individual seeks to maximize self-interest, the value of experienced utilities may decrease. Once the cost of this effortful focus of utility maximization is entered into the equation, a decreased emphasis on maximizing self-interest might actually increase net utilities even if it decreases the overall material output.

Although it might seem impossible to imagine a society in which the explicit pursuit of happiness was not the central driving force, it should be pointed out that there are cultures in which the explicit pursuit of happiness is not a central goal. For example, the orientation of Far Eastern cultures towards happiness is quite different from that of the Western societies. As Kityama and Markus (2000, p. 113) observe:

> ...in many American cultural contexts, the personal pursuit of happiness and the recognition of this pursuit by self and others are defining of the happiness itself... However, as exemplified in many East Asian cultures, happiness assumes a different subjective form—it is a state that emerges when taking a critical and disciplined stance to the personal self and thus engaging the sympathy of others.

In East Asian cultures, individuals hold the view, seemingly supported by the present analysis, that happiness does not require and is indeed undermined by the explicit pursuit of happiness. It must be noted that such cultures also often report *lower* overall levels of subjective well-being (e.g., Diener, 2000). However, as the present discussion indicates, we must be wary of taking subjective reports of well-being at face value. This is particularly true when comparing across cultures that may differ in the degree to which they view it as appropriate to acknowledge personal happiness. Despite the difficulties in comparing the actual experienced hedonics of members of different cultures, the examination of the East Asian cultures' orientations toward happiness suggest that an explicit focus on the pursuit of happiness is not a necessary element of human motivation.

5.2. Implications for Psychology

The present series of studies add to the growing body of evidence that thinking and reflection are not always productive activities. Although clearly invaluable for many activities, reflection has now been shown to disrupt a variety of activities that involve the automatic or the difficult to verbalize experiences including: face recognition (e.g., Schooler and Engstler-Schooler, 1990), taste recognition (Melcher and Schooler, 1995), insight problem solving (Schooler et al., 1993), affective decision making (e.g., Wilson and Schooler, 1991), and analogical reasoning (Sieck et al., 1999). The present research adds to this body of research by demonstrating that reflection can also lessen hedonic experience. Of course, the disruptive effects of reflection demonstrated here and elsewhere must be kept in perspective. Clearly, it would be rash to make major decisions without carefully thinking through their consequences. Moreover, the modest disruptions resulting from reflection reported here and elsewhere must be tempered by the fact that the individuals were given only limited amounts of time to reflect, and had little training on how to organize their thoughts on the topic at hand. Indeed, research on the disruptive effects of verbal reflection has found that such effects are mediated by individuals' expertise in articulating their experience (Melcher, 2000; Melcher and Schooler, 1996; Ryan and Schooler, 1998). For example, whereas untrained wine drinkers' memory for a previously consumed wine can be disrupted by efforts at translating that memory into words, trained experts show no such disruption (Melcher and Schooler, 1996). Thus, whereas unstructured verbal reflection may be disruptive for individuals with little formal training in introspecting on their hedonic experience, genuine insight into personal utilities might be gained from a more trained or guided reflection.

Although the present analysis poses some potentially serious difficulties for the empirical science of hedonics, it also suggests some potentially useful directions for overcoming these difficulties. Specifically, once we recognize that hedonic assessments can vary in the degree to which they draw on underlying hedonic experience vs. inference, we can begin to develop measures that provide maximal sensitivity to experienced hedonics. As suggested by studies reviewed in this chapter, two such techniques may be to encourage individuals to make very quick hedonic judgments, and to provide them with a visual feedback (a mirror). Both of these approaches may enable individuals to give self-reports that show a greater sensitivity to their visceral hedonic experience. It may also be possible to develop new forms of self-report measures that enable individuals to give more accurate appraisals of their underlying hedonic experience (see Green et al., 1993).

Additional investigations might look profitably at the relationship between various self-report measures and psycho-physiological responses. As noted, various measures such as eye-blink reflexes and heart blood flow may reflect hedonic experience. If so, future research might examine the relationship between various self-report measures and these psycho-physiological measures such as cardio-vascular blood flow (Tomaka et al., 1997) or eyeblink startle response (e.g., Lang, 1995) in order to develop a maximally valid measure of experienced hedonics. In addition, there are other indirect measures of hedonics, such as affective priming (e.g., Bargh et al., 1992; Fazio et al., 1995) that may also circumvent often questionable hedonic inferencing processes. Perhaps, if a combination of such indirect hedonic measures were used in concert, it might be possible to extract an underlying latent variable corresponding to hedonic experience. If so, it might be at long last possible to develop a science of utility that is unobstructed by many of the measurement problems outlined here (see Larsen and Fredrickson, 1999, for a discussion of the current limitations of indirect hedonic measurements).

More generally, the present analysis of the distinction between a hedonic experience and one's explicit meta-awareness of that experience illustrates the potentially broad applicability of the experiential consciousness/meta-consciousness distinction recently proposed by Schooler (in press). As Schooler points out, this distinction is exemplified by the case of mind wandering during reading. All readers are familiar with the experience of suddenly realizing that despite the best of intentions, one's mind has wandered, and one has no idea what they have been reading (like right now perhaps?). What is so striking about this experience is that although one consciously experiences the contents of the mind-wandering episode, one fails to notice that one's mind has wandered. Otherwise, one would have either stopped reading or stopped daydreaming. The fact that both activities continue demonstrates the absence of awareness that one is daydreaming, even though this is precisely what is occupying one's mind at the time. In short, the common everyday experience of mind wandering during reading illustrates that we can have an experience (i.e., experiential consciousness) without being explicitly aware (i.e., meta-conscious) of the fact that we are having that experience.

Within the present context, it seems quite reasonable to draw parallels between the experiential consciousness/meta-consciousness distinction as applied to daydreaming while reading and hedonics. Just as individuals may regularly daydream without realizing that they are doing so, so too individuals may regularly have hedonic experiences without explicitly apprehending their nature. Similarly, like catching one's mind wandering when it should not, the meta-awareness of hedonic experience may be most likely to occur when things are not going well. Indeed, perhaps, this is one additional reason why unhappy people tend to be introspective; unhappiness may be more likely to induce an explicit meta-awareness of one's hedonic state.

5.3. The Paradox of Introspection and the Pursuit of Happiness

As readers have likely surmised, our analysis suggests that there are several serious paradoxes surrounding the relationship between introspection, the pursuit of happiness, and actual hedonic experience. On the one hand, an explicit focus on the value of one's hedonic experience may both misrepresent and undermine its quality. On the other hand, a general lack of reflection may cause individuals to fail to recognize those experiences that provide them with the maximum utilities. A similar dilemma occurs with the pursuit of happiness, as the goal of maximizing utilities appears to be undermined by this very goal. Thus, it might seem that with respect to both monitoring and maximizing hedonics, individuals are damned if they do and damned if they do not.

There are several consideration that may ultimately help to resolve these paradoxes. For example, it may be that although the explicit pursuit and monitoring of happiness can be disruptive, that these processes can be carried out effectively at a more tacit level. There is now a growing body of evidence that goals can be activated and maintained without explicit awareness (e.g., Bargh and Chartrand, 1999). There is also evidence that the automatic monitoring systems can search for violations of goals (Wegner, 1994) and regulate affective states (Carver and Scheier, 1990). Thus, the activation of the automatic hedonic maximization goals and monitoring systems may be one way to maximize happiness, unimpeded by the costs of excessive evaluation and deliberation.

While automatic monitoring and goal maintenance processes may help afford hedonic maximization, it seems certain that from time to time it is necessary to explicitly appraise hedonic experience and adjust one's goals accordingly. Like a pilot who generally relies on the highly efficient auto-pilot system, but occasionally must shift to manual control, hedonic regulation may be best optimized when individuals periodically engage in a willful monitoring and control of their hedonic state. Of course, as our analysis suggests, introspection does not ensure that one will get an accurate reading of their hedonic state. Nevertheless, there are certainly some situations (e.g., enjoying a glorious sunset, suffering through a miserable meal) in which individuals do seem quite capable of accurately appraising their experience. Thus, despite its potential costs and inaccuracies, if timed appropriately *intermittent atttention* to one's hedonic situation may be critical for maximizing happiness. The challenge is determining when it is best to man the controls, and when it is better to simply enjoy the ride.

REFERENCES

Ariely, D. (1998). Combining experiences over time: The effects of duration, intensity changes and on-papers line measurements on retrospective pain evaluations. *Journal of Behavioral Decision Making, 11*, 19–45.

—— Loewenstein, G.F., and Prelec, D. (2000). *Coherent arbitrariness: Duration-sensitive pricing of hedonic stimuli around an arbitrary anchor.* Working paper, Department of Social and Decision Sciences, Carnegie Mellon University, Pittsburgh.

—— and Zauberman, G. (2000). On the making of an experience: The effects of breaking and combining experiences on their overall evaluation. *Journal of Behavioral Decision Making, 13*, 219–32.

Bargh, J.A., Chaiken, S., Govender, R., and Pratto, F. (1992). The generality of the attitude activation effect. *Journal of Personality and Social Psychology, 62*, 893–912.

—— and Chartrand, T.L. (1999). The unbearable automaticity of being. *American Psychologist, 54*, 462–79.

Becker, G.M., DeGroot, M.H., and Marschak, J., (1963). An experimental study of some stochastic models for wagers. *Behavioral Science, 8*, 199–202.

Bem, D.J. (1967). Self-perception: An alternative interpretation of cognitive dissonance phenomena. *Psychological Review, 74*(3), 183–2000.

—— (1972). Self-perception theory. In L. Berkowitz (Ed.), *Advances in experimental social psychology* (Vol. 6). New York: Academic Press.

Brickman, P. and Cambell, D.T. (1971). Hedonic relativism and planning the good society. In M.H. Appley (Ed.), *Adaptation-level theory*. New York: Academic Press.

Csikszentmihalyi, M. (1999). If we are so rich, why aren't we happy? *American Psychologist, 54*(10), 821–7.

Cupchik, G.C. and Leventhal, H. (1974). Consistency between expressive behavior and the evaluation of humorous stimuli: The role of sex and self-observation. *Journal of Personality and Social Psychology, 30*, 429–42.

Damasio, A.R. (1994). *Descartes' error: emotion, reason, and the human brain*. New York: G.P. Putnam.

Deci, E.L., Koestner, R., and Ryan, R.M. (1999). A meta-analytic review of experiments examining the effects of extrinsic rewards on intrinsic motivation. *Psychological Bulletin, 125*(6), 627–58.

Diener, E. (2000). Subjective well-being: The science of happiness and a proposal for a national index. *American Psychologist, 55*, 34–43.

Dutton, D.G. and Aaron, A.P. (1974). Some evidence for heightened sexual attraction under conditions of high anxiety. *Journal of Personality and Social Psychology, 30*, 510–17.

Duval, S. and Wicklund, R.A. (1972). *A theory of objective self-awareness*. New York: Academic Press.

Fazio, R.H. (1987). Self-perception theory: A current perspective. In M.P. Zanna, J.M. Olson, and C.P. Herman (Eds.), *Social influences: The Ontario Symposium* (Vol. 5, pp. 129–50). Hillsdale: Erlbaum.

—— Jackson, J.R., Dunton, B.C., and Williams, C.J. (1995). Variability in automatic activation as an unobtrusive measure of racial attitudes: A bona fide pipeline? *Journal of Personality and Social Psychology, 69*, 1013–27.

Festinger, L. (1957). *A theory of cognitive dissonance*. Stanford: Stanford University Press.

—— and Carlsmith, J.M. (1959). Cognitive consequences of forced compliance. *Journal of Abnormal and Social Psychology, 58*, 203–10.

Gilbert, D.T., Pinel, E.C., Wilson, T.D., Blumberg, S.J., and Wheatley, T.P. (1998). Immune neglect: A source of durability bias in affective forecasting. *Journal of Personality and Social Psychology, 75*(3), 617–38.

Green, B.G., Shaffer, G.S., and Gilmore, M.M. (1993). Derivation and evaluation of a semantic scale of oral sensation magnitude with apparent ratio properties. *Chemical Senses, 18*(6), 683–702.

Hicks, S.J. R. (1976). Some questions of time in economics. In A.M. Tang, F.M. Westfield, and J.S. Worley (Eds.), *Evolution, welfare, and times in economics: Essays in honor of Georgescu Roegen* (2nd ed.). Lexington: Lexington Books.

Ingram, R.E. (1990). Self-focused attention in clinical disorders: Review and a conceptual model. *Psychological Bulletin, 109*, 156–76.

James, W. (1884). What is an emotion. *Mind, 9*, 188–205.

Jevons, W.S. (1871). *Theory of political economy*. London: Macmillan.

Kahneman, D. (1999). Objective happiness. In D. Kahneman, E. Diener, and N. Schwarz (Eds.), *Well-being: The foundations of hedonic psychology* (pp. 3–25). New York: Russell Sage.

Kahneman, D. and Varey, C. (1991). Notes on the psychology of utility. In J. Elster and J. E. Roemer (Eds.), *Interpersonal comparisons of well-being: Studies in rationality and social change* (pp. 127–63). New York: Cambridge.

—— Wakker, P.P., and Sarin, R. (1997). Back to Bentham? Explorations of experienced utility. *The Quarterly Journal of Economics, May*, 375–405.

Kasser, T. and Ryan, R.M. (1993). A dark side of the American dream: Correlates of financial success as a central life aspiration. *Journal of Personality and Social Psychology, 65*(2), 41–422.

—— and —— (1996). Further examining the American dream: Differential correlates of intrinsic and extrinsic goals. *Journal of Personality and Social Psychology, 22*(3), 280–7.

Kityama, S. and Markus, H.R. (2000). The pursuit of happiness and the realization of sympathy: Cultural patterns of self, social relations, and well-being. In E. Deiner and Eukook Suh (Eds.), *Culture and subjective well-being*. Boston: MIT Press.

Konow, J. (2000). Fair shares: Accountability and cognitive dissonance in allocation decisions. *American Economic Review, 90*(4), 1072–91.

Lane, R.D., Reiman, E.M., Bradley, M.M., Lang, P.J., L., A.G., Davidson, R.J., and Schwartz, G.E. (1997). Neuroanatomical correlates of pleasant and unpleasant emotion. *Neuropsychologia, 35*(11), 1437–44.

Lang, P. (1995). The emotion probe: Studies of motivation and attention. *American Psychologist, 50*, 372–85.

Larsen, R.J. and Fredrickson, B.L. (1999). Measurement issues in emotion research. In D. Kahneman, E. Diener, and N. Schwarz (Eds.), *Well-being: The Foundations of hedonic psychology* (pp. 40–60). New York: Russell Sage Foundation.

Lazarus, R.S. (1984). On the primacy of cognition. *American Psychologist, 39*(2), 124–9.

Lepper, M.R., Greene, D., and Nisbett, R.E. (1973). Undermining children's intrinsic interest with extrinsic reward. *Journal of Personality and Social Psychology, 28*, 349–53.

Lewin, S.B. (1996). Economics and psychology: Lessons for our own day from the early twentieth century. *Journal of Economic Literature, 34*(3), 1293–323.

Little, I.M.D. (1957). *A critique of welfare economics* (2nd ed.). Oxford: Clarendon Press.

Loewenstein, G. (1992). The fall and rise of psychological explanations in the economics of intertemporal choice. In G. Loewenstein and J. Elster (Eds.), *Choice over time* (pp. 3–34). New York: Russell Sage Foundation.

Loewenstein, G. (1996). Out of control: Visceral influences on behavior. *Organizational Behavior and Human Decision Processes, 65*, 272–92.

—— and Frederick, S. (1997). Predicting reactions to environmental change. In M. H. Bazerman and D.M. Messick (Eds.), *Environment, ethics, and behavior: The psychology of environmental valuation and degradation* (pp. 52–72). San Francisco: The New Lexington Press/Jossey-Bass.

—— O'Donoghue, T., and Rabin, M. (2000). *Projection bias in the prediction of future utility*. Working paper, Department of Social and Decision Sciences, Carnegie Mellon University, Pittsburgh.

—— and Schkade, D. (1999). Wouldn't it be nice? Predicting future feelings. In D. Kahneman, E. Diener, and N. Schwarz (Eds.), *Well-being: The foundations of hedonic psychology*. New York: Russell Sage.

Lyubomirsky, S. and Lepper, H.S. (1999). A measure of subjective happiness: Preliminary reliability and construct validation. *Social Indicators Research, 46*, 137–55.

Melcher, J. and Schooler, J.W. (1996). The misremembrance of wines past: Verbal and perceptual expertise differentially mediate verbal overshadowing of taste. *Journal of Memory and Language, 35*, 231–45.

Musson, F.F. and Alloy, L.B. (1988). Depression and self-directed attention. In L.B. Alloy (Ed.), *Cognitive processes in depression* (pp. 193–220). New York: Guilford Press.

Myers, D.G. (1992). *The pursuit of happiness: Who is happy—and why.* New York: William Morrow.

——— (2000). *The American paradox: Spiritual hunger in an age of plenty.* New Haven: Yale University Press.

Olson, J. (1990). Self-inference processes in emotion. In J. Olson and M. Zanna (Eds.), *Self-inference: The Ontario symposium* (Vol. 6, pp. 17–42). Hillsdale: Lawrence Erlbaum.

Page, A.N. (1968). *Utility theory: A book of readings.* New York: Wiley.

Reisenzein, R. (1983). The Schachter theory of emotion: Two decades later. *Psychological Bulletin, 94*, 239–64.

Ryan, R.S. and Schooler, J.W. (1998). Whom do words hurt? Individual differences in susceptibility to verbal overshadowing. *Applied Cognitive Psychology, 12*, 105–25.

Schachter, S. and Singer, J.E. (1962). Cognitive, social and physiological determinants of emotional state. *Psychological Review, 69*, 379–99.

Scheier, M.F. and Carver, C.S. (1977). Self-focused attention and the experience of emotion: Attraction, repulsion, elation, and depression. *Journal of Personality and Social Psychology, 35*(9), 625–36.

Schooler, J.W. (2001). Discovering memories in the light of meta-awareness. *Journal of Aggression, Maltreatment and Trauma, 4*, 105–36.

——— (2002). Representing consciousness: Dissociations between consciousness and meta-consciousness. *Trends in Cognitive Science, 6*, 339–44.

——— and Engstler-Schooler, T.Y. (1990). Verbal overshadowing of visual memories: Some things are better left unsaid. *Cognitive Psychology, 17*, 36–71.

——— Ohlsson, S. and Brooks, K. (1993). Thoughts beyond words: When language overshadows insight. *Journal of Experimental Psychology, 122*, 166–83.

——— and Wilson, T.W. (1991). When words hurt: The disruptive effects of verbally analyzing reasons. *Proceedings of the Society for Consumer Psychology, 29*.

Schwarz, N. (1987). *Stimmung als information: Untersuchugen zum einfluss von stimmungen auf die Bewertung des eigenen Lebens.* Berlin: Springer.

——— and Clore, G.L. (1983). Mood, misattribution and judgments of well-being: Informative and directive functions of affective states. *Journal of Personality and Social Psychology, 45*, 513–23.

——— and Strack, F. (1999). Reports of subjective well-being: Judgmental processes and their methodological implications. In D. Kahneman, E. Diener, and N. Schwarz (Eds.), *Well-being: The foundations of hedonic psychology.* New York: Russell Sage.

——— Strack, F., Koomer, D., and Wagner, D. (1987). Soccer rooms, and the quality of your life: Mood effects on judgments of satisfaction with life in general and with specific life domains. *European Journal of Social Psychology, 17*, 69–79.

Sen, A. (1973). Behaviour and the concept of preference. *Economica, 40*, 241–59.

Sieck, W.R, Quinn, C.N., and Schooler, J.W. (1999). Justification effects on the judgment of analogy. *Memory and Cognition, 27*, 844–55

Stigler, G. (1965). The development of utility theory, *Essays in the history of economics.* Chicago: University of Chicago Press.

——— and Becker, G. (1977). De gustibus non est disputandum. *American Economic Review,* 67, 76–90.

Strack, F., Martin, L.L., and Stepper, S. (1988). Inhibiting and facilitating conditions of the human smile: A nonobtrusive test of the facial feedback hypothesis. *Journal of Personality and Social Psychology,* 54(5), 768–77.

Taylor, S.E. and Brown, J. (1994). Positive illusion and well-being revisited: Separating fact from fiction. *Psychological Bulletin,* 103, 193–210

Tomaka, J., Blascovich, J., Kibler, J., and Ernst, J.M. (1997). Cognitive and physiological antecedents of threat and challenge appraisal. *Journal of Personality and Social Psychology,* 73, 63–72.

Veenhoven, R. (1988). Utility of happiness. *Social Indicators Research,* 20, 333–54.

Wenzlaff, R.M. and Wegner, D.M. (2000). Thought suppression. *Annual Review of Psychology,* 51, 59–91.

Wegner, D.M. (1994). Ironic processes of mental control. *Psychological Review,* 101, 34–52.

——— Erber, R., and Zanakos, S. (1993). Ironic processes in the mental control of mood and mood related thought. *Journal of Personality and Social Psychology,* 6, 1093–104.

Wicklund, R. (1975). Objective self-awareness. In L. Berkowitz (Ed.), *Advances in experimental social psychology.* New York: Academic Press.

Wilson, T.D. (1990). Self-persuasion via self-reflection. In J. Olson and M. Zanna (Eds.), *Self-inference: The Ontario symposium* (Vol. 6, pp. 43–67). Hillsdale: Lawrence Erlbaum.

——— Dunn, D.S., Bybee, J.A., Hyman, D.B., and Rotondo, J.A. (1984). Effects of analyzing reasons on attitude-behavior consistency. *Journal of Personality and Social Psychology,* 47, 5–16.

——— Lindsey, S. and Schooler, T.Y. (2000). A model of dual attitudes. *Psychological Review,* 107(1), 101–26.

——— Lisle, D.J., Schooler, J.W., Hodges, S.D., Klaaren, K.J., and LaFleur, S.J. (1993). Introspecting about reasons can reduce post-choice satisfaction. *Personality and Social Psychology Bulletin,* 19, 331–9.

——— and Schooler, J.W. (1991). Thinking too much: Introspection can reduce the quality of preferences and decisions. *Journal of Personality and Social Psychology,* 60, 181–92.

Zajonc, R.B. (1984). On the primacy of affect. *American Psychologist,* 39(2), 117–23.

Zillman, D. (1978). Attribution and misattribution of excitalory reactions. In J.H. Harvey, W.J. Ickes, and R.F. Kidd (Eds.), *New directions in attribution research* (Vol. 2, pp. 335–68). Hillsdale: Lawrence Erlbaum.

PART II

IMPERFECT SELF-KNOWLEDGE AND THE ROLE OF INFORMATION

4

Behavioral Policy

ANDREW CAPLIN AND JOHN LEAHY

1. INTRODUCTION

Policy questions (such as when free trade among nations is beneficial) are central to economics. The economists have become very good at constructing models to address these questions. These models are often criticized as painting an idealized and unrealistic picture of the decision making process. Yet, it is this very idealism that makes them so valuable for designing optimal policies. By definition, suboptimal policies please no one.

In building their models, economists assume that human behavior derives from the effort to fulfill a few simple and transparent goals. Yet, a century of psychological experimentation points in an entirely different direction. Psychological research reveals the many complex mental processes that impact our understanding of the external world, our motivation, and our behavior. The intricacy of their research findings makes many psychologists see the simple economic man as an irrelevant abstraction. The economists, for their part, worry that it will be very hard to derive useful policy lessons from intricate psychological experiments. The psychologists may miss the forest for the trees.

The richest possibilities for collaboration between psychology and economics lie where strength meets strength. The economists can bring to the table their rich tradition of policy analysis, and the psychologists their equally rich tradition of analyzing human behavior. We argue that such a synthetic approach to behavioral policy is within our grasp, and that the resulting synthesis will open up whole new areas of research.

We pose three sets of policy questions, and explain why joint research will be required to address them. We begin Section 2 by posing a question from the field of behavioral medicine: how much information should a doctor supply to a patient prior to an operation? This small question perfectly illustrates the need for collaborative research. We outline our own integrative model that incorporates key psychological insights into an economic framework, and thereby provides deeper insight into policy than can be gleaned from either field in isolation (Caplin and Leahy, 1999).

We thank Daniel Gilbert, Daniel Kahneman, David Laibson, Yaacov Trope, and Ruth Wyatt for their valuable comments.

In the following sections, we turn to two questions that figure among the most burning policy questions of our era. Section 3 addresses policy issues raised by the ever-expanding availability of genetic tests that can provide subjects with an early warning of impending health problems. Section 4 addresses policy issues raised by the low US savings rate. In both cases, we argue that progress in policy analysis requires inter-disciplinary collaboration along the lines outlined in Section 2.

2. THE PROVISION OF MEDICAL INFORMATION

A (male) patient is facing an up-coming surgical procedure. The (female) doctor knows a great deal more about the procedure and its outcome than does the patient. The doctor's policy question is how much information to pass on to the patient before the operation. We first outline the quick and easy answer to the policy question were the doctor to follow the dictates of the standard economic theory, then the richer answer implied by psychological research, and finally the even richer answer offered by a synthetic approach.

2.1. Economics

A central result of the classical economic theory is Blackwell's theorem, which implies that more information can never be a bad thing. After all, the argument goes, information can only be an aid to planning, and if it is not an aid to planning it is simply irrelevant. Blackwell's theorem rests on the assumption that utility depends only on what actually ends up happening in the external world. Beliefs about what will happen have no independent effect on well-being, but serve merely as weights by which to average utility across external outcomes. Since only outcomes can be sources of utility, all forms of anxiety and fear, even the fear of death, are treated as irrational.[1]

In the medical context, Blackwell's theorem trivializes the question of information provision. If the information that the doctor possesses is important for some other decision by the patient (such as how soon after the operation he can go on a vacation), then she should pass it on. If the information is not relevant to decisions, it has no value whatsoever, and so it may not be worth taking the time to convey it.

2.2. Psychology

While anxiety plays no role in standard economics, it features heavily in psychological research on the supply of medical information. Janis (1958)

---

[1] Even Shakespeare's Caesar did not go quite this far. Being 'brave', he agreed with modern day economists in finding the fear of death hard to understand, 'Seeing that death, a necessary end, Will come when it will come'. Yet even he understood that the world contained many 'cowards' who 'die many times before their death'.

hypothesized that providing more information about an up-coming medical procedure would stimulate the 'work of worrying' that would initially raise patient anxiety, but subsequently lower it and thereby speed recovery. The more recent literature has focused attention on how individuals differ in their response to information. It has been shown that additional information serves to raise anxiety in some patients and lowers it in others (e.g., Miller and Mangan, 1983).

Researchers in behavioral medicine have extracted a policy recommendation from this research. They propose using questionnaire techniques to identify whether an individual generally finds medical information anxiety-inducing or anxiety-reducing. They recommend supplying information to the latter, not to the former. Morgan et al. (1998), investigated precisely this strategy in the case of a colonoscopy, a short yet stressful surgical procedure. They indeed found that those whose questionnaire answers revealed a desire for information did better (in a wide variety of psychological and medical measures) if they received more information, while those who revealed a lack of desire for information did better if they received less information.[2]

2.3. A Synthesis

Despite appearances to the contrary, psychological research cannot answer the policy question without the help of models from economics. One key limitation of the experimental techniques of psychologists is that results are of necessity derived in the *current* policy environment. If the policy were to change, so would the emotional response to information, and with it the policy recommendation itself.[3] Without a model, it is next to impossible to accommodate the policy implications of such complex spill-over effects. Yet, in principle, these effects can be handled in a suitably structured model.

In general, models are necessary laboratories for the kind of counter-factual analysis required to investigate the impact of policy changes. They also allow one to broaden the scope of the analysis to cover additional questions. Does the policy recommendation for a colonoscopy generalize to life-and-death operations? Should the questionnaire be enriched to include information on the patient's level of knowledge about the operation, and if so how such information should be used?

Our research program involves acknowledging the importance of psycho-logical forces such as fear and anxiety, while retaining the model-building philosophy of economics. Our 'psychological expected utility' model (henceforth

---

[2] Further psychological research in this area will be needed to deepen our understanding of patient anxiety. One issue is whether questioning patients immediately before the operation may itself pro-duce anxiety. After all, questioning patients about their preference for information allows them to infer that the doctor knows something of possible importance to them. This knowledge itself, although the patient remains uninformed, may be a source of stress.

[3] In economics, this interdependence between the current policy and observed responses to this policy is known as the 'Lucas critique'.

PEU) treats psychological states as prizes of equivalent status to the physical prizes that dominate the classical economic theory (Caplin and Leahy, 1997). Our work extends the ideas of Jevons (1905) and Loewenstein (1987) to settings with uncertainty.

In our model of how a doctor should supply information to a potentially anxious patient (Caplin and Leahy, 1999), we treat anxiety as resulting directly from the patient's information about the consequences of the operation. Even in its current simple form, our model provides some valuable insights.

We show that the questionnaire procedure proposed by psychologists does *not* apply to life-and-death operations. Consider a patient who finds information on the operation anxiety-inducing, yet whom the doctor believes to be unduly pessimistic. If good news would lower the patient's overall level of anxiety, then the doctor should pass it on at once, despite the patient's implicit request to be left in peace. The doctor must override the patient's preferences in such a case.

Our model also illuminates spill-over effects, whereby a policy of selectively revealing certain types of information may impact the state of mind, even of a patient who hears absolutely nothing. This effect is best brought to life in a somewhat different context. Consider a doctor who tests patients for AIDS, and who can either call them up immediately with the results, or wait for a week to schedule in-person interviews. The doctor tests two patients who are acquainted. One of the two patients gets called with good news on his test, while the other hears nothing. Knowing that good news is passed on quickly, the second patient spends the next week sitting by the phone, fearing that the lack of news means that his test is positive. To avoid creating this kind of anxiety, it may be better for the doctor to institute a general policy in which all news, good or bad, is revealed in precisely the same manner. Our model is well-suited to capturing the trade-off between committing to a uniform informational protocol and allowing for a more discretionary policy.

2.4. Challenges for Economics: Part I

On the one hand, we have argued that the classical economic theory has little of value to say on questions of information provision. On the other hand, we have shown that, when suitably amended, the economic modeling techniques are essential to policy analysis. So what are the critical amendments that account for this difference?

One amendment stems from the analysis of the spill-over effects outlined in Section 2.4. In the case of the HIV test, anxiety depends not only on what the doctor chooses to reveal, but what she chooses to suppress. If the doctor is believed to reveal only good news, then silence will induce anxiety, while if the doctor is believed to reveal only bad news, then silence will spell relief. Such effects have been ignored in the classical game theory, in which payoffs depend only on the state of the world at the *end* of the game. To allow for the impact of strategic uncertainty on payoffs, our model builds on the theory of psychological games introduced by Geanakoplos et al. (1989). Our game, however, is a simple one. Much work remains to be done before this class of models can be applied in richer, dynamic settings.

Our model makes a second and more fundamental departure from the standard economic theory. Our initial expectation had been that we would be able to shoe-horn the patient's dislike of information into the classical apparatus. After all, we were not the first to build a model that allows for exceptions to Blackwell's theorem. In particular, the Kreps–Porteus model allows one to capture a preference for the delayed revelation of information (Kreps and Porteus, 1978). We were surprised to find that their model was ill-suited to answer the question whether or not the doctor should reveal information to the patient. The only way to model the question was to use the PEU model.

There is a subtle yet profound difference of approach between the Psychological Expected Utility model and the Kreps–Porteus model that accounts for the difference. The modern choice theory is based on the principle of revealed preference, and is behaviorist in spirit. It is held that the only legitimate agenda for the theory is to describe choices among goods that are, or may potentially be, available in the market. Nothing less, and certainly nothing more. The Kreps–Porteus model adheres to this principle, and deliberately avoids the discussion of psychological states. In contrast the PEU model places these states on the center stage. Our policy problem exposes one limitation of the behaviorist program. By definition the patient cannot *choose* to be overly optimistic. So, the doctor cannot infer from his behavior alone whether or not to remain silent, if *she* knows he is overly optimistic.[4] She has to have a broader vision of his welfare, one that differentiates between the role that beliefs play as inputs into utility, and the role that they play in the calculation of expectations of future outcomes. The PEU theory formalizes such a vision.

3. GENETIC TESTING

The genetic revolution raises profound policy questions. Widespread testing has the potential to radically improve health outcomes, and lower health costs. At the same time testing can raise anxiety, and a negative result may be psychologically devastating. To what extent should public policy aim to promote testing, and how is this goal best accomplished? After presenting some of the existing research findings, we propose further research that is designed to connect more closely with key policy questions.

---

[4] In a similar manner, revealed preference cannot be used to decide whether or not to throw surprise parties for loved ones. By definition they are unable to choose whether or not to throw such parties for themselves.

3.1. Some Research Findings

Psychological research on genetic testing has focused on two of the first tests to be made widely available: the test for the genetic mutation responsible for Huntington's disease (HD) and the test for the so-called BRCA1 mutation. The BRCA1 mutation is implicated in many hereditary breast cancer cases, and carries with it an increased risk of ovarian cancer. Researchers have studied a wide range of questions including who gets tested, why subjects make the choices they do, and how well subjects understand the information conveyed by the test.

3.1.1. *Low Test Rates*

The first important question posed by researchers is how many subjects choose to undergo testing in the current policy climate. Survey evidence suggested that there would be high testing rates. Roughly 65 percent of those at risk for HD (Kessler et al., 1987) and fully 90 percent of those at risk for breast and ovarian cancer (Lerman et al., 1994) reported that they would be very interested in getting test results.

In practice, the uptake rate has turned our to be far lower than expected: about 40 percent in the case of breast cancer, and even lower in the case of HD. In one study of HD, only 15 percent of those who initially expressed interest ultimately followed through and got their results (Quaid and Morris, 1993).

3.1.2. *Research into Motivation*

For some, financial factors such as worries about the possible loss of health insurance coverage may be critical in the testing decision. For others, psychological factors may dominate. In psychological terms, the low acceptance rate of the HD test is, perhaps, not surprising. The test is unequivocal, and the disease is not only incurable but also terrifying. First symptoms appear at about age 40 with a gradual neurophysiological deterioration over the remaining life span of some 15 years.

Researchers have used surveys to try to understand motives for and against testing. Jacobsen et al. (1997) provide survey evidence on the importance of psychological factors in the case of the BRCA1 test, a test which is far less devastating than the HD test.[5] However, even in this case, the survey answers suggest that emotional considerations weighed at least as heavily against taking the test as did financial concerns. Fully 85 percent of the subjects in the study by Jacobsen et al. identified their reason for not taking the test as the resulting

---

[5] In contrast to the HD test, neither a positive nor a negative outcome of this test is unequivocal. The mutation is responsible for only 5 percent of all breast cancer cases, and the probability of a carrier getting breast cancer by the age of 70 is 85 percent, while the risk of getting ovarian cancer is 63 percent (Croyle et al., 1997). In addition, there are various measures that a carrier can take to reduce the probability of disease and death.

increased concerns about developing breast cancer; 72 percent increased worry about family members; 34 percent worried about losing health insurance coverage; and 27 percent felt that a bad result of the genetic test would leave them in a state of hopelessness and despair.

3.1.3. *Ignorance and Education*
The desire to avoid information was an important aspect of the medical example in Section 3.1.2. Such a 'head in the sand' behavior is even more important in the context of genetic testing. Lerman et al. (1996) surveyed subjects at risk on their understanding of the BRCA1 test. Despite the obvious importance of the issue, and despite having previously been sent literature on the test, the ignorance was pervasive. About 28 percent of the subjects were unaware that the BRCA1 gene caused an increased risk of ovarian cancer, while almost 80 percent were off by an order of magnitude in their belief that the BRCA1 gene causes 50 percent of all cases of breast cancer.

Following these findings, researchers have investigated the impact of education on understanding. Lerman et al. (1997) show that the understanding of genetic testing may be significantly enhanced by face-to-face education. Yet, the findings of Lerman and Croyle (1995) suggest that much ignorance may have affective rather than cognitive roots. They found that counselling raised the level of comprehension for only 20 percent of subjects who were highly anxious, yet for almost 80 percent of those who reported low levels of anxiety.

3.2. Policy Questions and Policy Research

We outline three issues for policy makers, and indicate how future research could shed a more direct light on policy questions if it incorporated economic reasoning (broadly interpreted).

3.2.1. *Should Health Insurance be Subsidized?*
The low rate of uptake of genetic testing has social ramifications that need to be considered by policy makers. Since society as a whole may have a stake in the testing decision, economic logic suggests that it may be wise to offer incentives for certain individuals to get tested. A simple way to accomplish this would be to subsidize the health insurance rates of such individuals, should they agree to testing. At the same time, this would dispose of the fear of 'genetic discrimination' in which the insurer is expected to raise health insurance rates in the face of a bad test result.

The question of subsidies pinpoints a methodological gap in the existing research in medical psychology. All experimental data are derived against the backdrop of the existing public policy. Researchers analyze how many subjects get tested in the current policy environment, but do not even attempt to answer the question of how testing rates would be impacted by a policy change, such as subsidizing health insurance. Policy analysis requires one to answer hypothetical questions such as the extent to which insurance subsidies would change decisions.

The key research question is how to accurately assess the impact of subsidies on decisions. This task of measurement presents a profound challenge, calling for a collaboration between the economists and the psychologists. There will be some subjects who tend to underestimate the subsidy required to induce testing, just as they overestimate their willingness to get tested. Others may overestimate the required level of compensation in the hope that this induces a large payment to be forthcoming. Designing experimental protocols that will correct such biases will be non-trivial.

3.2.2. *How to Match Policy with Motive?*

The survey evidence on motivation suggests that, there may be a limit to how much one could influence the acceptance rate for the HD and the BRCA1 tests with the use of reasonable financial incentives. Multiple motivations go with multiple policies. For the classical economic man, motivated by purely financial matters, the insurance subsidy should be adequate. However if an individual rejects testing to avoid being plunged into a state of hopelessness or despair, one might favor policies that include high levels of counseling at all stages of the process, with especially strong support services made available in the case of bad news.[6]

Again, this question highlights the need for research into counter-factuals. One needs a far more detailed investigation of the variety of motives involved in the decision, using innovative combinations of survey techniques and actual choice experiments. The economists can play a key role not only in ensuring the policy relevance of the resulting findings, but also in developing a menu of policies that are well-matched with the variety of motivations uncovered.

3.2.3. *Ignorance and Policy*

Existing research appears to be based on the idea that increasing understanding *per se* is the major goal of educational policy. Yet, Lerman and Croyle's finding that high anxiety interferes with learning calls into question the virtues of an aggressive educational effort. Persistent efforts to educate an already anxious subject may further raise his level of stress, with little to show in the form of increased knowledge.

A second question about the virtues of an across-the-board policy to increase knowledge is suggested by the fact that many at risk subjects vastly overestimate

---

[6] The importance of psychological motivations, further accentuates the limitations of the standard economic theory. While this theory correctly pinpoints how fear of an increase in health insurance rates may be a deterrent to testing (Sulgarnik and Zilcha, 1997), there is no place for feelings of despair. According to this vision, as soon as one neutralized the insurance issue, the preference for testing would become universal.

their risk of getting breast cancer. This form of misunderstanding is associated with a high level of interest in getting tested (Lerman et al., 1994). Since many of the public health arguments favor increased testing, it is far from clear how much effort should be made to correct these overestimates.[7]

In the end, the optimal educational policy is likely to be somewhat selective. Expenditures should be directed at correcting misunderstandings that are judged to be both important to overcome, and which can be overcome at a relatively low cost. Economic modeling is ideally suited to the task of policy design in this setting, given that there are several competing objectives and financial constraints.

3.3. Challenges for Economics: Part II

Since anxiety and stress are so important, a natural starting point for modeling is the PEU framework introduced in Section 2.[8,9] Yet, the modeling challenges are far more severe in the case of genetic testing. Some of these challenges stem from the far longer time horizon in the case of genetic testing, and others from the greater need to develop educational policies to counter certain forms of misunderstanding.

Given the long time horizon, it is important to consider the dynamics of anxiety, stress, and ignorance, and how they feed back onto medical behaviors. Tibben et al. (1993) found that the medium-term adverse impact of bad news was significantly higher for those who showed high levels of cancer-related distress prior to testing. Prolonged distress may in turn impact medical outcomes, since it has been shown to deter adherence to breast self-examination (Kash et al., 1992). Modeling anxiety, medical behaviors, and medical outcomes in a rich and empirically relevant dynamic structure will be profoundly challenging.

The long time horizon in the case of genetic testing presents economists with another challenge, this one in the normative arena. The economists are deeply attached to the concept of consumer sovereignty: the idea that each individual makes choices that are in his own best interests. A policy maker may believe that an individual who decides against getting tested is doing predictable damage to his own future health, but according to the principle of consumer sovereignty, the policy maker has no ethical grounds for intervening in this freely made decision.

---

[7] Similar issues show up in the case of smoking and lung cancer, since many smokers overestimate the risk of lung cancer. One does not see public health expenditures poured into a campaign to enhance informed decision-making by correcting these overestimates.

[8] Baum, Brown, Zakowski (1997) present a more textured psychological model.

[9] As with the medical questionnaire of Section 2, the current genetic testing policy can be criticized as needlessly raising stress. In the existing protocol, individuals are first told that the information on their genetic status is available. They are then asked whether or not they want the information. For those who seek to avoid any and all thought about their genetic status, this policy may serve only to raise distress, rather than influence the testing decision. Consistent with this hypothesis, Lerman et al. (1998) found a pattern of psychological deterioration among subjects who were offered and yet chose to reject information on the outcome of their BRCA1 test.

Employing a broader vision of human motivation than is normally employed in economics leads one to question consumer sovereignty. One issue concerns the stability of preferences over time. Individuals look at one and the same experience from many different viewpoints: prospectively as decision makers, contemporaneously in the realm of experience, and retrospectively through the filter of memory (Kahneman (Chapter 10, this volume)). The principle of consumer sovereignty hands all power to the prospective vision, and there may be room for bearing in mind that time changes everything (Caplin and Leahy, 2000). It is clearly possible to regret one's earlier choices. How responsive should policy be to this form of regret?

The psychological literature on 'affective forecasting' provides a second possible argument for restricting consumer sovereignty. This body of research suggests that many people overestimate how deep and long-lasting will be the impact of events that are currently perceived as traumatic (Wilson, Gilbert, and Centerbar, Chapter 10, this volume). Consistent with this, Tibben et al. (1993) found that even though post-test stress remained high for some who got bad news, it quickly fell back to normal for many others. It is possible that many subjects will have quicker than expected psychological recoveries, while the medical advantages will be profound and long lasting. Should policy makers take note of this asymmetry and offer subsidies to those who get tested, even when there are no obvious benefits to third parties?

Economic theory suggests a powerful, yet ultimately unsatisfactory, counter-argument to this form of intervention. In theory, if the policy maker believes that the subject is making a mistake in his assessment of the consequences of the test, she should fully communicate her grounds for disagreeing with him. If he persists despite her best efforts at persuasion, she must end up agreeing that he is making the correct decision. In practical terms, the problem with this form of logic is that it is based on an unrealistic vision of how easy it is to convey information. The evidence cited above suggests that it may be very difficult and costly to convey even the simplest piece of information. In some cases, the policy maker's informational advantage may be so large and difficult to reverse that the normal rules of sovereignty will need to be reconsidered. Of course, there are better and worse ways to use the informational advantage, and these too will need to be understood in a richer, psychological context.

This brings us back to the more general question of how to analyze educational policies in emotionally rich settings such as genetic testing. The challenge for economic theory is not only to allow for learning difficulties, but also to allow for the link between anxiety and learning identified by Lerman and Croyle (1995). This link is further complicated by possible feedback effects. The level of anxiety impedes the learning process. In turn, the resulting low level of understanding may increase uncertainty and exacerbate anxiety, making it still more difficult to learn. Are there policies that can break through this vicious circle?

4. SAVINGS AND PORTFOLIO CHOICE

The US personal savings rate fell to 3 percent in the early 1990s, and remains stuck at a historically low level. This low savings rate threatens to increase the poverty rate among elderly Americans, and further increase pressure on the public purse. Many Americans approach retirement with little personal wealth, and are therefore completely reliant on Social Security payments.

The appropriate policy response depends on what determines the level of savings. In the standard economic models, the central determinant of the savings rate is the utility function over the current and future consumption. In the classical life cycle model, the current consumption weighs heaviest in this function, with the importance of future consumption declining at a constant rate. The hyperbolic discounting model is a prominent alternative to the life cycle model (Strotz, 1955; Laibson, 1997). In this model, all future consumption is discounted not only according to how far in the future it lies, but also because it does not have the immediacy of current consumption. This double discounting implies that it is hard to implement optimal plans. A forty-year old may wish to save for consumption in retirement, yet fear that he would instead 'waste' these assets on impulsive spending in the years before retirement.

Both the life cycle and the hyperbolic models have relatively simple policy implications. In the former, the way to change the savings rate is to change tax rates, and thereby the rate of return to savings. In the latter, one can increase the savings rate by imposing harsh penalties for the early withdrawal of funds, as with the traditional IRA's. Both types of policies are in current use, and the savings rate has remained stubbornly low. Partly for this reason there are continuing challenges to both models, some of which call for a more direct focus on the psychological aspects of the savings decision.

4.1. Ignorance, Stress, and Policy

Standard models of savings treat households as if they are attentive to, and well informed about, the savings decision. To the contrary, Yakoboski and Dickemper (1997) found that only 36 percent of US workers had even tried to determine their retirement needs. Even among households with elderly people, approximately 30 percent report having hardly ever thought about retirement (Lusardi, 2000). These households had dramatically lower savings than those who had given the subject more thought.

What policy measures are suggested by these findings? Is the provision of additional educational materials about savings the best policy? In support, Bernheim and Garrett (1996) have shown that savings and participation in financial education counselling are strongly and positively correlated. What of the efforts to force households to give more attention to their level of retirement consumption? Kotlikoff (1992) proposed that each American worker receive an annual statement of projected Social Security benefits upon retirement, to focus attention on the urgent need for higher savings. A less direct proposal with similar goals is to allow Social Security recipients to have a certain portion of their benefits held in funds of their own choosing. To what extent would such a policy induce more households to pay attention to their savings and portfolio strategies?

It is clear that more research is needed to understand the virtues of these various proposals. As in the case of genetic testing, policy analysis rests on a deeper understanding of the sources of inattention and ignorance. Yakoboski and Dickemper (1997) report that one prevalent reason for not determining retirement needs was that subjects were afraid of the answer. Survey results presented by Lusardi (2000) suggest that the whole subject of retirement is surrounded by worries, with concerns about illness and disability being of particular importance. Constant efforts to force attention may produce little except anxiety, much in the same way as constant reminders of one's failure to undertake genetic testing may induce stress.

4.2. Challenges for Economics: Part III

As in the case of genetic testing, several of the challenges for economic theory stem from the long time horizon involved in the savings decision. Yet, the challenge is in many ways even deeper, since our ignorance about the psychology of savings is so comprehensive. To what extent is it stressful to contemplate being poor and sick in retirement, and how does this stress influence savings behavior? Is it stressful to learn *how* to save and invest, and if so does this cause complete withdrawal from the process? Is it stressful to have a savings portfolio that fluctuates in value, and if so does this account for the low holding of risky assets?

If the stress of contemplating poverty in retirement results in low savings, then this raises the possibility of feedback effects. For obvious reasons, low savings may heighten the stress associated with retirement. By making the activity of planning for retirement even more distressing, this may in turn further reduce the savings effort. How important are these feedback effects, and what, if anything, can be done about them?

The need to understand the psychology of savings immediately presents a second challenge. In the end, the economists will have to rely on experimental and questionnaire techniques to deepen their understanding. Choice data alone are not enough. These data reveal simply that many people save practically nothing, and end up with low consumption in retirement. The data cannot reveal why so many people get themselves into this situation. If low consumption in retirement is a matter of deliberative planning and leaves households overjoyed, there is no policy issue. Otherwise, policy makers may want to know why so many end up in such dire straits, to help determine a solution.

The need to use survey evidence in addition to choice data has not escaped economists' attention. Yet, the findings in Section 3 concerning overestimates of willingness to be tested suggest that survey results need to be interpreted with great caution. Indeed, a similar gap between stated preference and behavior is identified by Barsky et al. (1997). They asked respondents how they discounted the relative future to current consumption. Remarkably, the answers suggested that future consumption was more important to most respondents than was current consumption. If actual behaviors were dominated by such preferences, the savings rates would be far higher than it is.

In order to make the best use of survey evidence, the economists will have to join forces with the psychologists in exploring *why* survey answers differ systematically from actual decisions. In this respect, it is intriguing that in both the case of genetic testing and time discounting, survey answers suggest a greater concern with long-term benefits over short-term costs than do decisions. Does the high reported level of patience reflect a form of cognitive idealism in the survey answers, with short-term forces of an affective nature dominating actual behavior?[10] If one understands why survey answers differ from actual choices, the appropriate corrections can be used to improve the predictive value of such data.

5. CONCLUDING REMARKS

Working together, the economists and the psychologists can develop new tools of policy analysis. These tools will be applicable to a broad range of questions in the medical, financial, educational arenas, and beyond.

REFERENCES

Barsky, R., Kimball, M., Juster, T., and Shapiro, M. (1997). Preference parameters and behavioral heterogeneity. *Quarterly Journal of Economics, 112*, 537–79.

Baum, A., Brown, A., and Zakowski, S., 1997. Stress and genetic testing for disease risk. *Health Psychology, 16*, 8–19.

Bernheim, B. Douglas, and Garrett, D. (1996). The determinants and consequences of financial education in the workplace: Evidence from a survey of households. National Bureau of Economic Research, W P 5667, Cambridge, MA.

Caplin, A. and J. Leahy (1997). Psychological expected utility theory and anticipatory feelings, Research Report 97-37, C.V. Starr Center, New York University.

—— and —— 1999. The supply of information by a concerned expert, Research Report 99-08, C.V. Starr Center, New York University.

—— and —— 2000. The social discount rate. National Bureau of Economic Research, W P 7983, Cambridge, MA.

Croyle, R., Smith, K., Botkin, J., Baty, B., and Nash, J. (1997). Psychological responses to BRCA1 mutation testing: Preliminary findings. *Health Psychology, 16*, 63–72.

Geanakoplos, J., Pearce, D., and Stacchetti, E. (1989). Psychological games and sequential rationality. *Games and Economic Behavior, 1*, 60–79.

---

[10] The temporal construal theory (Trope and Liberman (Chapter 12, this volume)) makes a similar distinction. Distant benefits appear to be envisioned at a high level of abstraction, with stressful matters of process dominating the picture at a closer range.

Jacobsen, P., Valdimarsdottir, H., Brown, K., and Offits, K. (1997). Decision-making about genetic testing among women at familial risk for breast cancer. *Psychosomatic Medicine, 59*, 459–66.

Janis, I. (1958). *Psychological stress.* New York: Wiley.

Jevons, W. (1905). *Essays on economics.* London: Macmillan.

Kahneman, D. (2002). Experienced utility and objective happiness. In I. Brocas and J. D. Carrillo (Eds.), *The psychology of economic decisions.* Oxford: Oxford University Press.

Kash, K., Holland, J., Halper, M., and Miller, D. (1992). Psychological distress and surveillance behaviors of women with a family history of breast cancer. *Journal of the National Cancer Institute, 84*, 24–30.

Kessler, S., Field, T., Worth, L., and Mosbarger, H. (1987). Attitudes of persons at risk for Huntington's disease toward predictive testing. *American Journal of Medical Genetics, 26*, 259–70.

Kotlikoff, L., 1992. IRAs, savings, and the generational effects of fiscal policy. In M. Kosters (Ed.), *Personal saving, consumption, and tax policy.* Washington, DC: American Enterprise Institute.

Kreps, D. and E. Porteus (1978). Temporal Resolution of Uncertainty and Dynamic Choice Theory. *Econometrica, 46*, 185–200.

Laibson, D. (1997). Golden eggs and hyperbolic discounting. *Quarterly Journal of Economics, 112*, 443–79.

Lerman, C. and Croyle, R. (1995). Genetic testing for cancer predisposition: Behavioral science issues. *Journal of the National Cancer Institute*, monograph 17.

—— Narod, S., Schulman, K., Hughes, C., Gomez-Caminero, A., Bonney, G., Gold, K., Trock, B., Main, D., Lynch, J., Fulmore, C., Snyder, V., Lemon, S., Conway, T., Lenoir, G., and Lynch, H. (1996). BRCA1 testing in families with hereditary breast-ovarian cancer. *Journal of the American Medical Association, 275*, 1885–92.

—— Daly, M., Masny, M., and Balsheim, A. (1994). Attitudes about genetic testing for breast-ovarian cancer susceptibility. *Journal of Clinical Oncology, 12*, 843–50.

—— Bieseker, B., Benkendorf, J., Kerner, J., Gomez-Caminero, A., Hughes, C., and Reed, M. (1997). Controlled trial of pretest education approaches to enhance informed decision-making for BRCA1 gene testing. *Journal of the National Cancer Institute, 89*, 148–57.

—— Hughes, C., Lemon, S., Main, D., Snyder, C., Durham, C., Narod, S., Lynch, H. (1998). What you don't know can hurt you: Adverse psychological effects in members of BRCA1-linked and BRCA2-linked families who decline genetic testing. *Journal of Clinical Oncology, 16*, 1650–4.

Loewenstein, G. (1987). Anticipation and the valuation of delayed consumption. *Economic Journal, 97*, 666–84.

Lusardi, A. (2000). Explaining why so many households do not save. mimeo., Dartmouth College.

Miller, S. and Mangan, C. (1983). Interacting effects of information and coping style in adapting to gynecologic stress: Should the doctor tell all? *Journal of Personality and Social Psychology, 45*, 223–36.

Morgan, J., Roufeil, L., Kaushik, S., and Bassett, M. (1998). Influence of coping style and precolonoscopy information on pain and anxiety in colonoscopy. *Gastrointestinal Endoscopy, 48*, 119–27.

Quaid, K. and Morris, M. (1993). Reluctance to undergo predictive testing: The case of Huntington's disease. *American Journal of Medical Genetics, 45*, 41–5.

Strotz, R. (1955). Myopia and inconsistency in dynamic utility maximization. *Review of Economic Studies, 23*, 165–80.

Sulgarnik, E., and Zilcha, I. (1997). The value of information: The case of signal-dependent opportunity sets. *Journal of Economic Dynamics and Control, 21*, 1615–25.

Tibben, A., Duivenvoorden, H., Vegter-van der Vlis, M., et al. (1993). Presymptomatic DNA testing for Huntington disease: Identifying the need for psychological intervention. *American Journal of Medical Genetics, 48*, 137–44.

Trope, Y. and Lieberman, N. (2002). Temporal construal theory of time perspective effects on preference. In I. Brocas and J.D. Carrillo (Eds.), *The psychology of economic decisions.* Oxford: Oxford University Press.

Wilson, T., Gilbert, D., and Centerbar, D. (2002). Why happiness is like food, and why people don't know it. In I. Brocas and J.D. Carrillo (Eds.), *The psychology of economic decisions.* Oxford: Oxford University Press.

Yakoboski, P. and Dickemper, J., 1997. Increased saving but little planning: Results of the 1997 Retirement Confidence Survey. EBRI Issue Brief 191.

5

Information and Self-Control

ISABELLE BROCAS AND JUAN D. CARRILLO

1. INTRODUCTION

Nobody doubts that the behavior of agents often violates the most basic premises of rationality imposed in economics. Examples of such violations are provided in some of the essays in this volume. They suggest that looking for a purely rational explanation is sometimes either hopeless or absurd. On the other hand, labeling as irrational any conduct for which the explanation is not immediate, seems also a quite unsatisfactory strategy. In this essay, we show that if we keep the traditional ingredients of economic analysis and enrich these models in a few (and fairly natural) directions, then it is possible to rationalize some puzzling patterns of behavior.

There is considerable evidence that most smokers overestimate the risk of lung cancer, most entrepreneurs underestimate the risk of failure of their business activities, and most people overestimate the risk of transmission of the HIV virus during unprotected sexual intercourse. Should we deduce from these systematic biases that individuals are intrinsically optimistic in some situations (entrepreneurship) and intrinsically pessimistic in others (risks associated with pleasurable activities)? Can we conclude that there is a lack of rationality in the agents' capacity to process information? The answer is 'not necessarily'.

Impulse buying has also received a great deal of attention, especially in the management literature (see e.g., Bell, 1976). With the development of credit opportunities for the purchase of consumption goods, habits have been radically modified. Impulse buying has become so recurrent that some individuals are forced to freeze (in the literal sense) their own credit cards, in order to limit their spending. Is this behavior driven entirely by emotions and urges? Does it mean that agents are irrational and unable to anticipate the long run damaging consequences of this behavior? Again, the answer is 'not necessarily'.

The object of the exercise we propose is not to demonstrate the power of formal model-building or to reaffirm our confidence in the orthodox economic methodology. On the contrary, if our hypotheses are correct, then analyzing problems

We thank Andrew Caplin, Mathias Dewatripont, and Itzhak Gilboa for their helpful comments. Isabelle Brocas gratefully acknowledges financial support from the European Commission (TMR network FMRX-CT98-0203).

under this light has three main advantages. First, it offers unambiguous predictions concerning the class of situations in which a population of rational agents may look like intrinsic optimists, intrinsic pessimists, and impulsive. These behaviors, widely documented in psychology, have for a long time resisted economic analyses. In addition, one can use comparative static analysis to explore the impact of external factors on the magnitude of these apparent biases in judgments and behaviors. Second, the new ingredients of these enriched models may prove useful in explaining other apparently unrelated phenomena. Some of them are briefly discussed below, but clearly there is room for further research along these lines. Third, and maybe most important, once the underlying motivations for these original behaviors are understood, it is possible to conduct welfare analyses that will result in policy recommendations. In fact, identifying general patterns of behavior in order to isolate inefficiencies is probably the most standard methodology employed by economists. This, together with the conviction that the ultimate goal is to offer solutions in order to avoid suboptimal behaviors, are the two main differences with their fellow psychologists.

The plan of the paper is as follows. In Section 2, we discuss general issues about incentives to acquire information and their aggregate effects on the behavior of agents. In Section 3, we rationalize the willingness of agents to keep optimistic or pessimistic beliefs and we study its welfare implications. In Section 4, we analyze why agents may act impulsively. Some final remarks are presented in Section 5.

2. THE ROLE OF INFORMATION IN DECISION-MAKING

2.1. Unbiased Individual Beliefs and Biased Aggregate Behavior

The literature on self-perception suggests that most individuals hold excessively optimistic beliefs about their own qualities. One of the most popular among these studies claims that 90 percent of individuals consider themselves to be better than the average driver (see e.g., Köszegi, 2000, for a brief overview of this literature). Can we conclude on the basis of this observation that individuals are not rational processors of information? Of course we cannot. In fact, assuming that individuals with imperfect knowledge incorporate information in a rational way (or, formally stated, that they update information according to the Bayes rule), only implies that the beliefs in the population cannot be biased *on average*. Therefore, it does not preclude, for example, a situation in which the vast majority of individuals (say, 90 percent) has a slightly positive bias in their perceived ability, and the small minority (say, 10 percent) has a significant negative bias. The point of this observation is not to claim that Bayesian updating is a perfect predictor for the information processing behavior of agents. It only suggests that the Bayesian rationality imposes fewer constraints than one might think at first sight. Technically, under the Bayesian theory only the first order moment of the belief cannot be manipulated through the acquisition or avoidance of information. By contrast, higher order moments (and in particular the skewness of the distribution of beliefs) can be manipulated by rational agents.

This simple observation may have very powerful economic implications. Suppose that individuals drive more carefully the lower their belief about their own ability. As long as this negative relation between perceived ability and careful driving is linear, then the average attention paid by drivers is given by the *fixed* average belief about ability in the population. It will therefore be non-manipulable, that is, independent of the information acquired by individuals. On the contrary, suppose that there is a threshold in the perceived ability below which high attention is paid and above which low attention is paid. As already noted, the information possessed by each individual affects the skewness of the distribution of beliefs in the population. Therefore, in this second situation, the average attention paid by individuals will crucially depend on the beliefs held by each person. In particular, by strategically manipulating the information conveyed to a population of *rational* individuals, it may be possible to choose between inducing an average attention that is arbitrarily close to the high level and one that is arbitrarily close to the low level.

2.2. Self-Manipulation of Beliefs

It is clear, from the previous example, what the gains are for an individual (self-interested or social planner) by restricting the access to information to other agents and therefore manipulating their beliefs. A more intriguing issue is why any person would refrain from obtaining some information relevant for his own decision-making. From now on, we will call the situation in which a rational agent deliberately avoids free information that would reduce his uncertainty before acting as the 'self-manipulation of beliefs'.[1] There are at least three reasons for such behavior in the literature.

First, the simplest way to make self-manipulation desirable is to explicitly assume that individuals derive utility (directly or indirectly) from their beliefs. This issue has been explored in a number of papers. Caplin and Leahy (2001, 2002, Chapter 4, this volume) introduce anticipatory feelings in a standard expected utility framework, by allowing utility to depend on beliefs about the future states of the world. Information, then, becomes more desirable in some situations than in others, as it affects not only optimal decision-making but also the evolution of beliefs and therefore the anticipatory utility itself.[2] Köszegi (2000) also incorporates beliefs in the utility function by assuming that agents derive utility from having positive views about themselves. In his setting, individuals are likely to avoid information when they are satisfied with their current beliefs (self-image protection motive) and to seek evidence when they are dissatisfied (self-image enhancement motive). Last, Rabin (1995) considers the case of an individual without moral concerns, but with a self-restraining mechanism

---

[1] Obviously, one reason for avoiding information is that it may be costly. However, the question here is why would an individual be willing to pay not to get information.

[2] See also Gilboa and Schmeidler (1988) and Geanakoplos, Pearce, and Stacchetti (1989).

that forbids him to undertake actions whenever he believes that they exert a negative externality on others. In his model, the beliefs indirectly affect utility and therefore refusing information can be optimal. If negative beliefs are avoided, the self-restraining mechanism does not become operational, and the agent can engage in immoral (but optimal from his perspective) actions.

Second, from the economics of information literature, it is by now well known that obtaining (public or private) information can be hurtful in multi-person situations. For example, Hirshleifer (1971) points out that the revelation of public information may destroy the possibility of a mutually beneficial insurance agreement. Crémer (1995) shows that it can be optimal for an employer to commit not to acquire private information about the circumstances that affect the performance of his subordinate: the ex-post costs of coarser information can be outweighed by the ex-ante benefits due to the subordinate's higher incentives to put more effort into his job. Note that, in these models, the uncertainty is about a characteristic of the environment. However, if we postulate that individuals have an imperfect knowledge about some of their own personal traits, then it follows that the interacting agents may also benefit from avoiding private and public information about their own attributes.

Third, avoiding free information has also proved to be optimal in situations in which an individual has conflicting preferences. Intuitively, analyzing an individual with an intrapersonal conflict of preferences is not very different from analyzing a multi-person situation in which the preference of each person conflicts with those of his peers. It is, therefore, quite natural that individuals with internally conflicting goals may decide to manipulate their own beliefs, whenever this option is available. Intrapersonal disputes can be of a different nature. According to Thaler and Shefrin (1981), the agent is, at every period, composed of a planner who is interested in the agent's long-run utility and a doer who is only concerned with short-run payoffs. Since actions are taken by the doer, the planner restricts the set of alternatives in order to mitigate the doer's willingness to satiate immediate gratification at the expense of long-run welfare. Loewenstein (1996) argues that agents are often out of control due to visceral factors such as emotions, moods, and other somatic influences. These unanticipated states also result in discrepancies between the optimal and the realized behavior. In Bodner and Prelec (2002, Chapter 6, this volume), an agent infers his preferences from his own decisions. In other words, by means of his actions, the decision-making body signals to the mind what his true concerns are. Last, there is a growing literature starting with Strotz (1956), which argues that individuals discount short-term events relatively more heavily than long-term events. Formally, according to this theory, the discounting of future payoffs would be best approximated by hyperboles and not by the traditional exponential functions.[3] This type of discounting generates an intrapersonal conflict of preferences, because the optimal

---

[3] See Ainslie (1992) or Loewenstein and Prelec (1992) for a comprehensive theoretical and empirical discussion of hyperbolic discounting.

dynamic plan of actions of an individual at some date may no longer be optimal when reconsidered some time later. This intrapersonal conflict, in turn, creates severe welfare losses for the individual. As first pointed out by Carrillo and Mariotti (2000), a strategic self-manipulation of beliefs can alleviate this utility loss. In Section 3 we will review the main findings of this paper and the subsequent literature, relate them to the motivating examples presented in Section 1, and explain the implications for economics and psychology. The attention will be centered on the collection/avoidance of information of an individual with hyperbolic discounting. There are two main reasons for restricting the analysis to this case. First, the types of situations we have in mind are closely related to the individual's tendency to excessively satiate immediate gratification at the expense of future welfare, and excessively delay unpleasurable activities that are profitable in the long-run. Second, hyperbolic discounting has received wide support from the empirical and experimental literature (both in economics and in psychology) and, at the same time, it is a well-defined departure from the standard postulates of rationality.[4] However, there are definitely other interesting insights to be developed about the reasons and consequences of self-manipulation of beliefs in the various other settings described above.

3. STRATEGIC IGNORANCE AND SELF-CONTROL

3.1. The Value of Ignorance

We first start by considering a population of time-consistent utility maximizing individuals, who are choosing whether to invest in a risky project (the decision is binary). The investment requires some immediate cost and yields a delayed benefit that is proportional to the agent's talent. If agents know their own capacity perfectly, only those whose talent is above a certain threshold will choose to invest. If agents do not know their capacity but can learn it at no cost, then they will acquire this information and, just like before, act according to their revealed talent.

The problem is less trivial for an agent with time-inconsistent preferences. Given that, under hyperbolic discounting, immediate payoffs are overweighed relative to more distant ones, the agents' willingness to invest now depends on the date of reference. More precisely, the talent threshold above which an agent finds it profitable to invest in the next period (and get the benefits in two periods) is below the threshold above which he finds it profitable to invest in the current period (and get the benefits next period). In other words, for an intermediate level of talent, the agent would like to invest in a future date, but when the time of exerting effort arrives, the cost is overweighed and the agent reconsiders his decision. This is the standard procrastination problem first analyzed by

---

[4] It is partly for this reason that hyperbolic discounting has become, among economists, one of the least controversial departures. Naturally, this is not to say that all researchers accept its validity. See for instance Mulligan (1996) and Rubinstein (2000).

Akerlof (1991) and further developed by O'Donoghue and Rabin (1999) and others. Naturally, rational agents perfectly anticipate this change in their preferences. However, in the absence of exogenous commitment devices, nothing can be done to impose the previously optimal choice.

The situation becomes most interesting when we consider time-inconsistent preferences, imperfect self-knowledge, and the possibility of learning. As shown by Carrillo and Mariotti (2000), the combination of these three ingredients together with the binary nature of the investment decision can help in explaining some of the apparently irrational behaviors mentioned in Section 1. Consider an individual with an imperfect knowledge about his talent, who can acquire, at no cost, all the information about his ability on the date before making his investment decision. Recall that this agent faces a very specific conflict of preferences: some investments considered profitable the date before exerting effort are not undertaken when this date arrives. Because of this conflict, the agent may be interested in refusing information about his own talent. For instance, suppose that the expected talent is sufficiently high so that, in case of not getting information in the current period, the agent (who then maximizes expected utility) strictly prefers to invest in the next date. By learning his true talent, the agent may realize that his true ability takes an intermediate value, in which case he would like to invest in the next period, but when this date arrives he prefers not to do it anymore. To avoid such inefficient procrastination, the agent can rationally decide not to acquire the information. In other words, time-inconsistent preferences generate an endogenous cost of learning equal to the cost of inefficient procrastination. Naturally, ignorance has also some costs: if the agent's true talent is indeed sufficiently low, then by ignoring it and investing the agent is adopting a suboptimal behavior. Overall, under time-inconsistent preferences ignorance can act as a commitment device against the unavoidable change of preferences. The optimal learning decision will trade-off the benefits of avoiding inefficient procrastination and the usual costs of ignorance for decision-making.

Note that a necessary condition for the agent to remain ignorant is that, in case of not acquiring information, he must unambiguously prefer to invest in the next period. This is the key result of our analysis. Again, the reason is that the goal of ignorance is to avoid inefficient procrastination and induce future investment. Obviously, ignorance can then be only an effective mechanism if the agent is willing to invest given his current beliefs.

Now, consider an entire population of individuals, each of them with an imperfect knowledge about their ability. According to our previous analysis, two different behaviors can be observed depending on the shape of each individual's distribution of beliefs. Some agents will learn their ability, and invest only if they are sufficiently talented. Others will decide to remain ignorant and invest for sure. Overall, after making their learning decision, the skewness in the posterior distribution of beliefs in the population will be such that the vast majority of agents will consider themselves talented enough to invest. Interestingly, this biased aggregate behavior of the population, driven by a desire to avoid procrastination, occurs even though each agent is rational and has an unbiased belief about his own talent.[5]

3.2. Predicting Aggregate Behavior

We have seen that time-inconsistent preferences together with imperfect self-knowledge and the possibility of learning, predicts an aggregate tendency in the population to keep an optimistic attitude towards investment. Interestingly, the same mechanism predicts that the population will exhibit an aggregate tendency to keep excessively negative attitudes towards pleasurable but long-run damaging activities.

The crucial difference between a decision to invest in a risky business and a decision to consume something desirable but with negative side-effects is that, in the latter, the benefits of the activity come earlier than the costs while in the former it is the opposite. This may sound unimportant, however it has a crucial impact on the incentives of agents to gather information. In order to appreciate the difference, consider the decision of a time-inconsistent individual to smoke. Due to his intrapersonal conflict, the optimal consumption pattern may be to smoke in the current period and then stop forever. Naturally, and again without commitment devices, the agent will, in this case, end up smoking at every date; that is, the conflict of preferences induces a future excessive consumption from the current perspective. Now, suppose the agent has only an imperfect knowledge about the effects of tobacco on his own health. The only reason not to acquire information is to avoid an inefficient future consumption. Hence, a necessary condition for the agent's willingness not to acquire information is that the current beliefs must be sufficiently negative. In particular, given his current knowledge, the agent must prefer not to smoke not only in the future, but even in the present. As usual, these benefits of ignorance have to be compared to the costs of making choices with restricted information. Overall, in the smoking case, the population will consist of a fraction of agents who are perfectly informed about the side effects of smoking and consume accordingly, and a fraction of agents who retain their pessimistic beliefs and abstain.[6]

As a general conclusion, the vast majority of the population will believe that their health is too fragile to resist the effects of tobacco, and their talent high

---

[5] As discussed in Section 2.1, if the optimal level of investment were positive for all agents but proportional to their talent, then there would be no aggregate biased behavior. Yet, imposing a binary choice is not necessary either: an aggregate bias would occur for any non-linear relation between the talent parameter and the level of investment.

[6] The analysis predicts that only non-smokers may refrain from learning the true dangers of tobacco. This is because, in our example, individuals do not decide the amount of cigarettes they consume. If we relax the binary decision assumption, then some smokers may also decide to remain uninformed.

enough to succeed in risky businesses. Hence, time-inconsistency together with the endogenous decision to acquire information can explain both a feeling of optimism (in entrepreneurship) and a feeling of pessimism (for pleasurable but damaging activities), without any assumption of irrationality. The key to understand which situation applies, is to determine whether the costs come, on average, earlier or later than the benefits in the activity considered. These testable predictions can be pushed further: as the gap between the costs and the benefits of the activity increases, the strategic ignorance becomes a more useful self-disciplining device, and therefore it is more likely to observe an aggregate bias in the behavior of the population. Obviously, we do not believe that this approach can explain all the biases in judgment. For example, agents have a tendency to keep positive views about issues related to their own intelligence or leadership capacity. These are cases in which there is no clear delay between the costs and benefits of the activities involved, and therefore our analysis cannot be applied. What this theory offers, instead, is one possible explanation to a specific class of problems.

3.3. Welfare Implications and Social Interactions

In the previous analysis, each individual was studied in isolation. However, in many situations, the learning choices and the actions undertaken by each person affect the rest of the population. Therefore, if we want to understand the aggregate economic effects of strategic ignorance and its welfare implications, it is essential to take into account these endogenous interactions.

Brocas and Carrillo (1999) provide a first step towards this generalization. They consider the same investment decision as in the example above, except that the investment now requires some capital and individuals are cash constrained. This slight enrichment of the economic setting is sufficient to ensure that, the behavior resulting from the agents' intrapersonal conflict affects the welfare of all the individuals in the population. In other words, the agents are linked to each other by the inconsistency of their preferences.

The argument of the paper is as follows. If individuals are cash constrained, they need to resort to banks in order to finance their investment. In the standard (time-consistent) situation, agents learn their own ability to succeed, and those who are sufficiently talented apply for a loan. The banks are competitive and do not know the ability of the applicants, but they infer from their willingness to invest that it must be above a certain threshold. The interest rate of the money is then endogenously determined and inversely proportional to the expected talent of applicants (high talent implies a low risk of failure, therefore a low risk for banks of not being repaid, which in turn makes a low interest rate possible). By contrast, as already noted, the time-inconsistent agents have a tendency to procrastinate. To avoid this inefficient behavior they remain ignorant and retain their initial beliefs, as long as these are sufficiently positive. Naturally, the banks correctly anticipate that the agents are now excessively confident about their chances of success, so they increase the interest rate in order to counter this optimism. Overall, the endogenous decision of each agent to refuse information and apply for a loan is individually optimal, but it exerts a negative externality on the rest of the population by affecting the interest rates. The paper shows that, in some situations, the ex-ante welfare of all the individuals in the population is increased if the government forces them to learn their talent before deciding whether to invest. This measure eliminates the prevailing over-confidence of potential investors, and therefore induces banks to lower the interest rates.

In our view, this investment story is a good example of an analysis that can be of interest for both psychologists and economists. First, it suggests that it is possible to expand our understanding of human behavior and, in particular, of some apparently irrational conducts such as the willingness to keep optimistic prospects. Second, it indicates that understanding the reasons for such human behavior opens the door to the design of welfare-improving policy measures.

3.4. Available Information and Unavoidable Information

The literature on self-manipulation of beliefs provides an interesting implication about the value of information. There exist two different practical measures to encourage individuals to acquire information. The first one is to increase the sources of information at their disposal, that is to make more information available. The second one is to give incentives to incorporate the existing information, that is to make the available information unavoidable. When the public interest is congruent with the private interest of the agents, then both options are socially desirable and it is unclear which one has the greatest merits. However, in the case of a conflict between private and public interests, the outcomes can be radically different: the first alternative may be negative for social welfare and the second one positive.

Rabin's (1995) paper was the first to discuss these opposing effects. An agent who acts subject to a moral rule will try to avoid the beliefs where this moral constraint becomes binding. Having a better access to information then, increases his capacity to manipulate his own knowledge and, in particular, to avoid negative beliefs about the morality of his preferred action. Therefore, an agent with an unlimited access to information is more likely to exhibit immoral conduct than an agent with restricted access. On the contrary, forcing an agent to acquire information reduces his self-manipulation capacity, which is likely to improve his moral conduct.

These same differences between available and unavoidable information operate in the case of time-inconsistent individuals. Allowing better access to information, increases the capacity of potential investors to manipulate their beliefs and retain their optimistic prospects. On the contrary, forcing them to acquire some news destroys the possibility of using strategic ignorance in their own private interest. The main difference with Rabin's model is that this second alternative may not only be socially better, but even privately better as long as it is simultaneously imposed on all individuals in the society. As a policy implication, it means that governments should not facilitate the access to information to potential investors, but, rather, encourage the use of existing information (e.g., by requiring an accurate market study with every loan application).

3.5. Other Applications

The basic self-control and information gathering model developed above has been extended in a number of directions. Carrillo (1998) analyzes the decision of an individual to undertake activities that are pleasant in the short-run, but with a long-run negative effect on welfare. Examples include not only the ingestion of addictive substances, such as tobacco (as in the example discussed in Section 3.2), alcohol, or marijuana, but also the engagement in non-addictive activities like gambling, eating fat-food, or having extramarital relations. The basic postulate is that the pleasure derived from these activities is individual-specific and therefore it can only be evaluated after repeated exposure. In other words, there is learning through consumption. With these premises, the paper studies why abstinence and excessive exposure are both more frequently observed than moderate behavior, and reaches the following conclusions. As long as the agent is engaged in the activity, he learns about its net payoff. For example, by repeatedly smoking the agent updates the instantaneous pleasure and the negative effects on health. A time-inconsistent individual may then fall into a state of beliefs in which he wishes to have a high current consumption and a moderate future consumption (one pack of cigarettes today and a couple of cigarettes from tomorrow onwards). However, given the impossibility of commiting to a future behavior, he ends up consistently overconsuming. When beliefs are such that the expected intertemporal payoff under continual excesses (one pack a day) is smaller than the intertemporal payoff under abstention, the agent prefers not to consume at all. Abstention is only a second-best solution. By construction, moderate consumption at every period would be preferable, but this is not feasible due to hyperbolic discounting. Moreover, the strategy of abstaining is the agent's way of not learning. Therefore, it is his only possible commitment strategy to avoid sinful temptations in the future. To sum up, this theory explains not only convergence to but also persistence of abstention as the agent's optimal self-commitment device. It is important to realize that the 'complete abstention' strategy is not imposed, on the grounds that it acts better than any other personal rule as a focal point (as sometimes suggested in the literature). Rather, it endogenously becomes a basin of attraction due to its learning properties.

Benabou and Tirole (2000*a*) introduce imperfect memory and the possibility of increasing or decreasing the probability of remembering past events in the framework of Carrillo and Mariotti (2000). The paper shows that multiple equilibria might concur in the intrapersonal game, when memory management is costless. The idea is as follows. An individual does not want to remember information only if the news is likely to induce a future behavior suboptimal from the current perspective (i.e., if there is a high probability that the news will be 'bad'). However, the individual cannot fool himself, so this mechanism of strategically not remembering past signals is perfectly anticipated. Therefore, as the degree of censoring is increased, a lack of information is more likely to be interpreted in the future as 'bad news', which itself increases the incentives to censor information in the first place. This self-fulfilling mechanism immediately results in the coexistence of equilibria, with no repression, full repression, and partial repression of information.

The issue of willpower has also been studied in a similar context by Benabou and Tirole (2000*b*). The paper assumes that agents have an imperfect knowledge about their own capacity to resist impulses and short-run temptations. According to their current information, individuals have to decide whether to engage in a 'willpower-dependent' activity or not and, if they do, whether to resist or succumb to temptation. One of the main results is that in order to preserve their self-reputation, agents may end up adopting a compulsive, self-defeating behavior.[7]

4. IMPULSIVE BEHAVIOR AND SELF-CONTROL

We now analyze another puzzling pattern of behavior, namely the agent's willingness to engage in impulsive consumption. In Section 2.2, we argued that some authors (e.g., Loewenstein, 1996) have identified emotions and drives as the causes for some irrational, impulsive conducts. Here, by contrast, we provide a rational view for this behavior in a specific class of situations. We determine the type of circumstances in which impulsive actions are likely to occur and the possible remedies.

4.1. Exotic Holidays: An Example of Impulsive Behavior

Vacation time has arrived and I, a cash constrained and hyperbolic agent, have to decide where to go. This year and the next one are my two last opportunities to spend an entire month of holidays. I am, therefore, quite tempted to become indebted and travel to a distant exotic island, even though I do not know exactly how nice this trip will be. After considering the delayed costs and the current (thus overweighed) expected benefits, it turns out that the net present value (NPV) of this alternative is slightly negative. What should I do? There are three different variants of this situation, depending on the amount of information that I will receive about how enjoyable these vacations can be, if this year I refrain from making the trip. First, suppose that I will not get any extra news. Then, given its negative NPV, I go neither this year nor the next one. Second, suppose that a friend with very similar tastes to mine is traveling to that same place in half a year. My optimal decision is to wait for his news, learn with accuracy how pleasurable

---

[7] We refer to Bénabou and Tirole (2002, Chapter 8, this volume) for an exhaustive analysis of memory management and willpower.

the trip is, and then decide whether to go next year. Last and most interesting, consider the case in which I will get some meager and noisy information. If the news is slightly negative, it is optimal not to go at all. By contrast, if the news is slightly positive and I do not go this year, then I will choose to go the next year. This decision has expected benefits from next year's perspective (this is why I follow that option). However, from the current perspective, the benefits of a future holiday are not overweighed, and therefore the overall NPV of this future decision may be strongly negative. Anticipating such an inefficient behavior and in the absence of other commitment devices, my optimal decision may be to go this year, even if I know that the costs offset the expected benefits. Overall, the argument in favor of enjoying the current holidays is something like 'since I will go next year if I am given the smallest reason to go, I might as well go now'.

4.2. The General Case

The previous example suggests that impulsive behavior may not be the result of an irrational and unanticipated reaction to an urge or any other external cue. Instead, a fully rational individual with a self-control problem may engage in apparently suboptimal consumption decisions, only as a commitment against future actions that are even more inefficient.

This idea was first suggested by O'Donoghue and Rabin (1999) for consumption decisions in deterministic environments. Then, Brocas and Carrillo (1998) studied the role played by information in explaining this impulsive behavior. Their theory rests on three basic ingredients. First, as usual, a self-control problem. Second, the possibility of undertaking an irreversible (or partially irreversible) consumption decision that yields a short-run net benefit and a long-run net cost. Third, imperfect information about the net payoff of consuming and a per-period exogenous revelation of information, as long as the agent has not made his irreversible choice. Credit purchase is probably the clearest example of the situations we have in mind. However, the setting is sufficiently general to be adapted to other problems, such as the protection of the environment and the financing of public projects by official bodies.

In the absence of an intrapersonal conflict, the situation is characterized by a fundamental tradeoff: delaying consumption is costly because future payoffs are discounted, but it allows the acquisition of valuable information for future decision-making.[8] However, as we know, information is not always valuable if

---

[8] There is an extensive literature on this subject. The basic result is the existence of a cutoff value at each period, above which the agent consumes and below which he waits until the next date. The difference between the payoff at this cutoff and the expected payoff of never consuming is called the option value of waiting (OVW), and it is always non-negative. Moreover, when the consumption horizon is finite, then the OVW strictly decreases as the number of periods in which it can be exerted decreases and it becomes equal to zero in the last period. We refer to Dixit and Pindyck (1994) and the references therein for a review.

agents face a self-control problem. Therefore, the nature of the tradeoff is modified under time-inconsistency. The paper shows that the amount of information transmitted between periods is the key feature that will determine whether the agent will behave in an impulsive manner or not. The main idea is as follows. Under hyperbolic discounting, current benefits are overweighed relative to future costs. Due to the irreversibility of consumption, the optimal current decision of an individual depends on his future behavior in the case of postponing consumption (which determines his outside option). However, when the agent evaluates this outside option, he does not have to determine the effect on the current welfare of future choices optimal from the current perspective, but rather the effect on the current welfare of future choices optimal from the future perspective. Naturally, this future behavior will be a function of the signals received by the agent, which suggests that the amount of information transmitted between two periods must be a crucial variable. The most interesting situation arises when the flow of information is 'small', that is, when there are little variations from period to period in the expected profitability of consumption. Suppose that the agent's current beliefs are such that consuming has a current, slightly negative NPV. If he refrains from consuming and the information revealed is 'moderately positive', he will plunge into a state of beliefs where future consumption is desirable from the future perspective but highly undesirable from the current one. In order to avoid this situation, the individual prefers to rush and consume in the present period also with a negative (but at least close to zero) NPV. Summing up, consumption takes place not because of its intrinsic value but only as a commitment device against future choices.

The inefficiency of this two-period analysis is magnified in a multi-period situation. Indeed, a future consumption with a negative NPV from a future perspective is even more damaging from the current viewpoint. Hence, the agent is all the more willing to consume with the negative payoffs that he anticipates a future inefficient choice. Last, it is important to realize that the value of information is not monotonic in the amount of information transmitted. If the inter-period flow of news is sufficiently important, then the intrapersonal conflict is not a major problem: an agent who waits for information will learn, with a high probability, either that consumption is worthless or desirable both from a past and a current viewpoint. In other words, information, is on average, valuable because it is very unlikely that it directs the agent to the state of beliefs where present and future preferences are in conflict. On the other extreme, if no information ever flows in, the agent consumes either in the first period or never at all, but again there is no inefficiency.

4.3. Welfare Implications and Social Interactions

The main lesson of the previous analysis is that self-control problems may induce agents to adopt inefficient consumption decisions. The reason is the existence of a range of payoffs, such that consumption is profitable from the current perspective but highly detrimental from a past perspective. Naturally, this undesirable behavior is more likely to occur the greater the range of payoffs in which the intrapersonal conflict occurs and also, for a given range, the greater the chances of believing that payoffs are in this region. It is then possible to perform some comparative statics about the kind of situations in which agents will act impulsively. First and trivially, impulsive conduct will occur more often the stronger the agent's intrapersonal conflict and the bigger the delay between the costs and the benefits of the consumption goods. Second, the chances of eventually believing that payoffs are in the inefficient region are highest when the information transmitted between periods is small, and when the consumption decision can be delayed for a long period of time. Last, in decisions involving high stakes (i.e., both high current benefits and high delayed costs) the salience of current payoffs are more likely to trigger the self-defeating behavior.

Once the reasons for the impulsive behavior have been identified, it is possible to offer solutions in order to avoid or at least mitigate the inefficiencies. The most radical measure is to stay away from information. This is quite difficult to achieve: some news is often unavoidable and, once noticed, the information processing cannot be stopped. Moreover, information is sometimes extremely useful. Otherwise, a typical solution to self-control problems is to commit with third parties on future decisions (e.g., to freeze the credit card). One possible type of commitment is to make promises that are costly to break (e.g., due to reputation concerns as in Carrillo and Dewatripont (2000)). However, such commitments need to be renegotiation-proof and they also entail some implicit costs.

5. CONCLUDING REMARKS

The purpose of this essay has been to show that by enlarging the standard economic setting, it is possible to account for a number of puzzling patterns of behavior. The main new ingredients incorporated in the analysis are quite natural: hyperbolic discounting of future payoffs, imperfect knowledge about some of the agent's own attributes, and various possibilities of improving this self-knowledge. The combination of these factors is sufficient to explain some apparent biases in judgments and behaviors, like the tendency to keep optimistic or pessimistic prospects in some activities, to stick to restrictive personal rules of behavior, and to act impulsively. Naturally, some other behaviors could also be analyzed under this light.

Before concluding, we would like to insist on two points. First, as discussed all along in the paper, the explanations offered to these pervasive human behaviors are valid only for a specific class of situations. That is, our arguments make sense only if some precise conditions are met (activities with a natural delay between costs and benefits, imperfect information, etc). If individuals exhibit a similar behavior in settings where these conditions are not satisfied, then we need another (maybe complementary) explanation. Second, rationalizing human behavior is not a goal in itself. Our objective is to improve the understanding of human conduct in order to offer solutions for inefficient actions. Building a model as standard as possible with a minimum set of assumptions and which captures the main motivations of the individual is, in our view, an important step to reach this goal. Naturally, this is not always feasible, so one should not be opposed to incorporating some departures from rationality whenever it is appropriate.

REFERENCES

Ainslie, G. (1992). *Picoeconomics*. Cambridge: Cambridge University Press.

Akerlof, G.A. (1991). Procrastination and obedience. *American Economic Review, 81*, 1–19.

Bell, D. (1976). *The coming of post-industrial society: A venture in social forecasting*. New York: Basic Books.

Bénabou, R. and Tirole, J. (2000*a*). *Self-confidence: Intrapersonal strategies*, mimeo, Princeton.

——— and——— (2000*b*). *Personal rules*, mimeo, Princeton.

——— and ——— (2002). Self-knowledge and self-regulation and economic approach. In I. Brocas and J.D. Carrillo (Eds.), *The psychology of economic decisions*. Oxford: Oxford University Press.

Bodner R. and Prelec, D. (2002). Self-signaling and diagnostic utility in everyday decision-making. In I. Brocas and J.D. Carrillo (Eds.), *The psychology of economic decisions*. Oxford: Oxford University Press.

Brocas, I. and Carrillo, J.D. (1998). *A theory of haste with applications to impulse buying and destruction of the environment*, CEPR D.P. 2027, London.

——— and ——— (1999). *Entrepreneurial optimism and excessive investment*, mimeo, ECARES, Brussels.

Caplin, A. and Leahy, J. (2001). Psychological expected utility theory and anticipatory feelings. *Quarterly Journal of Economics*, 55–80.

——— and ——— (2002). *Behavioral policy*. In I. Brocas and J.D. Carrillo (Eds.), *The psychology of economic decisions*. Oxford: Oxford University Press.

Carrillo, J.D. (1998). *Self-control, moderate consumption, and craving*, CEPR D.P. 2017, London.

——— and Dewatripont, M. (2000). *Promises, promises . . .*, mimeo, ECARES, Brussels.

——— and Mariotti, T. (2000). Strategic ignorance as a self-disciplining device. *Review of Economic Studies, 67*, 529–44.

Crémer, J. (1995). Arm's length relationships. *Quarterly Journal of Economics, 110*, 275–95.

Dixit, A.K. and Pindyck, R.S. (1994). *Investment Under Uncertainty*. New Jersey: Princeton University Press.

Geanakoplos, J., Pearce, D., and Stacchetti, E. (1989). Psychological games and sequential rationality. *Games and Economic Behavior, 1*, 60–79.

Gilboa, I. and Schmeidler, D. (1988). Information dependent games: Can common sense be common knowledge? *Economics Letters, 27*(3), 215–21.

Hirshleifer, J. (1971). The private and social value of information and the reward from incentive activity. *American Economic Review, 61*, 561–74.

Köszegi, B. (2000). *Self-image and information acquisition*, mimeo, MIT.

Loewenstein, G. (1996). Out of control: Visceral influences on behavior. *Organizational Behavior and Human Decision Processes, 65*, 272–92.

Loewenstein, G. and Prelec, D. (1992). Anomalies in intertemporal choice: Evidence and an interpretation. *Quarterly Journal of Economics, 107,* 573–98.

Mulligan, C. (1996). *A logical economist's argument against hyperbolic discounting,* mimeo, University of Chicago.

O'Donoghue, T. and Rabin, M. (1999). Doing it now or later. *American Economic Review 89,* 103–24.

Rabin, M. (1995). *Moral preferences, moral constraints, and self-serving biases,* mimeo, UC Berkeley.

Rubinstein, A. (2000). *Is it Economics and Psychology?: The case of hyperbolic discounting,* mimeo, Tel Aviv and Princeton.

Strotz, R.H. (1956). Myopia and inconsistency in dynamic utility maximisation. *Review of Economic Studies, 23,* 166–80.

Thaler, R.H. and Shefrin, H.M. (1981). An economic theory of self-control. *Journal of Political Economy, 89,* 392–406.

6

Self-Signaling and Diagnostic Utility in Everyday Decision Making

RONIT BODNER AND DRAZEN PRELEC

1. PSYCHOLOGICAL EVIDENCE

By choosing one alternative over another, we reveal something about our preferences, not just to others but also to ourselves. In a previous paper (Bodner and Prelec, 1997), we described how the model of a utility maximizing individual could be expanded to include *diagnostic utility* as a distinct source of satisfaction. We review the basic elements of that proposal here. The inspiration comes directly from signaling games in which actions of one person provide an informative signal to others, which in turn affects esteem (Bernheim, 1994). Here, however, actions provide a signal to ourselves, that is, actions are *self-signaling*. For example, a person who takes a daily jog in spite of the rain may see that as a gratifying signal of willpower, dedication, or future well-being. For someone uncertain about where he or she stands with respect to these dispositions, each new choice can provide a bit of good or bad 'news'. We incorporate the value of such 'news' into the person's utility function.

The notion that a person may draw inferences from an action he enacted partially in order to gain that inference has been posed as a philosophical paradox (e.g., Campbell and Sawden, 1985; Elster, 1985, 1989). A key problem is the following: Suppose that the disposition in question is altruism, and a person interprets a 25-cent donation to a panhandler as evidence of altruism. If the boost in self-esteem makes it worth giving the quarter even when there is no concern for the poor, than clearly, such a donation is not valid evidence of altruism. Logically, giving is a valid evidence of high altruism only if a person with low altruism would not have given the quarter. This reasoning motivates our

The chapter draws on (co-authored) chapter 2 of Bodner's doctoral dissertation (Bodner, 1995) and an unpublished MIT working paper (Bodner and Prelec, 1997). The authors thank Bodner's dissertation advisors France Leclerc and Richard Thaler, workshop discussants Thomas Schelling, Russell Winer, and Mathias Dewatripont, and George Ainslie, Michael Bratman, Juan Carrillo, Itzakh Gilboa, George Loewenstein, Al Mela, Matthew Rabin, Duncan Simester, and Florian Zettelmeyer, for comments on these ideas (with the usual disclaimer). We are grateful to Birger Wernerfelt for drawing attention to Bernheim's work on social conformity.

equilibrium approach, in which inferences from actions are an *endogenous* part of the equilibrium choice.

As an empirical matter several studies have demonstrated that diagnostic considerations do indeed affect behavior (Quattrone and Tversky, 1984; Shafir and Tversky, 1992; Bodner, 1995). An elegant experiment by Quattrone and Tversky (1984) both defines the self-signaling phenomenon and demonstrates its existence. Quattrone and Tversky first asked each subject to take a cold pressor pain test, in which the subject's arm is submerged in a container of cold water until the subject can no longer tolerate the pain. Subsequently, the subject was told that recent medical studies had discovered a certain inborn heart condition, and that people with this condition are 'frequently ill, prone to heart-disease, and have a shorter-than-average life expectancy.' Subjects were also told that this type could be identified by the effect of exercise on the cold pressor test. Subjects were randomly assigned to one of two conditions in which they were told that the bad type of heart was associated with either increases or with decreases in tolerance to the cold water after exercise. Subjects then repeated the cold pressor test, after riding an Exercycle for one minute. As predicted, the vast majority of subjects showed changes in tolerance during the second cold pressor trial in the direction correlated with 'good news'—if told that decreased tolerance is diagnostic of a bad heart they endured the near-freezing water longer (and vice versa). The result shows that people are willing to bear painful consequences for a behavior that is a signal, though not a cause, of a medical condition.

An experiment by Shafir and Tversky (1992) on 'Newcomb's paradox' reinforces the same point. In the philosophical version of the paradox, a person is (hypothetically) presented with two boxes, A and B. Box A contains either nothing or some large amount of money deposited by an 'omniscient being'. Box B contains a small amount of money for sure. The decision-maker doesn't know what choice Box A contains, and has to choose whether to take the contents of that box (A) or of both boxes (A + B). What makes the problem a paradox is that the person is asked to believe that the omniscient being has already predicted her choice, and on that basis has already either 'punished' a greedy choice of (A + B) with no deposit in A or 'rewarded' a choice of (A) with a large deposit. The dominance principle argues in favor of choosing both boxes, because the deposits are fixed at the moment of choice.

This is the philosophical statement of the problem. In the actual experiment, Shafir and Tversky presented a variant of Newcomb's problem at the end of another, longer experiment, in which subjects repeatedly played a Prisoner's Dilemma game against (virtual) opponents via computer terminals. After finishing these games, a final 'bonus' problem appeared, with the two Newcomb boxes, and subjects had to choose whether to take money from one box or from both boxes. The experimental cover story did not mention an omniscient being but instead informed the subjects that 'a program developed at MIT recently was applied during the entire session [of Prisoner's Dilemma choices] to analyze the pattern of your preference.' Ostensibly, this mighty program could predict choices, one or two boxes, with 85 percent accuracy, and, of course, if the program predicted a choice of both boxes it would then put nothing in Box A. Although it was evident that the money amounts were already set at the moment of choice, most experimental subjects opted for the single box. It is 'as if' they believed that by declining to take the money in Box B, they could change the amount of money already deposited in Box A.

Although these are relatively recent experiments, their results are consistent with a long stream of psychological research, going back at least to the James–Lange theory of emotions, which claimed that people infer their own states from behavior (e.g., they feel afraid if they see themselves running). The notion that people adopt the perspective of an outside observer when interpreting their own actions has been extensively explored in the research on self-perception (Bem, 1972). In a similar vein, there is an extensive literature confirming the existence of 'self-handicapping' strategies, where a person might get too little sleep or under-prepare for an examination. In such a case, a successful performance could be attributed to ability, while unsuccessful performance could be externalized as due to the lack of proper preparation (e.g., Berglas and Jones, 1978; Berglas and Baumeister, 1993). This broader context of psychological research suggests that we should view the results of Quattrone and Tversky, and Shafir and Tversky not as mere curiosities, applying to only contrived experimental situations, but instead as evidence of a general motivational 'short circuit'. Motivation does not require causality, even when the lack of causality is utterly transparent. If anything, these experiments probably underestimate the impact of diagnosticity in realistic decisions, where the absence of causal links between actions and dispositions is less evident.

Formally, our model distinguishes between *outcome utility*—the utility of the anticipated causal consequences of choice—and *diagnostic utility*, which is the value of the adjusted estimate of one's disposition, adjusted in light of the choice. Individuals act so as to maximize some combination of the two sources of utility, and (in one version of the model) make correct inferences about what their choices imply about their dispositions. When diagnostic utility is sufficiently important, the individual chooses the same action independent of disposition. We interpret this as a personal rule. We describe other ways in which the behavior of self-signaling individuals is qualitatively different from that of standard economic agents. First, a self-signaling person will be more likely to reveal discrepancies between resolutions and actions, when resolutions pertain to actions that are contingent or delayed. Thus she might honestly commit to do some worthy action if the circumstances requiring the action were remote (temporally or probabilistically), but would in fact regret the commitment if those circumstances were obtained. Second, self-signaling gives rise to moral placebo effects, where a change in mere beliefs about one's traits or abilities may affect actions even though the new beliefs leave one's actual disposition unchanged.

2. DEFINITION OF SELF-SIGNALING

We begin with a general definition (Bodner and Prelec, 1997). A self-signaling person is characterized by: (1) a parameterized *outcome utility function, u(x, θ)*, where *x* is the outcome and *θ* the unknown parameter; (2) a *self-image distribution f(θ)*; (3) a *meta-utility function V(θ)*. The outcome utility function represents the expected value of the causal consequences of choosing *x*. The *θ*-parameter is an index of the unknown, momentary disposition (a 'type'). In the experiment by Quattrone and Tversky, it would be an index of the true, momentary tolerance for cold water following exercise. The self-image captures what the person knows about the disposition before making the choice. The meta-utility function represents the person's preferences over dispositions, which is to say, 'preferences-over-preferences,' given that dispositions are a preference parameter. In the Quattrone–Tversky experiment, subjects would naturally prefer to have tolerance levels of *θ* that are associated with healthy hearts.

The total utility created by choosing outcome *x* from a set, *C* = {*x, y, z* . . . }, equals the sum of the outcome utility of *x*, and the diagnostic utility of choosing *x* over all other outcomes *y, z* . . . etc. The outcome utility is simply the value *u(x, θ)*, computed with the actual *θ*. The diagnostic utility is the expectation of *V(θ)* calculated with respect to an *interpretation function, f(θ | x, C)*, which revises the self-image in light of the choice *x*. The total utility created by choosing *x* is:

Utility of choosing *x* from *C* = Outcome utility of *x*
$$+ \text{Diagnostic utility of choosing } x \text{ from } C$$

$$U(x, C, \theta) = u(x, \theta) = u(x, \theta) + \Sigma_\theta f(\theta | x, C) V(\theta). \tag{1}$$

Why do we not take an expectation of *u(x, θ)* over the unknown *θ* in eqn 1? The question brings to the surface the distinction between a standard unknown parameter and a parameter like *θ*, which has the property of being 'known' by the decision-making mechanism but which cannot be introspected before the choice.[1] The gut knows *θ*, but the mind does not. A *θ*-parameter, such as a person's cold water tolerance, willpower, disposition to alcoholism, altruism, exerts influence at the moment of choice, but cannot be deduced by merely imagining what one might do in a given situation. Precisely, it represents that part of uncertainty that can only be resolved by a *real*, as opposed to a hypothetical choice.

---

[1] The assumption that people only remember choices, but not the motivational and informational states that led to these choices, is invoked (in very different settings) by Ariely et al. (2000), Bénabou and Tirole (2000), Hirschleifer and Welch (1998), and Koszegi (1999). Koszegi, in particular, postulates an 'ego-utility' function, whose argument is the expectation of *θ*, conditional on past actions, i.e., Koszegi's agent evaluates *V(E{θ | x, C})* instead of *E{V(θ) | x, C}* as in our model. We discuss the work of Bénabou and Tirole in more detail in the concluding section of this paper.

Eqn 1 defines the self-signaling decision problem. To complete it, one has to specify the revised distribution, $f(\theta \mid x, C)$. There are several ways to do that, depending on how much rationality one wishes to ascribe to the decision-maker's interpretation of his choices.

2.1. Exogenous Interpretations

The most direct way to complete the model is to postulate an exogenous inter-pretation function $f(\theta \mid x, C)$. Psychologically, the function could be internalized through socialization or persuasion (e.g., as in the original formulation of Newcomb's paradox). On this zero-level model, the self-signaling implications of an action are independent of motives. The fact that feelings of shame or guilt can arise even in situations where a person is not 'at fault' suggests that such inter-pretations have psychological reality.

2.2. Face-Value Interpretations

One level up, we have 'face-value' interpretations, which derive $f(\theta \mid x, C)$ endo-genously from the assumption that an action reveals θ that maximizes the outcome-utility component of total utility. A person whose actions were made innocent of their diagnostic implications, would be justified in maintaining face-value inferences. Diagnostic utility would be experienced as an unintentional byproduct of choice, not something that consciously affected choice.

2.3. True Interpretations

A third possibility is that the revised distribution $f(\theta \mid x, C)$ is rational in a stronger sense, namely, that it is consistent with the maximization of *both* components of eqn 1 and with Bayes' rule. A choice reveals θ for which that choice is optimal.[2] We call these interpretations 'true' because they correctly discount the signaling value of an action for the fact that the action is partly motivated by self-signaling. They are 'true-to-reality,' so to speak.

---

[2] The only fine point is how to interpret actions that cannot be construed as optimal for any θ. To ensure that all actions have interpretations, we define 'plausibility of θ given choice x from C as the difference between the total utility of action x (assuming that θ is the actual disposition) and the highest total utility attainable from C (again, assuming θ):

Plausibility of θ given choice x from C = utility of x for θ

— maximum utility θ can gain from C

$$P(\theta, x, C) = U(x, \theta) - \underset{y \in C}{\text{Max}}\ U(y, C, \theta).$$

Interpretations are true if $f(\theta \mid x, C)$ places positive probability only on those θ for which x maximizes total utility, and if no such θ exists, on the most plausible θ. Bayes' rule resolves 'ties,' where more than one θ is maximally plausible. For face-value interpretations, the criterion would have the same form but with outcome utilities $u(x, \theta)$ replacing total utilities $U(x, C, \theta)$.

We can summarize the unbiased, fully rational self-signaling model with two assumptions:

Assumption 1 (Optimization)   I choose so as to maximize total utility (eqn 1), taking into account what my action might reveal about my true preferences.

Assumption 2 (True interpretations)   What my choice reveals about my true preferences is precisely that they are the preferences for which that choice maximizes total utility (or comes closest to maximizing total utility).

Readers familiar with economic theory will recognize here the concepts of signaling games (see Bodner and Prelec, 1997*a*, for a reduction of this problem to a degenerate signaling game).[3] Those not familiar with economic signaling models may be struck by the circularity in the assumptions: In order to know how to solve the optimization problem in Assumption 1, one needs to have ready an interpretation of each possible action, but the interoperations of actions in Assumption 2 presupposes a knowledge of which action is optimal for each θ. The circularity is intentional and tailor-made for game-theoretic analysis. The solutions are 'equilibria' in which actions are optimal in the light of how they will be interpreted, and interpretations are true given the optimality of actions.

2.4. Some Examples

Here are seven examples where self-signaling might play a role:

Example 1 x is '$ left at the casino' and θ 'disposition to gambling.'

Example 2 x is '$ donation to the United Way' and θ 'the level of true concern about the activities supported by United Way.'

Example 3 x is '$ spent on a wine bottle (no special occasion)' and θ is 'financial responsibility.'

Example 4 x is 'taking or not taking a drink before noon' and θ is disposition to alcoholism.

Example 5 x is 'embarking or not embarking on a dangerous mountain-climbing expedition,' and θ is 'perseverance.'

Example 6 x is 'quitting or not quitting your regular job' and θ is 'acting ability.'

Example 7 x is 'voting or not voting' and θ is 'dedication to the candidate.'

---

[3] The game is between a Sender that executes choices and a Receiver whose only function is to set the diagnostic utility term equal to the expectation of $V(\theta)$, as in eqn 1. Could we interpret the Receiver as a sort of Conscience or Superego struggling to control the Sender's baser impulses? We resist such an interpretation because any genuine model of a 'higher Self' should ascribe to it preferences over outcomes, presumably different from the preferences of the 'lower Self'. For example, in Thaler and Shefrin's Planner–Doer model (1981), the conflict between the Planner and the Doer arises because both sides have preferences over consumption streams, but the Planner's preferences exhibit a smaller discount rate. The Receiver here has no preferences over actions or over outcomes—it is simply a Bayesian calculator, enforcing a kind of objectivity on interpretations of actions.

Remark 1 In many, if not most of these examples, the act in question has significant causal consequences as well. Taking the drink in Example 4 changes body chemistry, increasing physiological dependence on alcohol. To the extent that this effect is recognized by the decision-maker, it would be absorbed in $u(x, \theta)$, along with any other causal consequences. However, in this example, and in many others like it, the purely causal consequences of the deviant action are slight, and a person's concern cannot be plausibly ascribed to it. Our model hopes to explain why seemingly trivial actions can have great subjective significance. In the self-signaling model, the diagnostic value of an action may be all out of proportion to its scale—a small gesture can reveal character quite effectively (e.g., stealing 25 cents still counts as theft).

Remark 2 In many, if not most of these examples, the person may not be intrinsically concerned about having the particular disposition; rather she is concerned about specific consequences that might result from having this disposition. For instance, a person may not care about endurance and perseverance *per se*, but only the career benefits that she expects to flow from this trait. One can distinguish therefore between *intrinsic* and *instrumental* self-signaling.[4] There is no difficulty in dealing with instrumental self-signaling provided that the future consequences of a given disposition do not involve any additional future decisions. The calculation of $V(\theta)$ would simply expand to include not just intrinsic concern about θ but also about all future consequences that derive from θ, adjusted by probability and time delay. This would be the natural way to model 'heart condition' in the Quattrone and Tversky experiment. If, however, these future consequences are predicated on additional decisions by that same person, then the problem would have to be analyzed as a dynamic game between a succession of multiple-selves, each of which is endowed with a self-signaling utility structure. The same applies to the final example, voting. The level of personal dedication to a candidate is not likely to have great intrinsic importance. However, to the extent that such dedication levels are correlated across the population, my dedication predicts the dedication of others, and hence their inclination to vote. Assuming other voters self-signal as well, in equilibrium my vote may be a valid evidence for whether others will vote.

Remark 3 Remark 2 notwithstanding, the distinction between intrinsic and instrumental self-signaling may not be as clear cut psychologically as it is logically. Consider an ostensibly instrumental disposition like willpower, and imagine that you have just scored in the top decile on some accurate psychological test of this trait. In order to feel happy about this news you don't need to elaborate in detail exactly how willpower might prove useful in the future. You have a rough sense that willpower will help in all kinds of situations, so the news is good. The decile rank in willpower functions exactly like the heart condition in

---

[4] Similarly, Koszegi (1999) distinguishes between 'pure self-image' and 'anxiety or worry about the future.'

the Quattrone and Tversky experiment—it is a general predictor of future quality of life on some important dimensions. Psychologically, therefore, the intrinsic self-signaling model may extend to forms of instrumental self-signaling, at least in situations where the underlying traits have diffuse potential benefits, contingent on unforeseeable opportunities and choices.

Remark 4   Example 3 raises issues of generalization, as discussed by Gilboa and Gilboa-Schechtman (2002, chapter 7, in this volume). Is the action diagnostic of 'general financial irresponsibility', or 'overindulgence on wines', or 'overindulgence on Burgundies after a hard day at the office'? There is nothing in the model that picks out one or another level of generalization. Formally, the level of generalization could be made endogenous by treating it as a cognitive decision variable, subject to similar diagnostic motivation as the action itself (i.e., narrow generalizations would facilitate excuses). Generalization involves the psychological notions of similarity and grouping, which fall outside standard economic modeling (Prelec, 1991; Gilboa and Schmeidler, 1995).

Remark 5   To the extent that a disposition is revealed through a series of choices, wouldn't a lifetime of behavioral evidence overwhelm the information content of a single action? Note, first, that as far as feelings are concerned, we often do seem to ignore the long-run track record and give excess weight to the most recent experience. This psychological bias would enhance diagnostic motivation. Second, and more important, the problem of drawing inferences from actions is not as simple as we had made it out to be. One can often choose how much to blame oneself and how much to blame outside circumstances.[5] A more realistic model would write the momentary disposition at time t as the sum of a stable component and an unobservable temptation, $\theta(t) = \theta + \varepsilon(t)$, and then consider how the person might extract the signal, θ, from the noisy behavioral record. Moreover, if θ is subject to drift, for example, as in: $\theta(t) = \theta(t-1) + \varepsilon(t)$, then the mere passage of time would create uncertainty about θ and restore diagnostic motivation. A person would periodically need to 'check' that $\theta(t)$ is still in the good range.

Remark 6   Finally, doesn't the true interpretation model require a weird combination of self-ignorance (i.e., of one's own dispositions) and self-awareness (i.e., of one's propensity to self-signal)? Well, as a matter of sheer cognitive skill, we are certainly able to discount behavioral signals *of other people* when we suspect ulterior motives on their part. What is less clear, however, is whether in fact we apply to our own actions the same rigorous interpretive standards that we apply to the actions of others. To the extent that we fail to do so, the face-value model of interpretations will be more correct.

---

[5] Bénabou and Tirole (2000) analyze the attribution-of-blame problem when memory of past actions and past temptation levels is imperfect. See also Bodner and Prelec (1997, section 5).

3. FACE-VALUE INTERPRETATIONS AND EXCESSIVE SELF-ESTEEM

Looking at eqn 1, one might think that the optimal choice would reflect a compromise between outcome and diagnostic utility, so that actions would diverge from the natural, outcome-utility maximizing levels in the direction that is diagnostic of preferred dispositions. This is how things turn out with 'face-value' interpretations, but not with 'true' interpretations. In the true-interpretations case, the signaling value of good actions is discounted for the diagnostic motive, which creates an escalating pressure for behavioral perfection. The generic result (described in Section 4) is that either diagnostic utility wins, and the person does the same 'perfect' thing irrespective of disposition, or natural impulses win, and the person simply ignores the diagnostic component of the utility structure.

Let us now consider the case where the disposition pertains to a nasty vice, such as gambling, and could be at one of three levels: *Low*, *Moderate*, and *High*, all equally likely. The level, x, of the problematic activity could be zero or any positive amount up to some maximum level. The meta-utility function $V(\theta)$ is decreasing in θ, so that lower dispositions are intrinsically preferred. Outcome utility, $u(x, \theta)$, is twice continuously differentiable, strictly concave, with $\partial u/\partial x$ increasing in θ, which indicates that higher θ implies more appetite for the activity. These assumptions ensure the existence of a unique equilibrium. We will refer to the consumption levels that maximize just outcome utility as the *natural consumption levels*, and, for the sake of interest, assume that they are positive for all θ, for example, even a person with the best *Low* disposition would prefer to gamble a small amount.

With these assumptions, and with face-value interpretations, we might observe an equilibrium such as described in Figure 6.1. The three natural levels are labeled as 'Light', 'Moderate', and 'Heavy', in the middle column. The first set of arrows indicates optimal actions for each disposition, and the second set of arrows the corresponding face-value interpretations. Solid arrows indicate interpretations of actions selected with positive probability in equilibrium, and dashed arrows actions never selected in equilibrium. In equilibrium, the person cuts back gambling by one step from the natural level. Face-value interpretations generously ignore the diagnostic motive for the reduction, and induce a self-image that is too good by one θ-step, except for the best disposition, which is correctly diagnosed.[6]

If the interpretations are true, then this obviously will not work. The rightmost column in Figure 6.1 gives the true interpretations in the postulated equilibrium. The Moderate level of consumption is diagnostic of the *High* rather than the *Moderate* disposition, and Light consumption of either *Low* or *Moderate*, rather than *Low* for sure.

---

[6] Other models that give rise to an excessively positive self-image are presented by Carrillo and Mariotti (2000), Brocas and Carrillo (1999, 2000), Bénabou and Tirole (1999), and Koszegi (1999).

$f(\theta)$	Disposition to vice	Consumption	Face-value interpretation	True interpretation
		Abstain - - - - - - →		
0.33	*Low* ——→	Light ——————→	*Low*	{*Low* or *Moderate*}
0.33	*Moderate* ——→	Moderate ————→	*Moderate*	*High*
0.33	*High* ——	Heavy - - - - - - - →	*High*	*High*

Figure 6.1. *An equilibrium that can arise only with face-value interpretations, and which produces on average an overly positive self-image (a 2/3 chance of Low and 1/3 chance of Moderate)*

As an empirical hypothesis, face-value interpretations may be closer to psychological reality. There is much evidence that self-assessments are excessively positive (e.g., Taylor and Brown, 1988). Furthermore, in the specific context of the Quattrone–Tversky experiment, which is our empirical cornerstone, most of the participants did not acknowledge ex-post any conscious efforts to influence the results of the cold-pressor test. The small minority of subjects who did confess to trying to bias the results were also relatively pessimistic about their own chances of having a good heart. The subject population apparently divided into a self-satisfied, face-value interpretations majority, and a pessimistic, true-interpretations minority.[7]

4. TRUE INTERPRETATIONS AND RULE-GOVERNED ACTION

What consumption levels would then be consistent with true interpretations? There are only three possibilities, identified in Figures 6.2–6.4. When diagnostic utility has no weight whatsoever, consumption is just at the natural levels, shown in Figure 6.2. The right column gives the obvious interpretations. In this case, you do as you please and what you do makes who you are transparent.

What happens when the weight of diagnostic utility is increased slightly from zero? Initially nothing—the optimal actions remain the same. A person with a *High* disposition would perhaps feel some inclination to reduce consumption, but could only generate a positive signal by reducing consumption to the moderate level, set by the *Moderate* disposition. If diagnostic utility is weak, it will not justify the discrete reduction in consumption. As diagnostic utility becomes stronger, a different, partially separating equilibrium emerges, in which consumption falls to zero for the two better dispositions, and remains Heavy for *High* (Figure 6.2). Notice that zero consumption does not maximize outcome utility for any disposition. The fact that it emerges as on optimal choice with self-signaling is an example of 'excessive virtue', sustained by the harsh interpretation of any positive level of consumption. The psychological intuition might go as follows: A

---

[7] To explain this kind of self-deception, it would be sufficient to hypothesize that the plausibility function in eqn 3 places less weight on diagnostic utility than does the optimal action rule in eqn 1.

$f(\theta)$	Disposition to vice	Consumption	True interpretation
		Abstain	
0.33	*Low*	Light	*Low*
0.33	*Moderate*	Moderate	*Moderate*
0.33	*High*	Heavy	*High*

Figure 6.2. *A separating equilibrium, when the diagnostic utility is weak*

$f(\theta)$	Disposition to vice	Consumption	True interpretation
		Abstain	
0.33	*Low*	Light	{*Low* or *Moderate*}
0.33	*Moderate*	Moderate	
0.33	*High*	Heavy	*High*

Figure 6.3. *A partially separating equilibrium*

person who is concerned about his inclination to gamble, and who has, as a result, never ventured into a casino, would treat even one lapse as evidence of a strong gambling urge. The person might say—'given how much I care not to discover that I have a taste for gambling, then I must indeed have a strong taste for it if I succumb on this occasion!' Moderation is not an option.[8]

Finally, when diagnostic utility is completely dominant, a person with a *High* disposition will also abstain (Figure 6.3). It is natural to interpret this pooling equilibrium as a rule, inasmuch as the same action is taken independent of disposition. In this situation, even though abstention is certain, this fact does not provide any reassurance about the underlying disposition—it is still equally likely to be any of the three types. Indeed, in a repeated choice setting, perfect compliance over many trials would still not reveal the underlying disposition, and it is this very fact that sustains the diagnostic motive. If one could infer that one had a perfect disposition after a certain number of abstentions, then one could afford 'to relax' and gamble occasionally. *Here, the rule remains in force precisely because following the rule is not informative.*

Figures 6.2–6.4 are the only possibilities that the model allows, if interpretations are true. Interestingly, one cannot have an equilibrium that pools on the Light or Moderate level. If, for example, pooling-on-Light is entertained as an equilibrium, then the best disposition (*Low*) would be motivated to reveal itself by reducing consumption just a tiny bit.

---

[8] A separate benefit of abstention is that it denies the person the opportunity to learn how much she really likes a potentially addictive substance. Carrillo (1998) shows how by 'enforcing ignorance' abstention can become the optimal second-best strategy in a situation where fully-informed hyperbolic-discounting agents cannot precommit to moderation.

$f(\theta)$	Disposition to vice	Consumption	True interpretation
0.33	*Low*	Abstain	
0.33	*Moderate*	Light	
0.33	*High*	Moderate	{*Low, Moderate* or *High*}
		Heavy	*High*

Figure 6.4. *Strong diagnostic utility promotes complete pooling—an 'abstention rule'*

$f(\theta)$	Disposition to vice	Consumption	True interpretation
0.33	*Low*	Abstain	
0.33	*Moderate*	Light	*Low*
0.33	*High*	Moderate	{*Low, Moderate* or *High*}
		Heavy	*High*

Figure 6.5. *An impossible equilibrium, with pooling on Light consumption. Interpretations are true but actions are not optimal. Any consumption level below Light signals the best disposition, so there is an incentive to reduce consumption by a small amount, from 'Light' to 'Light-ε.' Note how the impossibility result depends on x being a continuous variable*

Looking over the three equilibrium cases (Figures 6.1–6.3), we see that the motivational struggle between outcome and diagnostic utilities can be resolved in one of only two ways: Either outcome utility is stronger, and the person does as she pleases, or diagnostic utility is stronger, and the person chooses to abstain from consumption altogether.

Would these conclusions survive under different dimensional assumptions about x and θ? With continuous dispositions, we find separating equilibria with all dispositions consuming less than their natural, outcome-utility-maximizing level (Bodner and Prelec, 1997, section 4; see also Bernheim, 1994). With a discrete rather than continuous action set, a single utility structure (eqn 1) may yield multiple equilibria, including equilibria with pooling on positive consumption levels (e.g., something like Figure 6.5). Informally, the model seems more sensitive to dimensional assumptions about the action space than about the dispositional space.

5. RESOLUTIONS ARE MORE CONSISTENT WITH THE IDEAL SELF

True interpretations allow a short menu of three generic equilibria, and which one obtains will depend on the relative weight of outcome and diagnostic utility. One way in which this balance can be tilted is if mere 'intentions' or 'resolutions to act' replace actions. Now, by a resolution we usually mean one of two things. The first sense is that there is something that one intends to do at some time in the future.

A second sense is that there is something that one intends to do if called upon to do so (e.g., 'I resolve to abstain if the tempting occasion presents itself'). The first sense has to do with delay, and the second sense combines uncertainty and delay. In either case, we can compare resolutions, where consequences are uncertain and delayed, with actions having the same utility structure but where the outcomes are certain and immediate. In both cases, we imagine that the resolution is binding (i.e., there is no possibility of escaping the commitment ex-post).

Looking first at the case of a contingent resolution, the ex-ante decision problem is whether to commit to consume a given amount (or none at all) if the opportunity arises. Because the decision is binding, the self-signaling utility structure in eqn 1 is changed in only one respect—there is a probability, p, that the person will actually have to implement his resolution, and probability $(1 - p)$ that he will not. Hence, the only change is that outcome utilities are reduced by a factor of p, while the diagnostic part of the equation remains the same. The reduction in relative outcome weight promotes choices that are diagnostic of good dispositions, in equilibrium (Bodner and Prelec, 1997).

Bodner's experiments (Bodner, 1995) on contingent charitable pledges exhibit exactly this phenomenon. Contingent pledges are promises to give in the event that one is called upon to do so. Bodner found that the pledges of subjects who regarded themselves as insufficiently altruistic were relatively more sensitive to the stated probability of being called upon to give: they were relatively more generous when that probability was small. In effect, such subjects were purchasing self-esteem 'on the cheap', by pledging more when the likelihood of actual sacrifice was low.

Self-esteem can also be purchased on the cheap when the decisional consequences are far away in time. Outcome utility is now temporally, rather than probabilistically discounted, again making the good action a more likely choice. The chronic discrepancy between future plans and actual behavior may therefore be explained by two facts: (1) the diagnostic utility of a resolution is immediate while the outcome cost of that resolution is discounted, and (2) people fail to anticipate the reversal in preference, that is, that they are naïve in the sense of O'Donoghue and Rabin (1999).

This account provides a single explanation of what are otherwise different categories of dynamic inconsistency. Anything that selectively lowers the weight of outcome utility (low physical salience, uncertainty, time distance, and so forth) will result in choices being more driven by meta-utility. When the weight of outcome utility is restored (by making outcomes salient, certain, imminent, etc. . . .), the person may regret his earlier choice.

6. MORAL PLACEBOS

Consider the following problem: Imagine that you have a friend concerned about an underlying disposition to vice. He has abstained so far but is not sure whether he will be able to maintain this policy in the future. What beliefs would be most

$f(\theta)$	Disposition to vice	Consumption	True interpretation
		Abstain	
0.90	*Low*	Light	{Probably (90%) *Low*}
0.09	*Moderate*	Moderate	
0.01	*High*	Heavy	*High*

Figure 6.6. *An optimistic self-image increases the likelihood of an abstaining equilibrium*

$f(\theta)$	Disposition to vice	Consumption	True interpretation
		Abstain	
0.01	*Low*	Light	
0.09	*Moderate*	Moderate	{Probably (90%) *High*}
0.90	*High*	Heavy	*High*

Figure 6.7. *A pessimistic self-image is not likely to produce an abstaining equilibrium. The diagnostic benefits of abstaining are smaller than in Figure 6.6*

effective in maintaining his abstention policy, holding constant the combined utility structure, $u(x, \theta)$ and $V(\theta)$? Your only manner of influence is to shift $f(\theta)$ in some particular direction by reasoning and persuasion, that is, you cannot change his actual disposition.

Informally, one may identify two approaches here. The first approach, 'from fear', would say that it is good to increase the subjective probabilities of bad dispositions. The second approach, 'from self-worth', would say that boosting the probability of good dispositions increases the subjective stake in abstaining, making abstention more likely.

It turns out that the second approach is more effective if interpretations are true. Let us compare the plausibility of a pooling or 'abstain' equilibrium under optimistic and pessimistic prior beliefs. When the self-image is optimistic, then abstention is interpreted as a high likelihood (90 percent) of the best disposition, while any consumption triggers the most undesirable interpretation. Hence, the diagnostic 'stakes' are very high, increasing the chance that this equilibrium will be maintained (Figure 6.6).

When the self-image is pessimistic (Figure 6.7), then the diagnostic benefits of abstaining are slight. A person who abstains still faces a subjective 90 percent probability of having a bad disposition, hence the diagnostic penalty for indulging is small. The likelihood that this pooling equilibrium will arise with pessimistic beliefs is low. This constitutes an argument in favor of 'positive thinking' insofar as more favorable opinions about one's disposition provide a larger stake for abstaining.[9]

---

[9] Bénabou and Tirole (2000, proposition 1) derive a similar result in context of an intertemporal, multiple-selves model.

We can call the effect shown across Figures 6.6 and 6.7 a *moral placebo*, inasmuch as the ability to abstain is supported by a positive self-image that need not have any basis in reality. Consider a person having a bad *High* disposition, but who is not sure of that. At low levels of temptation (low weight on outcome utility), the pooling equilibrium in Figure 6.3 obtains and the person abstains from consumption. At high levels of temptation (high weight on outcome utility), the separating equilibrium in Figure 6.1 or 6.2 obtains, and he consumes heavily. At intermediate levels of temptation, however, whether one or the other equilibrium obtains depends on his self-image $f(\theta)$. By replacing the probabilities in Figure 6.7 with those in Figure 6.6 (i.e., consuming the 'moral placebo'), the person's ability to withstand temptation increases.

Moral placebo effects open the door to other nonstandard influences on actions. If dispositions are correlated across individuals in a particular group, then observing the actions of others in the group provides information about one's own disposition. For instance, if persons A and B believe that their dispositions are drawn from a common prior, $f(\theta^A, \theta^B)$, and if A sees B abstaining from consumption, that may make A's self-image more favorable, thereby increasing the likelihood that she will abstain. In other words, the information that someone else has resisted temptation promotes my own abstention, even if there are no causal connections between us and my action is entirely private.

Could a moral placebo effect be created by information provided by one's own earlier choices, that is, could past actions—decisional precedents—influence present choices purely by changing self-beliefs? The general answer is Yes, but the particulars will depend on how the intertemporal choice problem is set up, and on whether the intertemporal dependencies are themselves taken into account in the earlier choice (i.e., whether the individuals are 'naïve' or 'sophisticated' in the sense of O'Donoghue and Rabin (1999)). The extent that past choices can provide information about the current disposition depends also on whether a person believes in a fixed disposition ('Calvinism'), or whether she thinks that dispositions are variable. Under the Calvinist variant, once a bad θ is revealed no further action can repair the damage. If, however, θ is a stochastic process, then one's own earlier choice provides information in exactly the same way as do choices of other persons. If the information is positive, that is, if one has a good track record, the chances of abstaining in the future will tend to go up. When dispositions are not fixed, therefore, an action that is diagnostic of favored dispositions has a multiplier effect, increasing the probability that such an action will be repeated the second time that a similar choice opportunity arises. It is as if each moral success contributes an increment of 'moral capital', making future successes more likely.

7. ONE SELF OR MANY SELVES?

The conjecture that people can learn from their own actions has figured prominently in the psychological writings of George Ainslie (1992), and has, more recently, been given a different theoretical justification by Bénabou and

Tirole (2000, 2001). Because the objectives of Bénabou and Tirole overlap our own, we now briefly outline and compare their model.

Bénabou and Tirole (2000) work within an intertemporal, multiple-selves context, where each temporal self is strategically sophisticated with respect to its future incarnations. They distinguish between 'private' information, which one cannot communicate to future selves except through actions, and 'public' information, available to all selves (there are also intermediate cases, where information has some chance of being incorrectly recalled). The critical feature of this model relative to our own is that it upholds the rationality of the individual decision making process at a given point in time. A key issue for any such model is to reconcile two seemingly contradictory requirements:

(1) *Self-transparency*: Every Current Self knows it's own preferences (including 'willpower').

(2) *Self-signaling*: The Current Self is influenced by actions (that is, 'signals') of Past Selves, even though those actions do not affect her preferences *per se*.

(1) is an economic model-building principle, namely, that incomplete self-knowledge can only arise intertemporally, when you either forget your past actions or motives, or when you cannot forecast your future preferences. (2) is the desired result. The challenge is making the knowledge of past actions informationally useful to the current Self, notwithstanding its 'self-transparent' nature. Benabou and Tirole respond by dividing a stylized self-control problem into two subdecisions, a 'morning' decision whether to indulge all day or embark on a work project, and a second, 'afternoon' decision whether to finish the work or stop short of the goal. This scenario repeats on the second day (and could, in principle, be extended to subsequent days). Hyperbolic discounting (or 'weakness of will') makes the morning Self curious about what the afternoon Self will do: Specifically, the morning Self prefers to start working only if she believes the afternoon Self will follow through and finish the job. Even though the morning Self knows her willpower exactly, the morning decision is different from the afternoon decision, so the morning Self has to look backward to what happened 'under similar conditions' yesterday afternoon to estimate the chances that willpower *this* afternoon will be up to snuff. The imperfect correlation of willpower across time periods endows earlier decisions with informational value, even to a self-transparent Self. The morning Self conditions her actions on her expectations of what she will do later that afternoon, and her action yesterday afternoon provides the best evidence for that.

Bénabou and Tirole (2000) demonstrate that self-transparency and strategic sophistication are logically compatible with many of the self-reputation phenomena that have been discussed in the psychological literature, most notably by Ainslie (1975, 1986, 1992). The model is close in spirit if not in detail to Ainslie's story, in the sense that Ainslie also develops a rich psychology of self-control from hyperbolic discounting alone, without requiring any conflict between different personae *within* a given temporal Self (see, especially, the discussion of Freudian mechanisms in Ainslie, 1982).

Our model is based on a somewhat different set of psychological intuitions. Looking at the psychological evidence, we are impressed with the seamless quality of self-signaling and self-deception. When individuals manipulate their 'medical test' results (Quattrone and Tversky, 1984), personality self-reports (Sanitioso et al., 1990; Kunda, 1990; Dunning et al., 1995), or problem solving strategies in a desired direction (Ginossar and Trope, 1987), it is hard to discern two agents, the one who *signals* and the one who is *signaled to.*[10] For this reason, we favor the hypothesis that all acts of volition are *at the outset* biased by diagnostic motivation. This is a doctrine of volitional 'original sin' insofar as the desire for good news compromises thoughts and actions as they are formed and enter into consciousness. A person may be rationally aware of this biasing force, as in the 'true interpretations' version, or completely unaware of it, as in the 'face-value' version, but in either case there is no moment in time when he is truly self-transparent. Without self-transparency, the notion of self-signaling becomes more literal, involving one Self (at most).

REFERENCES

Ainslie, G. (1975). Specious reward: A behavioral theory of impulsiveness and impulse control. *Psychological Bulletin, 82,* 463–509.

—— (1982). A behavioral economic approach to the defense mechanisms: Freud's energy theory revisited. *Social Science Information, 21,* 735–79.

—— (1986). Beyond microeconomics: Conflict among interests in a multiple self as a determinant of value. In J. Elster (Ed.), *The multiple Self.* Cambridge: Cambridge University Press.

—— (1992). *Picoeconomics: The strategic interaction of successive motivational states within the person.* New York, Cambridge University Press.

Ariely, D., Loewenstein, G., and Prelec. D. (2000). *Coherent arbitrariness: Duration sensitive pricing around an arbitrary anchor,* MIT mimeo.

Bem, D.J. (1972). Self-perception theory. In L. Berkowitz (Ed.), *Advances in experimental social psychology* (Vol. 6). New York: Academic Press.

Bénabou, R. and Tirole, J. (1999). *Self-confidence: Intrapersonal strategies,* IDEI mimeo, June.

—— and —— (2000). *Willpower and personal rules,* Princeton mimeo, June.

—— and —— (2002). Self-knowledge and self-regulation: An economic approach. In I. Brocas and J.D. Carrillo (Eds.), *The psychology of economic decisions.* Oxford: Oxford University Press.

---

[10] To be fair, nothing in the intertemporal approach requires each Self to be fully conscious and to occupy an extended time period. Indeed, Ainslie (1992) has conjectured that the sensation of pain is produced by yielding to the temptation of an extremely brief attentional pleasure, a pleasure so brief that it cannot be detected consciously, yet sufficiently strong to 'lock' attention on the pain-producing stimulus.

Berglas, S. and Jones, E.E. (1978). Drug choice as a self-handicapping strategy in response to noncontingent success. *Journal of Personality and Social Psychology, 36*(4), 405–17.

—— and —— (1993). *Your own worst enemy: Understanding the paradox of self-defeating behavior.* New York: Basic Books.

Bernheim, D.B. (1994). A theory of conformity. *Journal of Political Economy, 102*(5), 841–77.

Bodner, R. (1995). *Self knowledge and the diagnostic value of actions: The case of donating to a charitable cause.* Unpublished doctoral dissertation, MIT, Sloan School of Management.

—— and Prelec, D. (1997). *The diagnostic value of actions in a self-signaling model,* MIT mimeo, January.

Bratman, M.E. (1995). Planning and temptation. In Friedman and Clark (Eds.), *Mind and Morals.* Bradford: MIT press.

Brocas, I. and Carrillo, J. (1999). *Entry mistakes, entrepreneurial boldness and optimism,* ULB-ECARES mimeo, June.

—— and —— (2000). Information and self-control, this volume.

Campbell, R. and Sowden, Lanning (Eds.), (1985). *Paradoxes of Rationality and Coopera-tion.* Vancouver: Vancouver University.

Carrillo, J. (1998). *Self control, moderate consumption, and craving,* CEPR D.P. 2017, November.

—— and Mariotti, T. (2000). Strategic ignorance as a self-disciplining device. *Review of Economic Studies, 76*(3), 529–44.

Elster, J. (1985). Weakness of will and the free-rider problem. *Economics and Philosophy.* 231–65.

Dunning, D., Leuenberger, A., and Sherman, D.A. (1995). A new look at motivated infer-ence: Are self-serving theories of success a product of motivational forces? *Journal of Personality and Social Psychology, 69,* 58–68.

Gilboa, I. and Gilboa-Schechtman, E. (2002) Mental accounting and the absentminded driver. In I. Brocas and J.D. Carrillo (Eds.), *The psychology of economic decisions.* Oxford: Oxford University Press.

—— and Schmeidler, D. (1995). Case-based decision theory. *Quarterly Journal of Eco-nomics, 110,* 605–39.

Ginossar, Z. and Trope, Y. (1987). Problem solving in judgment under uncertainty. *Journal of Personality and Social Psychology, 52,* 464–471.

Hirschleifer, D. and Welch, I. (1998). *A rational economic approach to the psychology of change: Amnesia, inertia, and impulsiveness,* mimeo, November.

Kunda, Z. (1990). The case for motivated reasoning. *Psychological Bulletin, 108,* 480–98.

Koszegi, B. (1999). *Self-image and economic behavior,* MIT mimeo, October.

Laibson, D.I. (1997). Golden eggs and hyperbolic discounting. *Quarterly Journal of Economics, 112,* 443–78.

Nozick, R. (1969). Newcomb's problem and two principles of choice. In Nicholas Rescher et al. (Eds.), *Essays in Honor of Carl G. Hempel.* Dordrecht: Reidel.

O'Donoghue, T. and Rabin, M. (1999). Doing it now or later. *American Economic Review, 89*(1), 103–24.

Prelec, D. (1991). Values and principles: Some limitations on traditional economic ana-lysis. In A. Etzioni and P. Lawrence (Eds.), *Socioeconomics: Toward a new synthesis.* New York.

Quattrone, G.A. and Tversky, A. (1984). Causal versus diagnostic contingencies: On self-deception and on the voter's illusion. *Journal of Personality and Social Psychology*, *46*(2), 237–48.

Sanitioso, R., Kunda, Z., and Fong, G.T. (1990). Motivated recruitment of autobiographical memory. *Journal of Personality and Social Psychology*, *59*, 229–41.

Shafir, E. and Tversky, A. (1992). Thinking through uncertainty: Nonconsequential reasoning and choice. *Cognitive Psychology*, *24*, 449–74.

Taylor, S.E. and Brown, J.D. (1988). Illusion and well-being: A social psychological perspective on mental health. *Psychological Bulletin*, *103*, 193–210.

Thaler, R. and Shefrin, H.M. (1981). An economic theory of self-control. *Journal of Political Economy*, *89*, 393–410.

PART III

IMPERFECT MEMORY AND LIMITED CAPACITY TO PROCESS INFORMATION

7

Mental Accounting and the Absent-minded Driver

ITZHAK GILBOA AND EVA GILBOA-SCHECHTMAN

1. MENTAL ACCOUNTING AND OVER-GENERALIZATIONS

The term 'mental accounting' refers to a variety of phenomena in which money is non-fungible. Since the pioneering works of Kahneman, Tversky, and Thaler (Kahneman and Tversky, 1979, 1984; Tversky and Kahneman, 1981; and Thaler, 1980, 1985) it has become abundantly clear that people do not treat all dollars alike. Rather, people manage different accounts in their minds, in which money has origins and goals that cannot be ignored when this money is spent.

There are many types of mental accounts and various rationales for drawing distinctions between seemingly identical resources. This chapter proposes that one type of mental accounting has to do with over-generalization, and that it can be viewed as an optimal strategy under a constraint of failing memory. The following example illustrates this.

Example 1 (Thaler, 1985) Mr. S admires a $125 cashmere sweater at the department store. He declines to buy it, feeling that it is too extravagant. Later that month he receives the same sweater from his wife for a birthday present. He is very happy. Mr. and Mrs. S have only joint bank accounts.

What goes on in Mr. S's mind when he declines to buy the sweater and when he later on receives it as a gift? It might be the case that, when Mr. S receives the gift from his wife, he is relieved of the moral responsibility that would normally be attached to consumption decisions. That is, if *he* makes the decision to buy the sweater, he should pay the mental and social cost of being a spendthrift. Having made such a decision may not conform to his self-image as a frugal person; it may also serve against him in his attempt to control his teenage daughter's spending, and so forth.

An alternative explanation is that Mr. S feels that it is acceptable to buy the cashmere sweater for his birthday, but unacceptable to buy it with no other reason apart from the fact that the sweater was there. One may consider two other

We wish to thank Michele Piccione and Drazen Prelec for comments and conversations. We are very grateful to Juan Carrillo for many specific comments. Israel Science Foundation grant no. 10110751 is gratefully acknowledged.

scenarios that might distinguish between the two explanations: first, Mrs. S may buy the sweater as a gift for Mr. S with no special occasion or special reason in mind. Second, Mr. S might consider buying the sweater himself for his own birthday.

The mental accounting theory suggests that control over and responsibility for choice are not the only reasons that money may differ from money. Thus, Mr. S may still feel uncomfortable with the sweater if it was bought by his wife without the birthday excuse, and may also feel that it is appropriate for him to indulge himself on the occasion of his birthday and buy the sweater himself. In both situations, Mr. S may say to himself, 'Well, I couldn't possibly walk into a store and grab whatever I like whenever I like it, but I can afford to spend a bit more once a year.' That is, according to this particular explanation, Mr. S's assessment of his choice does not depend only on the outcome of the present decision problem, but also on the hypothetical outcome of following the same mode of decision-making in many decision problems to come. It is as if Mr. S overgeneralizes his decision. Rather than asking himself 'Is it OK for me to buy this sweater', he asks, 'Is it OK for me *always* to buy things like that?' Obviously, 'things like that' is a very vague term. Indeed, propositions can normally be generalized in many different ways. The proposition 'Today Mr. S is buying a $125 cashmere sweater' may be generalized to 'Mr. S always buys $125 cashmere sweaters', to 'Every Monday Mr. S buys expensive clothes', or to 'Mr. S always buys whatever he fancies'. Which generalization should Mr. S use in assessing the current decision? One would expect that the details of the purchase decision will suggest what is the most natural generalization. Specifically, if Mr. S has no special reason for buying the sweater on this day, a rather sweeping generalization suggests itself. By contrast, if the sweater is a birthday gift, it is quite natural to think about a future in which 'Every year Mr. S spends $125 on a birthday gift'. Clearly, the second generalization is financially much less problematic than the first. Correspondingly, the prospect of spending $125 once a year on a birthday present is reasonable enough to allow Mr. S to enjoy the sweater. But the prospect of spending $125 every day is rather scary. So scary, that Mr. S would rather decline to purchase the sweater.

Let us assume that people do indeed tend to overgeneralize and to evaluate choices as if these choices are bound to be repeated in similar situations in the future. Based on this premise, one may explain several examples of mental accounting. Consider the following.

Example 2 (Thaler, 1980)   A family pays $40 for tickets to a basketball game to be played 60 miles from their home. On the day of the game there is a snowstorm. They decide to go anyway, but note in passing that had the tickets been given to them, they would have stayed home.

Why would this family insist on using tickets they have bought but allow themselves to forego the game in case the tickets were given as a gift? Assuming that they judge decisions based on the assumption of recurrence, the two situations turn out to be rather different. In one situation the generalization is 'We always/ often buy tickets we do not use' whereas in the other—'We always/often do not get to use tickets we have been given.' The first generalization is financially ominous. There is no bound on the sum of money one might lose if one were to buy tickets without using them. By contrast, one normally would not go bankrupt simply by failing to make the best use of gifts.

Example 3 (Thaler, 1985)   Mr. and Mrs. L and Mr. and Mrs. H went on a fishing trip in the northwest and caught some salmon. They packed the fish and sent it home on an airplane, but the fish were lost in transit. They received $300 from the airline. The couples take the money, go out to dinner and spend $225. They had never spent that much at a restaurant before.

Again, one possible explanation of this behavior is that the couples judge the choices available to them under the assumption that they will be repeated in the future. Spending $225 at a restaurant without the fish story suggests generalizations of the type 'We spend large amounts of money out of our income when we feel like it.' By contrast, spending the same amount in the story above generalizes more naturally to 'We spend windfall gains on luxurious items.' Whereas the former generalization hints at financial ruin, the latter bodes no ill. Hence, the $225 meal can be enjoyed in the story above, while the same meal without the fish story would taint pleasure with concern for the future.

Observe that in the example above the couples spend the money on a meal, rather than on some other luxurious consumption. Namely, they do not only have a mental account for 'easy come, easy go' money, but they seem to have an account dealing more specifically with food or with their lost salmon. The linkage between the source of the money (compensation for the lost salmon) and its use (a good meal) is reflected in the generalizations that are likely to be generated. If, for instance, the couples were to buy an expensive coat with the money they received from the airline, the effect of the mental account might have been diminished. This may be due to the fact that spending the airline money on a coat might be generalized to 'Spending money (that came from a generic source)' more easily than in the present example.

Undoubtedly, there are other explanations for these examples of mental accounting. Some involve self-discipline (see Thaler, 1980), while others have to do with self-signaling (Prelec and Bodner, 2002). In Section 4 we discuss the relationship between our explanation and these. We also comment on the optimality of decisions governed by mental accounting of the type discussed here. We first turn to discuss over-generalizations, to what extent they can be rationalized, and why they may be a prevalent mode of reasoning.

2. THE CATEGORICAL IMPERATIVE FOR MULTI-SELVES

The notion that people make single decisions as if they were to commit to the same decision over and over again in future decision problems may seem odd at first glance. Why would people overgeneralize their choices in this way? In this section we argue that this mode of reasoning about choice is not completely foreign to the human mind. The next section argues further that it can also be optimal under certain constraints.

A famous example of over-generalization in reasoning about choice is Kant's categorical imperative. This dictum, namely, that one should behave in a way that one would like everyone to behave, suggests that a decision maker evaluate her choice as if all other relevant decision makers make the same choice. This is an over-generalization because different decision makers are sovereign and independent. There is no causal relationship that would justify the generalization as a descriptive theory of what would actually be the outcome of a given choice. Yet, this is a common mode of reasoning.

One reason for making choices in accordance with the categorical imperative is attaching value to following rules as such. Suppose that Sally has to decide whether or not to pollute the environment. Knowing that her impact on the environment is miniscule, and that other decision makers are independent of her, she knows that others need not follow her decision. Yet, if she finds intrinsic value in behaving in a way that she would like others to behave in, she will make a choice as if she believed that others would follow her choice. This is an *over-generalization* to the extent that Sally knows that it is not supported by a causal relationship. But it may well be Sally's normative criterion for decision-making.

Another reason for over-generalization of choices may be more pragmatic. Consider the celebrated Prisoner's Dilemma (PD) game:

Player II

		C	D
	C	3,3	0,4
Player I	D	4,0	1,1

Whereas D is a dominant strategy for each of the two players, the outcome (D,D) is Pareto dominated by the outcome (C,C). Rational choice dictates that each player know what is and what is not under her control. For instance, since the player II's choice is not under player I's control, and, further, there is no causal relationship between I's choice and that of II's, player I is rightly comparing her payoffs in each column separately, and not along the diagonal.

Indeed, this is the problem exposed by the PD example: in many social situations the structure of the game is similar to the PD game. In these situations, one cannot trust individual optimization to result in a socially desired outcome. Rather, in order to obtain such an outcome, or at least to make it an equilibrium of the game, one has to change the game. One way to do so, and perhaps the most effective one, is to change the payoffs of the players by education, inculcation of guilt, and so forth. Specifically, if all parents in a society condition their children to vividly imagine 'what would happen if everybody behaved this way,' these children will, in essence, compare payoffs along the diagonal and prefer C to D.

Any two such children who play the game will engage in over-generalizations: they will behave *as if* the other followed their example, while in reality both are independent and sovereign decision makers. But, mistaken as they are, they will fare better than will two other children who were not trained to overgeneralize.[1]

It follows that, taking a social-evolutionary approach, one can justify over-generalization as a mode of reasoning about choice in certain situations, such as the PD game. Moreover, casual observation supports the conjecture that people do tend to think in terms of 'What would happen if everyone did the same as I do?' Observe that the over-generalization discussed in Section 1 employs this mode of reasoning, applied to future agents of the *same* decision maker, rather than to different people in a society. For instance, consider Mr. S of Example 1, who wonders whether he should buy the cashmere sweater. Mr. S considers his future decisions, and imagines the 'agent' or 'self' of himself in each of many decision periods in the future. If he considers these agents, or 'selves', as independent and sovereign decision makers, he can go ahead and buy the sweater as if this were a one-shot decision with no further repercussions. But if he imagines that all future selves will behave as he does, he performs an over-generalization that is very similar to following the categorical imperative, and he may consequently decide to forego the luring purchase.

The over-generalization of choice across individuals, as suggested by the categorical imperative, may seem less justifiable than the same over-generalization in the case of multi-selves of a single individual. First, one often tends to believe that different selves of the same individual will have a larger degree of affinity than will different individuals in a society. Selves that occupy the same mind may know more about each other and also care more about each other than do individuals who belong to the same society. Second, different selves of a single individual are called upon to act in a sequential manner, where they can, in principle, know the choices of past agents. Hence, future selves can, though they are by no means compelled to, decide to follow the example of earlier selves. By contrast, individuals in a society may often play a simultaneous move game (as the PD above), in which they do not have the information required to adopt such a strategy.

Naturally, the over-generalization employed by the categorical imperative is inherently ambiguous. For instance, the proposition 'John sits on his lawn on Sunday' may be generalized to 'Everyone sits on their lawn on Sunday', to 'Everyone sits on John's lawn on Sunday', to 'John sits on his lawn every day', and so forth. John may find the first generalization rather nice, the second—a physical nightmare, whereas the third—physically possible and even pleasurable but morally reproachable. Should John then sit on his lawn on Sunday? The answer depends on the type of generalization that John finds the most salient or compelling. By a similar token, the examples we discussed in Section 1 involve over-generalizations that are not uniquely defined. Our point is, precisely, that

---

[1] To the extent that parents identify with their own children, the decision whether or not to train one's child to overgeneralize generated a PD-like game among the parents. Each parent would prefer that her child would not overgeneralize, irrespective of the others. But all parents will be better off if they all train their children to overgeneralize than if they all train their children not to.

different contexts give rise to different rankings of generalizations in terms of their salience. Thus, we attempt to explain certain phenomena of mental accounting by the categorical imperative applied to multi-selves, in conjunction with the ambiguity of generalizations.

3.   ABSENT-MINDEDNESS IN GAME THEORY

Despite the similarity of over-generalizations in cases of mental accounting to those dictated by the categorical imperative, the question remains, why would people make these over-generalizations? After all, unless one takes a normative view that adopts the categorical imperative axiomatically, it remains erroneous reasoning. Why would people constantly engage in such an irrational mode of decision-making?

We suggest here that, should memory fail to be perfect, one may find that over-generalization is part of a procedure yielding optimal decisions. To see this, consider the example of the absentminded driver of Piccione and Rubinstein (1997a).[2] A driver is on a highway. She needs to take the second exit to get to her destination, which would result in a payoff of 1. Taking the first exit yields a payoff of zero, whereas staying on the highway past the second exit yields a payoff of -1.[3] This is a very simple choice problem. There is one twist, however: when the driver gets to the second exit, she will not remember that she has already gone past one exit. That is, she has an imperfect memory. The game may be described by the tree:

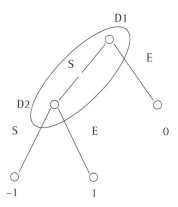

In this game there is a single player, who first moves in decision node D1 and then in decision node D2. In both nodes, she can either exit (E) or stay (S). The payoff is 1 if and only if she exits at node D2.

---

[2] Piccione and Rubinstein (1997a) present the example as a paradox. Several articles and comments in the same volume comment on the example and offer resolutions of the paradox. See Aumann et al. (1997a,b), Battigali (1997), Gilboa (1997), Grove and Halpern (1997), Halpern (1997), Lipman (1997), and Piccione and Rubinstein (1997b).

[3] The payoffs used here are slightly different from those in the original example of Piccione and Rubinstein.

However, when the driver is at D1 and when she is at D2 she only knows that she is either at D1 or at D2. This fact is reflected in that D1 and D2 belong to the same information set (denoted by the ellipse). It implies that the driver cannot choose a strategy that assigns a different move to the two nodes, since she knows in advance that she will not know which node she will be at.

Let us restrict attention to pure strategies.[4] The optimal strategy, namely to play S at D1 and then to play E at D2, is not feasible at all, as it selects different moves at D1 and at D2. One pure strategy is to select E at both nodes, which results in leaving at the first exit with a payoff of 0. The second pure strategy is to select S at both nodes, which results in a payoff of − 1. Thus, knowing that it is impossible to choose the second exit, the driver will choose to exit immediately.

Consider now the following example. John likes expensive wine, but he cannot afford to have it everyday. It would be optimal for him to buy a $30 bottle four times a month, and to buy a $10 bottle on the other days. But John is aware of his own limitations. Despite the fact that he can normally count up to three, he knows that he will not always be able to remember how many times he has bought an expensive bottle that month. He can easily implement a simple rule that says, 'Buy a $30 bottle' or one that says, 'Buy a $10 bottle'. But implementing a rule such as, 'Buy a $30 bottle if you haven't already bought such bottles four times this month, and otherwise buy a $10 bottle' requires a better memory than John's. Knowing this, John decides always to buy a $10 bottle.

Thus, when John selects a strategy for all his future selves, that is, when he chooses a rule, he is in a similar situation to the absent-minded driver above. He knows that any decision he makes at the current node may be repeated in all future nodes, and that he cannot signal to his future selves what is his current choice. If he were to choose instructions for his future selves, these instructions would have to be identical for the different selves. Under this constraint, it is optimal for John to always buy inexpensive wine (exit immediately) than to always buy expensive wine (stay throughout).

We have, thus, established that over-generalization is related to the ex-ante optimal strategy, given the constraint of imperfect memory. This simply follows from the assumption that memory does not allow the decision maker to give each future self a possibly different instruction. But it is still not clear that the ex-ante optimal strategy will indeed be followed. When John walks into the store on a particular day, he knows that he can afford the more expensive bottle *just this once*, and actually even four times each month. What, then, would prevent him from disobeying his own rule?

Indeed, the same question is raised by Piccione and Rubinstein (1997*a*) regarding the absent-minded driver when she is at a decision node.[5] Gilboa (1997)

---

[4] Piccione and Rubinstein (1997*a*) observe that, in a game of this type, a mixed strategy may yield a higher payoff than any of the pure strategies in its support.

[5] The paradox that Piccione and Rubinstein discuss, stems from the conflict between the notion of ex-ante optimality, and the interim calculations that the player will conduct while she is playing the game, and taking her strategy as given.

argues that the problem should be analyzed as a game among the agents of the driver, and that the problem bears some resemblance to the PD. Specifically, each agent has an incentive to disobey the rule, assuming the other agents obey it; but all agents are better off if they all obey the rule than if they all disobey it. Similarly, John will be better off if his future agents follow the categorical imperative than if they do not, just as a society may be better off if all its agents follow Kant's dictum than if they do not. Thus, behaving as if decisions will be repeated is an optimal strategy ex-ante. But, should each agent make her own choice optimally, this strategy need not be followed. Differently put, for future agents to follow this strategy, they need to exercise some degree of self-discipline.

4. SELF-DISCIPLINE, OPTIMALITY, AND SELF-SIGNALING

Self-discipline. We concluded that some notion of self-discipline is required in order to implement the ex-ante optimal strategy in the game of Section 3. It is, therefore, natural to ask, does one need the assumption of imperfect recall? Can we not explain why John buys only $10 bottles by self-discipline alone?

Indeed, one may try to suggest such an explanation. If John had unlimited self-discipline and infallible memory, he could choose four days a month on which to buy a more expensive wine, and follow this strategy with no difficulty. Why doesn't he? One explanation that relies solely on self-discipline would suggest that John can resist the temptation to buy a $30 bottle, but only as long as he hasn't started consuming such bottles. Once he has relished a few, he will not be able to resist buying more. That is, such an explanation would be along the lines of addiction: the expensive bottle can be resisted only before it has been consumed.

The addiction explanation seems counterintuitive in this example. John has probably enjoyed $30 wine bottles in the past. It seems more likely that John cannot restrict himself to four expensive bottles a month because his memory does not provide the technology to implement such a strategy, rather than that he will become addicted to expensive wine.[6]

Self-signaling. Some of the phenomena we discuss are closely related to issues of self-signaling as well (see Ainslie, 1992; Prelec and Bodner, 2002). For instance, the family that drives to the ball game may wish to prove to themselves that they are not the kind of people who spend money on products they do not need. Mr. S may also feel that walking into a store and buying an expensive sweater is not the kind of thing that he does. He may be upset to find out that he, too, and not only his teenage daughter, is a buying type.

Observe that self-signaling explanations also assume generalizations. Specifically, in a self-signaling model one observes one's actions and infers from them what is one's type. But the very notion of a 'type' presupposes that there are people who *generally* are prone to certain types of behavior. A model that employs types may provide another rationale for over-generalizations: the choice

---

[6] There are, however, other ways in which self-restraint can be explained. See, for instance, Asheim (1997), Caillaud et al. (1999), and Carrillo (2000).

in a given problem provides information regarding the decision maker's type, which, in turn, changes the probability of future actions, typically increasing the probability of repeating the same choices. However, in some of the examples above, self-signaling does not seem to be the most intuitive explanation. For instance, John knows that he prefers expensive to inexpensive wine. He chooses to restrain his consumption due to financial constraints alone, not in order to avoid certain realizations about himself.

Optimality. John's optimal strategy in the game of Section 3 is optimal ex-ante, but it does not induce an optimal choice for each agent of John's. But some of the mental accounting phenomena discussed here can be viewed as optimal strategies (for the player) that also induce optimal choices for each agent, despite memory limitations. For instance, if John decides to have an expensive bottle once over each weekend, he might be viewed as using the calendar as a memory aid for his wine consumption. He will end up choosing the optimal strategy without a memory constraint: he will buy expensive bottles precisely four times a month. Moreover, none of his agents will have an incentive to deviate from this strategy, as it is globally optimal. Similarly, Mr. S of Example 1 may like to buy a luxurious item only once a year. Choosing to do so on his birthday guarantees that he will not exceed this pre-assigned limit, without having to ask himself every day whether or not he has already bought a luxurious item this year. (Of course, he will have to ask himself every day whether it is his birthday.)

In the absence of sufficient memory aids, however, the optimal strategy under the memory constraint will, in general, be sub-optimal. For instance, Mr. S may be able to afford two cashmere sweaters a year. Due to imperfect memory he has to restrict himself to one sweater on his birthday, and to forego the second because he has no way to remember how many sweaters he bought himself as non-birthday presents. The sunk cost effects that make the family of Example 2 drive through a snowstorm to see a game do not lead to an optimal choice, even though they aid in the implementation of an ex-ante optimal strategy. Finally, John might wish to consume an expensive bottle of wine precisely once a week, but not necessarily on a weekend, or not even on a given day of the week. In this case, consuming an expensive bottle on the weekend is still a sub-optimal strategy.[7]

To conclude, imperfect memory may make the optimal choice of a player sub-optimal for some of her future agents. Mental accounting may be a way to implement the ex-ante optimal strategy. Moreover, when mental accounting is sophisticated enough to employ memory aids, it can help implement a strategy that is optimal for a player with perfect memory.

5. SUMMARY

Certain types of phenomena that fall under the broad category of mental accounting can be explained, based on the premise that decision makers evaluate

---

[7] This point is due to Juan Carrillo.

specific acts as if they were chosen not only once but repeatedly for a sequence of problems. This is a type of over-generalization that is reminiscent of the categorical imperative. Indeed, it is formally equivalent to it when one considers the society of selves, or the future agents of an individual. Moreover, if we assume that memory is imperfect, it turns out that not all strategies are implementable. Only those that are generalized enough may be considered, ex-ante, by an individual.

REFERENCES

Ainslie, G. (1992). *Picoeconomics: The strategic interaction of successive motivational states within the person.* Cambridge: Cambridge University Press.

Asheim, G. (1997). Individual and collective time-consistency. *Review of Economics Studies, 64*, 427–43.

Aumann, R.J., Hart, S., and Perry, M. (1997a). The absent-minded driver. *Games and Economic Behavior, 20*, 102–16.

—— —— and —— (1997b). The forgetful passenger. *Games and Economic Behavior, 20*, 117–20.

Battigali, P. (1997). Dynamic consistency and imperfect recall. *Games and Economic Behavior, 20*, 31–50.

Caillaud, B., Cohen, D., and Jullien, B. (1999). *Towards a theory of self-restraint*, mimeo.

Carrillo, J.D. (2000). *Self-control, moderate consumption, and craving*, mimeo.

Gilboa, I. (1997). A comment on the absent-minded driver paradox. *Games and Economic Behavior, 20*, 25–30.

Grove, A. and Halpern, J. (1997). On the expected value of games with absent-mindedness. *Games and Economic Behavior, 20*, 51–95.

Halpern, J. (1997). On ambiguities in the interpretation of game trees. *Games and Economic Behavior, 20*, 66–96.

Kahneman, D. and Tversky, A. (1979). Prospect theory: An analysis of decision under risk. *Econometrica, 47*, 263–91.

—— and —— (1984). Choices, values, and frames. *American Psychologist, 39*, 341–50.

Lipman, B. (1997). More absent-mindedness. *Games and Economic Behavior, 20*, 97–101.

Piccione, M. and Rubinstein, A. (1997a), On the interpretation of decision problems with imperfect recall. *Games and Economic Behavior, 20*, 3–24.

—— and —— (1997b). The absent-minded driver paradox: Synthesis and responses. *Games and Economic Behavior, 20*, 121–30.

Prelec, D. and Bodner, O. (2002). Self-signaling and diagnostic utility in everyday decision-making. In I. Brocas and J.D. Carrillo (Eds.), *The psychology of economic decisions*. Oxford: Oxford University Press.

Thaler, R. H. (1980). Toward a positive theory of consumer choice. *Journal of Economic Behavior and Organization, 1*, 39–60.

—— (1985). Mental accounting and consumer choice. *Marketing Science, 4*, 199–214.

Tversky, A. and Kahneman, D. (1981). The framing of decisions and the psychology of choice. *Science, 211*, 453–8.

8

Self-Knowledge and Self-Regulation: An Economic Approach

ROLAND BÉNABOU AND JEAN TIROLE

1. INTRODUCTION

In forecasting how *Homo Economicus* would evolve into *Homo Sapiens*, Thaler (2000) predicted that he would gradually 'begin losing IQ', but warned at the same time against simply 'making [him] dumber'. He recommended instead that economists pay closer attention to the actual processes of human cognition, which psychologists have shown to be subject to a number of specific imperfections and biases.

The research summarized in this chapter can be seen in the light of this overall agenda. Focusing on the links between self-judgment and self-regulation, our approach has been to develop an analytical framework with three main objectives: (i) to unify a number of findings from separate areas of psychology into a parsimonious model of cognition and motivation; (ii) to draw out their economic implications; (iii) conversely, to derive from the theory potential explanations for the lack of consensus among psychologists on certain empirical and policy-relevant questions, and suggest alternative experimental directions.

2. ENRICHING THE PSYCHOLOGICAL MAKEUP OF *HOMO ECONOMICUS*

We introduce three 'grains of sand' (or humanity) into the well-oiled mechanics of the ultra-rational economic agent: *imperfect self-knowledge, imperfect will-power*, and *imperfect recall*.

Incorporating these three ingredients—sometimes even only a subset of them—yields a surprisingly richer account of human behavior than that of the traditional *Homo Economicus*. We are first able to give a formal content to individual *traits* such as self-confidence, intrinsic motivation, dependence or autonomy, and power of will, as well as to cognitive *processes* such as wishful thinking or selective memory, self-monitoring, and the setting of personal rules (diets,

We are grateful for helpful comments to George Ainslie, Isabelle Brocas, and Danny Kahneman.

moral precepts, etc.). The resulting framework allows us to address the following array of questions. Why do individuals value self-confidence, both for themselves and for others towards whom they are not necessarily altruistic? At the same time, why do they sometimes sabotage their own performance, or deprecate their own accomplishments? Is it possible for a rational, Bayesian individual to deceive himself and hold self-serving beliefs? And if so, is such 'positive thinking' ultimately beneficial or harmful? How can we simultaneously account for undersaving and miserliness, procrastination and workaholism, overeating and anorexia? Why do extrinsic rewards (incentives) work well in some contexts, but appear counterproductive in others? Why do agents sometimes undermine the ego and self-confidence of others on whose effort and motivation they depend?

2.1. Imperfect Self-Knowledge

The agents who usually populate economic models have little doubt about 'who they are': they know their own abilities and basic preferences. Information economics is thus primarily concerned with how individuals can *signal to others* (e.g., employers, competitors, tax authorities), these privately known characteristics, or on the contrary attempt to keep them hidden.[1] Psychology, by contrast, gives a central role to the process of learning about oneself and to individuals' struggle with their own identity: self-esteem, depression, pride, guilt, and self-justification are but a few examples of introspective phenomena. The starting point for our research agenda is therefore the recognition of the fact that people face significant uncertainty about their own abilities and even preferences. That is, they do not know the ultimate costs and payoffs from their actions, and may not even be sure of what actions they would take in a given situation until the very moment when they actually experience it.

Thus, in Bénabou and Tirole (2002) an individual must decide whether or not to engage (or persevere) in a task that involves sure short-run costs but whose long-run payoff depends on his imperfectly known ability. Typically, the project will be undertaken only if the agent has sufficient self-confidence in his talent, or suitability for the task. In Bénabou and Tirole (2000), the individual is faced with a choice between a course of action that requires no self-restraint (e.g., slack off, drink, or smoke as he pleases), and a challenging one where his capacity to resist stress or temptation and hold out for larger, long-run payoffs, will be put to the test (taking on an ambitious project, attempting to quit smoking, going on a diet, etc.). The ability parameter on which uncertainty now bears is the degree to which his preferences may be subject, in certain circumstances, to a bias towards instant gratification.

---

[1] There are of course some exceptions: see, e.g., Holmström (1999) on workers who learn their abilities over time, Akerlof and Kranton (2000) on the economics of (socially constructed) 'identity', or Bodner and Prelec (2002, Chapter 6, this volume) on self-diagnostic in a 'planner–doer' context.

2.2. Imperfect Willpower

Because Economic Man always acts according to his own best interests (given the available information), there is no word in his vocabulary for anything like 'self-destructive' behavior, nor any meaning for statements such as 'I couldn't help myself'. By contrast, a major part of psychology has long been devoted to understanding—and helping alleviate—behaviors characterized by strong internal conflicts, harmful impulses to which the individual succumbs 'against his better judgement', or self-deceptions and self-punishments of varying degrees of severity (see Baumeister, 2002, Chapter 1, this volume). Furthermore, experimental psychologists have documented a robust feature of human time-preferences that commonly gives rise to self-control problems, namely people's tendency to discount payoffs much more steeply at long than at short horizons (hyperbolic-like discounting). In recent years, there has been growing recognition by economists of the relevance and explanatory power of such 'momentary' preferences that, by creating a conflict of interest between the individual's successive temporal selves, lead to ex-ante suboptimal behavior (preference reversal) and create a value of commitment.[2,3]

In Bénabou and Tirole (2000), we expand on the now standard quasi-hyperbolic specification by allowing the degree of present bias (or weakness of will) to be *state-dependent* and *imperfectly known*. Indeed, when deciding whether to go on a diet, embark on an ambitious project (intellectual, entrepreneurial, athletic, etc.), or invest himself in a personal relationship, a key source of uncertainty for the individual is whether he 'has it in him' to persevere once the going gets tough. If he is pessimistic as to the likelihood of his eventually caving in to temptation, he will ask himself 'what is the point?', and decide that he might as well start indulging himself right away rather than waste effort on a doomed attempt at self-restraint. Thus, once again, the individual's initial self-view is an essential determinant of his behavior. Moreover, because past conduct is a key source of information on one's own willpower, this unknown-preferences feature of the model allows us to capture and better understand the critical role of *self-monitoring* in regulating behavior, as well as the costs and benefits of finding *excuses* for oneself.

One may ask why, if temptation is recurrent, the individual cannot simply and directly recall the preferences (cravings, pain, exhaustion, etc.) that he previously

---

[2] See Ainslie (1992) and references therein for the evidence; Strotz (1956), Phelps and Pollack (1968), Laibson (1997) and O'Donoghue and Rabin (1999) for formal models and economic implications. Closest to our approach is the work of Carrillo and Mariotti (2000) and Brocas and Carrillo (1999), which we discuss in Section 3.1.

[3] There are alternative ways of representing intra-personal conflict, such as positing multiple contemporaneous selves (Id, Ego, and Superego, as in Freudian theory; 'Planner and Doer,' as in Thaler and Shefrin (1981); and Bodner and Prelec (2002, Chapter 6, this volume); or preferences characterized by the interplay of a 'decision utility' and a 'temptation utility', as in Gul and Pesendorfer (2001). We adopt (quasi) hyperbolic discounting because of its experimental validation, and because it is the simplest way to parametrize the key concept of *willpower*.

experienced, rather than having to infer them from past behavior and situational factors. The answer relates to the third cognitive 'imperfection' from which our simple model of Homo Sapiens suffers, compared to his Economicus cousin.

2.3. Imperfect Recall and Motivated Cognition

Standard economic agents may have only limited information, but (with a few notable exceptions) what is known or learned is never forgotten nor distorted in their later recollections.[4] In reality, memory is imperfect, attention is limited, and awareness can therefore only be selective. Of particular relevance for our purpose are the following two types of phenomena.

First, a lot of research (not to mention daily observation) has documented the fact that people's recollections of their past actions and performances are often *self-serving:* they tend to remember (be consciously aware of) their successes more than their failures, reframe their actions so as to see themselves as instrumental for good but not bad outcomes, and find ways of absolving themselves by attributing responsibility to others.[5] As explained in Section 3.2, such *motivated cognition* and its compatibility with rational inference represents a main focus of our analysis.

Second, it appears difficult for individuals to accurately recall from 'cold' introspection the intensity of stress, temptation, or other short-run feelings corresponding to 'hot' (visceral, emotional, not easily quantifiable) internal states that they experienced in the past. For instance, Kahneman et al.'s experiments (1997) on the recall of pain and discomfort, document a systematic divergence between what they term *experienced utility* and *decision utility.*[6] Such 'hot–cold empathy gaps', in the terminology of Loewenstein (1996), also arise in recollections and predictions about feelings such as hunger, exhaustion, drug or alcohol craving, or sexual arousal.[7] Just as people cannot accurately answer retrospective questions such as 'how much did it hurt?' or 'how much did you dislike that?', we think that asking oneself 'how much did I crave that cigarette, or that new dress yesterday?' or 'how cold and stiff was I when I went jogging last week?' is unlikely to be very informative, compared to asking *what one actually chose to do*—a 'revealed preference' approach familiar to economists.

There are, of course, steps that people can take to ensure that they do not forget a piece of data (feelings, actions, circumstances, or outcomes). They can keep written records, rehearse the information, share it with others who will remind

---

[4] For models with imperfect recall see Piccione and Rubinstein (2000) and Mullainathan (2002).

[5] On self-serving memory, see Korner (1950), Crary (1996), Mischel et al. (1976), Kunda and Sanitioso (1989), or Murray and Holmes (1994). On self-serving attributions, see Zuckerman (1979) and Snyder et al. (1983).

[6] The first is measured from the subject's moment-by-moment reports during a painful medical procedure or unpleasant laboratory experiment, while the latter correspond to his or her *retrospective evaluation* of the experience as a whole, and constitutes the informational basis for later decisions. See also Kahneman (2001), this volume.

[7] See Loewenstein and Schkade (1999) for a discussion and survey of the empirical evidence.

them of it, or surround themselves with cues that will trigger the relevant memory. These, however, are *decisions* that the individual may or may not choose to make. Furthermore, the very same strategies can be used to impede or offset the later recollection of unwanted news. There are also ways of interfering with the encoding of such data into memory and their later retrieval, ranging from distracting one's attention, to getting drunk, 'to forget'. The natural limitations of attention and decay of memory therefore give the individual some *discretion* about what data is more likely to still be present, later on, on the 'computer screen' of conscious awareness.

In line with these ideas and evidence, our model allows for differential rates of recall or accessibility for ego-favorable and ego-unfavorable informations, with the degree of selectivity (relative probability that bad news is forgotten) being either a fixed behavioral parameter, or the endogenous outcome of a (conscious or instinctive) cognitive process over which the individual yields some influence, and in which the benefits of self-esteem enhancement are weighed against the risks of overconfidence. We also allow different types of information to be subject to various degrees to this differential recall. Past internal states (sensations and feelings, i.e., 'experienced utility'), being the most 'soft' and least verifiable type of information, lead to the most unreliable and manipulable types of memories. External outcomes and circumstances can also be forgotten but less easily so, in the sense that speeding up the forgetting process or building up plausible excuses involves higher costs (destruction of evidence, active cue-management, selective interpersonal interactions, or even substance abuse—drinking to forget). Finally, memories of one's own past actions (especially significant ones) may be the most lasting and reliable, in particular, because they tend to leave more material 'tracks'. These memories also eventually decay, and can be repressed to some extent, but the process is slower and less easily manipulable.

2.4. Rationality

Is our 'psychologically enriched' individual, with his imperfect self-knowledge, lack of willpower, and selective recall, still rational? The label in itself is unimportant, but the fact that he retains a rather high level of IQ (cognitive and decision-making sophistication) should be emphasized.[8]

First, we maintain intertemporal utility maximization: at any point in time, the agent tries to do what is best for 'himself', given his current (often inaccurate) perceptions of his own interests and abilities. As usual, this optimizing behavior may be interpreted as a good first approximation to what instinct, education, or learning will ultimately produce. At the same time, we shall see that even this sophistication does not preclude the agent finding himself in harmful 'self-traps' (inferior personal equilibria).

[8] In a sense, we are still abstracting from a fourth 'grain of sand' (much harder to model than the other ones), which corresponds to a limited ability to assess probabilities and make the prospective calculations required to arrive at truly optimal decisions. See, e.g., Gabaix and Laibson (2000).

Second, we do not treat the individual as being naive about the systematic incentives to distort his information which he or other people might have. If a principal has a vested interest in an agent's accomplishing a task, the agent will not naively take all encouragements, assurances of success, and promises of rewards at face value, but is likely to infer from them some information about the nature of the task, or the principal's view of the agent's likelihood of success in the absence of such extrinsic motivators. Similarly, if a person consistently represses or manages not to think about negative news, he or she will likely become aware of this systematic tendency, and realize that the absence of adverse evidence or recollections should not be taken at face value. Formally, this skepticism with respect to others' messages and one's own memories or rationalizations (metacognition) is represented by Bayes' rule. Less sophisticated inference processes lead to similar results, as long as they are not too naive with respect to one's and other people's motives.

In summary, it could be said that in our model each temporal 'self' is both optimizing and Bayesian, yet, the whole intertemporal collection of such selves that describes the individual is neither, since his behavior is time-inconsistent and his cognition clouded by self-deception.[9]

3. SELF-CONFIDENCE AND INDIVIDUAL MOTIVATION

3.1. Why is Self-Confidence Valuable?

In most societies, self-confidence is widely regarded as a valuable individual asset.[10] Going back at least to William James (1890), an important strand in psychology has advocated 'believing in oneself' as a key to personal success. Today, an enormous 'self-help' industry flourishes, a sizeable part of which purports to help people improve their self-esteem, shed 'learned helplessness' and reap the benefits of 'learned optimism'.[11] American schools place such a strong emphasis on imparting children with self-confidence ('doing a great job!') that they are often criticized for giving it preeminence over the transmission of actual knowledge. Hence the general question: why is a positive view of oneself, as opposed to a fully accurate one, seen as such a good thing to have?

A first reason may be that thinking of oneself favorably just makes a person happier: self-image is, then, simply an additional argument in the utility function.[12] Indeed, psychologists emphasize the affective benefits of self-esteem as well as

---

[9] For psychologists, it may also be worth pointing out that our model is 'homunculus-free': at any point in time there is only one set of preferences and information that governs the individual's actions (as opposed to, say a conflicting Ego and Superego, Planner and Doer, etc.).

[10] Whether its open display or a more modest, even humble outward attitude, is considered socially appropriate is a rather different question, which varies much more across countries.

[11] These last two terms are borrowed from Seligman (1975, 1990).

[12] Following in the path of Akerlof and Dickens' (1982) celebrated model of dissonnance reduction, a number of recent papers such as Rabin (1995), Weinberg (1999), and Köszegi (1999) have also introduced self-beliefs as arguments of individual preferences.

the motivational ones on which we focus, and one might argue that such a 'consumption value' of beliefs could have arisen from a more functional (adaptive) mechanism, selected into preferences through evolution or education.[13] To fully operationalize the affective benefits approach, however, would require either an explicit model of preference selection, or empirical evidence imposing structure on the utility-from-beliefs. First, one needs to circumscribe the set of self-images that individuals care about, as there is a potential embarrassment of riches: they may want to perceive themselves as honest and compassionate individuals, good citizens, faithful spouses... or, on the contrary, pride themselves on being ruthless businessmen, ultra-rational economists, irresistible seducers, etc. Second, one would need to pin down the monotonicity and risk-attitude properties of the utility over beliefs. Whether the individual has a tendency towards blissful optimism or 'defensive pessimism' (see Section 3.4.2) will hinge on whether this function is increasing or decreasing; whether he is information-averse or information-loving will turn crucially on whether it is concave or convex.[14]

Another limitation of a purely affective theory of self-confidence is that it does not readily extend to *social and economic interactions*, where people clearly seek out optimistic, self-confident partners, rather than depressed, self-doubting ones, and spend substantial time and effort supporting the morale of those they end up matched with. If self-esteem just increases people's utility, something else must account for why we like not just ourselves and our family members to be self-confident, but also our coworkers, managers, employees, teammates, soldiers, and numerous others with whom we have only functional, non-altruistic interactions.

By contrast, the motivation-based theory, which we develop, offers a unified explanation of why (and when) self-confidence is valuable for ourselves *and* for others with whom we interact. The basic idea is that since a more optimistic view of his own abilities generally enhances an individual's expected return from effort, anyone with a vested interest in his performance has an incentive to build up and protect this self-esteem. This occurs in two classes of situations, corresponding respectively to *externalities* and '*internalities*' from the agent's effort.[15] First, the manipulator could be another person (parent, teacher, spouse, friend, colleague, boss, or relation) who would benefit from the agent's performance; such *interpersonal* issues are studied in Bénabou and Tirole (2001), and will be briefly discussed in Section 5. Second, as pointed out in Carrillo and Mariotti's (2000) seminal paper, an individual suffering from time inconsistency often has incentives to restrict his own information, as a way of indirectly controlling the

---

[13] For instance, the overconfidence that often results from such preferences may propel an individual to undertake activities (exploration, foraging, combat) that are more risky than warranted by their private material returns, but nonetheless evolutionarily successful because they confer important external benefits on the species.

[14] See Caplin and Leahy (2001) for a study of attitudes towards information and the resolution of uncertainty for a general class of preferences where beliefs over future lotteries enter into the intertemporal utility function.

[15] The term 'internalities' is due to Herrnstein et al. (1993).

behavior of his future selves. Building on this idea, we model in Bénabou and Tirole (2002) the following 'canonical' problem of *self-motivation.*[16]

An individual would like, ex-ante, to pursue a certain desirable project (professional, intellectual, athletic, health-related, etc.). However, he realizes that, due to his bias towards immediate gratification, he is too likely to give up along the way, thereby sacrificing significant expected long-run benefits for short-run relief from the effort costs of completing the task. That is, while he may not know in advance the effort cost that his future 'self' will face, he knows that the range of cost realizations for which the task will be abandoned is suboptimally large from a long-run point of view. At the same time, his sustained motivation for such endeavors will naturally depend on his assessment of his chances of success, or more generally of the costs and benefits he is likely to incur or reap from their pursuit. As a result, the individual's current 'self' has a vested interest in maintaining and enhancing the self-confidence of future selves, so as to counter their natural tendency to procrastinate or give up too easily. Imperfect self-knowledge and willpower thus combine to generate an endogenous, instrumental value of self-confidence. We discuss below a first round of implications involving a priori attitudes towards information, then turn to the issue of self-deception (ex-post belief manipulation) and present the main results obtained from the interaction of these two building blocks of our theory.

3.1.1. *Receptivity to Information*

As it counterbalances the deleterious effect of present-orientation on his motivation for effort, self-confidence is a valuable asset for the individual. Consequently, he may prefer to remain blissfully ignorant of his true abilities and past achievements than to endanger it, even when accurate information is freely available. This is of course a direct application of the general 'strategic ignorance' principle for time-inconsistent agents in Carrillo and Mariotti (2000). Conversely, someone with a very low initial self esteem will be desperate for good news that might lift him out of the 'procrastination trap', and his choices of tasks and social interactions will have the nature of '*gambles for resurrection*' of his self-esteem.

3.1.2. *Self-Handicapping*

It is not uncommon for people to sabotage their own performance—a behavior that, on its face, appears inconsistent with the rational pursuit of self-interest.[17] In experiments, subjects with a high but fragile self-confidence choose to take performance-impairing drugs before an intelligence test. In daily life, people withhold effort, prepare themselves inadequately (e.g., getting drunk or not sleeping enough the night before an exam), or select overambitious tasks where

---

[16] See also Brocas and Carrillo (1999, 2002, Chapter 5, this volume).

[17] See, Berglas and Jones (1978), Arkin and Baumgardner (1985), Fingarette (1985), or Gilovich (1991).

they are almost sure to fail. Test or performance anxiety is another example of self-handicapping behavior. Psychologists such as Berglas and Baumeister (1993) have suggested that self-handicapping is often a self-esteem maintenance strategy (instinctive or deliberate), directed both at oneself and at others. For economists, our model provides a validation of this insight by showing that it can be quite rational to sacrifice current performance in order to reduce the probability of a large negative inference about one's self. For psychologists, our analysis has implications for experiments on self-esteem maintenance, to which we now turn.

3.1.3. *Implications for Experimental Research*
There has been a significant amount of work examining whether it is high or low self-confidence individuals who are most likely to engage in self-esteem main-tenance strategies such as deliberate ignorance and self-handicapping. Although there seems to be somewhat more evidence in favor of the first hypothesis, our reading is that the sum of these experiments has not yielded any firm conclusion. Our model shows that this ambiguity is in fact to be expected, and suggests instead another variable whose correlation with such behaviors should be tested.

First, subjects' point-estimates of their abilities, whether self-reported or measured by scores on a self-esteem scale, are not sufficient statistics to predict attitudes towards information. Basic intuition makes clear that the extent of uncertainty around this estimate plays a crucial role; a similar point was already noted by Greenier et al. (1995). Furthermore, the analysis reveals that it is not even the variance of one's priors that matters, but a more subtle feature of the distribution (a likelihood ratio property). Such detailed information about how uncertain a person is of his own traits would not be easy to measure experimentally; and even if one could do it, there would remain a major difficulty: the value of information (the amount an agent is willing to sacrifice to obtain or avoid it) is typically not monotonic in his initial self-confidence.[18] Intuitively, those with very negative self-assessments have nothing to lose from information, while those with very positive and secure self-views have nothing to fear from it. For those with moderate and diffuse self-views, on the other hand, information may be dangerous.

Rather than initial self-esteem, the personal trait that the model suggests should be robustly correlated with a subject's propensity to engage in willful ignorance, self-handicapping and the like is their degree of undermotivation, that is, their (self-perceived) bias towards instant gratification. The economic approach to self-regulation—common to our work and that of Carrillo and Mariotti (2000) and Brocas and Carrillo (1999)—thus suggests a link between two hitherto disjoint

---

[18] The one case where a firm conclusion may be drawn is when information is available, or avoidable, at zero or minimal cost. Individuals with a higher self-esteem (in a monotone likelihood ratio sense) are then always the more likely ones to accept a signal about their ability, because they have more at stake in terms of motivation.

areas of experimental psychology, namely those on intertemporal preferences and self-esteem maintenance.

3.2. Can Rational Individuals Deceive Themselves?

Like it or not, in daily life we are subjected to a constant flux of feedback about our performance and abilities, be it from parents, teachers, spouses, coworkers, etc., or simply from observing our own performance and comparing it to that of others. The relevant issue is thus often not whether to seek or avoid information ex-ante (i.e., before knowing what it will turn out to say), but how to cope with the good and especially the bad news that one inevitably receives.

The answer might appear obvious: as Mark Twain succinctly put it, *'Denial aint' just a river in Egypt'*. Indeed psychologists, and before them writers and philosophers, have long documented people's universal tendency to deny, explain away, and selectively forget ego-threatening informations. Freudian repression into the unconscious is the now unfashionable archetype (or perhaps caricature) of such behavior, but various other forms of *motivated cognition* and *self-deception* feature prominently in contemporary psychology.[19]

At the same time, the impossibility of simply choosing the beliefs we like has always stood in the way of a fully consistent theory of self-deception. For instance, Sartre (1953) argued that the individual must simultaneously know and not know the same information. Gur and Sackeim (1979) defined self-deception as a situation in which: (a) the individual holds two contradictory beliefs; (b) he is not aware of holding one of the beliefs; (c) this lack of awareness is motivated.

Our dynamic model allows us to unbundle the 'self that knows' from the 'self that doesn't know', and thereby reconcile the motivation and cognition aspects of self-deception within a standard information-theoretic framework. The basic idea is that the individual can, within limits and at a cost, *affect the probability of remembering* a given piece of information. Under time-inconsistency, there is an incentive to try and remember signals that help sustain his long-run goals, and to forget those that undermine them. This is the motivation part.[20] On the other hand, we maintain the rational inference postulate, so people realize (at least to some extent) that they have a selective memory or attention. This is the cognition part.

To make things more concrete, suppose that the individual wishes to remember good news and forget bad ones. He can linger over praise or positive feedback, rehearse them, and choose to be more frequently in environments or with people who will remind him of his past successes.[21] Conversely, he can eschew

---

[19] See the references cited in Section 2.3. For a general discussion of self deception, see Baumeister (1998).

[20] Alternatively, it could arise from a purely affective value of self-esteem. The awareness-management component of our model could thus also be combined with a utility-for-beliefs approach.

[21] See Rhodewalt (1986) for a discussion of such self-presentation strategies and their link with self-enhancement.

situations and people who remind him of his failures, tear up the picture of a former girlfriend, or work unusually hard to 'forget' (really, not think about) a failed relationship or family problem—even use drugs and alcohol. The individual can also use a wide array of strategies to discount the bad news in the first place (question the motives of the newsbearer, search for contradicting evidence) or impair their accurate encoding and recollection (e.g., create a distraction, such as an emotional outburst that moves the interchange from 'talking to each other' to 'talking past each other').[22]

It is thus important to note at the outset that we need not *literally* assume that the individual can directly and mechanically suppress memories. Our model is equally consistent with a Freudian view where memories get buried in the unconscious (with some probability of reappearance), and with the more recent cognitive psychology view which holds that memory itself cannot be controlled, but emphasizes the different ways in which *awareness* can be affected: the choice of attention when the information accrues, the search for or avoidance of cues and the process of selective rehearsal afterwards, and again the choice of attention at the time the information is (voluntarily or accidentally) retrieved. While the means employed may be very different, the end-result of these two views of motivated belief formation is formally equivalent: the individual has differential rates of recall, or accessibility, depending on how helpful or hurtful the information is to his self-esteem and general efficacy.[23]

3.3. Intrapersonal Equilibrium

Recall the basic predicament of our time-inconsistent individual, whose bias towards immediate gratification means that he will always be too tempted (in a long-run welfare sense) to give up, procrastinate, or altogether shy away from hard tasks with delayed payoffs. As explained earlier, a greater degree of confidence in his likelihood of success if he does persevere, or in the size of the prize that this will yield, will tend to alleviate this underprovision of effort. Conversely, bad news about the expected payoffs from the project will further undermine his motivation.

Suppose the individual has, in fact, just received such bad news. In deciding, consciously or instinctively, whether to try and censor them, he faces a basic tradeoff between preserving the effort motivation of tomorrow's self (gain from confidence-maintenance) and the risk of becoming overconfident, meaning

---

[22] As Gilbert and Cooper (1985) argue, 'social interaction is a fertile context for self-deception because its very complexity often acts as a "smoke screen", keeping the self-deceptive process from becoming obvious'.

[23] It is also worth pointing out that allowing for the *possibility* of selective awareness or memory in the model's assumptions does not prejudge in any way whether (or when) such wishful thinking will actually be used. Our endogenous-memory, Bayesian model is thus very different from one where agents have a fixed, mechanical tendency to optimistically bias their interpretation of all self-relevant signals.

that he will blindly persevere even in circumstances so adverse that it would be (ex-ante) optimal to withdraw. Within the limitations of the available 'technology' of awareness manipulation, and given the costs involved, the individual's current self chooses the probability of recall so as to optimally balance these two effects. Consider next the inference problem faced by tomorrow's self: given that bad news is forgotten with a higher probability than good news, what credence should be given to the fact that only good news can be recalled? Assuming that the individual is not completely naive about his own motives and habits, his self-confidence and decisions will take into account the imperfect reliability of his memories. Conversely, the degree of selectivity chosen at any point in time will depend on how 'skeptical' the individual expects to be in the future. These two problems are interdependent, leading to a *game with private information* between today's and tomorrow's self.

We first highlight some important general features of the set of behaviors that will typically result, then turn in Sections 3.4 and 3.5 to the more specific questions of optimism, pessimism, and the welfare consequences of self-esteem maintenance.

3.3.1. *Self-Traps*

A first result emerging from the analysis is that multiple modes of cognitive behavior are often self-sustaining for the same person, or for otherwise identical subjects. Thus, an intrapersonal equilibrium with a low level of repression (self-honesty) often coexists with another one characterized by a high level of repression (positive thinking, denial), and an intermediate case in-between. Unless the individual can successfully coordinate the strategies and expectations of his temporal selves (a point on which we are agnostic), he or she may well be trapped in an inferior equilibrium.[24,25]

3.3.2. *Self-Doubt*

Repressing bad news more systematically makes recalling only good news more suspect, ultimately impairing the credible transmission of both types of signals. Just like a ruler whose entourage dares not bring him bad news, or a child whose parents praise him indiscriminately, an individual with some understanding of

---

[24] What makes all three equilibria self-fulfilling is thus precisely the *introspection* or 'metacognition' of the Bayesian individual, who understands that his cognitive process (in this instance, his memory) is subject to opportunistic distortions. The higher the degree of censoring by today's self, the more tomorrow's self discounts the 'no bad news to report' recollection, and therefore the lower the risk that he will be overconfident. As a result, the greater is today's self incentive to censor. Conversely, if today's self faithfully records all news in memory, tomorrow's self is more likely to be overconfident when he cannot recall any bad signals, and this incites today's self to be truthful.

[25] A closely related result is that small causes can have large effects: minor variations in preferences or incentives (time discounting, psychic or material costs of memory management, repression, etc.), can lead to large and sudden changes in cognitive strategies, self-confidence, and ultimately in performance.

the self-serving tendency in his attention or memory can never be sure that he *really* 'did great,' even in instances where this was actually true.[26]

3.3.3. *Testable Implication*

The model also shows that the tendency to engage in selective memory and similar forms of self-deception is greater for more time inconsistent (weak-willed) individuals. Indeed, the benefits of confidence-building rise with time inconsistency, while the risks of overconfidence decrease with it.

3.4. Optimism and Pessimism

3.4.1. *The Prevalence of Self-Serving Beliefs*

Surveys, experiments, and common observation consistently suggest that most people overestimate their past achievements, abilities, and other desirable characteristics, both in absolute terms and relative to others (e.g., Weinstein, 1980; Taylor and Brown, 1988). While this is often taken as evidence of pervasive irrationality in human inference, it turns out that *rational self-deception* by Bayesian agents can very well account for most people holding biased, self-serving beliefs.

To take a concrete example based on our endogenous-memory model, suppose that two-thirds of the population receive a signal that they are of low ability, while the remaining one-third receive no such signal (no news is then good news). If the costs of repression and awareness management are low enough, a large fraction, say three-quarters, of the low-ability group may successfully repress this bad news. Because of the self-doubt effect they will not be as optimistic as if they were certain that no adverse signal had occurred; but nonetheless the suppression of the adverse data will raise their self-assessments above the unconditional prior, which is also the population average. As a result, a majority of the total population ($3/4 \times 2/3$) will believe themselves to be *more able than they actually are, more able than average, and more able than two-thirds of the individuals*. Adding the one-third who had truly received and experienced good news (not received a negative signal), the fraction who think they are better than average is even larger, namely five-sixths; note, in passing, that the one-third able agents actually underestimate their true talent, due to the self-doubt effect. The remaining one-sixth of the population think, correctly, that they are worse than average; as a result they have low motivation and are unlikely to undertake challenging tasks. They fit the experimental findings of depressed people as 'sadder but wiser' realists, compared to their non-depressed counterparts who are much more likely to exhibit self-serving delusions (Alloy and Abrahamson, 1979).

---

[26] This coarsening of information is quite different from the a priori suppression of signals seen earlier with self-handicapping, or in Carrillo and Mariotti (2000). In particular, we shall see that it may end up doing the individual more harm than good, whereas the usual 'strategic ignorance' is only chosen when it improves ex-ante welfare.

The key intuition here is that Bayes' law does not constrain the skewness in the distribution of biases.[27] It only requires that the *average bias* across the over-confident and underconfident agents in the population (who number half and one-third in our example) sum to zero. Note also that, since decisions are typically non-linear in beliefs, a zero average bias in no way restricts self-esteem maintenance strategies from having aggregate economic and welfare effects.

3.4.2. *Defensive Pessimism*

While people are most often concerned with enhancing and protecting their self-esteem, there are also many instances where they seek to minimize their achievements, or convince themselves that the task at hand will be difficult rather than easy. A student studying for exams may thus discount his previous good grades as attributable to luck or lack of difficulty. A young researcher may understate the value of his prior achievements, compared to what will be required to obtain tenure. A dieting person who lost a moderate amount of weight may decide that he 'looks fatter than ever', no matter what others or the scale may say.

Such *defensive pessimism* can be captured with a very simple variant of our basic model. The above are situations where the underlying motive for information-manipulation is still the same, namely to alleviate the shirking incentives of future selves; the only difference is that ability is now a substitute rather than a complement to effort in generating future payoffs. This gives the agent an incentive to discount, ignore, and otherwise repress signals of *high* ability, as these would increase the temptation to 'coast' or 'slack off'. Substitutability will typically occur when the reward for performance is of a 'pass–fail' nature, such as in obtaining a diploma, making a sale, being hired or fired (tenure, partnership)—perhaps also in marriage and divorce. Note that this yields another *testable* prediction of the model, from which it could be distinguished from a purely hedonic theory of self-confidence: one could for instance compare subjects' confidence-maintenance behavior across experiments (or careers) where payoffs were complements and substitutes.

3.5. Is 'Positive Thinking' Good for You?

As noted earlier, there is an enormous industry of 'self-help' books, courses, gurus, and now web sites claiming to help people improve their self-esteem and that of their children. But is a person ultimately better off following a strategy of active self-esteem maintenance and 'positive thinking', or when he always faces the truth? Psychologists—both researchers and practitioners—appear sharply divided between these two conflicting views of self-deception. On one side are those who endorse and actively promote the self-efficacy/self-esteem movement (e.g., Bandura, 1977; Seligman, 1990), pointing to studies which tend to show that a moderate dose of 'positive illusions' has significant affective and functional

---

[27] This was first pointed out by Carrillo and Mariotti (2000) in a context of ex-ante strategic ignorance. See also Brocas and Carrillo (1999, 2002, Chapter 5, this volume) and Köszegi (1999).

benefits. On the other side are skeptics and outright critics (e.g., Baumeister, 1998; Swann, 1996), who see instead a lack of convincing evidence, and point to the dangers of overconfidence as well as the loss of standards that results when negative feedback is systematically withheld or discounted in the name of self-esteem preservation. Our formal analysis helps provide insights into the reasons for this ambiguity.

Recall that the benefit of a 'hear no evil-see no evil' strategy is that it helps the individual preserve motivation in the event of bad news. It does involve a risk that one will be overconfident, but the individual is aware of this tradeoff, and only censors signals when it leads to expected utility gains. This net *gain from forgetting bad news* is only one side of the coin, however: the other one is the *loss from disbelieving good news*, due to the self-doubt effect explained earlier. Thus, while the individual will be better or even over-motivated following a negative signal about his ability, he may actually be undermotivated following a good signal. Which effect dominates ex-ante welfare, therefore, depends on the general difficulty of the task (the distribution of effort costs) and on his degree of time-inconsistency. Our analysis establishes that:

1. When the tasks one faces are very difficult relative to one's willpower, an active strategy of self-esteem maintenance, selective memory, 'looking on the bright side', etc., can indeed pay off.
2. When the typical task is likely to be only moderately challenging, and time inconsistency is not too high, one can only lose by playing such games with oneself, and it would be better to always 'accept who you are'.

It is important to note that in the second case, the individual may *still* play such denial games, even though self-honesty would be better. First, he could be trapped in an inferior equilibrium. Second, motivated cognition may be the *only* equilibrium, yet still result in a lower welfare than if the individual could commit to never try to fool himself.

4. PERSONAL RULES AND TESTS OF WILLPOWER

4.1. Reasoned Self-Control

The cognitive strategies discussed until now represent attempts by the individual to manipulate his future self's *perception* of the payoffs attached to alternative courses of action: work or play, persevere or give up, abstain or drink, etc. Through strategic ignorance, self-handicapping, selective recall, and the like, he aims to minimize the intensity of future temptation, that is, to reduce the divergence between his ex-ante (or long-run) and his ex-post (or temporary) preferences. A closely related mode of self-regulation is *preparation of emotion,*[28] where the agent trains himself to care less about certain desires, or even to find them repulsive, by associating them with vivid, disgusting images (e.g., cigarettes

---

[28] This term is used by Ainslie (1992), and clearly emphasizes the ex-ante nature of this strategy.

and fatty foods with visions of diseased lungs and clogged arteries), and conversely by pairing positive images with delayed-gratification actions (receiving an award, achieving fame, etc.).

While undeniably important, these behaviors still fall short of fully capturing what is usually meant by self-control, namely the deliberate, reasoned and contemporaneous *overriding* of impulses, at the time they occur.[29] Thus, Baumeister et al. (1994) observe that most forms of self-control involve interrupting or suspending a naturally occurring physical or mental response to a desire or craving, and conclude that '*the essential nature of self-regulation is that of overriding*'. Similarly, Ainslie (1992) contrasts the use of either external commitments, which takes away the tempting option, or emotion control, which reduces its attractiveness, to '*the kind of impulse control which we call willpower, which allows a person to resist impulses while he is both attracted by them and able to pursue them*'.

So how do people resist the temptation that they are *currently* experiencing, and can our simple economic model also help understand these more direct forms of self-regulation? The answer likely tempting begins with the typical rationalization that accompanies *failed* attempts at self-restraint: 'just this time...'. Conversely, reasoned self-control requires perceiving a clear link between behavior today and behavior in the future, which transforms the impulsive act one is about to commit from an isolated decision into a *precedent* that bodes ill for all future such choices. 'If I eat this tempting desert, there goes my whole diet. If I cannot turn down this drink, I might as well admit that I am still a hopeless alcoholic'. As illuminatingly explained by Ainslie (1992, 2001), the way out of the time-inconsistency trap is to view choices between rewards not one by one, but as indissociable parts of more permanent patterns of behavior (impulsive versus reasoned, weak versus strong, moral versus immoral, etc.), which either affirm or violate long-lasting rules to which one would like to conform. Indeed, the setting and monitoring of *personal rules* and targets for oneself is perhaps the most prevalent strategy used by people to try and achieve self-restraint. Examples include diets, resolutions to smoke only after meals, jog four times a week, write five pages a day, always finish what you started, conduct your life in a way that would have made your mother proud, and all sorts of similar 'promises to oneself'. The question is, of course: given that these rules are entirely self-imposed, how (or when) can they actually constrain the individual's behavior? And, in particular, *why* should misbehavior today make it more likely that one will also misbehave tomorrow?

4.2. Self-Monitoring: Inferring One's Preferences from One's Actions

We have not found in our reading of the psychology literature a fully spelled out answer to these questions. Ainslie (1992) provides the most explicit clues, which

---

[29] By contrast, in what precedes the current self never attempts to restrain his own impulses, but only invests in information or disinformation that will help counteract the anticipated impulses of future selves.

suggest an important role for uncertainty and learning about one's preferences: '*In situations where temporary preferences are likely, [the individual] is apt to be genuinely ignorant of what his future choices will be. His best information is his knowledge of his past behavior under similar circumstances . . . Furthermore, if he has chosen the poorer reward often enough that he knows self-control will be an issue, but not so often as to give up hope that he may choose the richer rewards, his current choice is likely to be what will swing his expectation of future rewards one way or the other*'. Together with the emphasis placed by other psychologists such as Baumeister on the importance of self-monitoring for successful self-regulation, and on how devastating to a subject's self-view and subsequent behavior breaking a strict personal rule can be ('lapse-activated snowballing'), this quite naturally leads us to propose a theory of *self-reputation* over one's willpower, defined as the inverse of the bias towards immediate gratification.

The basic idea is that by breaking the rule the individual would *reveal himself*, in his own (future selves') eyes, as weak-willed—that is, incapable of resisting temptation. Such a loss in self-reputation would further undermine his resolve in the future, to the point where he may even abandon all attempts at self-restraint: what is the point of sticking to a diet today if, based on recent experience, it is likely to be broken tomorrow? Because of learning there can be no 'just this once', and the threat of triggering a significant and lasting loss of self-control can help limit or even override the individual's natural bias towards immediate gratification. While this intuitive description is still incomplete (we shall develop it further below), it already makes clear two important points.

First, a personal rule's power is predicated on the likelihood that a lapse today will later on be recalled and interpreted as denoting weakness of will, rather than forgotten or rationalized away (finding an excuse). Thus, the accuracy and reliability of the individual's monitoring and interpretation of his own actions are essential. Indeed, psychologists observe that most failures of self-regulation such as overeating, addiction, procrastination, etc., are associated with inaccurate or deficient self-monitoring (Baumeister et al., 1994). Conversely, simply adopting or being forced to adopt a more regular and accurate self-monitoring 'technology', such as keeping a journal of one's successes and lapses, often leads to a reduction in the occurrence of impulsive behavior (Ainslie, 1992). This will indeed be an implication of the model.

Second, and related to the first point, the fact that people commonly monitor and draw inferences from their own actions reveals that they must suffer from a deeper form of imperfect self-knowledge than the one discussed in previous sections. Whereas earlier they knew the underlying motives for their behavior but not all of its future consequences, they must now be uncertain about their very own preferences. Indeed, any time a person looks back to his past actions to infer what he is likely to do in the future, it *must* be that the preference ordering (motive) that led to the earlier decisions has some permanence (making it relevant to future choices), but nonetheless can *no longer be recalled* or accessed with complete accuracy or reliability. This kind of inaccessibility of one's preferences is quite different from the more transient kind of taste uncertainty found in economics, such as not knowing whether one will like a new food, product, or job (experience goods, learning by doing).[30] It is, on the other hand, very much in line with the evidence discussed earlier about people's inability to recollect their own past utilities, pain, cravings, etc. More generally, most psychologists view introspection as a very imperfect source of self-knowledge, leading individuals to commonly infer or reconstruct their own motives from their past actions (retrospective justification).

4.3. Personal Rules and Self-Reputation Over Willpower

Bringing together this convergent set of findings and ideas from psychology, we model in Bénabou and Tirole (2000) the behavior of individuals who are unsure of their willpower (ability to delay gratification) when under stress or confronted with intense temptation, and must therefore infer it from the extent to which their previous conduct conformed to, or strayed from, more or less stringent rules. We characterize the rules that can be sustained as intrapersonal equilibria, where impulses for immediate gratification are held in check by the fear of 'losing faith in oneself' (damaging one's self-reputation), which would lead to a further collapse of self-discipline. We also examine how they depend on the extent to which the individual's self-monitoring is subject to opportunistic distortions of memory or inference (such as finding excuses for oneself) of the type discussed in Section 3.2.

The basic model of imperfect self-knowledge, willpower, and recall outlined in Section 3.3 is thus extended as follows. The two basic periods—present and future or, for concreteness, 'today' and 'tomorrow'—are each subdivided into two subperiods—say morning and afternoon. Each morning, the individual first decides whether or not to try and exercise self-restraint that day. Trying means embarking on a willpower-dependent activity, where his capacity to defer gratification (or withstand discomfort) will be put to the test later in the day (second subperiod). Not trying means indulging his impulses right from the start, or more generally choosing some tempting activity where willpower will not be tested. Thus, for a smoker, attempting to exercise willpower means first abstaining from lighting up in the morning and then trying to hold fast through the afternoon, when the craving may become much more intense, or the temptation is heightened by the proximity of someone smoking. For a procrastinator, it means first setting to work on his book in the morning, and then trying to keep at it in the afternoon, when fatigue, boredom, and possible distractions will reach their peak. While the first phase of self-restraint is relatively easy, the second one is typically much harder, and the individual is generally uncertain of whether or not he will

---

[30] For instance in Carrillo (1998), a time-inconsistent individual may choose total abstinence with respect to goods such as alcohol or drugs in order to never find out that he (perhaps) finds them too tempting to resist.

have the willpower to ride it out.[31] Furthermore, if he expects to give up later in the day, the delayed benefits (incremental health, pages written) from only one morning of 'good behavior' may well be insufficient to compensate for his initial proclivity towards immediate gratification; in that case he will not even make the initial effort, but indulge his impulses right from the start. This, in turn, implies that much more than a half day's worth of delayed rewards rides on his persevering during the first afternoon. The individual knows that if he caves in (and if no extenuating circumstances can be invoked), he risks *appearing as weak-willed to himself* the next day, and his demoralized future self will then abandon all restraint and just start smoking or shirking first thing in the morning. A lapse today thus indeed acts, through its informational spillover, as a *precedent* that leads to a further deterioration in behavior tomorrow. Aware of these high stakes, the individual will then exercise greater self-restraint in the face of temptation. Thus, rules such as 'I don't smoke anymore' or 'I work on my book ten hours a day' are sustained through the force of self-reputation.[32]

Our simple model, thus, allows us to identify the key ingredients and mechanisms for a psychologically grounded, mathematically explicit, theory of rule-based behavior. In what follows, we emphasize some of its main results.

4.4. Lapses as Precedents

4.4.1. *The Value of Self-Confidence Once Again*
The model shows that the extent of self-discipline an individual will achieve (keeping constant his true preferences) is generally higher, the greater his confidence in his own willpower.[33] The intuition is that a greater reputational capital is then at stake in each decision, resulting in a more forward-looking behavior. As a result, ex-ante welfare is also higher. Thus, as with the assessment of one's productive ability, there arises an endogenous, instrumental value of confidence in one's 'character'.

4.4.2. *Dependence*
A closely related result concerns the notion of dependence and the conflict between extrinsic and intrinsic motivation.[34] Suppose that, during an initial phase (e.g., childhood), the individual's behavior is subject to tight external constraints—imposed for instance by 'controlling' parents or a society with rigid

---

[31] See Baumeister (e.g., 2002, Chapter 1 this volume) for evidence that willpower—which he compares to a muscle—depletes over time with stress and fatigue.

[32] The two-period setup is of course only a simplifying abstraction. A longer horizon would only amplify the effects identified here, as each lapse would put many periods' self-restraint at risk. Note that our non-cooperative, reputation-based model could be seen as providing an informational foundation for Caillaud et al.'s (1999) cooperative game-theoretic approach to self-restraint (cooperation or non-cooperation here is between temporal selves).

[33] As long as the problem of 'false excuses', which we discuss in the next section, is not too severe.

[34] See Section 5.1 for psychological references and further results in an interpersonal context.

norms. He will, of course, behave better, but be deprived of any opportunity to test his will and build up a reputation sufficient to ensure successful *self*-regulation later on, when he is left to his own devices. The externally enforced initial 'good behavior' thus comes at the expense of later autonomy (ability to make the right choices by oneself) and self-restraint. An excessively 'protected' childhood has the same effects.

4.4.3. *The Role of Self-Monitoring*

Once a lapse (succumbing to temptation) *has* occurred, it is a piece of 'bad news' about himself that the individual will often have strong incentives to try and forget or 'explain away', so as to avoid the costs associated with a damaged self-reputation. To capture this well-documented self-serving bias in memory we allow, much as in Section 3.2, each lapse to be forgotten with positive probability. We show that only when the recall probability is sufficiently high (in a well-defined sense) will behavioral rules with actual self-control be sustainable. There arises therefore a strong tension between the individual's ex-post incentives to forget lapses, and his ex-ante knowledge that he can only escape 'being the slave of passion' if he is able to prevent or limit such selective memory or attention. This points to the importance of choosing rules with good mnemonic properties (e.g., only one cigarette after each meal, rather than just three per day) and of rehearsing them often (e.g., religious principles) so as to *make lapses more salient* if they do occur. As noted earlier, people who fail at self-regulation are often those with poor self-monitoring, and conversely much of behavioral therapy involves endowing the patient with a more reliable, less manipulable 'technology' for monitoring his actions, such as keeping a journal or talking regularly with the therapist. Twelve-step programs and weekly confession in church are also, in large part, self-monitoring devices. Neither his peers in the group nor the priest in the confessional can (or even try) force the alcoholic or sinner to refrain from his vice (contrast this to, say, a rehabilitation clinic). Admittedly, there is some social or moral pressure, but the individual could avoid it by lying about his recent drinking or bad actions. He may perceive some probability of being found out and condemned by his peers, or punished by divine intervention, but the direct and inevitable effect of participating in such 'pure talk' sessions is that the individual is *forced to think about his own behavior*, even if he chooses to misrepresent it.

4.5. Excuses, Exceptions, and Compulsiveness

In sufficiently adverse circumstances, even the strongest-willed individual would, and perhaps even should, give up rather than persevere. When really feeling sick, or learning that a friend in trouble needs comfort, even a perfectly time-consistent person will postpone work to another day. If the weather is excessively cold, the jogging-every-day rule should be broken; if the host insists that one have some of his or her special dessert, it would be more impolite than heroic to refuse. In inferring one's strength of will from one's actions, attention must thus be paid to the circumstances under which they took place. This *signal-extraction* problem is further compounded by the fact that, once again, memory may be self-serving: an individual who recalls straying from his rule will generally have a strong incentive to come up with plausible 'excuses' that allow him to attribute the lapse to temporary, external factors, rather than enduring, personal ones.

These issues can be examined in our model by allowing the cost of perseverance (craving) to be stochastic: on any given day (afternoon) it can be either high, which constitutes a valid 'excuse' for giving in, or low, in which case there is no excuse, meaning that only a weak-willed individual would ever give up. Even in the latter case, however, the individual may still manage to come up ex-post (with some probability) with some plausible justification. Not being completely naive he will realize that this recollection could be self-serving rather than genuine, but this ambiguity is still better than not having any admissible excuse at all.

4.5.1. *Patterns of Self-Regulation*
The variability of situational factors allows us to distinguish between *flexible rules* (persevere except in really adverse circumstances) and *rigid rules* (never give in—take no excuses). The former corresponds to what an individual with no commitment problem would generally do. It can also be adopted by one with a relatively weak willpower who, by imitating ('pooling with') the strong-willpower type, is able to better restrain his own impulses. More novel at this point is the rigid type of behavior that occurs when an individual who has relatively high willpower, but is insecure about it, feels compelled to 'prove himself' in every instance by tolerating no exception to his rule.

4.5.2. *Compulsiveness*
The type of stringent rule described above could sometimes (depending on parameters) be desirable a priori. More interesting is the case where perseverance in the high-cost state is undesirable even ex-ante, that is, would never be chosen by a fully time-consistent, self-knowledgeable individual. In that case, it represents an unambiguous cost that the individual incurs for the sole purpose of reassuring himself about his own character. Such excessively rigid or 'legalistic' rules correspond well to *compulsive* or *obsessive* behaviors such as those of the miser, the workaholic, or the anorexic: the individual is so afraid of appearing weak to himself that every decision becomes a test of his willpower, even when the stakes are minor or when self-restraint is actually harmful.

4.5.3. *Overregulation and Underregulation: Two Sides of the Same Coin?*
The preceding result is important because it shows that the model is indeed able to account for over—as well as under—regulation within the same, simple, framework. Hyperbolic-type preferences are sometimes criticized for failing to explain common instances where individuals seem to *over*weigh distant payoffs; we show that this apparent 'salience of the future' is not only consistent, but actually generated by (a concern over) present-oriented preferences. Ainslie (1992) conjectured that compulsiveness is a 'side effect' of personal rules edicted to alleviate

the weakness of the will. Baumeister et al. (1994, pp. 85–6) summarize a similar view held by many psychologists, namely that '*Obsessions and compulsions are attempts to compensate for some self-regulatory deficit ... The quest for such structure [boundaries, limits, time markers, and the like] and the excessive adherence to such structure, which have been commonly observed among these individuals, may be a response to the inner sense that they cannot control themselves without those externals aids*'. Our model spells out formally the common cognitive mechanism through which *both* deficient and excessive self-restraint may occur. It also yields testable predictions, such as the fact that compulsive behavior is more likely when the individual's initial self-reputation is low relative to his true willpower, and when the veracity of self-excuses and ex-post rationalizations is difficult to ascertain (because he then does not 'trust his own judgement').

4.5.4. *Credibility of Excuses*
Indeed, suppose that the environment in which the individual operates becomes more permissive of (or conducive to) self-serving retrospective justifications: say, it is harder to ascertain later on whether extenuating circumstances did or did not apply; or, there is less probing and skeptical questioning of the individual's rationalizations by others (e.g., an experimenter). In terms of our model, this corresponds to a higher probability that a plausible (non-falsifiable) excuse can be found even when no extenuating circumstances existed for a previous lapse in behavior. How will this affect the extent of self-restraint by the individual? Our analysis suggests a clear dichotomy:

1. People with relatively low actual willpower (high susceptibility to temptation) respond by 'abusing' the excuses, and therefore *lose* self-restraint. Furthermore, this loss is more drastic, the *higher* the initial self-confidence. The intuition is that when the self-monitoring 'technology' is not very effective, a weak type with a good self-reputation can take full advantage of his 'principal's' (tomorrow's self) high level of trust, and misbehave without any adverse consequences. When initial reputation is low, however, tomorrow's self will apply a tougher standard, so the weak type must actually 'work at' passing for a strong one (exercising self-restraint).
2. For those with a relatively high actual willpower, by contrast, less reliable inference leads to a *tightening* of self-restraint, or *increased compulsiveness*. The idea is that the compulsive individual is trying to prove himself by systematically doing things 'the hard way'—that is, by taking actions that would be too costly for a weak-willed individual to mimic. When false excuses become easier to come by, he can only maintain a tough standard for himself by refusing to accept exceptions to the rule altogether.

These implications of the model should again be testable, provided one can: (i) assess subjects' initial self-perceptions of their willpower;[35] (ii) vary the extent to

---

[35] At least in terms of point-estimates and uncertainty. Ideally, one would also like to independently measure their true underlying preferences (susceptibility to temptation). This is likely to be quite

which the environment in which they must resist temptation offers arguments that could be invoked later on as excuses (e.g., tell them that most people give in, or do not give in; that this is a hard, or an easy task; visibly monitor, or not monitor, the conditions under which the test is done).

5. SOCIAL INTERACTIONS

A unified approach to social psychology should start from a single view of the individual's preferences, cognitive machinery, and basic problem-solving strategies. While incentives and feedback, and therefore behavior, are highly context-dependent, the underlying 'fundamentals' are the same whether the individual is engaged in self-regulation or interacting with others. Although a single unified model is surely an unattainable ideal, we briefly point out in this section how our simple theory, based on the interplay of self-knowledge and motivation, can also shed light on a number of psychological findings related to social interactions.

The common thread running through a wide variety of social situations is that one agent (or more) is trying to get another one (or more) to perform a certain task: study, work, buy or sell, consent to a relationship, etc. Conversely, the other party is interested in determining, and if possible maximizing, 'what is in it' for them. In such settings, which economists refer to as principal–agent relationships, psychologists have studied two types of interactions (going in opposite directions) between an individual's self-view and his social environment.

Self-presentation. Here, the individual attempts to manipulate others' behavior by conveying information about himself through self-promotion, intimidation, ingratiation, excuse-making, supplication, and the like. What allows such signaling is that an individual typically has private knowledge relevant to assessing his abilities, such as memories of his past performances and of how they were achieved (intensity of effort, circumstances that affected the results). For concreteness, suppose that this individual, called the 'agent' (he), interacts with a 'principal' (she), who can alter the attractiveness of a task (rewards, punishment, difficulty) for the agent, or even decide on the set of allowable tasks. The principal's decisions (offers) will generally depend on her assessment of the agent's motivation: his self-confidence in his ability to perform the task, and his beliefs about its difficulty or the personal payoffs (intrinsic rewards) attached to it. Consequently, the agent has an incentive to strategically represent his self-view to the principal: he may for instance signal high self-confidence when interviewing for a job or a new position, or low self-confidence when aspiring to an easy-going assignment.

The 'looking-glass self'.[36] Conversely, the individual's social environment often attempts to manipulate his self-view, or (very similarly) his perceptions of

---

difficult, however, precisely because the individual may be following a general rule that involves mimicking someone with higher willpower.

[36] This term is borrowed from Cooley (1902).

current and future activities. Thus, parents and educators try to boost children's confidence in their ability ('you can do it'), point at the large delayed payoff attached to a good education, or understate the unpleasantness of tasks ('math is fun'). Such strategies require that the principal hold information that is not available to the agent. For example, a teacher, thesis advisor, coach, or therapist may, due to her background and prior experience, be better able to judge the talent and prospects of success of a pupil, student, player, or patient. A parent is likely to have better information than their child about the monetary and non-monetary payoffs to education, and also be better at evaluating their achievements.[37] In all these situations, it is not just the principal's words (encouragement, praise, blame) but also the kinds of incentives (rewards, punishments) that she offers to the agent that provide the latter with a 'looking glass' from which he can learn about himself.

Both self-presentation and the looking-glass self are well amenable to standard economic analysis, based on signaling theory. In the rest of this section we shall focus on the latter situation, which is more original from an economic point of view, and also more directly related to this chapter's central concern with self-knowledge and motivation. As before, the agent's self-view is being manipulated in order to affect his performance, but the manipulator is now external (the principal) rather than internal (a previous incarnation). Consequently, the modeling of the looking-glass self and its implications requires only one of the three grains of sand introduced in Section 2, namely imperfect self-knowledge.[38]

The key point in the analysis is then that the agent views the principal's behavior as reflecting her information about him, and conversely the principal realizes that her words and deeds will lead the agent to revise his beliefs and alter his choices. For this looking-glass effect to operate, however, it is not sufficient that the principal have private information relevant to the agent's decision-making. As explained in the next section, two other conditions are required:

1. *Sorting.* The principal's incentives to offer different types of rewards or feedback must vary (preferably, monotonically) with what she knows about the agent or the task to be performed.

2. *Attribution.* The agent must understand—at least approximately—how the principal's motives impact her behavior.[39]

---

[37] Alternatively, she may be trying to convey information about her own preferences, ('I really want you to do well in school'), which in turn could be selfish ('make us proud') or altruistic ('I really care about your future').

[38] Of course, having the other two operate as well would only enrich the set of issues that can be addressed. For instance, one important role for altruistic principals (parents, teachers) could be to help the agent overcome his time-consistency problem; but of course, they also have their own agendas (e.g., morals, pride, reputation).

[39] Psychologists have accumulated a substantial amount of evidence on the variety and relative sophistication of inferences made by individuals in social environments. See, e.g., Festinger (1954), Heider (1958), Kelley (1971), or Gilbert and Silvera (1996).

5.1. Intrinsic Versus Extrinsic Motivation

In Bénabou and Tirole (2001) we study the provision of incentives (rewards, empowerment, feedback) in educational and workplace environments. A principal (parent, teacher, manager) possesses information relevant to the agent's (child, student, subordinate) decision-making, and the agent tries to see through the principal's ulterior motivation when responding to the incentive scheme he is offered.

Most of economics is built upon the premise that people respond to incentives, and there is a good amount of evidence that they usually do. In other words, rewards serve as 'positive reinforcers' for the desired behavior. In psychology, their effect is more controversial. Psychologists, while not denying that incentives often work (except for some who argue that rewards are alienating *per se*), point to a number of experiments and real-life situations to argue that they are only weak reinforcers in the short term, and negative reinforcers once they are withdrawn.[40] That is, rewards have hidden costs, which economists typically neglect.

An old-style behaviorist approach, mapping in reduced form the stimulus (reward) into a response (reduced effort) is unlikely to be productive, as it would say little as to how the response is altered with changes in the environment. For instance, how does a reward offered to a child for passing an exam differ from stock options held by a start-up entrepreneur? A cognitive/economic modeling of the question takes a more structural approach, reflecting the simple intuition that contingent rewards may 'send the wrong signal'. This is, for instance, why most parents realize that offering toys, candy, or even hugs and kisses to their child for each time they read a book, complete their homework, or clean up their room is usually a bad idea. The analysis thus brings to light the two key factors that help us understand when rewards are positive or negative reinforcers: the extent to which the principal holds *private information*, and the direction of her '*sorting condition*'. The first insight suggests for instance that one should expect performance rewards to have (on average) greater hidden costs in an educational environment than in the workplace. Indeed, a young person is typically quite uncertain about his self and the nature of the tasks that he faces, while the parent or educator can make judgments based on previous experience with other children or students. In the workplace, by contrast, both the nature of tasks and the reward scheme are usually less individual-specific and more publicly known, being part of a 'job description' or relatively standard contract.

Let us now illustrate the crucial role of the second insight, namely the sorting condition. Suppose, first, that the principal feels less of a need to offer a reward to the agent when she trusts in his ability. This may arise for two reasons. First,

---

[40] See, e.g. Deci (1975), Wilson et al. (1981), Kruglanski et al. (1971), Lepper et al. (1973), or Kohn (1993). Recent evidence by economists includes Gächter and Fehr (1998) and Gneezy and Rustichini (2000).

rewards may be more costly if they are handed out often, that is, if the agent is likely to succeed. Second, the principal may have private information but still be unsure about the agent's precise ability and/or motivation. A principal who has every reason to believe that the agent should feel good about himself or like his assignment need not provide much of a reward; conversely, if she is worried that the agent is or will become discouraged about his chances, she will need to offer him stronger incentives. However, if the agent, in turn, tries to read through the principal's choice of reward what she knows about him or his assignment, then an offer of reward represents bad news, and therefore has a hidden cost on the motivation side. It can in fact be shown in such settings that: (i) rewards are weak positive reinforcers in the current task; (ii) once withdrawn, a reward indeed becomes a negative reinforcer.

Result (i) means that the direct incentive effect of rewards must dominate the negative inferential effect; otherwise rewards would be self-defeating and would not be offered by rational principals—except by mistake, or in experiments. Result (ii) allows us to makes economic sense of the conflict between 'intrinsic' and 'extrinsic' motivation emphasized by a huge literature in psychology and sociology (e.g., Deci, 1975; Deci and Ryan, 1985). At the same time, however, it delineates *empirically testable* limits to its validity. In particular, we cannot stress too much the importance of the sorting condition. Indeed, one can think of cases where rewards are positive reinforcers even in the long term (i.e., once withdrawn). For example, suppose that effort in the current task allows the agent to 'learn by doing', and that this learning by doing is particularly effective for more talented agents. The sorting condition then operates in the opposite direction: the principal is more eager to reward, the more talented the agent. As a result, rewards are now interpreted as good news. Similarly, the principal may be signaling how much she cares about the agent's success in the task; if the agent somewhat internalizes the principal's utility, this generates a positive response of effort to reward. Yet another illustration is offered by the issue of help where, depending on the situation, a principal may have more of an incentive to lend a 'helping hand' when the agent is weak, or when he is strong. For example, some PhD supervisors spend substantial time with the weakest students (who will have trouble finishing their thesis in time) and with the strongest ones (in whose reflected glory they may bask, or whose work they find intellectually most pleasing). It is, therefore, not too surprising that help sometimes creates a pattern of dependency, while in other situations it is received as encouraging news.

5.2. Undermining the Other's Ego

While boosting or avoiding damage to others' self-confidence is a pervasive aspect of social interactions, people also often criticize or downplay the achievements of their spouse, child, colleague, subordinate, or teammate, and disclose information that is detrimental to their egos. In Bénabou and Tirole (2001) paper we, therefore, also address this kind of behavior, and show that it is not inconsistent with the need (stressed in the social psychology and human resource management literatures) to coach and boost the self-esteem of one's personal and professional partners. There are at least three rational motives for such ego-bashing: (i) the two agents may be in competition; (ii) the other may be tempted to 'rest on his laurels'; and (iii) more interestingly, the two may be engaged in a battle for dominance. Indeed, when decision-making relies on an agreement between the two parties, as is often the case in dyads, each may be tempted to demonstrate that he or she has a better judgment than the other (in the matter at hand, or in general), in order to impose his or her views and choices. The very fact that individuals attempt both to boost their partners' self-esteem at certain times, and to deflate it at others, demonstrates once again the need for an explicit, structural approach to the description of social interactions.

6. CONCLUDING COMMENTS

Economics has always been about making a small number of strong assumptions to allow for broad predictive power and policy analysis. At the same time, economists have been eager to extend their paradigm beyond its traditional realm in order to incorporate the lessons from other social sciences such as psychology, sociology, law, or political science. Indeed, the limits of the *Homo Economicus* paradigm are well known, and isolated pioneers—economists or psychologists working across boundaries—have long tried to broaden its scope. In doing so, they paved the way for the more systematic effort at cross-fertilization under-taken in recent years by both scientific communities, and reflected in particular by the present volume.

The value of this enterprise for economists is clear, and goes well beyond the 'private benefits' of entering new and intellectually challenging territory. We can surely expect to improve our understanding of numerous fields such as consumer behavior, product design, organizations, education, health, or finance. The real challenge will be to find a proper balance between the two methodological extremes: an ad hoc, hypothesis-intensive approach on the one hand, and a conservative (or compulsive?) attachment to rationality and functionalism on the other. The present chapter has tried to demonstrate how introducing a small number of key imperfections into the standard paradigm of Economic Man can go a long way towards reconciling it with a large body of disparate, and sometimes apparently conflicting, evidence from psychology. Needless to say, this work only scratches the surface; much remains to be done and—as evidenced by the con-tributions in his volume—there is room for many alternative approaches.

The value of the joint enterprise for psychologists is of course not for us to judge. We can only hope that they will find enough in it for them to sustain a lasting dialogue; at this point we can only speculate on what some of these potential benefits could be (aside from the intellectual satisfaction of seeing economists finally pay proper attention to their findings). First, there might be a revival of interest in developing a motivated and relatively unified approach to human behavior, bringing greater coherence to what sometimes seems like a collection of unrelated—sometimes even contradictory—effects and biases. Second, new models will lead to new predictions and therefore, down the line, to new experiments. We sketched several potential directions in this chapter, but in practice there is likely to be a lag while formal theory first struggles to satisfactorily incorporate the large corpus of preexisting evidence.

REFERENCES

Ainslie, G. (1992). *Picoeconomics: The strategic interaction of successive motivational states within the person (studies in rationality and social change)*. Cambridge, England and New York: Cambridge University Press.

—— (2001). *Breakdown of will*. Cambridge: Cambridge University Press.

Akerlof, G. and Dickens, W. (1982). The economic consequences of cognitive dissonance. *American Economic Review, 72*(3), 307–19.

—— and Kranton, R. (2000). Economics and identity. *Quarterly Journal of Economics, 115*(3), 715–53.

Alloy, L.B. and Abrahamson, L.Y. (1979). Judgement of contingency in depressed and nondepressed students: Sadder but wiser? *Journal of Experimental Psychology: General, 108*, 441–85.

Arkin, R.M. and Baumgardner, A.H. (1985). Self-handicapping. In J. Harvey and G. Weary (Eds.), *Attribution: Basic issues and applications*. New York: Academic Press.

Bandura, A. (1977). *Self efficacy: The exercise of control*. San Franciso, CA: Freeman Company.

Baumeister, R. (1998). The self. In D. Gilbert, S. Fiske, and G. Lindzez (Eds.), *The Handbook of Social Psychology*. Boston: McGraw-Hill.

Baumeister (2001). The psychology of irrationality: Why people make foolish, self-defeating choices, this volume.

—— Heatherton, T., and Tice, D. (1994). *Losing control: How and why people fail at self-regulation*. San Diego, CA: Academic Press.

Bénabou, R. and Tirole, J. (2002). Self-confidence and personal motivation. *Quarterly Journal of Economics, 117*(3), in press.

—— and —— (2001). *Intrinsic and Extrinsic Motivation*, Princeton University mimeo, December.

—— and —— (2000). *Willpower and personal rules*, Princeton University mimeo, June.

Berglas, S., and Baumeister, R. (1993). Your own worst enemy: Understanding the paradox of self-defeating behavior. New York: BasicBooks.

—— and Jones, E. (1978). Drug choice as a self-handicapping strategy in response to non-contingent success. *Journal of Personality and Social Psychology, 36*, 405–17.

Bodner, R., and Prelec, D. (2002). A neo-Calvinist model of conscience. In I. Brocas and J.D. Carrillo (Eds.), *The psychology of economic decisions*. Oxford: Oxford University Press.

Brocas, I., and Carrillo, J. (1999). *Entry mistakes, entrepreneurial boldness and optimism*, ULB-ECARES mimeo, June.

—— and —— (2002). Information and self-control. In I. Brocas and J.D. Carrillo (Eds.), *The psychology of economic decisions*. Oxford: Oxford University Press.

Caillaud, B., Cohen, D., and Jullien, B. (1999). *Towards a theory of self-restraint*, CERAS mimeo, December.

Caplin, A. and Leahy, J. (2001). *Psychological expected utility theory, Quarterly Journal of Economics, 116,* 55–79.

Carrillo, J. (1998). *Self control, moderate consumption, and craving*, CEPR D.P. 2017, November.

—— and Mariotti, T. (2000). Strategic ignorance as a self-disciplining device. *Review of Economic Studies, 67*(3), 529–44.

Cooley, C. (1902). *Human Nature and the Social Order*. New York: Scribner's.

Crary, W.G. (1996). Reactions to incongruent self-experiments. *Journal of Consulting Psychology, 30,* 246–52.

Deci, E. (1975). *Intrinsic motivation*. New York: Plenum Press.

—— and Ryan, R. (1985). *Intrinsic motivation and self-determination in human behavior*. New York: Plenum Press.

Festinger, L. (1954). A theory of social comparison processes. *Human Relations, 7,* 117–40.

Fingarette, H. (1985). Alcoholism and self-deception. In M. Martin (Ed.), *Self-deception and self-understanding*. Kansas: University Press of Kansas.

Gabaix, X. and Laibson, D. (2000). *Bounded rationality and directed cognition*, Harvard University mimeo.

Gächter, S., and Fehr, E. (1998). How effective are trust- and reciprocity-based incentives? In A. Ben-Ner and L. Putterman (Eds.), *Economics values and organizations*. Cambridge: Cambridge University Press.

Gilbert, D. and Cooper, J. (1985). Social psychological strategies of self-deception. In M. Martin (Ed.), *Self-deception and self-understanding.* Kansas: University Press of Kansas.

—— and Silvera, D. (1996). Overhelping. *Journal of Personality and Social Psychology, 70,* 678–90.

Gilovich, T. (1991). *How we know what isn't so*. New York: Free Press.

Gneezy, U. and Rustichini (2000). Pay enough or don't pay at all. *Quarterly Journal of Economics, 115*(3), 797–810.

Greenier, K., Kernis, M., and Wasschull, S. (1995). Not all high (or low) self-esteem people are the same: Theory and research on the stability of self-esteem. In M. Kernis (Ed.), *Efficacy, agency and self-esteem*. New York: Plenum Press.

Gul, F. and Pesendorfer, W. (2001). *An economic theory of self-control. Econometrica, 69*(6), 1403–36.

Gur, R. and Sackeim, H. (1979). Self-deception: A concept in search of a phenomenon. *Journal of Personality and Social Psychology, 37,* 147–69.

Heider, F. (1958). *The Psychology of Interpersonal Relations*. New York: Wiley.

Herrnstein. R., Loewenstein, G., Prelec, D., and Vaughan, W. (1993). Utility maximization and melioration: Internalities in individual choice. *Journal of Behavioral Decision Making, 6,* 149–85.

Holmström, B. (1999). Managerial incentive problems: A dynamic perspective. *Review of Economic Studies, 66*(1), 169–82.

James, W. (1890). *The Principles of Psychology*. Cleveland, OH: World Publishing.

Kahneman, D., Wakker, P., and Sarin, R. (1997). Back to Bentham? Explorations of experienced utility. *Quarterly Journal of Economics, 112*(2), 375–407.

—— (2001). Experienced utility and objective happiness: a moment-based approach, this volume.

Kelley, H. (1971). Causal schemata and the attribution process. In E. Jones et al. (Eds.), *Attribution: Perceiving the causes of behavior.* Morristown, NJ: General Learning Press.

Kohn, A. (1993). *Punished by rewards.* New York: Plenum Press.

Korner, I. (1950). *Experimental investigation of some aspects of the problem of repression: Repressive forgetting.* New York, NY: Contributions to Education, Bureau of Publications, Teacher's College, Columbia University.

Köszegi, B. (1999). *Self-image and economic behavior,* MIT mimeo, October.

Kruglanski, A., Friedman, I., and Zeevi, G. (1971). The effect of extrinsic incentives on some qualitative aspects of task performance. *Journal of Personality, 39,* 608–17.

Kunda, Z. and Sanitioso, R. (1989). Motivated changes in the self-concept. *Journal of Personality and Social Psychology, 61,* 884–97.

Laibson, D. (1997). Golden eggs and hyperbolic discounting. *Quarterly Journal of Economics, 112,* 443–78.

Lepper, M., Greene, D., and Nisbett, R. (1973). Undermining children's interest with extrinsic rewards: A test of the overjustification hypothesis. *Journal of Personality and Social Psychology, 28,* 129–37.

Loewenstein, G., (1996). Out of control: Visceral influences in behavior. *Organizational Behavior and Human Decision Processes, 65*(3), 272–92.

—— and Schkade, D. (1999). Wouldn't it be nice? Predicting future feelings. In D. Kahneman, E. Diener and N. Schwartz (Eds.), *Well-being: Foundations of hedonic psychology.* New York: Russel Sage Foundation.

Mischel, W., Ebbesen, E.B., and Zeiss, A.R. (1976). Determinants of selective memory about the self. *Journal of Consulting and Clinical Psychology, 44,* 92–103.

Mullainathan, S. (2002). *A memory based model of bounded rationality, Quarterly Journal of Economics, 117*(3), in press.

Murray, S.L. and Holmes, J.G. (1994). Seeing virtues in faults: Negativity and the transformation of interpersonal narratives in close relationships. *Journal of Personality and Social Psychology, 20,* 650–63.

O'Donoghue, T. and Rabin, M. (1999). Doing it now or later. *American Economic Review, 89*(1), 103–24.

Phelps, E. and Pollack, R. (1968). On second-best national savings and game-equilibrium growth. *Review of Economic Studies, 35,* 185–99.

Piccione, M. and Rubinstein, A. (2000). On the interpretation of decision problems with imperfect recall. *Games and Economic Behavior, 20,* 3–24.

Rabin, M. (1995). *Moral preferences, moral rules, and belief manipulation,* University of California mimeo, April.

Rhodewalt, F.T. (1986). Self-presentation and the Phenomenal self: On the stability and malleability of self-conceptions. In R. Baumeister (Ed.), *Public Self and Private Self.* New York: Springer.

Sartre, J.P. (1953). *The existential psychoanalysis* (H.E. Barnes, trans.). New York: Philosophical Library.

Seligman, M. (1975). *Helplessness: On depression, development, and death.* San Francisco, CA: Freeman.

Seligman, E. (1990). *Learned optimism: How to change your mind and your life.* New York: Simon and Schuster.

Snyder, C., Higgins, R., and Stucky, R. (1983). *Excuses: Masquerades in search of grace.* New York: John Wiley.

Strotz, R. (1956). Myopia and inconsistency in dynamic utility maximization. *Review of Economic Studies, 23,* 165–80.

Swann Jr., W.B. (1996). *Self traps: The elusive quest for higher self-esteem.* New York: Freeman.

Taylor, S.E., and Brown, J.D. (1988). Illusion and well-being: A social psychological perspective on mental health. *Psychological Bulletin, 103,* 193–210.

Thaler, R.H. (2000). From Homo Economicus to Homo Sapiens. *Journal of Economic Perspectives, 14*(1), 114–42.

—— and Shefrin, H.M. (1981). *An economic theory of self control.* Journal of Political Economy, *89*(2), 392–406.

Weinberg, B. (1999). *A model of overconfidence,* Ohio State University mimeo, August.

Weinstein, N. (1980). Unrealistic optimism about future life events. *Journal of Personality and Psychology, 39*(5), 806–20.

Wilson, T., Hull, J., and Johnson, J. (1981). Awareness and self-perception: Verbal reports on internal states. *Journal of Personality and Social Psychology, 40,* 53–71.

Zuckerman, M. (1979). Attribution of success and failure revisited, or the motivational bias is alive and well in attribution theory. *Journal of Personality, 47,* 245–87.

9

A New Challenge for Economics: 'The Frame Problem'

XAVIER GABAIX AND DAVID LAIBSON

1. INTRODUCTION: THE FRAME PROBLEM

Consider the problem of a travelling salesman who must map out a route that includes visits to K cities. If an economist were asked to predict the path chosen by the traveller, the economist might begin by conceptualizing an optimization problem. 'Order the cities so that the resulting route minimizes total trip time.' However, the economist would soon realize that the number of possible paths grows so quickly in K that this optimization problem is effectively unsolvable. For example, with $K = 30$, the problem yields $3 \times 10^{32} = K!$ distinct paths, enough to overwhelm any supercomputer.[1]

Real decision makers confront versions of the travelling salesman's problem every day and most of the time the problem does not overwhelm *them*. They use numerous simplifications to 'solve' this problem. For example, they may rule out certain classes of paths right from the start. They may use heuristics to identify promising candidate paths. They may stop their analysis when their current best path is unlikely to be substantially improved by further analysis.

Three features of the traveller's problem interest us. First, the problem is complex in the sense that the theoretical optimum is time-consuming to calculate. Second, the optimal solution can be approximated using a few sensible rules of thumb. Third, sometimes these simplifying heuristics actually generate a suboptimal choice. Such poor choices represent the price of simplification.

In the past twenty years, economists and psychologists have made substantial progress toward understanding the heuristics that humans use to analyze decision

We are grateful for the suggestions of Isabelle Brocas and participants at the Economics and Psychology Conference at ECARE. Numerous research assistants contributed to this paper. We are particularly indebted to John Friedman, Guillermo Moloche, Rebecca Thornton, and Stephen Weinberg. Laibson acknowledges financial support from the National Institutes of Health (R01-AG-16605), the MacArthur Foundation, and the Olin Foundation. Gabaix and Laibson acknowledge support from the National Science Foundation.

[1] The most powerful current supercomputers execute one trillion calculations per second (one teraflops). If each path is evaluated with a single calculation, then analysis of the $K = 30$ case would require 10^{13} years.

problems. The work of Daniel Kahneman and Amos Tversky (1974) stands out within this literature.[2] They showed that a few basic heuristics (e.g., representativeness, availability, and anchoring) lie behind many of our intuitive inferences. We view such heuristics as powerful simplifying tools that enable computationally limited organisms to make sensible judgments. However, such simplifications naturally distort our inferences, invariably causing deviations from perfect rationality and sometimes generating decisions that dramatically lower welfare relative to the rational benchmark.

Our current research studies the process by which humans simplify and approximately solve complex decision problems. We want to understand both the set of heuristics that decision makers use and the ways that those heuristics are applied to complex problems. For example, how does a decision-maker represent a complex problem? What information does the decision-maker use and what information is overlooked? How is the analyzed information cognitively manipulated? When does the decision-maker decide to stop working on a complex problem and act on her best guess? More generally, how does the decision-maker decide how deeply to analyze a problem?

These questions relate closely to a set of questions in cognitive science known as the 'frame problem'. The frame problem arises in any model of cognition, but it is sometimes motivated as a challenge for the designers of a robot. How should the robot be programmed to decide which information to analyze and which information to overlook? Failing to analyze relevant information can lead to bad choices. Analyzing all of the potentially relevant information takes too long and effectively paralyzes the system. In a famous essay, Daniel Dennett motivates the frame problem with the following story:

Once upon a time there was a robot, named R1 by its creators. Its only task was to fend for itself. One day its designers arranged for it to learn that its spare battery, its precious energy supply, was locked in a room with a time bomb set to go off soon. R1 located the room, and the key to the door, and formulated a plan to rescue its battery. There was a wagon in the room, and the battery was on the wagon, and R1 hypothesized that a certain action which it called PULLOUT (WAGON,ROOM) would result in the battery being removed from the room. Straightaway it acted, and did succeed in getting the battery out of the room before the bomb went off. Unfortunately, however, the bomb was also on the wagon. R1 knew that the bomb was on the wagon in the room, but didn't realize that pulling the wagon would bring the bomb out along with the battery. Poor R1 had missed that obvious implication of its planned act.

Back to the drawing board. 'The solution is obvious,' said the designers. 'Our next robot must be made to recognize not just the intended implications of its acts, but also the implications about their side-effects, by deducing these implications from the descriptions it uses in formulating its plans.' They called their next model, the robot-deducer, R1D1. They placed R1D1 in much the same predicament that R1 had succumbed to, and as it too

[2] For a few examples of other seminal contributions to our understanding of bounded rationality see Conlisk (1996), Payne et al. (1993), Shugan (1980), Simon (1955), and Thaler (1991, 1994). All of these authors discuss both the costs and benefits of simplification.

hit upon the idea of PULLOUT (WAGON,ROOM) it began, as designed, to consider the implications of such a course of action. It had just finished deducing that pulling the wagon out of the room would not change the color of the room's walls, and was embarking on a proof of the further implication that pulling the wagon out would cause its wheels to turn more revolutions than there were wheels on the wagon—when the bomb exploded. (Dennett, 1987, pp. 41–2)

Finding an effective middle ground between too little and too much cognitive analysis has proved to be a difficult challenge for cognitive scientists. How can artificially intelligent machines be designed to quickly and *effectively* identify the right depth of analysis? Humans do it all the time. What kind of model can describe or replicate this remarkable ability? The challenge of developing such a model has been described as 'the most important problem in cognitive science' (Dietrich and Fields, 1996, p. 13).

To further illustrate the frame problem, consider an even more complex version of the travelling salesman problem. Real travellers consider many more attributes than the distance between two points. If a traveller had infinite cognitive capacity he would consider the financial costs of road tolls, the variability of travel times, the probability of an accident, the depreciation to his car caused by road disrepair, the presence of amenities during the trip (e.g., road-side diners or motels), the option value of alternative routes in case the chosen route turns out to be congested, the relationship between travel time and weather conditions (e.g., some roads are bad in snow), the proximity to repair services if the car breaks down, and so on.

Somehow, decision makers wrestle with such highly complex problems and come up with useful solutions. Moreover, people are not mechanistic in their analysis of such problems. They know when to work hard to come up with a sophisticated decision (e.g., when they are picking a route to drive from New York to San Francisco) and when to go with their first instinct (e.g., when travelling a few blocks in a familiar neighborhood).

Even when decision makers analyze a decision in depth, they still have to decide which information to consider and which information to ignore. For example, the Rocky Mountains receive 300 in. of snow per year. A winter coast-to-coast trip through the Rockies may generate snow delays. That is worth considering. By contrast, no normal traveller would incorporate the incremental effects of global warming in their estimate of the likelihood of snow delays. A solution to the frame problem must avoid an analysis of every conceivable issue that might bear, however remotely, on our payoffs.

A solution to the frame problem must also avoid the paralysis that would arise if we had to separately identify and decide to ignore all of the inconsequential issues that do *not* bear on our decision problems. For every relevant fact, like snowfall in Colorado, there are untold irrelevant facts, like Colorado's date of statehood. Identifying everything that we know about Colorado and determining the relevance of all of those facts is a cognitive waste.

For the purposes of this essay, we conceptualize the frame problem as the simultaneous challenge of thinking effectively *and* quickly about a complex problem. This definition matches the approach that Dennett has taken in a series of influential essays over the past two decades: 'A creature that can solve any problem given enough time—say a million years—is not in fact intelligent at all. We live in a time-pressured world and must be able to think quickly before we leap (1987, p. 49).' 'I see the frame problem as arising most naturally and inevitably as a problem of finding a *useful*, compact representation of the world—providing actual *anticipations in real time* for purposes of planning and control' (1996, p. 1, original emphasis).[3]

Five motivations heighten our interest in the frame problem. First, the frame problem represents a basic economic question. In essence, the frame problem describes the way that individuals allocate particularly important scarce resources: attention and cognition.

Second, without a solution to the frame problem, economic models are necessarily *incomplete*. For example, the standard economic maximization model makes no practical quantitative prediction in the traveller's problem, since the maximization problem can not be solved on any modern computer.

Third, a century of cognitive psychology research suggests that decision-makers use short-cuts to solve complex problems. We want to understand that simplification process.

Fourth, solving the frame problem is an important input to the study and development of artificial intelligence. To build intelligent machines we need to understand how to efficiently simplify complex problems.

Fifth, and perhaps most importantly, the frame problem provides a micro-foundation for many of the systematic errors that humans make when solving hard problems. Sensible cognitive shortcuts necessarily generate imperfect judgments. Ultimately, we believe that understanding endogenous mental shortcuts will lead to a general framework for understanding many of the ways that humans deviate from the rational benchmark.

The remainder of this essay summarizes a modeling approach that addresses some of the issues raised by the frame problem. We discuss an economic model of attention allocation that is based on the standard *option value* calculations (Gabaix and Laibson, 2000b).[4] The option value approach quantifies the economic value of the option to collect additional information.[5] In our model, actors think more

---

[3] Other authors use the label 'frame problem', to describe a narrower set of issues, particularly representations of information in dynamic environments in which an agent changes the environment through his actions. See Pylyshyn (1987), and Ford and Pylyshyn (1996) for discussions of various conceptualizations of the frame problem. For example, Glymour (1996), writes, 'The central questions about planning and the frame problem are: (a) How can causal structure be learned reliably, efficiently and feasibly? and (b) How can complete or partial knowledge of causal structure be used to reliably and feasibly predict the effects of interventions in the causal system' (p. 32). See McCarthy and Hayes (1969) for the first description of the frame problem. See also Shanahan (1997) for a thorough treatment in a particular context.

[4] An earlier paper (Gabaix and Laibson, 2000a) analyzes the same phenomena, but applies a mechanistic model, which does not provide a theory of endogenous simplification.

[5] See Dixit and Pindyck (1994) for an introduction to the option value approach to investment under uncertainty.

deeply about problems when additional analysis is likely to reveal a large amount of new information or when no obvious winner has emerged from a class of competing alternatives. We describe the intuition behind this model, sketch the formal structure of the model, and review an experiment that we have conducted to test the model.

2. DIRECTED COGNITION

Our 'directed cognition' model applies two simple economic ideas that derive from the option value literature. These ideas provide a framework for deciding how deeply to analyze a complex decision problem.

First, when cognitive analysis yields little new insight, the option value of continued analysis declines. Second, when many different choices are being compared and a particular choice gains a large edge over the available alternatives, the option value of continued analysis also declines. Our directed cognition model quantifies these two effects and integrates them in a formal framework that makes sharp quantitative predictions about boundedly rational choices. We have successfully tested these predictions in an experiment conducted on Harvard undergraduates.

To illustrate the two basic ideas in our model, consider the complex decision tree in Figure 9.1.[6] This is one of twelve randomly generated trees that we asked our subjects to analyze. Each starting box in the left-hand column leads probabilistically to boxes in the second column. Branches connect boxes and each branch is associated with a given probability. For example, the first box in the last row contains a 5. From this box there are two branches with respective probabilities .65 and .35. The numbers inside the boxes represent flow payoffs. Starting from the last row, there exist 7776 outcome paths. For example, the outcome path that follows the highest probability branch at each node is (5, 4, 4, 3, 1, − 2, 5, 5, −3, 4). Integrating with appropriate probability weights over all 7776 paths, the expected payoff of starting from row five is 4.12 (where the subject receives the payoff in every box through which he travels).

We asked undergraduate subjects to choose one of the boxes in the first column of Figure 9.1. We told the subjects that they would be paid the expected value associated with whatever starting row they chose.

The directed cognition model can be used to analyze trees like those in Figure 9.1. We informally describe this application of the model in this essay. We refer interested readers to Gabaix and Laibson (2000b) for a detailed description of the model.

Our application is built on a basic cognitive operation: extending a partially examined path one column deeper into the tree. Such extensions enable the decision-maker to improve her forecast of the expected value of any given

---

[6] Decision trees are difficult to solve, but they are not in the same class of problems (NP-problems) as the travelling salesman problem.

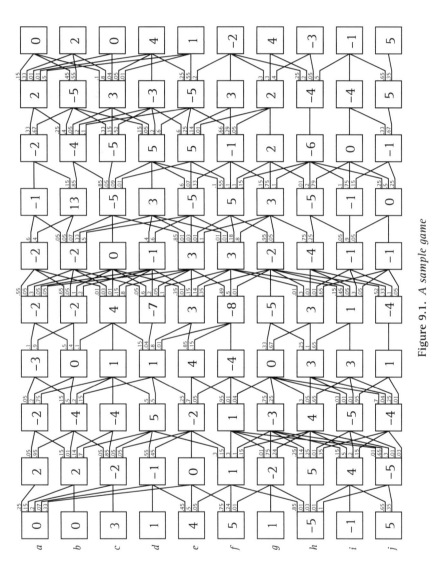

Figure 9.1. *A sample game*

Subjects choose a row with payoffs represented by the probabilistic continuation paths moving from left to right.

starting row.[7] For example, consider again the last row of Figure 9.1. Imagine that a decision-maker is trying to approximate the expected value of that starting row, and that he has calculated only the expected value of the two truncated paths leading from column 1 to column 2. Hence, the estimated value would be: $a = 5 + (.65)(4) + (.35)(-5)$. Following the highest probability path (i.e., the upper path with probability .65), the decision maker could look ahead one additional column and come up with a revised estimated value:

$$a' = a + .65[.15(-3) + .5(4) + .2(-5) + .15(-4)].$$

Each path extension refines the decision-maker's expectations about the value of a starting row. We assume that each path extension requires some time and generates cost q.

We will also allow concatenated path extensions. Specifically, if the decision-maker executes a two-step path extension from a particular node, he twice follows the branch with the highest probability. Hence, starting from the last row of Figure 9.1, his updated estimate would be:

$$a'' = a' + (.65)(.5)[.3(0) + .05(3) + .65(3)].$$

Such concatenated path extensions generalize naturally. A τ-step path extension looks τ columns more deeply into the tree. At each intermediate node the extension follows the branch with highest probability.

A given path from a particular starting node can be extended in many different ways, since a path will generally have many subpaths. Let f represent one such path extension; f embeds information about the starting row, the subpath which is to be extended, and the number of steps in that extension. Let σ represent the standard deviation of the updated estimate resulting from the application of f:

$$\sigma^2 = E(a' - a)^2,$$

where a' represents the updated value of a after application of path extension f. We assume that the decision-maker thinks about the update as if

$$a' = a + x,$$

where x has a normal distribution with mean zero and standard deviation σ.

We now derive the ex-ante expected value of path extension f. Consider the simple case in which the decision-maker faces a choice between two rows: A and B. Assume that the agent knows that choosing row B will generate a certain payoff of b.

The payoff from choosing row A is uncertain. Call this expected payoff a. The agent can learn more about this expected payoff if she executes a path extension f. Specifically, executing the path extension will enable her to update the expected payoff of row A from a to $a' = a + x$.

---

[7] Such forward induction is motivated by experimental work by Colin Camerer et al. (1994) and theoretical work by Philippe Jéhiel (1995), which argue that decision-makers may solve problems by looking forward. Our framework can generalize to also include cognitive operations based on backwards induction.

If the agent doesn't execute the path extension, she'll need to pick between A and B without observing x. So her expected payoff will be

$$\max(E[a'], b) = \max(a, b).$$

If the agent executes the path extension, her expected payoff will be

$$E[\max(a', b)] - q_f,$$

where q_f is the cost of executing the path extension. The value of executing the path extension is the difference between the previous two expressions:

$$E[\max(a', b)] - \max(a, b) - q_f.$$

This can be rewritten as,

$$\int_{-\infty}^{-|a-b|} \frac{|x| - |a-b|}{\sigma} \phi\left(\frac{x}{\sigma}\right) dx - q_f. \tag{1}$$

Here $\phi(\cdot)$ is the standard normal density function.[8]

To gain intuition for eqn 1, begin by assuming (without loss of generality) that $a \geq b$. In this case, the decision-maker only learns something useful when the new analysis leads to a revised value a' that lies below the next best alternative b. Since x represents the new information (i.e., $a' = a + x$), eqn 1 integrates over x values that are less than $-|a - b|$. Finally, $(1/\sigma)\, \phi\,(x/\sigma)$ represents the density of x, since $x \sim N(0, \sigma)$.

For additional intuition consider Figure 9.2, which represents

$$\int_{-\infty}^{-|a-b|} \frac{|x| - |a-b|}{\sigma} \phi\left(\frac{x}{\sigma}\right) dx$$

graphically. The shaded area under the density in Figure 2 represents the probability densities of states of the world in which row a has been revealed to be inferior to row b: that is, $a' < b$. Naturally these are the states of the world in which it is ex-post useful to have analyzed row a. In these states the decision-maker learns that row b is a better choice than row a.

Three fundamental comparative statics are captured in this option value framework. First, the value of a path exploration declines as the cost q_f of the exploration rises.

Second, the value of a path exploration falls with the variability of the information that will be obtained: σ. In other words, the less information that is likely to be revealed by a path exploration, the less valuable such a path exploration becomes. This can be seen graphically by comparing Figures 9.2 and 9.3.

---

[8] Integration yields the alternative expression

$$-|a - b|\Phi\left(-\frac{|a-b|}{\sigma}\right) + \sigma\phi\left(\frac{a-b}{\sigma}\right) - q_f,$$

where $\Phi(\cdot)$ is the cumulative of the standard normal distribution.

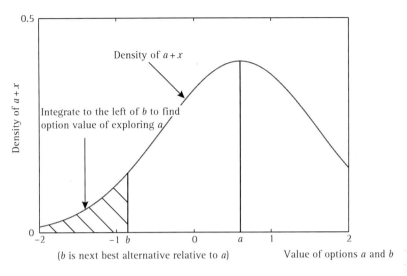

Figure 9.2. *Calculation of the option value*

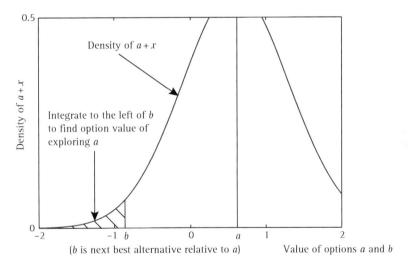

Figure 9.3. *Calculation of the option value (low variance case)*

Figure 9.3 represents

$$\int_{-\infty}^{-|a-b|} \frac{|x| - |a-b|}{\sigma^-} \phi\left(\frac{x}{\sigma^-}\right) dx,$$

for $\sigma^- < \sigma$. As σ falls, so does the probability of reaching states in which $x < -|a-b|$.

Third, the value of a path exploration falls the larger the gap between a and b. As the gap rises, the interval of states for which $x < -|a - b|$ grows smaller. This can be seen graphically by comparing Figures 9.2 and 9.4. Figure 9.4 represents $\int_{-\infty}^{-|a-b|} |-|x|-|a - b^-|/\phi(x/\sigma)\mathrm{d}x$, for $b^- < b$. As b falls, so does the measure of states in which $x < -|a - b|$.

In Gabaix and Laibson (2000*b*), we apply these option theoretic considerations to twelve tree games including the game reproduced in Figure 9.1. We use the option value calculation in eqn 1 to measure the ex-ante expected value of a wide range of path extensions. The directed cognition algorithm then executes the path extension with the highest expected value net of cognition cost, q. The algorithm continues in this way—evaluating the expected value of path extensions and executing the most promising path extension—until no remaining path extension has a positive expected value net of cognition cost.

This procedure radically simplifies analysis of our decision trees. Each unsimplified tree has approximately 100 000 paths leading from the first column to the last column. Our directed cognition algorithm, restricts attention to only a handful of these paths. For example, Figure 9.5 plots the path extensions generated by the directed cognition model for the game in Figure 9.1. Using ex-ante option-theoretic considerations, the algorithm restricts analysis to 7/100 000 of the possible paths in this tree. After these seven path extensions are executed, the algorithm stops. In this sense, the directed cognition provides a partial solution to the frame problem. Option-theoretic intuitions enable the decision-maker to

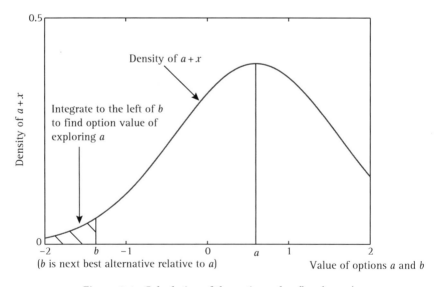

Figure 9.4. *Calculation of the option value (low b case)*

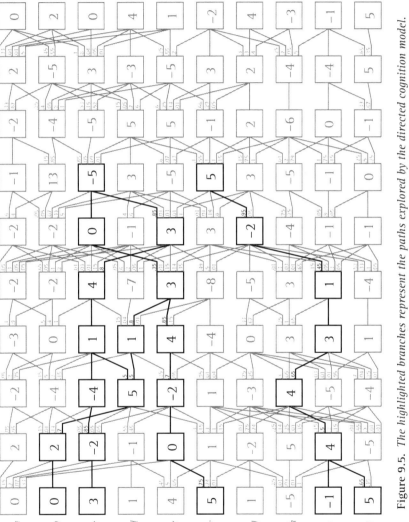

Figure 9.5. *The highlighted branches represent the paths explored by the directed cognition model.*

simplify his problem by restricting attention to a tiny fraction of the available information.

We have tested the directed cognition model by comparing the predictions of the model to the actual experimental choices made by 252 Harvard under-graduates. We measured the Euclidean distance between the model predictions and the empirical choices of our subjects. We then measured the Euclidean distance between the predictions of the rational choice model (with zero cognition cost) and the empirical subject choices. Using this metric, the directed cognition model outperformed the rational choice model with an associated *t*-statistic of 5.2.

We also compared the directed cognition model to three variants of the rational model that prune the decision trees by discarding information in the right-most columns of the trees: the *column cutoff model*, the *column discounting model*, and the *follow the leaders model*.

The column cutoff model assumes that decision-makers calculate perfectly rationally but pay attention to only the first Q columns of the C-column tree, completely ignoring the remaining $C-Q$ columns. The parameter Q is estimated to maximize the fit of the model. The column discounting model assumes that decision-makers follow all paths, but exponentially discount payoffs according to the column in which those payoffs arise. The discount factor is estimated to maximize the fit of the model. Finally, the follow the leaders model only follows branches that have a marginal probability greater than or equal to some threshold probability. The threshold probability is estimated to maximize the fit of the model.[9]

These three algorithms are designed to capture the idea that decision-makers ignore information that is relatively less likely to be useful. For example, the dis-counting model can be interpreted as a model in which the decision-maker has a reduced probability of seeing payoffs in 'later' columns. The directed cognition model significantly outperforms the column cutoff model and the column discounting model. The directed cognition model statistically ties the follow the leaders model.

The directed cognition model simplifies the analysis of complex problems and partially replicates the decisions that subjects make. The directed cognition model exploits three basic principles. First, cognition is costly. Second, cognition is more useful when it reveals a lot of new information. Third, cognition is more useful when it reveals information about choices that are relatively close competitors. Using these basic ideas we were able to dramatically simplify the analysis of complex decision trees, generating behavioral predictions that match subject choices.

In addition, the directed cognition model can be easily generalized. In the version of the model described above, the cognitive operation in which the

---

[9] From any starting box *b* follow all branches that have a probability greater than or equal to *p*. Continue in this way, moving from left to right across the columns in the decision tree. If a branch has a probability less than *p*, consider the box to which the branch leads but do not advance beyond that box. Weight all boxes that you consider with their associated cumulative probabilities, and calculate the weighted sum of the boxes.

decision-maker engages is to look forward into the tree. To generalize the model, other cognitive operations could also be considered. For example, if the middle of the decision tree contained occasional large outlier payoffs, it might make sense for the decision-maker to start at those large payoff boxes and then backwards induct back toward the first column. Such backward induction is a cognitive operation that can be evaluated using the same option value calculations described above.

Although the directed cognition model can be applied to a wide range of choice problems (e.g., all decision trees and sequential extensive form games), the model has several critical limitations, which jointly imply that the model is *not* a general solution to the frame problem. Most importantly, the directed cognition model relies on option values that may take substantial time to calculate, and which can only be calculated with a sophisticated knowledge about the decision problem. For example, the model assumes that the decision maker has rational expectations about σ, the standard deviation of signals arising from additional analysis of the problem. Real actors may not have such prior knowledge, though we believe that they intuitively, crudely infer such standard deviations from their previous experience with analogous problems. We imagine that our model's formal option value calculations represent proxies for the informal option value intuitions that guide real decision makers. These informal intuitions are undoubtedly more experienced-based and backward looking than the rationally forward-looking calculations implied by the model.

Finally, we believe that decision makers use a wide range of complementary tools to limit the number of option-value intuitions/calculations that they execute. For example, agents may only execute option value analysis on concepts called to mind by environmental cues. We don't think about global warming (while planning a cross-country trip), unless an explicit cue calls this issue to our attention. Without such attention filters our agent might be paralyzed by myriad option value calculations, which would have the unintended consequence of slowing down his analysis instead of speeding it up.

A true resolution of the frame problem would need to explicitly model such attention filters. We did not need attention filters in our decision tree analysis, since the number of option value calculations were limited by the forward induction framework that we adopted. Branching paths leaving a particular starting row in Figure 9.1 were endogenously pruned by the model before they had branched too finely. In more general problems, the analysis is not so well-ordered and the potential option value calculations are not so tightly bounded. For these general problems (e.g., walking across Central Park in Manhattan), attention filters are probably necessary equipment.

Zenon Pylyshyn, one leading contributor to the frame problem literature, recounts a shaggy dog story in which an engineer boasts that he has invented a perpetual motion machine. The complicated machine is revealed with great fanfare but no parts are moving and one onlooker asks why. The inventor responds, 'Well the machine is all finished except for one minor little piece that is still on order and is expected any day now. It's just a small ratchet that fits in here and goes back and forth forever (1996, p. xii).' Pylyshyn suggests that solutions to the frame problem suffer from the same problem. 'It usually ends up with the critical element being on order.' Attention filters are one of the missing ratchets in our machine.

We hope that our model's shortcomings will serve primarily to entice other economic researchers to enter the fray. The frame problem represents a fundamental challenge to researchers who build models of intelligent agents: How do agents allocate scarce resources like cognition and attention? We imagine that economists may have something useful to say about this interesting and important allocation problem.

3. CONCLUSION

The frame problem is the challenge of developing intelligent machines that can think quickly *and* effectively about complex problems. A solution to the frame problem would provide a theory of endogenous simplification of complex problems.

The option value approach provides a small step in this direction. Our directed cognition model provides a framework for deciding how deeply to analyze decision problems. When cognitive analysis is likely to yield little new insight, the option value of continued analysis declines. This option value also declines when a particular choice gains a large edge over the available alternatives. Our directed cognition model quantifies these two effects and integrates them in a formal framework that makes sharp quantitative predictions about behavior. We have successfully tested these predictions in an experiment conducted on Harvard undergraduates.

Future work will sharpen this analysis by actually measuring the allocation of *attention* within decision problems. Computer based experiments enable researchers to determine exactly what information subjects are analyzing moment by moment.[10] With these kind of real time observations, we will be able to directly test the attention allocation predictions of the option value approach.

Ultimately, we expect that theories of endogenous simplification will explain many deviations from pure rationality. In Gabaix and Laibson (2000*b*) we use the directed cognition model to explain psychological phenomena like myopia, salience, and anchoring. Understanding how decision-makers simplify complex problems will reveal why they occassionally make mistakes, providing a possible microfoundation for anomalous decision-making.

---

[10]   We are currently running experiments (Gabaix et al. 2002) that ask subjects to analyze problems on a computer screen. By using Mouselab (Payne et al., 1993), a programming language that enables experimenters to record the exact location of the mouse cursor, and by only revealing information in a neighborhood of the cursor, we can determine what information subjects are using from moment to

REFERENCES

Camerer, C., Johnson, E.J., Rymon, T., and Sen, S. (1994). Cognition and framing in sequential bargaining for gains and losses. In K. Binmore, A. Kirman, and P. Tani (Eds.), *Frontiers of game theory* (pp. 27–47). Cambridge, MA: MIT Press.

Conlisk, John. (1996). Why bounded rationality? *Journal of Economic Literature, 34*(2), 669–700.

Dennett, D. (1987). Cognitive wheels: The frame problem of AI. In Z.W. Pylyshyn (Ed.), *The Robot's Dilemma: The Frame Problem in Artificial Intelligence* (pp. 41-64). Norwood, NJ: Ablex Publishing Corporation.

—— (1996). Producing future by telling stories. In K.M. Ford, Z.W. Pylyshyn (Eds.), *The Robot's Dilemma Revisited: The Frame Problem in Artificial Intelligence*. Norwood, NJ: Ablex Publishing Corporation.

Dietrich, E. and Chris F. (1996). The role of the frame problem in Fodor's modularity thesis: A case study of rationalist cognitive science. In K.M. Ford and Z.W. Pylyshyn (Eds.), *The Robot's Dilemma Revisited: The Frame Problem in Artificial Intelligence*. Norwood, NJ: Ablex Publishing Corporation.

Dixit, A.K. and Pindyck, R.S. (1994). *Investment under uncertainty*. Princeton, NJ: Princeton University Press.

Ford, K.M. and Pylyshyn, Z.W. (Eds.) (1996). *The robot's dilemma revisited: The frame problem in artificial intelligence*. Norwood, NJ: Ablex Publishing Corporation.

Gabaix, X. and Laibson, D. (2000a). A boundedly rational decision algorithm, *AER Papers and Proceedings*, May, 433–8.

—— and —— (2000b). Bounded rationality and directed cognition, MIT and Harvard mimeo.

—— —— Moloche, G., and Weinberg, S. (2002) 'The Allocation of Attention: Theory and Evidence' Harvard: mimeo.

Glymour, C. (1996). The adventures among the asteroids of angela android, series 8400XF with an afterword on planning, prediction, learning the frame problem, and a few other subjects. In K.M. Ford and Z.W. Pylyshyn (Eds.), *The robot's dilemma revisited: The frame problem in artificial intelligence* (pp. 25–34). Norwood, NJ: Ablex Publishing Corporation.

Jéhiel, P. (1995). Limited horizon forecast in repeated alternate games. *Journal of Economic Theory, 67*, 497–519.

Kahneman, D. and Tversky, A. (1974). Judgment under uncertainty: Heuristics and biases. *Science, 185*, 1124–31.

McCarthy, J. and Hayes, P.J. (1969). Some philosophical problems from the standpoint of artificial intelligence. In B. Meltzer and D. Michie (Eds.), *Machine Intelligence* (Vol. 4, pp. 463–502). Edinburgh: University of Edinburgh Press.

Payne, J.W., Bettman, J.R., and Johnson, E.J. (1993). *The Adaptive Decision Maker*. Cambridge: Cambridge University Press.

Pylyshyn, Z.W. (Ed.) (1987). *The robot's dilemma: The frame problem in artificial intelligence*. Norwood, NJ: Ablex Publishing Corporation.

Shanahan, M. (1997). *Solving the frame problem: A mathematical investigation of the common sense law of inertia*. Cambridge, MA: MIT Press.

Shugan, S.M. (1980). The cost of thinking. *Journal of Consumer Research, 7*(2), 99–111.

Simon, H. (1955). A behavioral model of rational choice. *Quarterly Journal of Economics, 69*(1), 99–118.

Thaler, R. (1994). *Quasi rational economics*. New York: Russell Sage.

——(1994). *The winner's curse*. New York: Russell Sage.

PART IV

TIME AND UTILITY

10

Experienced Utility and Objective Happiness: A Moment-Based Approach

DANIEL KAHNEMAN

The concept of utility has carried two different meanings in its long history. As Bentham (1789) used it, utility refers to the experiences of pleasure and pain, the 'sovereign masters' that 'point out what we ought to do, as well as determine what we shall do.' In modern decision research, however, the utility of outcomes refers to their weight in decisions: utility is inferred from observed choices and is in turn used to explain choices. To distinguish the two notions I refer to Bentham's concept as *experienced utility* and to the modern usage as *decision utility*. Experienced utility is the focus of this chapter. Contrary to the behaviorist position that led to the abandonment of Bentham's notion (Loewenstein, 1992), the claim made here is that experienced utility can be usefully measured. The chapter presents arguments to support that claim, and speculates about its implications.

This essay has three main goals: (1) to present a detailed analysis of the concept of experienced utility and of the relation between the pleasure and pain of moments and the utility of more extended episodes; (2) to argue that experienced utility is best measured by moment-based methods that assess the experience of the present; (3) to develop a moment-based conception of an aspect of human well-being that I will call 'objective happiness'. The chapter also introduces several unfamiliar concepts that will be used in some of the chapters that follow.

Pleasure and pain are attributes of a moment of experience, but the outcomes that people value extend over time. It is therefore necessary to establish a concept

This chapter was previously published as chapter 37 in D. Kahneman and A. Tversky (Eds.) (2000), *Choices, Values and Frames.* New York: Cambridge University Press and the Russell Sage Foundation. Reprinted with the permission of Cambridge University Press.

I thank Shane Frederick, Barbara Fredrickson, Laura Gibson, David Laibson, Nathan Novemsky, David Schkade, Cass Sunstein, Richard Thaler, Anne Treisman, and Peter Wakker for helpful comments. I also thank Peter Wakker for allowing me to use ideas and sentences that we had fashioned together, and Peter McGraw for extremely valuable assistance and useful suggestions.

of experienced utility that applies to temporally extended outcomes. Two approaches to this task will be compared here.

(i) The *memory-based* approach accepts the subject's retrospective evaluations of past episodes and situations as valid data. The *remembered utility* of an episode of experience is defined by the subject's retrospective global assessment of it.

(ii) The *moment-based* approach derives the experienced utility of an episode from real-time measures of the pleasure and pain that the subject experienced during that episode. *Moment-utility* refers to the valence (good or bad) and to the intensity (mild to extreme) of current affective or hedonic experience. The *total utility* of an episode is derived exclusively from the record of moment-utilities during that episode.

The main novelty of the treatment proposed here is that it is thoroughly moment-based. Section 1 reviews some of the evidence that raises doubts about the validity of memory-based assessments. Section 2 presents the conditions that must be satisfied to permit an assessment of the total experienced utility of episodes from the utilities of their constituent moments. Section 3 introduces a moment-based concept of objective happiness, and examines the feasibility of its measurement. Section 4 exposes the ambiguity of a central idea of the well-being literature—the hedonic treadmill—and discusses how measures of objective happiness could contribute to the resolution of that ambiguity. A research agenda and some major objections are discussed in Section 5.

The main concepts of the present treatment are illustrated by Figure 10.1, which is drawn from a study of immediate and retrospective reports of the pain of medical procedures (Redelmeier and Kahneman, 1996). Patients undergoing colonoscopy were asked every 60 s to report the intensity of their current pain, on a scale where 10 was 'intolerable pain' and 0 was 'no pain at all'. These ratings were used to construct the profiles of *moment-utility* shown in the figure. The patients later provided several measures of the *remembered utility* of the procedure. They evaluated the entire experience on a scale, and they also compared it to a standard set of aversive experiences. The *total utility* associated with each patient's colonoscopy has a different nature. Unlike moment-utility and remembered utility, it is not an expression of a subjective feeling or judgment. Total utility is an objective assessment of the statistics of a utility profile.

The cases of patients A and B also illustrate the contrast between remembered utility and total utility. It is immediately apparent from inspection of Figure 10.1 that patient B had a worse experience than patient A,[1] and this impression will be confirmed by the analysis of total utility in Section 2 (see Figure 10.2). However, patient A in fact retained a worse evaluation of the procedure than patient B. In this case, as in many others, remembered utility and total utility do not coincide,

---

[1] On the assumption that the two patients used the pain scale similarly. This issue is discussed further in Section 2.

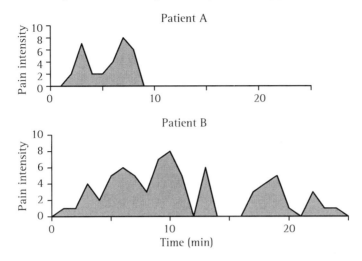

Figure 10.1. *Pain intensity reported by two colonoscopy patients*

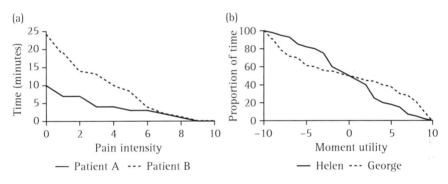

Figure 10.2. *(a) Decumulative temporal function representing pain profiles of Patients A and B. (b) Fictitious decumulative functions representing the objective happiness of two individuals over a period of time*

and outcomes will be ranked differently depending on whether experienced utility is assessed by a memory-based or by a moment-based method.

1. MEMORY-BASED ASSESSMENT: REMEMBERED UTILITY

Anyone who has cared for an elderly relative whose memory is failing has learned that there is a crucial difference between two ostensibly similar questions. The question 'How are you now?' may elicit a confident and cogent answer while the question 'How have you been?' evokes only confusion. This distinction is rarely drawn in other settings. We normally expect people to know how they have been as well as they know how they are. Memory-based evaluations of experience and reports of current pleasure and pain are treated with equal respect in routine conversations—but the respect for memory is less deserved. Studies of the psychology of remembered utility are reviewed in detail in the next chapter. The main conclusions of this research are listed below, and illustrated by the colonoscopy study from which Figure 10.1 was drawn.

Duration neglect. No one would deny that it is generally better for a colonoscopy to be short than to be long. At least in principle, then, the duration of a colonoscopy is relevant to its overall utility. However, memory-based assessments do not generally conform to this principle. For example, the colonoscopies studied by Redelmeier and Kahneman (1996) varied in duration between 4 and 69 min, but the correlation between the duration of a procedure and the patient's subsequent evaluation of it was only .03. Furthermore, the duration of the colonoscopy had no effect on patients' hypothetical choice between a repeat colonoscopy and a barium enema. Complete, or nearly complete neglect of duration has been found in other studies, using a variety of different research designs. A hypothesis of 'evaluation by moments' is introduced in chapter 38 to explain these findings: it asserts that the remembered utility of an episode is determined by constructing a composite representative moment, and by assessing the utility of that moment.

The Peak/End rule. The patients' subsequent evaluation of the procedure was predicted with relatively high accuracy ($r = 0.67$) from the average of the most intense level of pain reported during the procedure, and of the mean pain level reported over the last three minutes. Because the Peak/End average was higher for patient A than for patient B, this empirical rule predicts—correctly—that patient A would retain a more aversive memory of the colonoscopy than would patient B. Strong support for the Peak/End rule was obtained in several other studies, reviewed in detail in the following chapter.

Violations of dominance. The Peak/End rule implies a counter-intuitive prediction: adding a period of pain to an aversive episode will actually improve its remembered utility, if it lowers the Peak/End average. For example, several extra minutes at pain level 4 would be expected to improve patient A's global evaluation of the procedure. A clinical experiment with 682 patients undergoing colonoscopy tested this prediction. Half of the patients were randomly selected for an experimental treatment, in which the examining physician left the colonoscope in place for about a minute after terminating the examination. The patient was not informed of the manipulation (Katz et al., 1997).[2] The extra minute is distinctly uncomfortable, but not very painful. The effect of the experimental treatment was to reduce the Peak/End average for patients, such as patient A, who would otherwise have experienced considerable pain in the final moments of the procedure. As predicted by the Peak/End rule, retrospective

---

[2] The ethical justification for the experiment was the observation of poor compliance among patients who have had a painful colonoscopy and are instructed to schedule another.

evaluations of the procedure were significantly more favorable in the group that experienced the prolonged procedure than in the group that was treated conventionally.

Similar violations of dominance were also observed in choices: in one experiment, participants were exposed in immediate succession to two unpleasant sounds of similar composition. One of them lasted for 10 s at 78 db; the other consisted of the same 10 s at 78 db, followed by 4 s at 66 db. When given an opportunity to choose which of the two sounds would be repeated later, most participants chose the longer (Schreiber and Kahneman, 2000; [ch. 38]). This choice is odd, because 4 s of silence would clearly be preferable to 4 s of 66 db noise. In this simple situation, decision utility appears to be determined directly by remembered utility: people choose to repeat the sound they dislike least, and the Peak/End rule determines that.

2. MOMENT-BASED ASSESSMENT: TOTAL UTILITY

The evidence reviewed in the preceding section suggested that memory-based assessments of experienced utility should not be taken at face value. The present section introduces a moment-based alternative, in which the *total utility* of an episode is derived from a temporal profile of moment-utility. The same analysis extends to related episodes separated in time, because utility profiles may be concatenated. For example, the total utility of a Kenya safari should include subsequent occasions of slide-showing and reminiscing.

Figure 10.2a presents the data of Figure 10.1 in the form of a decumulative function, which shows the amount of time spent at or above each pain level. If the measure of moment-utility on which it is based satisfies a stringent set of conditions, total utility can be derived from the type of representation illustrated in Figure 10.2 (Kahneman et al., 1997). Six conditions are listed below. The first four impose requirements on the measure of moment-utility. The last two conditions are normative in character; they specify how total utility is constructed from moment-utilities.

Inclusiveness. In a moment-based approach the utility profile is a 'sufficient statistic' to determine the experienced utility of an extended outcome. The measure of moment-utility should therefore incorporate all the aspects of experience that are relevant to this evaluation. In particular, a measure of moment-utility should reflect the affective consequences of prior events (e.g., satiation, adaptation, fatigue), as well as the affect associated with the anticipation of future events (fear, hope).

Ordinal measurement across situations. The measurement of moment-utility must be ordinal or better. Experiences of different types (e.g., a stubbed toe and a humiliating rebuke) must be measured on a common scale.

Distinctive neutral point. The pain scale that was used in the colonoscopy study has a natural zero point. However, the dimension of moment-utility is bipolar, ranging from intensely positive to neutral, and from neutral to intensely negative affect. A distinctive neutral point ('neither pleasant nor unpleasant', 'neither approach nor avoid') anchors the scale and permits comparisons across situations and persons.[3] As will be seen later, a stable zero is also essential for cardinal measurement of moment-utility on a ratio scale.

Interpersonal comparability. The scale must permit comparisons of individuals and groups. The next section shows that this requirement may be more tractable than is commonly thought.

The next two requirements are of a different nature. They involve normative assumptions about the nature of total utility. The assumptions of separability and time-neutrality are required to justify the transformation of utility profiles (e.g., Figure 10.1) into the decumulative format (e.g., Figure 10.2). The discussion of these assumptions highlights a critical difference between the present analysis and economic models of the utility of sequences of outcomes. These models generally describe outcomes as physical events. The analysis of total utility, in contrast, describes outcomes as moment-utilities.

Separability: the order in which moment-utilities are experienced does not affect total utility. Order effects are ubiquitous in experienced utility. For example, a strenuous tennis game and a large lunch yield a better experience in one order than in the other, because the enjoyment of the tennis game is sharply reduced when it follows lunch. The condition of separability states that the contribution of an element to the global utility of the sequence is independent of the elements that preceded and followed it. This condition is often violated when the sequences are described in terms of physical events, such as lunch and a tennis game. In a moment-based treatment, however, the elements of the sequence that is to be evaluated are not events—they are moment-utilities associated with events. Because *all* the effects of the order of events are already incorporated into moment-utilities, separability can be assumed for these moment-utilities. Separability is necessary for the decumulative representation, which does not preserve order information. To appreciate the intuition, consider an individual who receives two unexpected prizes in immediate succession, one of $500, the other of $10 000, then promptly dies, or loses his memory. In evaluating the total utility of these experiences, we recognize that it would be better for the two prizes to arrive in ascending rather than in descending order—presumably because the enjoyment of the smaller prize is greater when it comes first. Now imagine that all you know is that just before he died (or became amnesic) an individual had two pleasurable experiences with utilities U_a and U_b, where $U_a \gg U_b$, would we still think that their order matters? When outcomes are moment-utilities, there is no compelling reason to reject separability.

Time neutrality: all moments are weighted alike in total utility. Total utility is a measure on completed outcomes, and is therefore always assessed after the fact. Unlike decision making, in which the temporal distance between the moment of decision and the outcome may matter, the temporal distance between an outcome

---

[3] Some authors consider valence as bi-valent rather than bipolar (e.g., Cacioppo et al., 1999).

and its retrospective assessment is entirely irrelevant to its evaluation. Total utility is therefore *time neutral.* In this important respect, it is unlike decision utility and remembered utility, which both assign more weight to some parts of the sequence than to others. The decision utility of outcomes that occur late in a sequence is often heavily discounted. In remembered utility, on the other hand, the last parts of a sequence are weighted more than those that came earlier— a bias that is incorporated in the Peak/End rule. The normative status of both weighting schemes is dubious. If the benefits are obtained before the costs must be paid, discounting of delayed outcomes in decisions favors myopic preferences for options that do not maximize total utility. The overweighting of endings may be equally unreasonable: an experience that ended very badly could still have positive utility overall, if it was sufficiently good for a sufficiently long time (Kahneman et al., 1997).

2.1. Measures of Total Utility

The representation of Figure 10.2 assumes both that a utility profile can be rearranged at will and that all its parts are weighted equally. Separability and time neutrality are therefore necessary, and together with the assumptions of inclusiveness and ordinal measurement, sufficient for the representation of utility profiles as decumulative temporal distributions. The total utility of episodes is a measure on these distributions.

Figure 10.2 illustrates two representations of temporal distributions of utility, which differ in their ordinates: time is shown in absolute units in panel (a), but in proportional units in panel (b). The representation of panel 2a is appropriate when the duration of the episode is relevant to its evaluation. Thus, it is reasonable to say that the colonoscopy of patient B was worse than that of patient A because it lasted longer. On the other hand, it does not make sense to say that Helen was happier last week than she was last Sunday because last week was longer than last Sunday. The representation of Figure 10.2b is correct when the duration of the period of evaluation is not relevant to its evaluation. It is the appropriate representation in the assessment of the well-being of individuals and groups, which is discussed in the next section.[4]

As Figure 10.2a illustrates, the ordinal measurement of moment-utility permits the detection of distributional dominance. By this simple test, patient B had a worse colonoscopy than patient A. The decumulative distribution can also be characterized by non-parametric statistics, such as the median and other fractiles. However, distributional dominance is a blunt measuring instrument, and no single non-parametric index captures all the relevant information contained in a

---

[4] There are situations in which both representations are relevant. The total utility (or happiness) that Alan enjoyed while he was married to Helen may depend on how long they were married before she died in an accident. On the other hand, an assessment of how happy Alan was in his marriage should not be influenced by how long it lasted.

temporal distribution of moment-utilities. Figure 10.2b presents decumulative distributions of moment-utility for two individuals, George and Helen. There is no dominance in this comparison, and the medians are close. The main conclusion that can be drawn is that George experienced more extremes of affect than Helen did.

Cardinal measurement of moment-utility would be desirable, of course. With cardinal measurement, the most natural index of total utility could be calculated: the temporal integral of moment-utility. The idea has a long history (Edgeworth discussed it in 1881) but it effectively requires a rescaling of moment-utility in terms of physical time, which is difficult to implement. This reasoning is explicit in the use of QALYs (Quality Adjusted Life Years) in medical decision making. QALY's are derived from judgments of equivalence between periods of survival that vary in duration and in level of health. For example, two years of survival at a QALY of 0.5 are equally desirable as one year in normal health (Broome, 1993).

A formal analysis of the temporal integration rule was offered by Kahneman, et al. (1997). Their treatment invoked all the assumptions that were discussed in this section, including separability and temporal neutrality. In addition, it introduced an idealized objective observer, who assesses the total utility of utility profiles, such as those of Figure 10.1. The following axioms specify the logic of this assessment.

1. *The global utility of a utility profile is not affected by concatenation with a neutral utility profile.*
2. *Increases of moment-utility do not decrease the global utility of a utility profile.*
3. *In a concatenation of two utility profiles, replacing one profile by another with a higher global utility will increase the global utility of the concatenation.*

The following theorem can be proved: 'The three axioms above hold if and only if there exists a non-decreasing ('value') transformation function of moment-utility, assigning value 0 to 0, such that global utility orders utility profiles according to the integral of the value of moment-utility over time.' The proof is due to Peter Wakker.

The representation of total utility as a temporal integral implies a scale of moment-utility, monotonically related to the original scale, but now calibrated by its relation to duration. For example, suppose that an idealized observer who conforms to the axioms judges that 1 minute of pain that had been rated 7 on the original scale is equivalent to 2 minutes at a rating of 6. On the transformed scale, the value that corresponds to the original rating of 7 will be double the value assigned to a rating of 6. Idealized observers are hard to find, of course, and cardinal scaling of utility is therefore a conceptual exercise rather than a practical procedure. Fortunately, the decumulative representation is adequate for many purposes. The conditions identified by Kahneman et al. (1997) are sufficient to guarantee this representation, without attempting cardinal measurement and without involving observers.

3. OBJECTIVE HAPPINESS: CONCEPT AND MEASURE

Moment-utility is the building block of the broader construct of experienced utility. It is also the building block for a construct of *objective happiness*, with which the remainder of this chapter is concerned. Like total utility, objective happiness is to be derived from a distribution of moment-utility (see Figure 10.2b for an example) that characterizes an individual (George or Helen), a group (Californians, midwesterners, paraplegics), or a setting (the Washington subway, the New York subway). Like total utility, objective happiness is a moment-based concept, which is operationalized exclusively by measures of the affective state of individuals at particular moments in time. In this essential respect, objective happiness differs from standard measures of subjective well-being, which are memory-based and require the subject to report a global evaluation of the recent past. The term 'objective' is used because the judgment of happiness is made according to objective rules. The ultimate data for the judgment are, of course, subjective experiences.

In the special conditions of the clinic or laboratory it is sometimes possible to obtain continuous or almost continuous reports of experienced utility from patients or experimental subjects. Continuous measures are of course impractical for the measurement of objective happiness over a period of time. Sampling techniques must be used to obtain a set of values of moment-utility that adequately represents the intended population of individuals, times, and occasions. For example, a study of the objective happiness of Californians should use a sample of observations that reflects the relative amounts of time spent on the freeway and in hot tubs. Techniques for sampling times and occasions have been developed in the context of Experience Sampling Methodology (ESM) (Csikszentmihalyi, 1990; Stone et al., 1999).[5]

Reporting the sign and intensity of current hedonic and affective experience is not essentially different from the standard psychophysical tasks of reporting color or smell. The report of affect is probably intermediate in difficulty between these tasks: somewhat more difficult than labeling colors, but much easier than describing smells. The worlds of affective experience and of color experience are similar in another important respect: they combine phenomenological richness with a simple underlying structure. A non-intuitive finding of color research is that, in spite of the enormous variety of subjective color experience, the world of color can be represented in a two-dimensional space—the color circle—with additional information provided in a third dimension of luminance. A major result of research on affect is that a similarly simple structure is found in that domain as well. Much of the variation among affective states is captured by specifying their positions in a two-dimensional space, which is defined by the major dimensions

---

[5] Participants in studies using ESM carry a palmtop computer that beeps at random times during the day. The palmtop computer then displays questions that elicit information about the current setting and about the subject's present affective state.

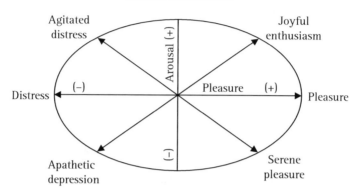

Figure 10.3. *A representation of affective space*

of valence (good to neutral to bad) and arousal (from frenetic to lethargic) (Plutchik and Conte, 1997; Russell, 1980; Russell and Carroll, 1999; Stone, 1995; Warr, 1999). As Figure 10.3 illustrates, the two-dimensional structure permits a distinction between two forms of positive affect—exuberant joy or serene bliss—and two forms of negative affect—agitated distress or apathetic depression.

A significant limitation of the two-dimensional representation of affect is that it does not capture the nature of primary emotions, such as surprise or anger. Another objection to this scheme questions the assumption that valence is a single bipolar dimension. Cacioppo et al. (1999) point out that positive and negative affect are processed by different neural systems and may be activated concurrently. They suggest that a three-dimensional representation may be necessary, in which 'good' and 'bad' are independent dimensions. However, the systems are not functionally independent, and there is evidence that they inhibit each other. Lang (1995) has shown, for example, that watching pleasant pictures of food or smiling babies attenuates the startle response to a loud sound, whereas startle is actually enhanced in the presence of disgusting or otherwise awful pictures. For the present purposes, the description of valence as a bipolar dimension can be retained as a useful approximation, even if it is not perfectly correct (Russell and Carroll, 1999; Tellegen et al., 1999). Later in this section, I discuss a physiological measure that can provide convergent validation of the measurement of valence.

The simplest method for eliciting a self-report of current affective state is undoubtedly the *affect grid*: respondents describe their state by marking a single position on a grid defined by the two dimensions of valence and arousal (Russell et al., 1989). The affect grid appears to be applicable in all situations: any moment of life can be characterized by the attributes of valence and arousal. The characterization is incomplete, of course, but hardly irrelevant to an analysis of well-being. The affect grid can be used to derive a unidimensional distribution of affective values, as in Figure 10.2. Of course, finer-grain analyses that do not collapse over the arousal dimension are likely to be even more informative.

Next, I attempt to evaluate the affect grid in terms of the four criteria of adequate measurement of moment-utility that were considered in the preceding section. The purpose of this speculative discussion is to illustrate both the problems and the promise of measurement in this domain, not to endorse any particular measure.

Inclusiveness. Defining happiness by the temporal distribution of experienced affect appears very narrow, and so it is. The concept of objective happiness is not intended to stand on its own, and is proposed only as a necessary element of a theory of human well-being. A comprehensive account of well-being inevitably brings in philosophical considerations (Ryff and Singer, 1998) and a moral conception of 'the good life' (Brock, 1993; Nussbaum and Sen, 1993), which are not easily reduced to experienced utility. However, good mood and enjoyment of life are not incompatible with other psychological criteria of well-being that have been proposed, such as the maintenance of personal goals, social involvement, intense absorption in activities, and a sense that life is meaningful (Argyle, 1999; Cantor and Sanderson, 1999; Csikszentmihalyi, 1990; Fredrickson, 1999). Clearly, a life that is meaningful, satisfying, and cheerful should rank higher on the scale of well-being than a life that is equally meaningful and satisfying, but sad or tense. Objective happiness is only one constituent of the quality of human life, but it is a significant one.

Ordinal measurement across situations. The experiences of a stubbed toe and of a humiliating rebuke are both likely to be described on the affect grid as negative in valence and high in arousal—but can the valence and the arousal be compared? It is a familiar psychological fact that comparison along a single attribute is especially difficult if the objects compared differ in other attributes as well. For example, it is more difficult—but not impossible—to compare the loudness of sounds that differ in pitch and timbre than to compare sounds that share these attributes. The question of whether people can compare physical and emotional pain, or the thrills of food and of music is ultimately empirical. In general, the coherence of judgments across categories is tested by examining the correspondence between ranking of objects in explicit comparisons and ratings of the same objects, considered one at a time. This test is applicable to ratings and rankings of the utility of different kinds of experience, although it is complicated by the necessity of relying on memory for the comparison task.

Absolute zero point. Bipolar scales of judgment comprise scales for two qualitatively different attributes, separated by a distinctive neutral point. Familiar examples include the dimensions that run from hot to cold and from red to green. The neutral point that separates the reddish zone from the greenish zone of the red-green dimension is 'colorless gray or white'. Similarly, 'neither cold nor warm' is the natural zero of the scale of subjective temperature. The stimulus that gives rise to a neutral experience may be different in different contexts, but the neutral experience itself is constant. For example, people can completely adapt to a range of different temperatures, and within that range any temperature to which one has fully adapted will evoke the same neutral experience. The natural zero of the scale of moment-utility should be 'neither pleasant nor unpleasant—neither approach nor avoid.' A distinctive zero permits a crude but useful assessment of well-being in terms of the amount of time spent on the positive and on the negative side of the neutral point (Diener et al., 1991; Parducci, 1995). Because it is distinctive, the neutral value can be used with some confidence to match experiences—whether thermal or hedonic—across time for a given individual, and even across individuals (Kahneman and Varey, 1991).

Interpersonal comparability. Interpersonal comparisons of subjective experience can never be fully satisfactory, but the success of psychophysical research suggests that these comparisons do not present an intractable problem. Three illustrative lines of evidence will be mentioned in support of this conclusion. (i) There is substantial inter-subject agreement on the psychophysical functions that relate reports of the intensity of subjective experience to the physical intensity of the stimulus. For example, the relation between a measure of the physical strength of labor contractions during childbirth and self-reports of pain was generally similar for different women (Algom and Lubel, 1994). (ii) The design of the colonoscopy study (Redelmeier and Kahneman, 1996) included a group of 50 patients who were not required to report their pain every minute during the procedure. Assessments of the pain of these patients were made every 60 s by a minimally trained assistant, on the basis of what she could see and hear of the patient's reactions. The remarkable result was that the Peak/End average of the observer's ratings correlated quite highly ($r = .70$) with the patients' own global evaluations of the procedure, reported after its termination. The observer was evidently capable of meaningful comparisons of the immediate experiences of different patients. Furthermore, the pattern of results implies considerable agreement among patients in the use of the response scales. (iii) The observation of high correlations between self-reports and physiological measures, which is discussed next, provides further support of the feasibility of interpersonal comparisons.

3.1. Physiological Validation

The fundamental simplicity of affective space and the speed of developments in brain research make it likely that physiological correlates of moment-utility (affective valence) will be found. The difference between levels of electrical activity in the left and right hemispheres of the prefrontal cortex appears to meet most criteria for such a measure (Davidson, 1998). Positive and negative affect are respectively associated with greater activity in the left and in the right prefrontal regions. Neurologists have long known that the misery of a stroke that affects the prefrontal area is much worse if the damage is in the left hemisphere—the happier region, where opportunities for approach appear to be calculated (Sutton and Davidson, 1998). A simple measure of the difference in the levels of activity in the two hemispheres has been validated as a measure of mood and of the response to affectively relevant stimuli. Stable individual differences in the characteristic value of this difference are highly correlated with differences in individual temperament and personality, both in adults (Davidson and Tomarken, 1989; Sutton and Davidson, 1997) and in babies (Davidson and Fox, 1989). Correlations with questionnaire measures of approach and avoidance tendencies, and of positive and negative affect are strikingly high (Sutton and Davidson, 1997; Tomarken et al., 1992). This result demonstrates, in passing, that the function that relates self-reports to brain states must be quite similar across people.

A different approach to the physiology of well-being has been adopted by investigators who study physiological markers of long-term cumulative load on coping resources (Ryff and Singer, 1998; Sapolsky, 1999). It is tempting to speculate that these measures of stress-induced physiological wear and tear could be correlates of long-term objective happiness. It is not science fiction to imagine that physiological measures will eventually contribute to the solution of enduring puzzles in the study of experienced utility and of well-being, and provide a criterion for the validation of self-report measures.

In conclusion, the prospects are reasonably good for an index of the valence and intensity of current experience, which will be sensitive to the many kinds of pleasure and anguish in people's lives: moods of contentment or misery, feelings of pride or regret, aesthetic thrills, experiences of 'flow', worrying thoughts, and physical pleasures. However, the limits of what is claimed here should be made explicit. No one will wish to argue that the affect grid or a measure of prefrontal electrocortical asymmetry convey all that we would wish to know about an individual's affective and hedonic experience, just as no one would argue that a measure of the pooled activity levels in the red-green and blue-yellow channels convey the experience of seeing a view. The claim made here is not that the dimension of valence in experience is all we need to know—only that we need to know the valence of experience.

4. THE AMBIGUITY OF TREADMILL EFFECTS

The fundamental surprise of well-being research is the robust finding that life circumstances make only a small contribution to the variance of happiness—far smaller than the contribution of inherited temperament or personality (Diener et al., 1999; Lykken and Tellegen, 1996; Myers and Diener, 1995). Although people have intense emotional reactions to major changes in the circumstances of their lives, these reactions appear to subside more or less completely, and often quite quickly (Headey and Wearing, 1992; Frederick and Loewenstein, 1999). As a consequence, cross-sectional correlations between life circumstances and sub-jective happiness are low. Between 1958 and 1987, for example, real income in Japan increased fivefold, but self-reported happiness did not increase at all (Easterlin, 1995). The most famous observations in this vein were made by Brickman et al. (1978), who reported that after a period of adjustment lottery winners are not much happier than a control group and paraplegics not much unhappier. In a now classic essay, Brickman and Campbell (1971) used the term *hedonic treadmill* both to describe and to interpret such observations. I will use the term *treadmill effect* to refer to the general observation, while reserving the term hedonic treadmill to refer to a particular explanation of the effect.

4.1. Treadmill Effects

Brickman and Campbell (1971) based their conception of the hedonic treadmill on a notion of adaptation level, which Helson (1964) had introduced earlier to explain phenomena of adaptation in perception and judgment. Anyone who has bathed in a cool pool, or in a warm sea, will recognize the basic phenomenon. As one adapts, the experience of the temperature of the water gradually drifts toward 'neither hot nor cold', and the experience of other temperatures changes accordingly. A temperature that would be called warm in one context may feel cool in another. Brickman and Campbell proposed that a similar process of adaptation applies to the hedonic value of life circumstances.

The prevalence of treadmill effects is of psychological interest for two separate reasons. First, because of the ironic light it sheds on the pursuit of happiness. Second, because its surprise value is itself surprising: if the treadmill effect is a common fact of life, why do people not seem to know about it? As the next chapter shows, the extent and the speed of treadmill effects in self-reported happiness are not anticipated. A study conducted among students in California and in the Midwest was designed to examine both the reality of regional effects in life satisfaction and beliefs about these effects (Schkade and Kahneman, 1998). The results showed no trace of a difference between Californians and Midwesterners in overall life satisfaction. However, they revealed a widespread expectation, shared by residents of both regions, that the self-reports of Californians would indicate more happiness than the self-reports of Midwesterners.

Beside their robustness and their unexpectedness, studies of treadmill effects share a third characteristic: they are not entirely persuasive. Skeptics argue that the null results are due, at least in part, to differences in the use of scales of happiness and life satisfaction. If people whose life circumstances differ use the scales differently, there may be less hedonic adaptation to circumstances than surveys of subjective well-being suggest. Frederick and Loewenstein (1999) present an extensive list of reasons that may lead paraplegics to overstate their 'true happiness.' The main claim of the present section is that these doubts are not mere quibbles, and that demonstrations of treadmill effects are subject to a critical ambiguity, which can only be resolved by measuring objective happiness.

What do people mean when they assert that Californians are, in fact, happier than other people, although Californians do not report themselves as happier? The possibility that Californians have more meaningful lives than others is rarely advanced. Rather, the proposition that Californians are happier appears to mean that Californians are objectively happier: their lives are richer in pleasures and less burdened by hassles, and they are consequently in a better mood, on average, than most other people. In this view, a treadmill effect is observed because

Californians use the happiness scale differently than other people. The same argument could of course be extended to the Japanese who reported equal happiness in 1987 and in 1958 despite a large increase in standard of living. It could also apply to paraplegics. If this view is accepted, the evidence for a happiness treadmill unravels. Perhaps life circumstances do, after all, have a greater effect on well-being than surveys of subjective happiness indicate. A specific hypothesis about a mechanism that could produce spurious evidence for a hedonic treadmill is introduced next.

4.2. The Satisfaction Treadmill

Brickman and Campbell explained treadmill effects by invoking the notion of an adaptation level (Helson, 1964). I propose an alternative hypothesis, called a *satisfaction treadmill*, which draws on another venerable psychological concept: the aspiration level (Irwin, 1944). The aspiration level is a value on a scale of achievement or attainment that lies somewhere between realistic expectation and reasonable hope. The essential observation is that people are always satisfied when they attain their aspiration level, and usually quite satisfied with slightly less. The best-established finding about aspiration levels is that they are closely correlated with past attainments. Current income, for example, is the single most important determinant of the income that is considered satisfactory for one's household (Van Praag and Frijters, 1999).

To illustrate the difference between a hedonic treadmill and a satisfaction treadmill, consider a former graduate student, who will be called Helen. Assume that Helen regularly eats in restaurants, and that she has a well-defined ranking of experienced utility for a set of entrées, which is perfectly correlated with their price. In her graduate-student days Helen was constrained by her budget to consume mostly mediocre dishes. Now she has taken a lucrative job which allows her to consume food of higher quality. In tracking her overall satisfaction with food over the transition period, we observe that her satisfaction rises initially, then settles back to its original level. This is the standard pattern of a treadmill effect. Now consider two mechanisms that could produce this effect.

1. The hedonic treadmill hypothesis invokes the hypothesis of an *adaptation level* for palatability, which is determined by a weighted average of the palatability experienced on recent occasions. Helen's pleasure from food rises initially, because the food she consumes exceeds the adaptation level that was established in her graduate-student days. As time passes, however, her adaptation level will catch up to her consumption, and her pleasure from food will return to its original level. After she has adapted to the new level of pleasure, she will consume better entrées than she did as a graduate student, but will enjoy each of them less than she had in the past. On the hypothesis of a hedonic treadmill, Helen's reports of subjective satisfaction correctly reflect the changes in her enjoyment of food.

2. The hypothesis of a satisfaction treadmill invokes the notion of a changing *aspiration level*, which is determined in large part by the level of pleasure recently derived from food. For the sake of an extreme example, assume now that there is no hedonic adaptation at all, and that the experienced utility that Helen derives from any entrée does not change. As the quality of her entrées improves, so does the overall pleasure that she derives from them. Suppose, however, that Helen has an aspiration level for *food pleasure*: as the pleasure that she obtains from food increases, her aspiration level gradually follows, eventually adjusting to her higher level of enjoyment. After this adjustment of aspirations, Helen reports no more *satisfaction* with food than she did when she was poorer, although she actually draws more pleasure from food now than she had done earlier.

The concept of a satisfaction treadmill extends readily from food pleasure to happiness. Only one additional assumption is needed: that people require a certain balance of pleasures and pains to report themselves happy or satisfied with their lives. On this hypothesis, Californians could indeed enjoy life more than others. However, if they also require more enjoyment than others to declare themselves happy, they will not report higher subjective happiness. Californians might be happier than other people objectively, but not subjectively.

The statistical test for the hypothesis of a satisfaction treadmill is straightforward: if such a treadmill exists, the regression lines that describe the relation between subjective and objective happiness will not be the same for groups in different circumstances. At any level of objective happiness, people with a higher aspiration level will report themselves less happy and less satisfied than others whose aspirations are lower. If the results for both groups fall on the same regression line, there is no satisfaction treadmill.

A satisfaction treadmill and a hedonic treadmill may co-occur, both contributing to observed treadmill effects. The critical conclusion of the analysis is that the relative contributions of the two mechanisms cannot be determined without direct measurements of experienced utility. The hypothesis of a satisfaction treadmill is both plausible and effectively untested, and the interpretation of treadmill effects observed with measures of satisfaction and subjective happiness is correspondingly indeterminate. A substantial amount of well-being research might have to be redone to resolve this ambiguity.

5. DISCUSSION

The premise of this essay was a distinction between two meanings of the term 'utility', which were labeled experienced utility and decision utility. Decision utility is about wanting, experienced utility is about enjoyment. This basic dichotomy has been discussed elsewhere (Kahneman 1994; Kahneman, 1999). The focus of the present discussion was the further distinction between two approaches to the interpretation and measurement of experienced utility, which were called moment-based and memory-based.

Wanting or not wanting is not the only orientation to future outcomes. People sometimes also attempt to forecast the affective or hedonic experience—the experienced utility—that is associated with various life circumstances. These are judgments of *predicted utility* (Kahneman et al., 1997), or affective forecasting (Gilbert et al., 1998). With the inclusion of predicted utility, the number of distinct concepts of the utility of extended outcomes—bounded episodes or states of indefinite duration—rises to four. The concepts are distinguished by the operations on which they are based:

(i) *Decision utility* is inferred from observed preferences.
(ii) *Predicted utility* is a belief about future experienced utility.
(iii) *Total utility* is a *moment-based* measure of experienced utility. It is derived from measurements of moment-utility, statistically aggregated by an objective rule.
(iv) *Remembered utility* is a *memory-based* measure of experienced utility, which is based on retrospective assessments of episodes or periods of life.

Decision utility is the almost exclusive topic of study in decision research and economics, and memory-based self-reports are the almost exclusive topic of study in the domain of Subjective Well-Being (SWB) research. The various concepts of utility suggest a rich and complex agenda of research; they also suggest different interpretations of utility maximization.

To extend an example already discussed, consider families that move (or might move) from California to Ohio. The decision utility of families that consider relocation could be studied by eliciting their global preferences, as well as their preferences for different attributes of the two locations. Whether or not people maximize utility is interpreted in this context as a question about the coherence of preferences: would the choice that the family makes survive reframing, or a new context? The predicted utility which the decision makers associate with the alternative locations could be studied by eliciting their general beliefs about the experience of living in the two places, and their particular beliefs about what they might enjoy or dislike. There is considerable evidence that this task of affective forecasting is not one in which people excel (see, Gilbert et al., 1998; Kahneman, 1999; Kahneman and Schkade, 1999; Loewenstein and Adler, 1995; Loewenstein and Schkade, 1999; Schkade and Kahneman, 1998). Another question of some importance is whether people even consider the uncertainty of their future tastes as part of the activity of decision making (March, 1978; Simonson, 1990.

As we have seen in preceding sections, different conclusions about the outcomes of families that did move to California could be reached, depending on whether the outcomes are assessed by moment-based or by memory-based techniques—by measures of total utility or objective happiness on the one hand, of remembered utility or subjective happiness on the other. Self-selection and dissonance reduction would predict high subjective happiness among people who moved voluntarily. Treadmill effects, on the other hand, predict that people who moved will eventually return to their characteristic level of subjective happiness. The argument of the preceding section was that these memory-based measures do not tell us what we would really want to know: whether people who move to California are *really* happier there than they were earlier. In the approach adopted here, this question must be answered by obtaining moment-based measures, using either self-reports or physiological techniques.

The distinctions that have been drawn between variant concepts of utility are directly relevant to normative issues in the domain of policy, as the following list of questions illustrates. 'Does the presence of trees in a city street affect the mood of pedestrians?' 'What is the contribution of an attractive subway system to the well-being of city residents?' 'What are the well-being consequences of inflation, unemployment, or unreliable health insurance?' Here again, it is possible to ask what the public wants, perhaps by asking people how much they are willing to pay for the provision of some goods. It is also possible to elicit people's opinions about the welfare effects of particular public goods, to obtain a measure of predicted utility. Finally, it is sometimes possible to measure the experienced utility associated with public goods. Again, this can be done either by moment-based or by memory-based methods.

Conventional economic analyses of policy recognize only one measure of the value of public goods: the aggregate willingness of the public to pay for them. There are serious doubts about the coherence of this concept and the feasibility of measuring willingness to pay (see, e.g., Kahneman et al., 1999). A more funda-mental question is whether willingness to pay should remain the only measure of value. The present analysis suggests that moment-based measures of the actual experience of consequences should be included in assessments of outcomes and as one of the criteria for the quality of decisions, both public and private.

Treadmill effects raise difficult normative questions. If there is a hedonic treadmill, then changes in circumstances will often have less long-term effects on human welfare than might be inferred from their *ex-ante* desirability or from the initial hedonic response that they evoke. Should policy resist calls for the pro-vision of desirable goods that convey no long-term utility benefits? And if there is a satisfaction treadmill, then clients of policies will never be satisfied very long even when an improvement in their circumstances makes them permanently (objectively) happier. Furthermore, false negatives occur in all prediction tasks: people may fail to identify some circumstances that would actually make them happier. Do policy makers have a duty to provide goods that make people truly better off, even if they are neither desired *ex-ante* nor appreciated *ex-post*? The easy answer is no, but it is perhaps too easy. Dilemmas of paternalism were discussed in Kahneman (1994).

The moment-based approach to experienced utility and happiness which has been presented here runs into two strong objections. The first is that there is more to human well-being than good mood. The second is that the moment-based view is based on abstract arguments and on logical construction, and fails to reflect the role of memory in the subjective reality of mental life. Both objections have much merit, but neither should block the judicious use of moment-based measures.

Objective happiness is not proposed as a comprehensive concept of human well-being, only as a significant constituent of it. Maximizing the time spent on the right side of the affect grid is not the most significant value in life, and adopting this criterion as a guide to life may be morally wrong, and perhaps also self-defeating. However, the proposition that the right side of the grid is a more desirable place to be is not particularly controversial. Indeed, there may be more differences among cultures and systems of thought about the optimal position on the arousal dimension—some prefer the bliss of serenity, others favor the exultation of faith or the joys of participation. Objective happiness is a common denominator for various conceptions of well-being. Furthermore, when it comes to comparisons of groups, such as Californians and others, or to assessments of the value of public goods such as health insurance or tree-lined streets, experienced utility and objective happiness may be the correct measure of welfare.

In a memory-centered view of life, the accumulation of memories is an end in itself. A clear statement of this position is offered by Tversky and Griffin (1991), who speak of the stock of memories as an endowment, which is enriched by storing new memories of good experiences. The moment-centered approach that has been proposed here does not deny the importance of memory in life, but it suggests a metaphor of consumption rather than of wealth. Without a doubt, the traveler who goes to a Kenya safari may continue to derive utility from that episode long after it ends, whether directly—by 'consuming' the memories in pleasant or unpleasant reminiscing—or, perhaps more importantly, by consuming the experience of the self as it has been altered by the event (Elster and Loewenstein, 1992). However, the moment-based approach raises a question that should not be dismissed too lightly: how much time will be spent in such consumption of memories, relative to the duration of the original experience? The weight of memory relative to actual experience is likely to be reduced when time is taken seriously.

The memory-based and the moment-based views draw on different intuitions about what counts as real. There is an obvious sense in which present experience is real and memories are not. But memories have an attribute of permanence which lends them a weightiness that the fleeting present lacks: they endure and populate the mind. In the words of the novelist Penelope Lively (1993, p.15), 'A narrative is a sequence of present moments but the present does not exist.' Because memories and stories of the past are all we ultimately get to keep, memories and stories often appear to be all that matters. These common intuitions are part of the appeal of Fredrickson's (2000) eloquent critique of the idea—central to the notion of total utility and objective happiness—that all moments of time are weighted equally. The argument for meaning is memory-based: memory certainly does not treat all moments equally, and meaningful moments must be memorable. Indeed, the statement 'I will always remember this' is often proffered, not always correctly, at meaningful moments. Futhermore, the immense importance that most of us attach to deathbed reconciliations suggests that who does the remembering may not greatly matter in conferring meaning, so long as someone does.

The goal of this discussion is not to reject the memory-based view, which is indeed irresistibly appealing, but to point out that intuition is strongly biased against a moment-based view. The approach proposed here is bound to be counter-intuitive even if it has merit—that was one of the reasons for proposing it. Although wholly devoid of permanence, the experiencing subject deserves a voice.

REFERENCES

Algom, D. and Lubel, S. (1994). Psychopysics in the field: Perception and memory for labor pain. *Perception and Memory, 55,* 133–41.

Argyle, M. (1999). Causes and correlates of happiness. In D. Kahneman, E. Diener, and N. Schwarz (Eds.), *Well being: The foundation of hedonic psychology* (pp. 353–73). New York: Russell Sage.

Bentham, J. (1789). *An Introduction to the principle of morals and legislations.* (Reprinted) Oxford, UK: Blackwell, 1948.

Broome, J. (1993). Qalys. *Journal of Public Economics, 50,* 149–67.

Brickman, P. and Campbell, D.T. (1971). Hedonic relativism and planning the good society. In M.H. Apley (Ed.), *Adaptation-level theory: A symposium* (pp. 287–301). New York: Academic Press.

—— Coates, D., and Janoff-Bulman, R. (1978). Lottery winners and accident victims: is happiness relative? *Journal of Personality and Social Psychology, 37,* 917–27.

Brock, D. (1993). Quality of life measures in health care and medical ethics. In M.C. Nussbaum and A. Sen (Eds.), *The quality of life* (pp. 95–132). Oxford: Clarendon Press.

Cacioppo, J.T., Gardner, W.C., and Berntson, G. (1999). The affect system has parallel and integrative processing components: Form follows function. *Journal of Personality and Social Psychology, 76,* 839–55.

Cantor, N. and Sanderson, C.A. (1999). Life task participation and well-being: The importance of taking part in daily life. In D. Kahneman, E. Diener, and N. Scharwz, (Eds.), *Well-being: The foundations of hedonic psychology* (pp. 230–43). New York: Cambridge University Press.

Csikszentmihalyi, M. (1990). *Flow: The psychology of optimal experience.* New York: Harper and Row.

Davidson, R.J. (1998). Affective style and affective disorders: Perspectives from affective neuroscience. *Cognition and Emotion, 12,* 307–30.

—— and Fox, N.A. (1989). Frontal brain asymmetry predicts infants' response to maternal separation. *Journal of Abnormal Psychology, 98,* 127–31.

—— and Tomarken, A.J. (1989). Laterality and emotion: An electrophysiological approach. In F. Boller and J. Grafman (Eds.), *Handbook of neuropsychology.* Amsterdam: Elsevier.

Diener, E., Sandvik, E., and Pavot, W. (1991). Happiness is the frequency, not the intensity, of positive versus negative affect. In F. Strack, M. Argyle, and N. Schwarz (Eds.), *Subjective Well-Being* (pp. 119–40). New York: Pergamon Press.

—— Suh, E.M., Lucas, R.E., and Smith, H.E. (1999). Subjective well-being: Three decades of progress. *Psychological Bulletin, 125,* 577–606.

Easterlin, R.A. (1995). Will raising the income of all increase the happiness of all? *Journal of Economic Behavior and Organization, 27*, 35–47.

Edgeworth, F. Y. (1881). *Mathematical Psychics: An essay in the application of mathematics to the moral sciences* (reprinted), New York: M. Kelly, 1967.

Elster J. and Loewenstein, G. (1992). Utility from memory and anticipation. In J. Elster and G. Loewenstein (Eds.), *Choice over time* (pp. 213–24). New York: Russell Sage Foundation.

Fredrickson, B.L. (2000). Extracting meaning from past affective experiences: The importance of peaks, ends, and specific emotions. *Cognition and Emotion, 14*, 577–606.

Frederick, S. and Loewenstein, G. (1999). Hedonic adaptation. In D. Kahneman, E. Diener, and N. Scharwz (Eds.), *Well-being: The foundations of hedonic psychology* (pp. 302–29). New York: Cambridge University Press.

Gilbert, D.T., Pinel, E.C., Wilson, T.D., Blumberg, S.J., and Wheatley, T. (1998). Immune neglect: A source of durability bias in affective forecasting. *Journal of Personality and Social Psychology, 75*, 617–38.

Headey, B. and Wearing, A. (1992). *Understanding happiness: A theory of subjective well-being.* Melbourne: Longman Cheshire.

Helson, H. (1964). *Adaptation-level theory.* New York: Harper and Row.

Irwin, F.W. (1944). The realism of expectations. *Psychological Review, 51*, 120–6.

Kahneman, D. (1994). New challenges to the rationality assumption. *Journal of Institutional and Theoretical Economics, 150*, 18–36.

—— (1999). Objective happiness. In D. Kahneman, E. Diener, and N. Schwartz (Eds.), *Well-being: Foundations of hedonic psychology* (pp. 3–27). New York: Russell Sage Foundation.

—— Ritov, I., and Schkade, D. (1999). Economic preferences or attitude expressions? An analysis of dollar responses to public issues. *Journal of Risk and Uncertainty*, forthcoming.

—— and Schkade, D. (1999). *Predicting the well-being effect of new circumstances: Changes are proxies for states*, working paper, Princeton University.

—— and Varey, C. (1991). Notes on the psychology of utility. In J. Roemer and J. Elster (Eds.), *Interpersonal comparisons of well-being* (pp. 127–63). New York: Cambridge University Press.

—— Wakker, P.P., and Sarin, R. (1997). Back to Bentham? Explorations of experienced utility. *Quarterly Journal of Economics, 112*, 375–405.

Katz J., Redelmeier D.A, and Kahneman D. (1997). Memories of painful medical procedures [abstract]. American Pain Society 15th Annual Scientific Meeting.

Lang, P. (1995). The emotion probe: studies of motivation and attention. *American Psychologist, 50*, 372–85.

Lively, P. (1993). *Cleopatra's sister.* New York: Harper's Perennial.

Loewenstein, G. (1992). The fall and rise of psychological explanations in the economics of intertemporal choice. In G. Loewenstein and J. Elster (Eds.), *Choice over time* (pp. 3–34). New York: Russell Sage Foundation.

——and Adler, D. (1995). A bias in the prediction of tastes. *Economic Journal, 105*, 929–37.

—— and Schkade, D. (1999). Wouldn't it be nice: Predicting future feelings. In D. Kahneman, E. Diener, and N. Schwarz (Eds.), *Well being: The foundation of hedonic psychology* (pp. 85–108). New York: Russell Sage.

Lykken, D. and Tellegen, A. (1996). Happiness is a stochastic phenomenon. *Psychological Science, 7*, 186–9.

Myers, D.G. and Diener, E. (1995). Who is happy? *Psychological Science, 6*, 10–19.

Nussbaum, M.C. and Sen, A.K. (Eds.), (1993). *The quality of life.* Oxford: Clarendon Press.

Parducci, A. (1995). *Happiness, pleasure, and judgment: The contextual theory and its applications*. Hillsdale, NJ: Erlbaum.

Plutchik, R. and Conte, H.R. (Eds.), (1997). *Circumplex models of personality and emotions*. Washington, DC: American Psychological Association.

Redelmeier, D. and Kahneman, D. (1996). Patients' memories of painful medical treatments: Real-time an retrospective evaluations of two minimally invasive procedures. *Pain, 116*, 3–8.

Russell, J.A. (1980). A circumplex model of affect. *Journal of Personality and Social Psychology, 39*, 1161–78.

—— and Carroll, J.M. (1999). On the bipolarity of positive and negative affect, *Psychological Bulletin, 125*, 3–30.

—— Wess, A., and Mendelsohn, G.A. (1989). Affect grid: A single item scale of pleasure and arousal. *Journal of Personality and Social Psychology, 57*, 493–502.

Ryff, C. and Singer, B. (1998). The contours of positive human health. *Psychological Inquiry, 9*, 1–28.

Sapolsky, R.M. (1999). The physiology and pathophysiology of unhappiness. In D. Kahneman, E. Diener, and N. Scharwz (Eds.), *Well-being: The foundations of hedonic psychology* (pp. 453–69). New York: Cambridge University Press.

Schkade, D. and Kahneman, D. (1998). Does living in California make people happy? A focusing illusion in judgments of life satisfaction. *Psychological Science, 9*, 340–6.

Schreiber, C.A. and Kahneman, D. (2000). Determinants of the remembered utility of aversive sounds, *Journal of Experimental Psychology, 129*, 27–42.

Simonson, I. (1990). The effect of purchase quantity and timing on variety-seeking behavior. *Journal of Marketing Research, 17*, 150–62.

Stone, A.A. and Shiffman, S.S. (1994). Ecological Momentary Assessment (EMA) in the behavioral medicine. *Annals of Behavioral Medicine, 16*, 199–202.

—— (1995). Measures of affective response. In S. Cohen, R. Kessler, and L. Gordon (Eds.), *Measuring stress: A guide for social and health scientists* (pp. 148–71). New York: Cambridge University Press.

—— Shiffman, S.S., and DeVries, M. (1999). Rethinking self-report assessment methodologies. In D. Kahneman, E. Diener, and N. Scharwz (Eds.), *Well-being: The foundations of hedonic psychology* (pp. 26–39). New York: Cambridge University Press.

Sutton, S.K. and Davidson, R.J. (1997). Prefrontal brain asymmetry: A biological substrate of behavioral approach and inhibition systems. *Psychological Science, 8*, 204–10.

Tellegen, A., Watson, D., and Clark, L.A. (1999). On the dimensional and hierarchical structure of affect. *Psychological Science, 10*(4), 297–303.

Tomarken, A.J., Davidson, R.J., Wheeler, R.E., and Doss, R.C. (1992). Individual differences in anterior brain assymetry and fundamental dimensions of emotion. *Journal of Personality and Social Psychology, 62*, 676–87.

Tversky, A. and Griffin, D. (1991). Endowment and contrast in judgments of well-being. In F. Strack, M. Argyle, and N. Scharwtz (Eds.), *Subjective well-being*. Elmsford, NY: Pergamon Press.

Van Praag, B.M.S. and Frijters, P. (1999). The measurement of welfare and well-being: The Leyden approach. In D. Kahneman, E. Diener, N. Scharwz (Eds.), *Well-being: The foundations of hedonic psychology* (pp. 413–33). New York: Cambridge University Press.

Warr, P. (1999). Well-being and the workplace. In D. Kahneman, E. Diener, and N. Scharwz (Eds.), *Well-being: The foundations of hedonic psychology* (pp. 392–412). New York: Cambridge University Press.

11

Making Sense: The Causes of Emotional Evanescence

TIMOTHY D. WILSON, DANIEL T. GILBERT,
AND DAVID B. CENTERBAR

> The mind of every man, in a longer or shorter time, returns to its natural and usual state of tranquillity. In prosperity, after a certain time, it falls back to that state; in adversity, after a certain time, it rises up to it.   Adam Smith, *The Theory of Moral Sentiments*

Psychology and economics generally agree about the importance of two fundamental human motives, the desire to reduce uncertainty and the desire to obtain pleasure (though to be sure, there are differences in views between and within the fields on the definitions of these motives and the importance attributed to them). In this chapter, we explore some overlooked implications of these two motives that lead to a paradox: People seek happiness, but as soon as they obtain it, psychological mechanisms are activated to reduce it. Unfortunately, there may be limits to the duration of the pleasure we obtain from positive life events.

That is the bad news. The good news is that these same mechanisms place limits on the duration of displeasure caused by negative life events. Humans are built in such a way that emotional reactions to positive and negative events wear off fairly quickly, more quickly than people think. We first document that emotional reactions are, in fact, relatively short-lived, and then argue that (i) emotional evanescence is functional, allowing people to remain vigilant to important changes in the environment, and (ii) emotional evanescence is the byproduct of the human need to make sense out of the world and reduce uncertainty, which robs events of their emotional power. We conclude with a discussion of some recent work on how to prolong emotional reactions to positive events, and with a discussion of the implications of our work for economic theory.

1. EMOTIONAL EVANESCENCE

To be sure some life events, such as the death of a loved one, can have emotional reverberations that last for years. And, some people are chronically depressed. There is considerable evidence, however, that emotional reactions to external events are surprisingly short-lived, and that sooner rather than later, people return to their baseline levels of happiness.

In a study by Suh et al. (1996), for example, college students reported their level of subjective well-being and whether a large number of positive and negative life events had occurred in the previous four years. Many of the students had experienced significant events in their lives. Fifty-five percent had experienced the end of a romantic relationship, 29 percent had experienced the death of a close family member, 52 percent had gained at least 10 lb, and 42 percent had been unable to locate a job. Eighty-two percent became involved in a romantic relationship that lasted at least two months, 20 percent became engaged or were married, and 28 percent were admitted to graduate school. If these events had occurred six months or longer in the past, neither the number of negative nor the number of positive events people experienced were correlated with people's subjective well being. If the events had occurred in the previous three months, the correlations with subjective well-being were significant but modest (.25 for the number of positive events, − .28 for negative events). As Suh et al. put it, 'only recent events matter', and recent events did not matter very much (1996, p. 1091).

A number of other studies have examined people's reactions to specific events and found that on an average, their emotional reactions are surprisingly short-lived (Frederick and Loewenstein, 1999). Two major life events that have received a lot of attention are the death of a loved one, and winning a very large sum of money in the lottery. The literature on bereavement indicates that many people are either not affected at all by the loss of a loved one or recover relatively quickly from intense grief. One study found that 30 percent of parents who lost babies due to the sudden infant death syndrome never experienced significant depression. Another found that 82 percent of bereaved spouses were doing well two years after the death (Lund et al., 1989; Wortman et al., 1993). Similarly, winning huge sums of money in the lottery does not seem to make people happy for very long; in fact, there is some evidence that lottery winners are less happy after the major disruption of sudden wealth in their lives (Brickman et al., 1978; Kaplan, 1978).

These studies are surprising because they violate most people's intuitions about how long emotional reactions to such major events should last. None of them, however, specifically measured people's affective forecasts and compared them to the actual duration of the emotional events. We have done just this in several studies, in which people forecast how happy they will be at specified times after an emotional event, and these forecasts are compared to people's actual happiness at those time points. We have documented a robust *durability bias*, which is the tendency for people to overestimate the duration of their reactions to emotional events. People have exhibited the durability bias when they predict their emotional reactions to major life events (e.g., achieving academic tenure, being denied tenure, the end of a romantic relationship), as well as more minor events (e.g., receiving negative feedback on a personality test, watching a favorite sports team win or lose a game). The durability bias has been found for both negative and positive events (Gilbert et al., 1998; Wilson et al., 2000).

1.1. Why are Emotional Reactions Short-Lived?

A number of reasons have been offered for why emotional reactions to external events do not last for very long. These explanations include the view that happiness is more of a dispositional trait than a reaction to external events (Costa & McCrae, 1984; Lykken & Tellegen, 1996); that people adapt to repeated experiences of the same event, because that event becomes the baseline to which new experiences are compared (Brickman and Campbell, 1971; Parducci, 1995; Kahneman and Tversky, 1979); that happiness results more from the pursuit of a goal than from the attainment of a goal (e.g., Davidson, 1994; Diener, 2000; Emmons, 1986; Ryan et al., 1996); that people possess a psychological immune system that speeds their recovery from negative emotional events (e.g., Festinger, 1957; Freud, 1937; Gilbert et al., 1998; Taylor, 1991; Vaillant, 2000); and that people who experience an intense negative affect are more likely to experience an intense positive affect as well, thereby 'canceling out' prolonged emotional reactions of one valence (Diener et al., 1991).

Each of these viewpoints can explain a part of the puzzle of emotional evanescence, but do not provide complete explanations. Even if happiness is partly dispositional, for example, that does not explain why external events make people happy or unhappy, or why people return quickly to their baseline level of happiness. Adaptation-level theories explain why an event loses some of its emotional power when experienced repeatedly (because it establishes a new comparison level), but not why affective reactions to a single event wear off quickly. The fact that goal pursuit is often as pleasurable as goal attainment does not explain why people recover rapidly from negative events that impede their goals. Finally, the existence of a psychological immune system explains why people recover quickly from negative events (i.e., because people rationalize or reconstrue the events in ways that make them less painful), but not why people recover quickly from positive events (cf. Taylor, 1991). None of these approaches offers a complete explanation of emotional evanescence.

1.2. Making Sense

The main reason for emotional evanescence, we suggest, is because people reduce the emotional power of events by making sense of them, a process we call 'ordinization.' When a novel event occurs, people automatically engage in cognitive work to make the event seem predictable and explainable. Although this process has been widely discussed in the psychology and economics literatures, its implications for people's emotional lives has been largely overlooked. By turning the extraordinary into the ordinary, people rob events of their emotional power.

We suggest that this ordinization process occurs for two reasons. First, it may be to people's advantage to recover quickly from emotional events, and the cognitive mechanism of making sense is an important way in which this is accomplished. Second, the need to make sense of novel events may have other benefits, and emotional evanescence is a byproduct of this useful tendency to turn novel events into ones that seem predictable.

2. THE ADVANTAGES OF AFFECTIVE STABILITY

It may be to one's advantage to recover quickly from emotional events, and that human sense making ability is one way in which this is accomplished. Such an argument is straightforward when applied to negative emotions. It is easy to imagine why it is advantageous to recover quickly from negative events, and why humans have mechanisms (i.e., the psychological immune system) that orchestrate this recovery. It is not as obvious why it is to people's advantage to 'recover' quickly from positive events, because this would seem to violate the fundamental principle that people seek to obtain pleasure and avoid pain. We believe, however, that a case can be made that it is important that people's emotional reactions to both positive and negative events not last too long.

2.1. Why Happiness is Like Food

Happiness may be like food, in that we can have too little or too much of it. Food is a powerful operant, of course, and without it we would die. As noted by Woods (1991), there is an 'eating paradox' whereby people are motivated to ingest food, but doing so disrupts a number of important homeostatic, physiological systems (e.g., the level of blood sugar) and the human body has a number of mechanisms designed to minimize its impact (e.g., the secretion of insulin to lower blood sugar). In Woods's (1991, p. 500) words, 'Food intake has many attributes of a particularly disruptive event. Just as people learn to tolerate the administration of dangerous drugs, so they learn to tolerate the intake of food.' In support of the idea that food can be too much of a good thing, the risk of a heart attack increases ten fold in the hour after a heavy meal ('Heavy meal increases risk,' 2000).

Perhaps human happiness is a homeostatic system as well, whereby disruptions in a downward or upward direction trigger mechanisms to restore happiness to a set level. As we have seen, it is difficult for people to function with too little happiness (i.e., if one is severely depressed), and there are mechanisms in place to ameliorate the emotional impact of negative events. Similarly, there may be mechanisms in place to ameliorate the impact of positive events.

2.2. Why Happiness is Like Blood Pressure

Before detailing what these mechanisms are, it is worth noting that there may be a better analogy than happiness-as-food. Happiness, we suggest, may be more like blood pressure, which is an allostatic instead of a homeostatic system. In homeostatic systems, there is an optimal set point, and deviations from this point trigger negative feedback processes that attempt to restore it. The normal level of blood sugar in humans, for example, is about 80 mg/ml. Deviations ineither direction trigger physiological mechanisms that return it to this optimal level. When people ingest food and blood sugar increases, their pancreas releases insulin, which causes a greater uptake of glucose by the liver and the muscles.

Sterling and Eyer (1988) introduced the term allostasis to describe a different type of feedback system. Rather than trying to maintain a set point, the purpose of allostatic systems is to keep a variable within a healthy range, but at the same time to let it vary in response to environmental demands. For example, there is no single set point for blood pressure that the body tries to maintain at all times; instead, pressure rises when physical activity is high, such as when a person exercises, and drops when a person rests. Obviously, however, there need to be mechanisms that keep blood pressure within a healthy range. If it rises or falls too much the person would die, and neither chronic hypertension nor hypotension are desirable states. Sterling and Eyer (1988) detail a number of physiological mechanisms designed to do just this with the regulation of blood pressure.

We suggest that the regulation of human happiness is also an allostatic system. Just as there are mechanisms that keep blood pressure from dropping too low or rising too high, there are mechanisms to keep people from being too dysphoric or euphoric for too long a time, for three reasons. First, changes in emotion serve to signal the onset of critical events in the environment (Frijda, 1988; Ortony et al., 1988), and if the emotional system is to retain its signaling capacity, it must not get 'stuck' in an extreme emotional state. People who remain euphoric or depressed by what happened yesterday are less likely to be tuned in to emotional changes in their environment today. Second, intense emotional reactions can impede higher order cognitive processing, because it is difficult to think clearly when in a state of extreme dysphoria or euphoria— as anyone knows who has tried to review a journal article while severely depressed or wildly in love. Although moderately positive states seem to enhance creative problem solving (Fredrickson, 1998; Isen, 1993), extreme states make it difficult to engage in rational decision making. Third, it would be physiologically taxing to be in a constant state of dysphoria or euphoria. Euphoria is accompanied by increases in arousal, for example, that the body cannot maintain indefinitely. For all three reasons, then, people seem designed to have hedonic reactions to the objects and events in their environment, and then return quickly to the baseline.

2.3. Mechanisms of Affective Allostasis

We believe that there are a number of mechanisms that accomplish this goal, ranging from basic physiological processes to conscious, deliberative, choices on the part of the individual.

The opponent process theory. One mechanism of affective allostasis occurs at the physiological level. According to Solomon's (1980) opponent process theory, physical events that cause extreme affective responses trigger an opponent process that produces the opposite affective response, to avoid prolonged, extreme reactions. When people ingest cocaine, for example, physiological processes occur that cause an extreme positive affective reaction. An opponent process is also triggered that neutralizes this reaction. According to Solomon, the opponent process is initially weak but is strengthened with repeated exposure, which explains habituation to an event or substance. When people first ingest cocaine the opponent process is weak, such that they experience a prolonged positive affective response. The more they take the drug the stronger the opponent process, however, which serves to diminish the positive response. Furthermore, because the opponent process take a long time to extinguish when the event no longer occurs, the theory can explain withdrawal symptoms. When a cocaine addict stops ingesting the drug the pleasure-inducing response no longer occurs, but the opponent, pleasure-reducing response does, producing considerable dysphoria.

The opponent process theory has become a popular account of responses to physical stimuli such as drugs (e.g., Koob et al., 1997), and appears to offer a good explanation of how the body regulates extreme physical perturbations to the affective system, in both a positive and negative direction. The theory has been less successful in explaining people's reactions to psychological events (Sandvik et al., 1985). That is, the opponent process theory may explain what happens at a physiological level when the bodily systems are disrupted, such as neurochemical responses to drug ingestion, but it does not deal as well with the psychological responses to complex emotional events such as winning a lottery, falling in love, or losing a loved one. In order to explain why the emotions that such complex events trigger are often short-lived, we need to examine the kinds of psychological and behavioral responses people have to them.

Conscious, deliberative regulation of emotion. Sometimes people keep their emotions in check in a quite deliberative fashion. This is obvious when it comes to negative emotions; people do not like to feel bad and often take steps to improve their moods, such as visiting a friend or renting a funny movie. It is less obvious with positive emotions—why would people deliberately rain on their own parades? Although such cases may be rare, they do occur. Laughing uproariously at a funeral is unlikely to engender good will, and people might take steps to lower their moods before entering the funeral parlor (e.g., by thinking sad thoughts; Hochschild, 1979). Similarly, if people know they have to concentrate on a task, they purposefully avoid putting themselves in too good a mood (Erber, 1996).

Neither physiological processes nor deliberative behavioral strategies, however, can account fully for people's resilience in the face of positive and negative life events. We believe a mechanism has been overlooked, namely a set of automatic, nonconscious processes by which people make sense of and ordinize their environments. By turning novel events into predictable, ordinary ones, people rob those events of their emotional power and return quickly to their emotional baselines.

One view of this ordinization process is that it developed in order to maintain affective stability. Another is that it is a quite functional process in its own right, because it increases people's sense of control over their environments. It is worth reviewing the idea that people seek to reduce ambiguity in their environments, because it is prevalent in psychology and economics. The consequences of this process on people's emotional lives, however, has been largely overlooked.

3. THE UNCERTAINTY AVERSION PRINCIPLE

As succinctly stated by Gilovich (1991, p. 9), 'We are predisposed to see order, pattern, and meaning in the world, and we find randomness, chaos, and mean-inglessness unsatisfying. Human nature abhors a lack of predictability and the absence of meaning.' This *uncertainty aversion principle* is fundamental to many psychological theories. Attribution theorists argue that people have a funda-mental need to view the world as predictable and controllable, and that the pervasive attempt to explain the causes of other people's behavior occurs in the service of this need (Gilbert, 1991; Heider, 1958; Jones and Davis, 1965; Kelley, 1967). In Heider's words, people make causal attributions 'not only because of intellectual curiosity, but also because such attribution allows him to understand his world, to predict and control events involving himself and others' (Heider, 1958, p. 146). Research on perceived control and the learned helplessness theory has demonstrated that if people feel that they cannot control or predict their environments, they are at risk for severe motivational and cognitive deficits, such as depression (Abramson et al., 1978; Langer and Rodin, 1976; Schulz, 1976; Seligman, 1975; Taylor and Brown, 1988; Thompson et al., 1998).

In fact, it could be argued that the attempt to understand and predict the world is the overriding purpose of the cognitive system (Pittman, 1998). Piaget pointed out that the processes of assimilation and accommodation are fundamental to cog-nitive development (Piaget, 1952; Piaget and Inhelder, 1969). Children and adults assimilate new events to existing knowledge structures, or, if that is not possible, alter their knowledge structures to accommodate the new information. The idea of *people as sense makers* is pervasive in philosophy, the social sciences, and the humanities as well. Dennett (1991, p. 177, his emphasis) argued that 'all brains, are, in essence, *anticipation machines*' that try to predict what is going to happen next. And one of the chief functions of art and religion is to help people make sense out of a confusing, unpredictable world (e.g., Jobes, 1974; Pfeiffer, 1982).

Loewenstein (1994) reviewed a wide body of evidence that people are sense-seeking organisms who have a low tolerance for uncertainty. The need for certainty, he argues, is a major underpinning of curiosity. One reason people voluntarily seek to make themselves curious, he argues, is because it is so pleasurable to resolve it. Just as people sometimes fast to maximize the pleasure of a well-prepared meal, so will people seek uncertainty in order to obtain the pleasure of reducing it. Unsatisfied curiosity, like hunger, is a particularly aversive state.

Sometimes curiosity even gets the best of hunger. A few years ago, a homeless man in New York was rummaging through a trash dumpster, looking for unspoiled food, when he came across a bundle of letters and poems a man had written to his lover. Hungry as he was, the homeless man became fascinated with the letters and sat down and read them all. What happened to such a promising relationship, he wondered? How could two people who were so in love have gotten to the point where one of them threw the love letters in the trash, along with the onion peels and coffee grinds?

The homeless man called the author of the letters (after finding a phone number in one of the letters), and asked him how his beautiful prose and poetry could have ended up in a dumpster. It turned out that a relationship with a woman in his office had just ended, and the woman had thrown the letters away. 'I would have called you sooner,' the homeless man said, 'but this was the first quarter I was given today' (DeMarco, 1994; quoted in Aronson et al., 1999, p. 105). The man's desire to satisfy his curiosity was so strong that he was willing to go hungry a little longer.

3.1. Uncertainty Reduction in Economics

The idea that people abhor uncertainty is also prevalent in economics, usually under the rubric of aversion to ambiguity. Within the area of judgment under uncertainty, a number of investigators have noted examples of people's aversion to uncertain or ambiguous situations, including the *certainty effect* (Kahneman and Tversky, 1979), the *Allais paradox* (Allais, 1953), and the *Ellsberg paradox* (Ellsberg, 1961), which all have in common a descriptive account of the ways in which people avoid uncertainty and ambiguity at the expense of normatively preferable outcomes (Baron, 1994).

Ellsberg found that people violated the assumptions of the expected utility theory by preferring to avoid situations in which the probability of possible outcomes is unknown, and called the effect *ambiguity aversion*. For example, in one variation of the Ellsberg paradigm employed by Keren and Gerritsen (1999), people were asked to imagine an urn containing ninety marbles, thirty of which were red and the remainder of which were an unknown number of blue or green marbles. They were told that they would win a monetary prize if they correctly guessed the color of one marble drawn at random. Participants should be indifferent to the color of the marble they select, as the expected prior probability of winning is one-third for each color. In fact, most people preferred to guess red, because of the uncertainty as to the number of blue or green marbles.

In follow-up studies, Keren and Gerritsen (1999) further demonstrated that people preferred a non-ambiguous option, even when it was inferior in terms of expected utility. In one study they manipulated the amount of information associated with ambiguity. An interesting finding was that the inclusion of useless information about an ambiguous alternative (simply describing how the hypothetical machine that selects the ball from the urn at random, mechanically operates) improved its attractiveness to subjects. The authors conclude that, 'Uncertainty, in whatever form, is an undesirable situation that, although inherent in our daily life, is one that we try to reduce or minimize' (p. 170).

Others have noted that people find information value in certainty, and weigh this in their decision making (Fox and Tversky, 1995; Frisch and Baron, 1988; Heath and Tversky, 1991). As Baron (1994) notes, when useful additional information is available, of course, it is rational to pursue it. However, additional information is not always available; and when available it is not always useful. As demonstrated by Bastardi and Shafir (1998), people will sometimes pursue information that clearly has no value for their decisions. There is a pervasive motivation for people to avoid uncertainty in their lives, although, as we will suggest, doing so may lead to paradoxical effects on people's happiness.

Economists have focused primarily on the ways in which people attempt to reduce uncertainty *prior* to making a decision, in the attempt to maximize utility. In contrast, psychologists have focused a good deal of attention on the ways in which people reduce uncertainty *after* an outcome or decision, as a way of promoting the view that the world is a predictable and controllable place. It is this latter, post-outcome uncertainty reduction with which we are primarily concerned, specifically with the ways in which it dampens people's emotional reactions to the event.

3.2. The Pleasure Principle

It is instructive to consider how the uncertainty aversion principle relates to what is probably the most fundamental motive of all, the pleasure principle. This motive is fundamental to virtually all psychological theories, including such diverse approaches as psychoanalysis and behaviorism. 'Our entire psychical activity is bent upon *procuring pleasure* and *avoiding pain*,' Freud (1924/1968, p. 365, emphasis in the original) argued, and termed this the pleasure principle. Learning theories, from Thorndike (1911) to Skinner (1938) and beyond, similarly assume that humans (and indeed, all animals) are motivated to seek out and maintain pleasurable states and to avoid negative ones. This assumption may be the only thing that psychoanalysis and behaviorism have in common, and there are, of course, many debates over the generality of the pleasure principle and exactly how it operates in humans. But no psychologist would deny that it is a fundamental human motive.

The status of the pleasure principle in economics has been more checkered. A central tenet in economics is the notion that individuals seek to maximize utility. Although its definition can be a source of some disagreement, utility to some is synonymous with satisfaction. The construct has been traced to Bernoulli (1738/ 1954), who observed that people act as if the pleasure or utility of a gain of a certain amount is less than the potential pain or disutility of a loss of the same amount. Its relationship to the pleasure principle was furthered by Bentham (1789/1948), for whom social and economic behavior could be explained in terms of a *principle of utility*, defined in terms of the ability of objects to produce pain or pleasure.

For some early economists, namely Jevons, Walras, and Marshall, the notion was entertained that the pleasure derived from economic pursuit was both real and measurable. As with the degree in temperature and the pound in weight, satisfaction utility was given its own unit of measurement, the util (Sher and Pinola, 1981). Similarly, Adam Smith (1776/1976, p. 18) noted that the pursuit of self-interest is a fundamental economic motive. In his words, 'It is not from the benevolence of the butcher, the brewer, or the baker that we expect our dinner, but from their regard to their own interest'. The idea was not that people act selfishly and without altruism, but rather that in the pursuit of those ends that provide self-satisfaction, individuals thereby produce goods and services of value to others, providing mutual gain from their exchanges.

With the development of the expected utility theory, many modern economic approaches no longer equate utility with the simple desire for pleasure, partly out of concern about how to measure pleasure. As noted by Mellers (2000), however, the idea that people base decisions on anticipated pleasures and pain, and the importance of measuring and modeling these anticipated emotions, is gaining favor in the economic theories of judgment and decision making.

3.3. Two Motives or One?

If we assume that uncertainty is always aversive to people, then the uncertainty aversion principle is really just another form of the pleasure principle. Uncertainty may simply be one of the many forms of displeasure that people seek to avoid. Consistent with this view, several theories assume that there are severe affective consequences to a failure to achieve uncertainty reduction. Kagan (1972), for example, argued that by reducing uncertainty, people avoid a negative affect:

Most of the popular motives normally ascribed to children and adults by novelists or psychologists in Western culture, such as achievement, affiliation, power, dependency, nurturance, or succorance, can be derivatives of a primary motive to resolve uncertainty and alleviate subsequent affective distress. The affective distress, be it anxiety, fear, shame, or guilt, only emerges when the person cannot assimilate, remove, or act upon—in short, cope with—the original source of uncertainty. (Kagan, 1972, p. 56)

We suspect that the uncertainty aversion principle does, in fact, have its roots in the pleasure principle. Why would humans have such a strong aversion to uncertainty? At some level, the reason may well be to promote pleasure, in the sense of avoiding danger and furthering one's survival, by working to understand and predict one's environment. It makes more sense, for example, to argue that people reduce uncertainty in order to obtain pleasure and avoid pain, than to argue the reverse, that people seek pleasure in order to reduce uncertainty.

This is different than saying, however, that uncertainty aversion and the pleasure principle always go hand in hand, and that every time people reduce uncertainty, they obtain immediate pleasure. Our argument is that whereas uncertainty is often aversive and people gain pleasure by reducing it, there are important exceptions in which reducing uncertainty also reduces pleasure. As just seen, one way that the sense maker reduces uncertainty is by turning events that are novel into ones that are commonplace; in short, by psychologically 'ordinizing' events. By so doing, events lose some of their emotional power, because ordinary events do not produce as strong an emotional response as novel, unexpected ones (Berlyne, 1971; Frijda, 1988). This process has positive hedonic consequences when the event is negative, by reducing the extent to which the event causes pain. It has negative hedonic consequences when the event is positive, by reducing the extent to which the event causes pleasure. That is, there is a paradoxical effect of the human sense-making process: people try to discover the meaning of the things that happen to them so that they can repeat their best experiences and avoid repeating their worst, but by so doing they rob these experiences of their future hedonic power.

3.4. Ordinization and Negative Events

Through the process of assimilation, accommodation, and 'sense making', an event that is painful at first gradually becomes less so, by virtue of seeming less novel and unpredictable. In a short story by D. Eisenberg, for example, a woman named Francie has this reaction just after learning that her mother has died:

If you were to break, for example, your hip, there would be the pain, the proof, telling you all the time it was true: *that's then and this is now.* But this thing—each second it had to be true all over again; she was getting hurled against each second. *Now.* And *now again—twack!* Maybe one of these seconds she'd smash right through and find herself in the clear place where her mother was alive, scowling, criticizing. (Eisenberg, 1994, p. 109)

We have all had this 'twack' experience after a negative life event. We can hardly think about anything else, and when we do, the event and the negative emotions it engenders suddenly slam back into consciousness.

Little by little, however, the sense maker does its work. The event becomes woven into our life story and no longer seems so surprising or novel. The 'twacks' diminish, and we find ourselves thinking about the event less and less. Although we might be sad when we do think of the death of loved ones and other negative events, the strength of these emotional reactions gradually diminish. In colloquial language we 'come to terms' with the event after we 'let it sink in', which are other ways of saying that the sense maker has succeeded, through the process of assimilation and accommodation, in transforming a novel, unexpected event into a familiar, more understandable one.

3.5. Ordinization and Positive Events

We will have more to say later about how the sense maker accomplishes this task. For now, the important point is that the same process occurs when people experience positive events. Unfortunately, the sense maker does its work well here as well, such that novel events that cause a good deal of pleasure soon come to seem ordinary and, consequently, not as pleasurable. What seems like an amazing and unpredictable event at first quickly seems like old news, as it becomes woven into our world view and our attention turns to new events.

Consider two recent political events, the impeachment of President Clinton in early 1999 and the results of the presidential election in the November of 2000. Both events were virtually unprecedented in American history and received a tremendous amount of media attention. At the time, many Americans viewed these events as momentous, fantastic, chapters in history whose effects would reverberate for years. And although they certainly were momentous events in many ways, it is interesting how quickly they faded from people's attention. A few months after the impeachment trials, Clinton's presidency seemed to go on as before, with hardly a reference to the fact that he was nearly voted out of office by the Senate. A few months after the 2000 presidential election, many people did not think about it nearly as much as they thought they would.

The fact that big news events quickly fade from memory is due in part to the way the media operates; it is always looking for the next big story, and by tomorrow, today's cataclysmic event is old news. Our point is that the sense maker operates in much the same way. What seems like big news today is quickly ordinized through the processes of assimilation and accommodation, such that it quickly seems like old news, with little emotional power.

To appreciate the implications of this process when positive life events occur, consider a young professional who achieves a life-long dream, namely to attend the Stanford University Business School. When she reads the letter of acceptance she screams with joy, calls her parents, and tells all her friends. She experiences genuine euphoria, as evidenced by a marked increase in her heartbeat, blood pressure, and other indices of arousal. She cannot think of anything else, and in fact takes the afternoon off, knowing that she would not be able to concentrate.

Sooner rather than later, her life returns to normal. She calms down, physiologically and emotionally. In the hours and days after her acceptance, she experiences several twacks of pleasure whenever she thinks about it. As the weeks pass, however, she thinks about it less and less, and when she does, the thoughts are not accompanied by the ping of pleasure. The knowledge that 'I will be a Stanford MBA student' recedes to the background of her identity. It is an important part of her life story, to be sure, but it becomes woven into her storyline in such a way that it seems normal and ordinary, not novel and exciting. When she matriculates and begins attending business school classes in the fall, the thought that 'I am a Stanford MBA student' barely causes a ripple in her emotional life.

3.6. The Sense Maker at Work

Some of the most direct evidence for the human sense making process comes from research on the hindsight bias, whereby an event that seems uncertain in prospect often seems more inevitable in retrospect. A stock broker might be quite uncertain, for example, whether technology stocks will rise or fall in value in the next year. After a major correction in which stocks lose 20 percent of their value, the stock broker is likely to believe that he or she should have seen this coming and to blame him or herself for not predicting it. Fischhoff (1975) termed this the hindsight bias or 'creeping determinism,' a phenomenon that has proved to be quite robust (Carli, 1999; Hawkins and Hastie, 1990; Roese and Olson, 1996).

One explanation of the hindsight bias is that as soon as an event occurs, people begin to explain and make sense of it. 'Upon receipt of outcome knowledge,' Fischhoff (1975, p. 297) argued, 'judges immediately assimilate it with what they already know about the event in question. In other words, the retrospective judge attempts to make sense, or a coherent whole, out of what he knows about the event.' Roese and Olson (1996, p. 201) argue that, 'People perceive the occurrence of an outcome and are compelled to make sense of it' (see also Wasserman et al., 1991).

In our terms, the hindsight bias is a major component of the human sense making system, whereby people strive to make sense of their environments. When outcomes occur people do their best to explain them and put them in context. One consequence of this is that the outcomes seem more predictable in retrospect than they did in prospect. Another consequence—one that has been overlooked in the literature on the hindsight bias—is that the event loses some of its emotional power. An event that is unexpected and novel has more emotional impact than one that is expected and ordinary, as in our earlier example of the young professional whose joy at being accepted to graduate school fades relatively quickly.

But exactly how does explaining an event and making it seem more predictable reduce its hedonic power? One way, as we have argued, is that an event that seems ordinary and predictable elicits a less intense emotional reaction than one that seems novel and unpredictable. Another way is by reducing the frequency and duration of thought about the event; ordinary events command less attention than extraordinary ones, and are easier to file away in memory. Consider, for example, the woman who was accepted by the Stanford Business School. A week later, compared to the day she received the acceptance letter, she thinks about her acceptance less frequently and for shorter periods of time, and when she does think about it, her emotional reaction is less intense. Consequently, the event causes less pleasure than it did.[1]

---

[1] The hypothesis that the more ordinary and familiar an event seems, the less its emotional power, may seem inconsistent with the mere exposure effect. A considerable amount of research shows that the more people are exposed to a physical stimulus, such as a word, picture, or song, the more they like it. As argued by Zajonc (1998), this is a fundamental, precognitive process that is common to animals and humans alike. In contrast, we refer to a cognitive process whereby an event is transformed psychologically from one that is surprising, novel, and attention-demanding to one that is commonplace, ordinary, and not attention-demanding. This ordinization process, we suggest, often overpowers any increase in the positive affect due to the mere exposure process.

3.7. The Sense-Making Process Occurs Automatically

In the above quotations about the hindsight bias, researchers used words such as 'immediately assimilate' and 'compelled' to describe the process by which people come to view events as inevitable. The implication is that people automatically explain events in such a way that makes them seem more probable. There is some support for the idea that the hindsight bias is a result of nonconscious, automatic mental processes (e.g., Pohl and Hell, 1996). More generally, there is considerable evidence that the attribution process, whereby people strive to understand and explain each others' behavior, requires little or no mental effort, is unintentional, and occurs outside of awareness (Gilbert, 1998; Gilbert et al., 1988).

An important property of the sense-making apparatus, we argue, is that it operates automatically. When novel events occur, people do not have to stop and deliberate about them consciously to make sense of them. Instead, assimilation, accommodation, and explanation occur outside of conscious awareness, such that events seem more predictable and ordinary. The fact that sense making occurs automatically and nonconsciously has implications for people's understanding of their own emotional lives, which we will discuss later.

To summarize, uncertainty reduction and the pleasure principle operate in tandem for negative events; by finding meaning in such occurrences and ordinizing them, people succeed both in reducing uncertainty and in reducing the negative affect. However, these motives are at cross purposes when people experience positive events. In such cases, we argue, the uncertainty principle usually trumps the pleasure principle. People reduce uncertainty by ordinizing positive events, and thereby reduce the amount of pleasure that they derive from them.

4. EMPIRICAL TESTS AND IMPLICATIONS

An implication of our argument is that recovery from emotional events can be sped up or slowed down by facilitating or inhibiting the sense-making apparatus. Although there is very little research directly testing this hypothesis, there are some relevant findings, and we have conducted some initial studies in our lab.

4.1. Facilitating Sense-Making to Reduce the Duration of Negative Affect

If our arguments are correct, then when negative events occur, emotional recovery can be facilitated by speeding up the process whereby people ordinize the events. There is very little direct research on this hypothesis, and indeed, there are more questions than answers. Must we let the ordinization process take its natural course, or is there some way of speeding it up? Given that sense making processes are largely automatic and nonconscious, to what extent can they be influenced by a conscious, deliberate attempt to facilitate them?

Research by Pennebaker on 'opening up' suggests one strategy that can help, namely writing about one's thoughts and emotions over a period of days. In numerous studies, Pennebaker has asked people to spend about 15 minutes, on three consecutive days, writing about 'your very deepest thoughts and feelings about an extremely important emotional issue that has affected you and your life' (Pennebaker, 1997, p. 162). People often write about quite negative events, such as the death of loved ones or sexual or physical abuse. Not surprisingly, writing about events such as these is initially upsetting; people who do so report more distress than control participants who write about superficial topics (such as their plans for their day). As time goes by, however, people show remarkable benefits from the writing exercise. Compared to people in the control condition, those who write about emotional experiences report better moods, get better grades in college, miss fewer days of work, show improvements in immune system functioning, and are less likely to visit physicians (Pennebaker, 1990, 1997; Smyth, 1998).

The reason that writing has such beneficial effects is that it seems to help people make sense of a negative event by constructing a meaningful narrative that explains it. Pennebaker has analyzed the hundreds of pages of writing his participants provided, and found that the people who improved the most were those who began with rather incoherent, disorganized descriptions of their problem and ended with coherent, organized stories that explained the event and gave it meaning. Further, people who write about current traumas tend to benefit more than people who write about past ones, possibly because people have not had as much of a chance to explain and find meaning in current traumas.

One interpretation of these findings is that sometimes, the sense maker cannot make sense of a disturbing event, and its emotional effects, thus, linger. Some life events are random and unpredictable and difficult to reconcile. Perhaps, Pennebaker's writing exercise allows people to reexamine these events in a way that imposes some meaning on them. The events come to seem a little more understandable, and as a result lose their emotional power.

4.2. Inhibiting Sense-Making to Increase the Duration of Positive Affect

As we have discussed, when people experience positive events, they automatically ordinize these events to the point where they no longer produce much pleasure. If so, then anything that makes an event difficult to assimilate or explain should slow down the ordinizing process, prolonging people's pleasurable reactions to positive events. Paradoxically, uncertainty may prolong pleasure, to the extent that it increases the frequency and duration of thought about a positive event, and the intensity of emotional reactions to that event.

But how might the nonconscious sense maker be stymied when positive events occur? One possibility is to engage in counterfactual reasoning, whereby people mentally undo the past by imagining alternative outcomes (e.g., 'If the admissions committee at Stanford Business School had paid more attention to my low GPA from my first year of college, I would have never gotten in.') The relationship between counterfactual thinking and sense-making is complex, because there are conditions under which it increases people's confidence that the actual outcome was inevitable, and conditions under which it decreases confidence. As noted by Roese and Olson (1996), to the extent that counterfactual thinking focuses people's attention on the reasons why the actual outcome occurred, they will become more confident in the inevitability of that outcome. For example, thinking about how an admissions committee might have reached a different decision can direct attention to why the committee made the decision they did ('Sure I had a low GPA in my freshman year, but I got all As after that, and had great scores on the Graduate Management Admission Test'), thereby making the outcome seem more inevitable ('How could they have done anything else but accept me?'). In our terms, counterfactual reasoning can speed up the process by which a novel event is ordinized, to the extent that it stimulates thinking about why the actual event occurred.

Roese and Olson (1996) also note that counterfactual thinking can decrease people's certainty that an outcome was inevitable, if the alternative scenarios people imagine reinforce the idea that the actual outcome was arbitrary or random, and that other outcomes might well have occurred. Sometimes, for example, people think about arbitrary decisions or events that lead to a desired outcome, but easily could not have occurred. 'If I stayed home instead of going to Bob's party a few years ago,' someone might think, 'I never would have met Sarah and fallen in love.' Note that this counterfactual thought does not focus people's attention on a causal explanation for the desired event; instead, it emphasizes how arbitrary the event was and how it easily might not have occurred. In our terms, it slows down or undoes the ordinizing process of the sense maker, which should prolong the pleasure people obtain from positive events.

Ironically, trying not to think about a positive event might prolong the pleasure it causes, by increasing the accessibility of thoughts about the event. Wegner (1994) and his colleagues have shown that trying to suppress a thought about something can increase the accessibility of thoughts about that topic, especially when people are under a mental load. Wegner et al., (1994) demonstrated that keeping a positive topic secret (e.g., a romantic relationship) can increase the accessibility of thoughts about that topic and increase the pleasure that people derive from it. In our terminology, attempts at thought suppression might thwart the process by which people ordinize events and no longer think about them very often. Instead, thought suppression initiates both the conscious attempt to avoid thinking about a topic and a nonconscious, automatic search for thoughts about that very topic, in order to alert the conscious system that further attempts at suppression are necessary. When people are under a mental load, however, the conscious suppression process breaks down whereas the nonconscious search continues, increasing the accessibility of the topic. This is not a good thing when people are trying to avoid thoughts about anxiety-provoking topics or negative events. If people want to prolong the pleasure they get from positive events, however, then one successful strategy might be to try not to think about it.

Another way to inhibit the nonconscious sense maker is to make it difficult for people to explain why a positive event occurred. We (Wilson et al., 2001) have tested this hypothesis in a recent study in which we first created a positive affect, and then manipulated the ease of assimilating and explaining its causes.

We improved people's mood by providing them with a feedback indicating that several other college students had evaluated them very positively in an impression formation study. Ostensibly as part of a study on how people form impressions using modern communication technology, participants believed that they were communicating over the internet with five students at other universities. They saw photographs of these students, and we scanned a photo of the participant allegedly for the other students to see. In fact there was only one real participant; the responses of the other students' responses were preprogrammed.

Once connected to the messaging program, participants saw the photos and first names of the other students and then responded to questions prompted by the program, such as, 'Please tell the opposite-sex participants about some of your interests. What are your career goals? What do you do in your spare time?' After composing and sending the messages, people read what the other students had ostensibly written. Participants then rated their liking for each student, selected one opposite-sex student as their choice of 'best potential friend', and sent a message to the students that explained their choice.

The participant then learned that all three of the opposite-sex students had selected him or her as their best potential friend, and read flattering messages from the students explaining the reasons for their choice. In the easy to assimilate condition, participants were informed as to which student had written which explanation. The photo and name of the other students accompanied the message that they had supposedly written. In the difficult to assimilate condition, people read the identical explanations, but were not told which student had written which explanation (supposedly to preserve confidentiality). Thus, people in both conditions learned that all three opposite-sex students had chosen them as their best potential friend, and read flattering explanations as to why. The only difference was that in one condition people knew which student had written which paragraph, whereas in the other condition they did not.

We predicted that the immediate effects of receiving the feedback would be to improve people's mood in both conditions, because in both cases the feedback was very positive. This was in fact the case. As seen in Figure 11.1, people's reported mood right after receiving the feedback was extremely positive, with a mean of about 7.9 on a 9-point scale. There was no significant difference between the easy and difficult to assimilate conditions. Further, in a follow-up study, both conditions were significantly higher than a control condition that did not receive any feedback from the other students.

We predicted that there would be a difference in how quickly this positive affect dissipated. In the easy to assimilate condition, people could explain the

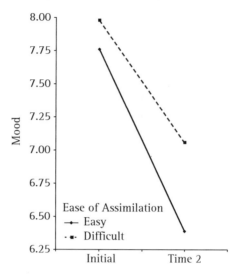

Figure 11.1. *The change in affect over time, as a function of how easily participants could assimilate the information about why people preferred them as their best potential friend*

feedback relatively quickly, by matching each paragraph with the person who ostensibly provided it. That is, regardless of which of the three students ostensibly wrote each paragraph (which was, in fact, counterbalanced), people's sense-making apparatus could find an explanation (e.g., 'That makes sense that Sam would talk about our similar values; now that I think about it, he did seem to share many of my life goals'). Consequently, the feedback should become 'ordinized' (i.e., explainable, predictable). People in the difficult to assimilate condition, however, should find it more difficult to ordinize the feedback, because they could not match the explanations with their authors. Consequently, they might think about the feedback more and derive pleasure from it longer.

To test this hypothesis we assessed people's affect 15 min later, after they completed an unrelated filler task. As predicted, the positive affect had dissipated significantly more in the difficult to assimilate condition than in the easy to assimilate condition (see Figure 11.1). To test the hypothesis that people in the difficult to assimilate condition were less likely to ordinize the feedback and store it in memory, we also gave participants a word completion task at the end of the study, in which they had to make words out of stems such as 'ROM___.' People in the difficult to assimilate condition were more likely to complete this stem with the word 'romance,' suggesting that thoughts about the positive feedback from the opposite-sex students were more accessible in this condition.

This result is preliminary, and clearly more work is needed to provide a clearer understanding of the way in which the human sense-making apparatus can be facilitated or inhibited. Nevertheless, the study is consistent with the possibility that there can be positive hedonic consequences to uncertainty. By making a positive event more difficult to explain and assimilate, the event may have remained more accessible in people's minds and caused a more lasting positive affect. Whereas it is unlikely that any manipulation will cause people to remain happy indefinitely, perhaps there are times when some degree of uncertainty about the causes and meaning of positive events is a good thing, extending people's experience of the pleasure they bring. If so, there may be some situations in which the uncertainty aversion and pleasure principles operate at cross purposes.

5. SUMMARY AND IMPLICATIONS FOR ECONOMICS

As noted earlier, a key attribute of the sense maker is that it occurs largely outside of conscious awareness. Consequently, when people predict their future reactions to emotional events, they fail to take into account the degree to which they will transform the events from extraordinary to ordinary ones. This fact is one of the major reasons for the durability bias, the tendency for people to overestimate the duration of their reactions to emotional events. People assume that the events will retain their emotional power for longer than they in fact do.

This process was demonstrated by Gilbert et al. (1998), in a series of studies on affective forecasts about negative events, such as receiving unflattering feedback on a personality test. People failed to take into account the extent to which their psychological immune systems would ameliorate their reactions to the event, and thus predicted that their negative reactions would last longer than they in fact did. In this chapter, we discussed this process in a larger context, namely one in which the nonconscious sense maker ordinizes both negative and positive events. There may well be an extra motivation to minimize negative events, given the pain they cause (Taylor, 1991). Nonetheless, one of our central points is that the sense maker ordinizes positive events as well, thereby reducing their emotional power.

The implications of these ideas to economic decision making remain to be explored, but we can offer a few speculations here. Many consumer decisions are based at least in part on people's predictions about the affect these decisions will cause (Mellers, 2000). People buy television sets, automobiles, and clothing in part because they believe that these goods will bring them lasting pleasure. Consumers would be unlikely to spend $1000 on a new high definition television set, for example, if they believed that it would increase their happiness for only a few days. At least implicitly, the amounts that people are willing to pay for a product are based on forecasts about the duration of the pleasure they will obtain from it (Della Vigna, 2000).

If so, research on the durability bias suggests that people often pay too much, by overestimating the amount of time that this pleasure will last. For the reasons we have outlined in this chapter, the positive affect people obtain from new sweaters, televisions, and cars is likely to wear off quickly. If they were aware of this fact, they might not be willing to pay as much as they do, such as $1000 for a new television set.

This raises the question of why people do not learn from experience that their affective reactions to durable goods do not last as long as they expect. There are a number of reasons why they might not (see Gilbert et al., 1998, and Wilson et al., in press, for a more complete discussion of this issue). People might remember that the pleasure they received from a new television set wore off quickly, but attribute this to the particular product ('High definition TV is not all that it was cracked up to be'), rather than to the workings of their nonconscious sense making processes. That is, they might fail to generalize from several such experiences, realizing that it is something inside their heads that is reducing their pleasure, rather than something about the specific products they buy.

Further, as time passes after a consumer choice, people might fail to remember that the product did not make them as happy for as long as they anticipated. Meyers et al. (2000) and Mitchell et al. (1997) found evidence for a retrospective durability bias, whereby people overestimated the duration of their happiness after positive emotional events in the past. Meyers et al., for example, surveyed people interested in politics at three points in time: A few weeks before the 1996 United States presidential election, right after the election, and three months later. Democrats showed a strong durability bias before the election, predicting that they would be much happier following Bill Clinton's victory than they in fact were. They also showed a retrospective durability bias, whereby three months after the election, they recalled being happier following Bill Clinton's victory than they in fact had been.

The reason why people exaggerated the duration of their pleasure in both prospect and retrospect may be that there was a common mechanism involved, *focalism*, whereby people think too much about the event in question and fail to consider the consequences of other events that are likely to occur. When predicting how they will feel in the future after an emotional event, people fail to take into account that there will be many other things going on in their lives that will influence their thoughts and feelings (Schkade and Kahneman, 1998; Wilson et al., 2000). Similarly, when trying to reconstruct how happy they were in the past, people may focus too much on the event and not enough on other events that occurred at the time, thereby overestimating the emotional impact of the event.

Interestingly, in both the Mitchell et al. (1997) and Meyers et al. (2000) studies, the retrospective durability bias was not as strong as the prospective one. One possible explanation for this is that the nonconscious sense maker had transformed people's view of the event over time, such that it seemed more ordinary and commonplace in retrospect than prospect, leading people to recollect that it must not have influenced them for very long. Nonetheless, a retrospective durability bias was still found. An implication of this finding is that it may not be easy to teach people that they are overestimating the duration of the pleasure that they will receive from consumer purchases. Although this may be undesirable for individual consumers, it may not be such a bad thing for the economy as a whole, given its dependence on consumer spending.

In sum, we argue that humans are built in such a way that limits the duration of their emotional experiences. One reason for this is that emotional stability may be adaptive, such that it is not to people's advantage to be dysphoric or euphoric for too long. Emotional evanescence may also be a byproduct of uncertainty aversion. The nonconscious sense maker automatically ordinizes events so as to make them seem more predictable, with the side effect of reducing the emotional power of the events.

We discussed some ways in which the sense maker might be sped up or slowed down, in order to speed recovery from negative events and prolong the pleasure derived from positive events. The extent to which it is possible to alter the course of such a fundamental process for any length of time, or even whether it is desirable to do so, remains to be seen.

REFERENCES

Abramson, L.Y., Seligman, M.E.P., and Teasdale, J.D. (1978). Learned helplessness in humans: Critique and reformulation. *Journal of Abnormal Psychology, 87*, 49–74.

Allais, M. (1953). Le comportment de l'homme rationnel devant le risque: Critique des postulates et axioms de l'ecole americaine. *Econometrica, 21*, 503–46.

Aronson, E., Wilson, T.D., and Akert, R.M. (1999). *Social psychology* (3rd ed.). New York: Longman.

Baron, J. (1994). *Thinking and deciding* (2nd ed.). New York: Cambridge University Press.

Bastardi, A. and Shafir, E. (1998). On the pursuit and misuse of useless information. *Journal of Personality and Social Psychology, 75*, 19–32.

Bentham, J. (1948). *An introduction to the principles of morals and legislation.* Oxford: Blackwell. (Original work published 1789.)

Berlyne, D.E. (1971). *Aesthetics and psychobiology.* New York: Appleton.

Bernoulli, D. (1954). Specimen theoriae novae de mensura sortis [Exposition of a new theory of the measurement of risk]. *Econometrica, 22*, 23–36. (Original work published 1738.)

Brickman, P. and Campbell, D.T. (1971). Hedonic relativism and planning the good society. In M.H. Appley (Ed.), *Adaptation-level theory* (pp. 287–305). New York: Academic Press.

—— Coates, D., and Janoff-Bulman, R. (1978). Lottery winners and accident victims: Is happiness relative? *Journal of Personality and Social Psychology, 36*, 917–27.

Carli, L.L. (1999). Cognitive reconstruction, hindsight, and reactions to victims and perpetrators. *Personality and Social Psychology Bulletin, 25*, 966–79.

Costa, Jr., P.T. and McCrae, R.R. (1984). Personality is a lifelong determinant of well-being. In C. Malatesta and C. Izard (Eds.), *Affective processes in adult development and aging* (pp. 141–56). Beverly Hills, CA: Sage.

Davidson, R.J. (1994). Asymmetric brain function, affective style, and psychopathology: The role of early experience and plasticity. *Development and Psychopathology, 6*, 741–58.

230 Timothy D. Wilson, Daniel T. Gilbert, and David B. Centerbar

Della Vigna, S. (2000). *Comments on 'Why Happiness is Like Food, and Why People Don't Know It'*. Paper presented at the Centre for Economic Policy Research Conference on Psychology and Economics, Brussels, Belgium.

Dennett, D.C. (1991). *Consciousness explained*. Boston: Little Brown.

Diener, E. (2000). Subjective well-being: The science of happiness and a proposal for a national index. *American Psychologist, 55*, 34–43.

—— Colvin, R., Pavot, W.G., and Allman, A. (1991). The psychic costs of intense positive affect. *Journal of Personality and Social Psychology, 61*, 492–503.

Eisenberg, D. (1994). The girl who left her sock on the floor. *The New Yorker* (pp.108–24).

Ellsberg, D. (1961). Risk, ambiguity, and the Savage axioms. *Quarterly Journal of Economics, 75*, 643–69.

Emmons, R.A. (1986). Personal strivings: An approach to personality and subjective well-being. *Journal of Personality and Social Psychology, 51*, 1058–68.

Erber, R. (1996). The self-regulation of moods. In L.L. Martin and A. Tesser (Eds.), *Striving and feeling: Interactions among goals, affect, and self-regulation* (pp. 251–75). Mahwah, NJ: Erlbaum.

Festinger, L. (1957). *A theory of cognitive dissonance*. Stanford, CA: Stanford University Press.

Fischhoff, B. (1975). Hindsight foresight: The effect of outcome knowledge on judgment under uncertainty. *Journal of Experimental Psychology: Human Perception and Performance, 1*, 288–99.

Fox, C.R. and Tversky, A. (1995). Ambiguity aversion and comparative ignorance. *Quarterly Journal of Economics, 110*(3), 585–603.

Fredrickson, B.L. (1998). What good are positive emotions? *Review of General Psychology, 2*, 300–19.

Frederick, S. and Loewenstein, G. (1999). Hedonic adaptation. In D. Kahneman, E. Diener, and N. Schwarz (Eds.), *Well being: The foundations of hedonic psychology* (pp. 302–29). New York: Russell Sage Foundation.

Freud, A. (1937). *The ego and the mechanisms of defense*. London: Hogarth Press.

Freud, S. (1968). *A general introduction to psychoanalysis* (J. Riviere, Trans.). New York: Washington Square Press. (Original work published 1924.)

Frijda, N.H. (1988). The laws of emotion. *American Psychologist, 43*, 349–58.

Frisch, D. and Baron, J. (1988). Ambiguity and rationality. *Journal of Behavioral Decision Making, 1*, 149–57.

Gilbert, D.T. (1991). How mental systems believe. *American Psychologist, 46*, 107–19.

—— (1998). Ordinary personology. In D. Gilbert, S. Fiske, and G. Lindzey (Eds.), *The handbook of social psychology* (4th ed., Vol. 2, pp. 89–150). New York: Random House.

—— Pelham, B.W., and Krull, D.S. (1988). On cognitive busyness: When person perceivers meet persons perceived. *Journal of Personality and Social Psychology, 54*, 733–40.

—— Pinel, E.C., Wilson, T.D., Blumberg, S.J., and Wheatley, T.P. (1998). Immune neglect: A source of durability bias in affective forecasting. *Journal of Personality and Social Psychology, 75*, 617–38.

Gilovich, T. (1991). *How we know what isn't so: The fallibility of human reason in everyday life*. New York: The Free Press.

Heath, C. and Tversky, A. (1991). Preference and belief: Ambiguity and competence in choice under uncertainty. *Journal of Risk and Uncertainty, 4*, 5–28.

'Heavy meal increases risk of a heart attack'. *Washington Post* (2000, Nov. 15), p. A11.

Hochschild, A.R. (1979). Emotion work, feeling rules, and social structure. *American Journal of Sociology, 85*, 551–75.

Hawkins, S.A. and Hastie, R. (1990). Hindsight: Biased judgments of past events after the events are known. *Psychological Bulletin, 107*, 311–27.

Heider, F. (1958). *The psychology of interpersonal relations*. New York: Wiley.

Isen, A.M. (1993). Positive affect and decision making. In M. Lewis and J.M. Haviland (Eds.), *Handbook of emotions* (pp. 261–77). New York: Guilford Press.

Jobes, J. (1974). A revelatory function of art. *The British Journal of Aesthetics, 14*, 24–133.

Jones, E.E. and Davis, K.E. (1965). From acts to dispositions: The attribution process in social psychology. In L. Berkowitz (Ed.), *Advances in experimental social psychology* (Vol. 2, pp. 219–66). New York: Academic Press.

Kahneman, D. and Tversky, A. (1979). Prospect theory: An analysis of decision under risk. *Econometrica, 47*, 263–91.

Kagan, J. (1972). Motives and development. *Journal of Personality and Social Psychology, 22*, 51–66.

Kaplan, H.R. (1978). *Lottery winners: How they won and how winning changed their lives*. New York: Harper and Row.

Kelley, H.H. (1967). Attribution theory in social psychology. In D. Levine (Ed.), *Nebraska symposium on motivation* (Vol. 15, pp. 192–238). Lincoln, NB: University of Nebraska Press.

Keren, G. and Gerritsen, L.E.M. (1999). On the robustness and possible accounts of ambiguity aversion. *Acta Psychologica, 103*, 149–72.

Koob, G.F., Caine, S.B., Parsons, L., Markou, A., and Weiss, F. (1997). Opponent process model and psychostimulant addiction. *Pharmacology Biochemistry and Behavior, 57*, 513–21.

Langer, E.J. and Rodin, J. (1976). The effects of choice and enhanced personal responsibility for the aged: A field experiment. *Journal of Personality and Social Psychology, 34*, 191–8.

Loewenstein, G. (1994). The psychology of curiosity: A review and reinterpretation. *Psychological Bulletin, 116*, 75–98.

Lund, D.A., Caserta, M.S., and Dimond, M.F. (1989). Impact of spousal bereavement on the subjective well-being of older adults. In D.A. Lund (Ed.), *Older bereaved spouses: Research with practical implications* (pp. 3–15). New York: Hemisphere.

Lykken, D. and Tellegen, A. (1996). Happiness is a stochastic phenomenon. *Psychological Science, 7*, 186–9.

Mellers, B.A. (2000). Choice and the relative pleasure of consequences. *Psychological Bulletin, 126*, 910–24.

Meyers, J.M., Wilson, T.D., and Gilbert, D.T. (2000). *The accuracy of predicted and recollected happiness after emotional events*. Unpublished raw data.

Mitchell, T.R., Thompson, L., Peterson, E., and Cronk, R. (1997). Temporal adjustments in the evaluation of events: The 'rosy view'. *Journal of Experimental Social Psychology, 33*, 421–48.

Ortony, A., Clore, G.L., and Collins, A. (1988). *The cognitive structure of emotions*. New York: Cambridge University Press.

Parducci, A. (1995). *Happiness, pleasure, and judgment: The contextual theory and its applications*. Mahwah, NJ: Erlbaum.

Pennebaker, J.W. (1990). *Opening up: The healing power of expressing emotions.* New York: Guilford.

—— (1997). Writing about emotional experiences as a therapeutic process. *Psychological Science, 8,* 162–6.

Pfeiffer, J.E. (1982). *Explosion: An inquiry into the origins of art and religion.* New York: Harper & Row.

Piaget, J. (1952). *The origins of intelligence in children.* New York: International Universities Press.

Piaget, J. and Inhelder, B. (1969). *The psychology of the child.* New York: Basic Books.

Pittman, T.S. (1998). Motivation. In D. Gilbert, S. Fiske, and G. Lindzey (Eds.), *The handbook of social psychology* (4th ed., Vol. 1, pp. 549–90). New York: Random House.

Pohl, R.F. and Hell, W. (1996). No reduction in hindsight bias after complete information and repeated testing. *Organizational Behavior and Human Decision Processes, 67,* 49–58.

Roese, N.J. and Olson, J.M. (1996). Counterfactuals, causal attributions, and the hindsight bias: A conceptual integration. *Journal of Experimental Social Psychology, 32,* 197–227.

Ryan, R.M., Sheldon, K.M., Kasser, T., and Deci, E.L. (1996). All goals are not created equal: An organismic perspective on the nature of goals and their regulation. In P.M. Gollwitzer and J.A. Bargh (Eds.), *The psychology of action: Linking cognition and motivation to behavior* (pp. 7–26). New York: Guilford Press.

Sandvik, E., Diener, E., and Larson, R.J. (1985). The opponent process theory and affective reactions. *Motivation and Emotion, 94,* 407–18.

Schkade, D. and Kahneman, D. (1998). Does living in California make people happy? A focusing illusion in judgments of life satisfaction. *Psychological Science, 9,* 340–6.

Schulz, R. (1976). Effects of control and predictability on the physical and psychological well-being of the institutionalized aged. *Journal of Personality and Social Psychology, 33,* 563–73.

Seligman, M.E.P. (1975). *Helplessness: On depression, development, and death.* San Francisco: Freeman.

Sher, W.T. and Pinola, R. (1981). *Microeconomic theory: A synthesis of classical theory and the modern approach.* New York: North Holland.

Skinner, B.F. (1938). *Behavior of organisms.* New York: Appleton-Century-Crofts.

Smith, A. (1976). *An inquiry into the nature and causes of the wealth of nations.* (E. Cannan, Ed.). Chicago: University of Chicago Press. (Original work published 1776.)

Smyth, J.M. (1998). Written emotional expression: Effect sizes, outcome types, and moderating variables. *Journal of Consulting and Clinical Psychology, 66,* 174–84.

Solomon, R.L. (1980). The opponent-process theory of acquired motivation. *American Psychologist, 35,* 691–712.

Sterling, P. and Eyer, J. (1988). Allostasis: A new paradigm to explain arousal pathology. In S. Fisher and J. Reason (Eds.), *Handbook of life stress, cognition and health* (pp. 629–48). Chichester, UK: John Wiley and Sons.

Suh, E., Diener, E., and Fujita, F. (1996). Events and subjective well-being: Only recent events matter. *Journal of Personality and Social Psychology, 70,* 1091–102.

Taylor, S.E. (1991). Asymmetrical effects of positive and negative events: The mobilization-minimization hypothesis. *Psychological Bulletin, 110,* 67–85.

—— and Brown, J.D. (1988). Illusion and well-being: A social psychological perspective on mental health. *Psychological Bulletin, 103,* 193–210.

Thompson, S.C., Armstrong, W., and Thomas, C. (1998). Illusions of control, under-estimations, and accuracy: A control heuristic explanation. *Psychological Bulletin, 123,* 143–61.

Thorndike, E.L. (1911). *Animal intelligence.* New York: Macmillan.

Vaillant, G. (2000). Adaptive mental mechanisms: Their role in positive psychology. *American Psychologist, 55,* 89–98.

Wasserman, D., Lempert, R.O., and Hastie, R. (1991). Hindsight and causality. *Personality and Social Psychology Bulletin, 17,* 30–5.

Wegner, D.M. (1994). Ironic process of mental control. *Psychological Review, 101,* 34–52.

——Lane, J.D., and Dimitri, S. (1994). The allure of secret relationships. *Journal of Personality and Social Psychology, 66,* 287–300.

Wilson, T.D., Centerbar, D., and Gilbert, D.T. (2001). *The pleasures of uncertainty.* Unpublished raw data, University of Virginia.

——Meyers, J., and Gilbert, D.T. (2001). Lessons from the past: Do people learn from experience that emotional reactions are short lived? *Personality and Social Psychology Bulletin, 27,* 1648–61.

——Wheatley, T.P., Meyers, J.M., Gilbert, D.T., and Axsom, D. (2000). Focalism: A Source of durability bias in affective forecasting. *Journal of Personality and Social Psychology, 78,* 821–36.

Woods, S.C. (1991). The eating paradox: How we tolerate food. *Psychological Review, 98,* 488–505.

Wortman, C.B., Silver, R.C., and Kessler, R.C. (1993). The meaning of loss and adjustment to bereavement. In M.S. Stroebe, W. Stroebe, and R.O. Hansson (Eds.), *Handbook of bereavement: Theory, research, and intervention* (pp. 349–66). New York: Cambridge University Press.

Zajonc, R.B. (1998). Emotions. In D. Gilbert, S. Fiske, and G. Lindzey (Eds.), *The handbook of social psychology* (4th ed., Vol. 1, pp. 591–632). New York: Random House.

Temporal Construal Theory of Time-Dependent Preferences

YAACOV TROPE AND NIRA LIBERMAN

For more than a century, questions about the psychological consequences of time perspective have provided the impetus for a large amount of research in the behavioral sciences (see review by Loewenstein, 1993). This research has been conducted by investigators across different disciplines, including psychology (e.g., Ainslie, 1975; Ainslie and Haslam, 1992; Baumeister and Heatherton, 1996; Metcalf and Mischel, 1999; Rachlin, 1995; Read and Loewenstein, 2000), behavioral economics (e.g., O'Donoghue and Rabin, 2000; Thaler, 1981), and political science (e.g., Elster and Loewenstein, 1992; Schelling, 1984). Investigators in these disciplines have used a wide range of laboratory, survey, and econometric methods to study time perspective phenomena. Within psychology, time perspective issues have played a central role in all the three major schools of thought, as exemplified by the psychodynamic analyses of primary vs. secondary processes (see Freud, 1959), behaviorist analyses of self-control (see Ainslie, 1975; Rachlin, 1995), and cognitive analyses of delay of gratification (Mischel, 1974).

Over the years, research has documented reliable time-dependent changes in preference. A course of action that seems desirable in the distant future often seems undesirable in the near future, and vice versa. As a result, past decisions may sometimes seem regretful and even puzzling as one gets closer in time to implementing those decisions. Traditionally, such inter-temporal inconsistencies have been explained in terms of time-discounting theories. These theories assume that preferences change with temporal distance because different types of value have different rates of discounting over time. Thus, according to valence-dependent time-discounting, near future decisions give more weight to negative outcomes, whereas distant future decisions give more weight to positive outcomes because negative outcomes are discounted more steeply than positive outcomes (Lewin, 1951; Miller, 1944). According to affect-dependent time-discounting, near future decisions give more weight to affective value, whereas distant future decisions give more weight to cognitive value because affective value is discounted more

The research reported in this article was supported by NIMH Grant #1R01MH59030-01A1 and NSF Grant # SBR-9808675.

steeply than cognitive value (Loewenstein, 1996; Metcalfe and Mischel, 1999; Mischel et al., 1989). And according to hyperbolic time-discounting, near future decisions give more weight to immediate outcomes, whereas distant future decisions give more weight to delayed outcomes because negative outcomes are discounted more steeply than positive outcomes (Ainslie and Haslam, 1992; Loewenstein and Prelec, 1997; Rachlin, 1995; Read et al., 1999).

The temporal construal theory (TCT) proposes a different approach, one that emphasizes the construal of future events (Liberman and Trope, 1998; Trope and Liberman, 2000). According to the TCT, temporal distance changes individuals' preferences because it changes the way individuals mentally represent future events (see Gilbert et al., 1998; Gilbert and Wilson, 2000; Kahneman and Lovallo, 1991; Wilson, Gilbert, and Wheatley, 1998). The greater the temporal distance from future events, the more likely are the events to be represented in terms of a few abstract and essential features (high-level construals), rather than in terms of more concrete and superficial features (low-level construals). As temporal distance increases, the value attached to the high-level construals of events receives more weight and the value attached to the low-level construals of events receives less weight. Thus, the TCT proposes that temporal distance changes preferences because distant future preferences, compared to near future preferences, are more likely to reflect the value attached to high-level construals than the value attached to low-level construals. When the high-level construal of an option is less positive than its low-level construal, the value of the option should be *diminished* when delayed, but when the high-level construal of an option is more positive than its low-level construal, the value of the option should be augmented when delayed.

Consider, for example, an activity consisting of two parts: A main task (e.g., reading) that constitutes the purpose of the activity and an unrelated filler task (e.g., coloring) to be performed during a break in the reading. Reading is the goal of the activity and as such is part of a high-level construal of the activity. Coloring is unrelated to the goal of the activity, and thus is part of a low-level construal of the activity. The TCT therefore predicts that temporal distance will increase the weight of the value of the main task (reading) relative to the weight of the value of the filler task (coloring) in determining the overall attractiveness of the activity. Thus, if reading is more interesting than coloring, the activity should be more attractive in the distant future than in the near future, but if coloring is more attractive than reading, then the activity should be more attractive in the near future than in the distant future. In general, an activity consisting of an interesting main part and a boring filler part would become more attractive over temporal delay. In contrast, an activity consisting of a boring main part and an interesting filler part would become less attractive over temporal delay.

Valence-dependent time-discounting and affect-dependent time-discounting make different predictions. Based on the conflict models theories (Lewin, 1951; Miller, 1944), valence-dependent time-discounting assumes that negative value undergoes steeper time-discounting than does positive value; that is, the temporal distance decreases the weight of negative aspects and increases the weight of positive aspects of an activity, regardless of their construal level. Therefore, according to valence-dependent time-discounting, options with positive and negative aspects would always seem more attractive from a distant time perspective than from a close time perspective. This should be the case regardless of whether these aspects comprise high-level or low-level construals. In our example, temporal distance should always increase the attractiveness of an activity consisting of interesting and boring tasks.

Affect dependent time-discounting (Metcalfe and Mischel, 1999; Loewenstein, 1996) assumes that the rate of value time-discounting depends on whether the value is affect-based or cognitive-based. Affect-based value presumably undergoes steeper time-discounting than does cognitive-based value. Therefore, temporal distance should always increase the weight of the cognitive value relative to the weight of the affective value in preference. The TCT, on the other hand, proposes that temporal changes in the weight of the cognitive and affective value depend on the level of construal to which these values are attached. When the cognitive value is attached to high-level construals and affective value to a low-level construals (e.g., the main task has cognitive value and the filler has affective value), the temporal distance will increase the relative weight of the cognitive (vs. affective) value. However, when affective value is attached to high-level construals and cognitive value to low-level construals (e.g., the main task has affective value and the filler has cognitive value), the temporal distance will increase the relative weight of affective (vs. cognitive) value.

A series of five studies tested the predictions of the TCT regarding time-dependent preferences (Trope and Liberman, 2000). The first four studies contrasted the predictions of the TCT and value-dependent time-discounting. The fifth study tested the predictions of the TCT against those of affect-dependent time-discounting.

1. TIME-DEPENDENT TASK PREFERENCES

This study presented participants with pairs of activities consisting of a main and filler task. One activity consisted of an interesting main task and a boring filler task, whereas the other activity consisted of a main boring task and an interesting filler task. As argued above, the main task is more central to the activity than the filler task, and therefore constitutes a high-level construal of an activity. Based on this assumption, we predicted that the preference for the activity with the interesting main task over the activity with the boring main task would be stronger in the distant future than in the near future, so that the attractiveness of the former activity should increase and the attractiveness of the latter activity should decrease with temporal distance.

Based on a pretest, we selected four interesting tasks (e.g., 'Judging humor: Evaluating cartoons for their funniness') and four boring tasks (e.g., 'Data checking: Comparing two lists of numbers to check for discrepancies'). Each of the interesting tasks was paired with each of the uninteresting tasks, creating

16 different activities. For each activity, one of the tasks was described as the main task, and the other task was describes as a filler task. Reversing the roles of the main task and the filler created two versions of each activity. A total of 32 different activities were thus generated, with the content of the main and filler tasks fully counterbalanced. Each activity was described as consisting of three sessions of performing the main task, with the filler task performed between these sessions to provide rest and distraction from the main task. For example, an activity entitled 'Judging humor' was described as follows: 'The main task is judging humor, and will ask you to evaluate the funniness of cartoons. The filler task in between the three sessions is checking data, and will ask you to compare two lists of numbers to check for discrepancies.' In the other version of this activity, the roles of the same tasks as main and filler were reversed. Thus, the activity was entitled 'Checking data,' and was described as follows: 'The main task is checking data, and will ask you to compare two lists of numbers to check for discrepancies. The filler task in between the three sessions is judging humor, and will ask you to evaluate the funniness of cartoons.'

Participants indicated their preferences regarding two activities, one consisting of an interesting main task and a boring filler, and the other consisting of a boring main task and an interesting filler. In the near future condition, participants expected to perform the chosen activity in the same experimental session, whereas in the distant future condition, they expected to perform this activity in the next session, 4–6 weeks later. Participants rated on 1–9 scales the extent to which they were interested in performing each activity. These ratings were said to determine which of the two activities participants would actually perform. The present study thus manipulated time (near future vs. distant future) between-participants and type of activity (interesting main task with a boring filler vs. boring main task with an interesting filler) within-participants.

A 2(time) × 2(type of activity) ANOVA on the attractiveness ratings of the activities revealed a main effect for type of activity, $F(1, 60) = 93.50$, $p < .0001$, indicating a preference for the interesting activity with a boring filler ($M = 8.15$) over the boring activity with an interesting filler ($M = 4.23$). This confirmed that the main task was more central than the filler task in evaluating the activities. However, a type of activity × time interaction, $F(1, 60) = 4.17$, $p < .05$, indicated that the preference for the activity with an interesting main task over the activity with a boring main task was more pronounced in the distant future ($Ms = 8.53$ vs. 3.78) than in the near future ($Ms = 7.78$ vs. 4.69). Thus, as predicted by the TCT, temporal distance enhanced the tendency to evaluate activities in terms of their main task rather than their filler task, so that over time delay the activity with an interesting main task became more attractive and the one with a boring main task became less attractive.

This pattern of results is predicted by the TCT but not by valence-dependent time-discounting. Both activities had both positive (interesting) and negative (boring) features. The conflict models theory predicts that both activities would seem more attractive in the distant future than in the near future, because negative features presumably undergo steeper time-discounting than positive features. This prediction was not confirmed. Moreover, this study manipulated the values of the high- and low-level construals in the same way. It seems, then, that level of construal, rather than valence or some content property, is the critical factor that determines time-dependent changes in preference.

2. TIME-DEPENDENT PRODUCT PREFERENCES

This study examined the effect of temporal distance on interest in products with multiple features. We reasoned that features that are related to the primary function of the product, compared to features that are unrelated to this function, constitute a higher level of construal of the product. Suppose, for example, that one wants to buy a radio set in order to listen to music and news and has a choice between a radio set that has good sound but a poor built-in clock, and a radio set that has poor sound but a good clock. Given one's goal, sound quality should be more central than the quality of the clock in the construal of the radio set. The TCT therefore predicts that the preference for the radio that has good sound over the radio that has poor sound should be stronger in the distant than near future, with the attractiveness of the former increasing and the attractiveness of the latter decreasing with temporal distance. Valence-dependent time-discounting would predict that both products would be evaluated more positively in the distant future than in the near future, because both give rise to a conflict between positive and negative features.

To test these predictions, one group of participants received a description of a radio set with good sound and a poor built in clock, whereas another group received a description of a set with poor sound and a good clock. The first group read: 'Imagine that tomorrow you will buy a radio set. You need a simple set in the kitchen to listen to morning programs and music when you get up. When you arrive home, you discover that it fits just great in the place you wanted to put it, and the sound is really good. However, the clock that is built into the set turns out to be pretty useless. The digits are too small and can be hardly seen unless you stand right in front of it.' The second group read: 'Imagine that tomorrow you would buy a radio set. You need a simple set in the kitchen to listen to morning programs and music when you get up. When you arrive home, you discover that if you put the set in the place you wanted, the reception is bad, and to get a reasonable reception you have to put it in a rather inconvenient place. However, the clock that is built into the set turns out to be pretty useful. It has large clear digits that can be easily seen from anywhere in the kitchen.' In the distant future condition, 'tomorrow' was replaced with 'a year from now.' After reading the scenarios, participants indicated to what extent they would be satisfied with their purchase on a 1–9 (not at all satisfied to very satisfied) scale.

A 2(time) × 2(type of product) ANOVA on the satisfaction ratings revealed a main effect of type of product, $F(1, 186) = 21.69$, $p < .001$, indicating that overall participants preferred the set with good sound and a poor clock over the set with poor sound and a good clock. This confirmed our assumption that the quality of the radio was generally more central than the quality of the built-in clock. However, a time × type of product interaction, $F(1, 186) = 4.19$, $p < .05$, indicated that this preference was stronger in the distant future ($Ms = 5.48$ vs. 3.46) than in the near future ($Ms = 4.91$ vs. 4.13). Thus, as predicted by the TCT, temporal distance increased the tendency to evaluate products according to their primary function rather than their secondary function. Over time delay, the radio with the good sound became more attractive despite its poor clock, and the radio with the poor sound became less attractive despite its good clock. Like the results of the earlier study on task preferences, the present results are inconsistent with the conflict models theories. Both radio sets entailed a conflict between a positive and a negative feature. Hence, according to the conflict models theories, both sets should have seemed more attractive in the distant future than in the near future. The present results failed to show this main effect of time on evaluations.

3. TIME-DEPENDENT JOB PREFERENCES

This study examined the effect of temporal distance on preferences for two work-study options. One option offered an interesting job with an uninteresting training period, whereas the other option offered an uninteresting job with an interesting training period. We assumed that the job is more central than the training, and therefore constitutes a higher level of construal of the work-study option. Based on this assumption, we predicted that the preference for the interesting job option over the uninteresting job option would be greater in the distant future than in the near future, with attractiveness of the former option increasing and the attractiveness of the latter option decreasing over time delay. Valence-dependent time-discounting, on the other hand, predicts that both options would seem more attractive in the distant future than in the near future.

In a pretest, participants rated the attractiveness of six different jobs and six different training programs on scales ranging from 1–9 (very unattractive to very attractive). Based on these ratings we selected an attractive and an unattractive job ($M = 7.68$ and $M = 3.00$, respectively), and an attractive and an unattractive training ($M = 6.06$ and $M = 4.25$, respectively). Two descriptions of work-study options were composed for the main study from these pretested jobs and training programs. The *interesting job with uninteresting training* was described as '...judging and measuring individuals' evaluations of the funniness of cartoons, movies and jokes...' and as requiring '...preliminary training that involves a few sessions of learning the basics of attitude measurement...' The *uninteresting job with interesting training* was described as '...entering data, and examining whether attitudes elicited by the different types of measurement are similar or not...' and as requiring '...preliminary training that involves a few sessions of learning the basics of attitude change through analyzing commercial ads in papers and TV...'

Participants in the near future condition were told that the jobs were immediately available, and participants in the distant future condition were told that the jobs would be available a year later. Participants then received either the description of the interesting job with uninteresting training, or the description of the uninteresting job with interesting training. After reading the description, participants were asked to imagine that they were looking for a work-study job (or would be looking for a work-study job a year later) and indicate how much they would like to take the job on a 1–9 (not at all to very much) scale.

A 2(time: near vs. distant future) × 2(type of job) between-participants ANOVA on the preference ratings of the work-study options yielded a main effect for type of job, $F(1, 109) = 10.44$, $p < .001$, indicating an overall preference for the interesting job over the uninteresting job. This confirmed our assumption that the job was more central than the training for the job. However, a significant time type of job interaction, $F(1, 109) = 6.30$, $p < .01$, indicated that the preference for the interesting job over the uninteresting job was more pronounced in the distant future ($Ms = 6.72$ vs. 4.74) than in the near future ($Ms = 6.44$ vs. 6.13). Thus, as predicted by the TCT, over time delay, job preferences became increasingly more in line with the quality of the jobs rather than the training for the jobs. The interesting job became more attractive and the boring job less attractive over time delay. This pattern of results is inconsistent with the valence-dependent time-discounting prediction of the conflict models theories (Miller, 1944; Lewin, 1951). According to these theories, both the interesting and boring jobs elicit an approach-avoidance conflict because they have both positive and negative aspects, and therefore both jobs should have seemed more attractive in the distant future than in the near future. The present results failed to show this main effect of time on job preferences.

4. TIME-DEPENDENT PREFERENCES FOR EVERYDAY-LIFE SITUATIONS

This study tested the ability of the TCT to predict which events would look more attractive when delayed than when immediate, and which events would show the reverse pattern. The first, pretest stage of the study was designed to determine the values associated with the high- and the low-level construals of different events (e.g., 'eating a cake,' 'having houseguests'). Participants described either the general meaning and broad implications of events (i.e., high-level construals of the event) or its concrete details and circumstances (i.e., low-level construals), and then indicated how positive or negative the event was. For the second stage of the study, we selected the events that had a different valence at the high and low levels of construal. In this second stage, participants evaluated how positive or negative would each of these events be if it happened in the near future (tomorrow) or in the distant future (the next year). The TCT predicts that the events that had a more positive high-level construal than low-level construal would seem more attractive in the distant future than in the near future (i.e., would be augmented over time delay), whereas events that had a less positive high-level construal than low-level construal would seem less attractive in the distant future than in the near future (i.e., would be discounted over time delay).

Six events were selected on the basis of the pretesting. The following three events had more negative high-level construals than low-level of construals:

My roommate cleaned the apartment. Imagine that your apartment has been a real mess, and for the last few days your roommate has been urging you to clean the apartment together. Each day you kept telling him that you would do the cleaning together tomorrow. You have the feeling that finally the day has come. The cleaning will have to be done today. However, when you come home you realize that your roommate has cleaned the apartment himself. Probably he got really irritated. At least now you don't have to do the cleaning.

Eating a cake. Imagine that after spending the break at your parents', you made a resolution not to eat fattening food any more, and especially to stay away from rich desserts. Imagine that it is lunchtime, and you are at a nice coffee shop with a friend. You feel hungry and your friend takes a fresh, big muffin with his coffee. You look at him, and then decide to take a piece of cake, just this one time.

My mother's party. Imagine that your mother has a party, which she has been planning for a long time. You, the whole family, and some friends are supposed to be there. Just before the party you realize that you have to prepare for an exam you have in a few days, and therefore you decide not to go to your mother's party. Now, you call your mother to tell her that you won't come.

The following three events had more positive high-level construals than low-level construals:

Studying in the library. Imagine that you have to write a paper for an important course. Just before the deadline you go to the library. You will spend a few hours reading books you need and working on your paper.

Having houseguests. Imagine that three of your friends are coming to spend their vacation in NYC. They are going to stay at your place for a week or so. You really like them, and you actually invited them to stay with you when they are in the city.

A letter to my parents. You know that your parents expect a letter from you. You've been promising to write them in detail about your life. Finally, you get to do that. Imagine yourself sitting at your desk, trying to get this letter written.

Participants in the main study rated how much they would like to experience each of the events either a year from now (the distant future condition) or tomorrow (the near future condition). We first examined the three events that had a more positive low-level construal than high-level construal. A MANOVA on the desirability ratings of these events, with time as a between-participants factor and event as a within-participants factor, yielded a significant effect of time, $F(1, 54) = 7.01$, $p < .01$. Consistent with the TCT, these events were rated as less positive in the distant future than the near future. Participants rated the experience of finding out that their roommate has cleaned their apartment as more positive when it pertained to the near future ($M = 8.00$) than the distant future ($M = 6.71$). Breaking a diet was also more attractive tomorrow ($M = 5.21$) than a year later ($M = 4.57$). And not going to their mother's birthday party tomorrow was less aversive ($M = 2.46$) than in a year ($M = 1.71$).

We then examined the three events that had a more positive high-level construal than low-level construal. A MANOVA on the desirability ratings of these events yielded a significant effect of time, $F(1, 54) = 13.08$, $p < .001$, indicating that these events were rated as more positive in the distant future than the near future. As predicted by the TCT, participants felt that studying in the library would be more positive in the distant future ($M = 5.29$) than the near future ($M = 4.18$). Having houseguests also seemed more attractive when expected a year from now ($M = 6.71$) than tomorrow ($M = 4.79$). And writing a letter to one's parents in the next year seemed like a more positive experience ($M = 5.39$) than writing it tomorrow ($M = 3.79$).

These results demonstrate that as temporal distance increases, the weight of high-level construals is enhanced and the weight of low-level construals is reduced in determining preference. Thus, when high-level construals of events are more positive than low-level construals of the events, temporal distance enhances the desirability of the events, but when high-level construals of events are less positive than low-level construal of the events, temporal distance diminishes the desirability of the events. In other words, temporal distance shifts the value of events closer to the value of their high-level construal.

5. TEMPORAL CONSTRUAL AND AFFECT-DEPENDENT TIME-DISCOUNTING

We now relate temporal construal to affect-dependent time-discounting. This hypothesis has been proposed by self-regulation theories as an explanation of variations in the effect of time on preference (Metcalfe and Mischel, 1999; Mischel et al., 1989). As discussed earlier, affect-dependent time-discounting assumes that cognitive-based value (i.e., 'cold' value) is discounted less steeply (and even augmented) with temporal distance than is affect-based value (i.e., 'hot' value). Therefore, temporal distance should always increase the relative weight of cognitive (vs. affective) value in preference. According to the TCT, the way temporal distance changes the weight of affective and cognitive value depends on the level of construal to which the two types of value are linked. When the cognitive value is linked to high-level construals and affective value to low-level construals, temporal distance will indeed increase the relative weight of cognitive vs. affective value, as affect-dependent time-discounting predicts. However, when affective value is linked to high-level construals and cognitive value to low-level construals, temporal distance should increase the relative weight of affective vs. cognitive value, contrary to what affect-dependent time-discounting predicts.

To test these predictions, we assessed preferences regarding films varying in affective value (funniness) and cognitive value (informativeness). The goal of watching the films was either affective (getting oneself into a good mood) or cognitive (learning about a topic). Depending on the goal, either affective features or cognitive features of the films were more central, and thus constituted the high-level construal of the films, whereas the other type of features was rendered goal-irrelevant and, thus, part of the low-level construal of the films.

In the cognitive goal condition, participants were told that the study was on information exchange in informal interactions, and that they would discuss the 'principles of comic films' after they learn about the subject by watching a short film. Participants in the affective goal condition were told that the study was on the effects of mood on social interaction, and that they would watch a short film that was designed to induce a good mood before the interaction. Participants in each goal condition were told that they would watch the film in either a few minutes or one month later.

All of the participants were told that there were four films prepared by film students as a final project in their course on 'principles of comic films'. The films were described as 15 min long and as explaining some comic principles and exemplifying comic scenes. Participants received four or five written evaluations of the films, ostensibly obtained from 'pretest students'. The following are examples of these evaluations: 'It was a very helpful explanation and great funny examples' (informative and funny); 'I really enjoyed the jokes, but could not make sense of the guy's explanations' (funny but uninformative); 'it wasn't really funny, probably because the explanations made it all so clear and transparent' (funny but uninformative); 'The explanation was pretty boring and confusing, and they selected pretty dull examples, too' (uninformative and not funny). Participants then rated the extent to which they would like to see each film.

The TCT predicts that over time delay, the effect of goal-relevant value would increase relative to the effect of goal-irrelevant value. Thus, temporal distance should increase the influence of the informativeness vs. the funniness of the films when the goal is cognitive, but decrease the influence of informativeness vs. the funniness of the films when the goal is affective. To test this prediction, we examined the preferences for the mixed options (the informative/not funny film and uninformative/funny film). A time × goal × option ANOVA yielded the predicted three-way interaction, $F(1, 75) = 6.68$, $p < .01$, indicating that preferences for the two options changed in opposite directions over time, depending on the goal condition (see Figure 12.1). Specifically, in the cognitive goal condition, temporal distance increased the preference for the informative/not-funny film over the uninformative/funny film, $Ms = 6.75$ vs. 5.05 in the distant future, whereas both $Ms = 6.26$, in the near future. In contrast, in the affective goal condition, temporal distance increased the preference for the uninformative/funny film over the informative/not-funny film, $Ms = 6.75$ vs. 3.95, in the distant future, whereas $Ms = 6.60$ vs. 5.15, in the near future.

Overall, the preference for films that had a positive goal-relevant value over films that had a negative goal-relevant value was stronger in the distant future ($Ms = 6.75$ vs. 4.50) than in the near future ($Ms = 6.43$ vs. 5.69), $F(1, 75) = 6.88$,

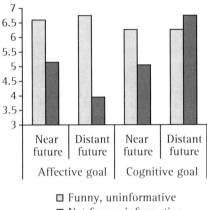

Figure 12.1. *Preferences for films varying in affective and informational value under affective and cognitive goals in the near and distant future*

$p < .01$. This pattern of results is predicted by the TCT, but not by affect-dependent time-discounting. The latter hypothesis predicts that regardless of the goal, the preference for the uninformative/funny film over the informative/not-funny film should be stronger in the near than distant future. However, the time × option interaction predicted by this hypothesis was insignificant, $F < 1$.

The results of this study support TCT in that participants' preferences revealed that low-level, goal-irrelevant aspects, compared to high-level, goal-relevant aspects, were more influential in the near future compared to distant future decisions. In other words, distant future decisions were less influenced by the value of low-level construals, either affective or cognitive. These results are inconsistent with affect-dependent time-discounting, which assumes that near future decisions compared to distant future decisions are more influenced by affective value and less influenced by cognitive value.

6. DISCUSSION

The present studies demonstrate that the weight of high-level value, compared to the weight of low-level value, is greater in the distant future than in the near future decisions. Thus, when high-level construals of mixed options (options with both positive and negative features) were positive, the options were more attractive in the distant future than in the near future. But when high-level construals of the mixed options were negative, they were more attractive in the near future than in the distant future. This pattern of temporal changes in preference was obtained across different manipulations of level of construal. Temporal distance increased the tendency to choose according to main rather than filler tasks, superordinate rather than subordinate aspects of job offers, primary rather than secondary functions of products, abstract rather than concrete value of everyday life situations, and goal-relevant rather than goal-irrelevant aspects of films. Toge-ther, these findings provide converging evidence for the TCT prediction that value is augmented or discounted with temporal distance depending on whether the value is associated with high- or low-level construals of an activity.

According to the conflict models theories (Lewin, 1951; Miller, 1944), negative aspects of options are discounted over time delay more steeply than positive aspects, and therefore ambivalent options (i.e., options with both positive and negative aspects) should be more attractive in the distant future than in the near future. The results of all of our studies show that this was true only for those options that had a positive high-level construal and a negative low-level con-strual. Options that had a negative high-level construal and a positive low-level construal showed the reverse pattern. It should be pointed out, however, that although the present research disentangles valence and level of construal, there are many situations in which the two factors are correlated. For example, positive outcomes are often part of individuals' goals, whereas negative outcomes are often incidental and imposed by circumstances. In such situations, positive outcomes constitute a higher level of construal than negative outcomes, and, as a result, would be discounted over time delay less steeply than negative outcomes. Temporal construal may thus contribute to the occurrence and intuitive appeal of valence-dependent time-discounting.

The present research also addresses affect-dependent time-discounting. This hypothesis assumes that affect-based value ('hot' value) is discounted more steeply than cognitive-based value ('cold' value) over time delay (Loewenstein, 1996; Metcalfe and Mischel, 1999; Mischel et al., 1989; Read et al. 1999). Therefore, temporal distance should increase the weight of the cognitive value and decrease the weight of the affective value in determining preferences regarding future options. The present findings fail to support this hypothesis. The change in the relative weight of cognitive vs. affective value over time delay, depended on whether these two types of value were goal-relevant (and therefore related to a high-level construal of the activity) or goal-irrelevant (and therefore related to a low-level construal of the activity). However, like valence, type of valence (affective vs. cognitive) may be often correlated with the level of construal. Thus, it has been proposed that affective ('hot') value is represented at a concrete level, whereas cognitive ('cold') value is represented more abstractly (e.g., Metcalfe and Mischel, 1999). Moreover, affective value (e.g., funniness) can be consumed for its own sake, without considering higher-level goals, whereas cognitive value (e.g., informativeness) derives its positivity from higher level goals (e.g., doing well in an exam) and, therefore, has to be represented in terms of these goals in order to be appreciated. It is possible, then, that such differences in the construal level contribute to the greater time-discounting of affective value than cognitive value.

Some of the present findings may be interpreted in terms of hyperbolic time-discounting (see e.g., Ainslie and Haslam, 1992; Loewenstein and Prelec, 1997; Rachlin, 1995; Read et al., 1999). This hypothesis assumes that the discounting rate changes over temporal distance. The discounting rate is initially steep, and then becomes more moderate. Therefore, when a future activity has immediate and delayed outcomes, more weight should be given to the immediate outcomes than to delayed outcomes in near compared to distant future decisions. As a result, temporal distance should increase the preference for activities with relatively more valuable delayed outcomes and decrease the preference for activities with relatively more valuable immediate outcomes.

It might be argued that the activities in some of our studies had immediate and delayed outcomes. For example, in the study on everyday life preferences, eating a cake may have immediate positive value ('tasty'), but delayed negative value ('fattening'), whereas studying in the library may have immediate negative value ('tiring'), but delayed positive value ('getting high grades'). Hyperbolic time-discounting would therefore entail decreased interest in the cake and increased interest in studying in the distant future compared to the near future, as this study found. Similarly, in the study on job preferences, training was immediate whereas the job itself was delayed. Therefore, by hyperbolic discounting, the weight of the quality of the job (vs. the quality of training) should receive greater weight in the distant future than in near future decisions, so that temporal distance should increase the preference for an interesting job with boring training over a boring job with interesting training, as this study found. It should be pointed out, however, that in the other three studies low- and high-level outcomes were concurrent. For example, participants in the task preference study expected to experience the boring or interesting main and filler task on the same occasion. The same holds true for the quality of the sound and the quality of the clock in the product preference study and the goal-relevant vs. goal-irrelevant features of the films in the film preference study. Thus, hyperbolic time-discounting can account for only some of our findings.

The present findings have important implications for real-life decision situations in which the available options entail a trade-off between one's central and peripheral interests. For example, one may need to choose between an interesting job with uninteresting training and an uninteresting job with interesting training. As predicted by the TCT, the present research demonstrates that central interests, compared to peripheral interests, carry more weight in the distant future than in near future decisions. For example, in the distant future, the good job was clearly preferred to the bad job, but in the near future this preference vanished. It seems, then, that the secondary advantages or disadvantages of distant future options do not prevent individuals from making unequivocal decisions according to their primary interests. However, as one gets closer in time to the available options, secondary considerations become increasingly influential and capable of inducing conflict and hesitation. Preferences for the near future are thus more contaminated by peripheral considerations than distant future preferences. Interestingly, despite the uncertainty that is inherent in evaluating the distant future, the temporal construal actually produces clearer preferences regarding the distant future than the near future.

In our studies, centrality was defined by content: We assumed that goal-related features are more central than goal-irrelevant features. It is quite possible, however, that other factors, beyond goal-relevance, also affect centrality. For example, it could be that in continuous hedonic experiences, the experience at the peak and the end points are more central than experiences at other points in time (Kahneman, 2002, Chapter 10, this volume). It could be also that other procedures, such as explicit noting or segmentation may single out certain points during the course of an experience thereby rendering them more central (Ariely and Carmon, 2000; Ariely and Zauberman, 2000). Kahneman and his colleagues found that these prominent points in the course of an experience have a disproportionate weight in retrospective evaluations of the experience. It would be interesting to examine in future research whether this over-weighting is further enhanced over time (i.e., as the event becomes more distant in the past), as well as whether the same relation holds for the future: Are peak and end points weighted more in evaluating distant future experiences than near future experiences?

REFERENCES

Ainslie, G. (1975). Specious reward: A behavioral theory of impulsiveness and impulse control. *Psychological Bulletin, 82*, 463–96.

Ainslie, G. and Haslam, N. (1992). Hyperbolic discounting. In G. Loewenstein and J. Elster (Eds.), *Choice over Time* (pp. 57–92). New York: Russel Sage Foundation.

Ariely, D. and Carmon, Z. (2000). Gestalt characteristics of experiences: The defining features of summarized events. *Journal of Behavioral Decision Making, 13*, 191–201.

—— and Zauberman, G. (2000). On the making of an experience: The effects of breaking and combining experiences on their overall evaluation. *Journal of Behavioral Decision Making, 13*, 219–32.

Baumeister, R.F. and Heatherton, T.F. (1996). Self regulation failure: An overview. *Psychological inquiry, 7*, 1–15.

Elster, J. and Loewenstein, G. (1992). Utility from memory and anticipation. In G. Loewenstein and J. Elster (Eds.), *Choice Over Time* (pp. 213–34). New York: Russel Sage Foundation.

Freud, S. (1959). In S. Freud (Ed.) *Collected papers* (vol.4, pp. 13–21). New York: Basic Books.

Gilbert, D.T., Pinel, E.C., Wilson, T.D., Blumberg, S.J., and Wheatley, T.P. (1998). Immune neglect: A source of durability bias in affective forecasting. *Journal of Personality and Social Psychology, 75*, 617–38.

—— and Wilson, T.D. (2000). Miswanting: Problems in affective forecasting. In J. Forgas (Ed.), *Thinking and feeling: The role of affect in social cognition*. New York: Cambridge University Press.

Kahneman, D. and Lovallo, D. (1991). Timid choices and bold forecasts: A cognitive perspective on risk taking. *Management Science, 39*, 17–31.

Lewin, K. (1951). Field theory in social science. In D. Cartwright (Ed.), *Field theory in social science*. Chicago: The University of Chicago Press.

Liberman, N. and Trope, Y. (1998). The role of feasibility and desirability considerations in near and distant future decisions: A test of Temporal Construal Theory. *Journal of Personality and Social Psychology, 75,* 5–18.

Loewenstein, G.F. (1996). Out of control: Visceral influences on behavior. *Organizational behavior and human decision processes, 65,* 272–92.

Loewenstein, G.F. and Prelec, D. (1997). Anomalies of intertemporal choice: Evidence and interpretation. *Quarterly Journal of Economics, 107,* 573–97.

—— and —— (1993). Preferences for sequences of outcomes. *Psychological Review, 100,* 91–108.

Metcalfe, J. and Mischel, W. (1999). A hot/cool system analysis of delay of gratification: Dynamics of willpower. *Psychological Review, 106,* 3–19.

Miller, N.E. (1944). Experimental studies of conflict. In McV. Hunt (Ed.), *Personality and the behavior disorders.* New York: Ronald Press.

Mischel, W. (1974). Processes in delay of gratification. In L. Berkowitz (Ed.), *Advances in experimental social psychology* (Vol. 7, pp. 249–92). New York: Academic Press.

—— Shoda, Y., and Rodriguez, M.L. (1989). Delay of gratification in children. *Science, 244,* 933–8.

O'Donoghue, T. and Rabin, M. (2000). The economics of immediate gratification. *Journal of Behavioral Decision Making, 13,* 233–50.

Rachlin, H. (1995). Self control: Beyond commitment. *Behavioral and Brain Sciences, 18,* 109–59.

—— and Raineri, A. (1992). Irrationality, impulsiveness and selfishness as discount reversal effects. In G. Loewenstein and J. Elster (Eds.), *Choice over time* (pp. 93–118). New York: Russel Sage Foundation.

Read, D., Loewenstein, G., and Kalyanaraman, S. (1999). Mixing virtue and vice: Combining the immediacy effect and the diversification heuristic. *Journal of Behavioral Decision Making, 12,* 257–73.

—— and —— (2000). Time and decision: Introduction to the Special Issue. *Journal of Behavioral Decision Making, 13,* 141–4.

—— —— and Kalyanaraman, S. (1999). Mixing virtue with vice: Combining the immediacy effect and the diversification heuristic. *Journal of Behavioral Decision Making, 12,* 257–73.

Schelling, T. (1984). Self command in practice, in theory and in a theory of rational choice. *American Economic Review, 74,* 1–11.

Thaler, R. H. (1981). Some empirical evidence on dynamic inconsistency. *Economic Letters, 8,* 201–7.

Trope, Y. and Liberman, N. (2000). Temporal construal and time-dependent changes in preference. *Journal of Personality and Social Psychology, 79,* 876–89.

—— and Liberman, N. (2000). Temporal construal and time-dependent changes in preference. *Journal of Personality and Social Psychology, 79,* 876–89.

Wilson, T.D., Gilbert, D.T., and Wheatley, T.P. (1998). Protecting our minds: the role of lay beliefs. In Vincent Y. Yzerbyt and Guy Lories (Eds.), *Metacognition: Cognitive and social dimension* (pp. 171–201). Thousand Oaks, CA: Sage Publications.

PART V

EXPERIMENTAL PRACTICES IN PSYCHOLOGY, ECONOMICS, AND FINANCE

13

Economists' and Psychologists' Experimental Practices: How They Differ, Why They Differ, and How They Could Converge

RALPH HERTWIG AND ANDREAS ORTMANN

1. INTRODUCTION

We all value the notion of interdisciplinarity. But, principles notwithstanding, dialogues across borders do not occur very often. Why is this so? There are myriad hurdles that stand in the way of transcending the limits of our disciplines, ranging from the incommensurability of theoretical frameworks and languages to differences in subject matters to mundane institutional barriers (e.g., interdisciplinary work is not a good bet for getting tenured). Yet another hindrance is the fact that different disciplines often employ different tools in the production of scientific knowledge. And, unfortunately, we often move quickly from recognizing the other tribe's different methodological tools and conventions to a suspicion of their epistemological soundness. Needless to say this suspicion tends to grow larger when the findings generated by alien practices challenge one's own long-held beliefs and assumptions. Interactions between experimental economists and psychologists are not exempt from this phenomenon. Fortunately, however, one's own beliefs about proper methodological conduct, as much as suspicions about the other tribe's practices, can be empirically scrutinized.

The goal of this chapter is to subject some of our beliefs to such an analysis. Specifically, we will discuss economists' and psychologists' different conceptions of proper experimentation in terms of two key variables of experimental design—the use (or lack thereof) of financial incentives and deception. Both variables have been suggested to epitomize the conflicting methodological views of economists and psychologists. Moreover, these variables figure prominently in economists'

We would like to thank Juan Carrillo and Daniel Gilbert for constructive comments. Special thanks are due to Anita Todd for improving the readability of the manuscript, and the Deutsche Forschungsgemeinschaft for financial support to the first author (Forschungsstipendium He 2768/6–1).

debates about the reliability of empirical results from psychology (e.g., Grether and Plott, 1979). We will address two questions: First, do psychologists and economists, in fact, realize these variables differently, and if so, why? Second, do the different realizations matter in terms of the outcome of the experiments? We conclude the discussion of each of these questions with a policy recommendation.

Two caveats are in order. The fact that we focus on two key variables of experimental design does not make others irrelevant. In fact, elsewhere we have discussed additional variables (Hertwig and Ortmann, 2001). Moreover, whenever we speak of standard experimental practices in 'psychology', we mean those used in research on behavioral decision-making (an area relevant to both psychologists and economists; e.g., Rabin, 1998) and related research areas in social and cognitive psychology, such as social cognition, problem solving, and reasoning. The practices discussed do not apply, or apply to a much lesser degree, to the research practices in other fields of psychology (such as biological psychology or psychophysics).

2. WHY FINANCIAL INCENTIVES AND WHY DECEPTION?

The few exchanges over methodological issues between economists and psychologists have been intimately linked to a contentious debate. This debate concerns the question of to what extent, if at all, individual decision-makers depart from the principles of rational economic behavior. Psychologists have accumulated experimental evidence since the 1970s that suggests that 'behavioral assumptions employed by economists are simply wrong' (Grether, 1978, p. 70; see Camerer, 1995; Hogarth and Reder, 1987; and Rabin, 1998, for a summary). Economists have countered by challenging the relevance of this evidence. One prominent reply is that even if individuals' decision-making is flawed, the market will correct for errors and biases (e.g., by averaging out violations that may essentially be random mistakes, or by driving agents who make mistakes from the market; see Camerer, 1990, for a summary and discussion of these and other arguments).

Another prominent reply, and the one that is most relevant for the present discussion, questions the validity of the experimental evidence itself. Experimentally observed violations of rational choice models, so the argument goes, could be peculiar to the methodological customs and rituals of psychologists. David Grether and Charles Plott (1979) are among the economists who have given voice to the misgivings about psychologists' methodologies. In a classic article published in the *American Economic Review*, they explored the robustness of one of the violations psychologists had documented, the *preference reversal* phenomenon. Among others, two features of psychological experimentation raised their suspicion: the lack of financial incentives and the use of deception. Here is why:

1. *Mis-specified Incentives.* Almost all economic theory is applied to situations where the agent choosing is seriously concerned or is at least choosing from among options that in some sense matter.... Thus, the results of experiments

where subjects may be bored, playing games, or otherwise not motivated, present no immediate challenges to theory.

2. *The Experimenters were Psychologists.* In a very real sense this can be a problem. Subjects nearly always speculate about the purpose of experiments and psychologists have the reputation for deceiving subjects.... In order to give the results additional credibility, we felt that the experimental setting should be removed from psychology (Grether and Plott, 1979, pp. 624, 629).

On the basis of their own experimental studies, Grether and Plott (1979) observed that preference reversals survive under experimental conditions that conform to economists' methodological preferences (but see Chu and Chu, 1990). Nevertheless, the lack of performance-based monetary payments (henceforth, *financial incentives*) and the use of deception in psychological experimentation have remained a concern. More than ten years later, the economist Vernon Smith, for instance, concluded that the fact that financial incentives 'are commonly absent in the research of psychologists... has made their work vulnerable to the criticism that the results are not meaningful' (Smith 1991, p. 887). In what follows, we examine the claim that incentives are not commonly used in psychological experimentation and then address the question of to what extent financial incentives matter for the results obtained.

3. FINANCIAL INCENTIVES: HOW DIVERGENT ARE ECONOMISTS' AND PSYCHOLOGISTS' PRACTICES, AND WHY?

Unlike psychologists, experimental economists who do not use financial incentives are pretty much assured that their results will not be published in respected journals. According to Camerer and Hogarth (1999), during 1970–97, every published experimental study in the *American Economic Review* paid its participants according to performance. What motivates this strict norm? Arguably, the most important reason is the one stated by Grether and Plott (1979). Economic theory applies to situations in which there is something at stake for the decision maker (see also Smith, 1991, p. 887). If nothing or too little is at stake in an experimental setting, so the argument goes, participants may not bother to think carefully about the problem and will respond in an offhand, unreliable fashion.

The rationale behind this belief is that economists think of 'cognitive effort' as a scarce resource that people allocate strategically. If participants are not paid contingent on their performance, then they will not invest the cognitive effort necessary to avoid judgment errors. In contrast, if payoffs are provided that satisfy certain requirements such as 'payoff dominance' (Smith, 1976, 1982), participants will invest cognitive effort.[1] As a consequence, performance variability will

---

[1] Smith (1982) proposed several precepts to define what is meant by a controlled microeconomic experiment. Harrison (1989, 1992) argued that experiments in economics that provide financial incentives nevertheless often fail to operationalize satisfactorily one of these precepts, namely, 'payoff

be reduced (Davis and Holt, 1993, p. 25), and performance will be closer to the predictions of the economic theory (Smith and Walker, 1993). Other arguments for financial incentives are derivatives of this general argument: for instance, the assumption that the saliency of financial incentives is easier to gauge and implement than most alternative incentives, or the assumption that most of us want more money, and thus there is no satiation over the course of an experiment.

Compared to economists' strict norm, what is the practice in psychology? Though they are frequently a bone of contention, we know very little about how often (performance-based) financial incentives have been used in psychological experimentation. In a first attempt to quantify the actual practice, we examined all the articles published in the *Journal of Behavioral Decision Making (JBDM)* in the years 1988–97. The *JBDM* is a major publication for behavioral decision researchers in psychology. We included 186 studies in the analysis (see Hertwig and Ortmann, 2001, for details of the procedure).

In this large pool of studies, were financial incentives in fact 'commonly absent' (Smith, 1991, p. 887)? Of those 186 studies, about a quarter (48, or 26 percent) employed financial incentives. However, one quarter is likely to be an upper-bound estimate for the prevalence of financial incentives in psychology, because *JBDM* publishes articles at the intersection of psychology, management science, and economics, and experimental economists are on the editorial board. Indeed, in another large sample of 106 empirical studies on Bayesian reasoning, published in a wide cross-section of psychology journals, we (Hertwig and Ortmann, 2001) found that fewer than three percent provided financial incentives (the sample of studies was drawn from a recent review of Bayesian reasoning studies by Koehler, 1996). In sum, while Smith's assertion that financial incentives are commonly absent in psychology sounds harsh, the evidence seems to support him.

Why are financial incentives rarely used by psychologists? The considerations frequently raised in conversations and writing are pragmatic, theoretical, and ethical. On a pragmatic level, some psychologists fear that the cost of experiments will become prohibitive, limiting the ability of young investigators to conduct empirical studies. Regular financial incentives appear even more unacceptable when coupled with the belief that 'our subjects are the usual middle-class achievement-oriented people who wish to provide (maximal performance)' (Dawes 1996, p. 20). Such a belief suggests that financial incentives are redundant.

---

dominance'. Lack of payoff dominance describes essentially flat maxima, which make it relatively inexpensive for participants not to choose the theoretically optimal action. Thus, for payoffs to satisfy the dominance requirement (Smith, 1976), the difference between the payoff for participants' actual behavior and that for optimal behavior in an experiment needs to be monetarily significant to participants. For instance, if the difference between the payoff for the participant's actual behavior and that for optimal behavior is small (see Harrison, 1994, for examples), one could argue that the payoff decrement participants accept by not behaving optimally is too trivial to be considered meaningful.

A theoretical consideration is that the imposition of a monetary structure on experiments unduly restricts people's wide range of motivations to just one, and may even crowd out intrinsic motivation (see Deci et al., 1999; but also Eisenberger and Cameron, 1996). In addition, incentives in the experimental situation may provide cues to the experimenter's intent ('demand characteristics') and thus bias participants' responses. As a consequence, participants' behavior may conform to the experimenter's hypotheses, for reasons independent of the hypotheses the experimenter intends to test (e.g., Dawes, 1999). Finally, it has been argued that performance-contingent financial incentives have ethical implications. Public payment, for instance, can be akin to an announcement of poor test performance and, thus, might violate a number of ethical standards. We will return to these objections later, but first will consider the question of the effects of financial incentives.

4. FINANCIAL INCENTIVES: DO THE DIFFERENT PRACTICES MATTER?

The impact (or lack thereof) of financial incentives is an important but also contentious issue, with each side of the debate pointing to empirical evidence that supports its particular claims. Tversky and Kahneman (1987, p. 90), for instance, argued that 'experimental findings provide little support' for the view that 'observed failures of rational models are attributable to the cost of thinking and will thus be eliminated by proper incentives . . . . In particular, elementary blunders of probabilistic reasoning . . . are hardly reduced by incentives.' Referring to this conclusion, Smith (1991, p. 887) responded that 'strangely missing, since it is said that there *is* a "little" evidence, are any of the many citations that could have been offered showing that monetary rewards matter.'

Not surprisingly, the fact that the results are mixed contributes to the suspicion on each side that the other is selectively citing evidence. A lack of review studies that rely on the representative samples of experiments certainly does not allay this skepticism. Our ten-year sample of empirical studies published in *JBDM*, however, should be unbiased insofar as its purpose was to quantify the frequency of financial incentives and not to demonstrate that they either matter or do not matter. In the *JBDM* sample, 48 of 186 studies employed financial incentives, but only 10 of those 48 studies systematically explored the effect of financial incentives (by comparing either a payment to a nonpayment condition or different payment schemes).

In a relatively small sample that nevertheless covers a wide range of research topics, such as framing effects, auctions, evaluations of gambles, preference reversal, and information search, what kind of effects did we find? In the majority of cases in which financial incentives made a difference, they *improved* participants' performance, that is, it brought decisions closer to the predictions of the normative models (see Hertwig and Ortmann's, 2001, Table 2 and their text for the detailed results). In only two cases did financial incentives seem to impair performance (but one of the two cases was compromised by methodological problems), and in a few cases, they did not affect performance at all.

In other words, what we found is that although financial incentives certainly do not guarantee optimal decisions, in many cases they bring decisions closer to the predictions of the normative models. Equally important, some studies in our sample reported that financial incentives substantially reduce data variability. These results are in line with the central conclusions from a recent survey by Smith and Walker (1993). Their survey, however, did not specify the inclusion criteria for the studies sampled.

Aside from the Smith and Walker study, only a few other recent review articles have explored the effects of financial incentives (e.g., Jenkins et al., 1998; Prendergast, 1999). We focus here on the analysis by Camerer and Hogarth (1999) because they considered studies both from psychology and economics. They compiled a total of 59 studies, using what they call an 'opportunistic sampling' approach (i.e., a nonrandom sampling insofar as they included studies they knew of and that came to their attention). The studies came from three different research domains, namely, 'judgments and decisions'. 'games and markets', and 'individual choice'. Taken together, the three research domains yielded mixed results: In 45 percent of the studies, financial incentives did not make a difference; in 40 percent they helped; and in 15 percent their effects were negative. But when we consider the first two domains separately, interesting differences emerge.

As Figure 13.1 shows, the largest effect of financial incentives occurred for 'judgment and decision' studies: In 15 of 28 studies (53 percent), the financial

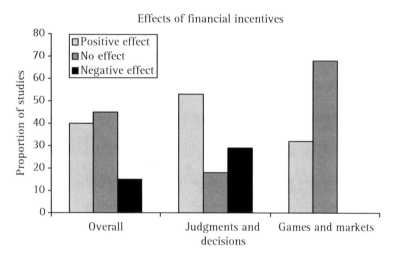

Figure 13.1. *The proportion of studies exhibiting various incentive effects in Camerer and Hogarth's (1999) sample of studies. The graphs show the results averaged across all studies (left), and for two subset of studies ('judgments and decisions' vs. 'games and markets' studies)*

incentives had positive effects, in 5 (18 percent) they had no effect, and in 8 (29 percent) they had negative effects. Regarding the latter studies, however, Camerer and Hogarth (1999, pp. 6 and 8; emphasis is theirs) concluded that the 'effects are often unclear for various methodological reasons.' Moreover, they reported that in 'many of the studies where incentives did not affect mean performance, added incentives *did* reduce variation.'

In contrast to the 'judgment and decision' studies, Camerer and Hogarth (1999) observed that among the 'game and market' studies the effect of financial incentives appears to be substantially weaker. In only 7 of 22 studies (32 percent) did incentives have positive effects, while in 15 (68 percent) they had no effect (this lack of effect was even more pronounced for the few 'individual choice' studies, see Camerer and Hogarth, 1999, table 2). To the extent that one accepts Camerer and Hogarth's nonrandom sample as representative of the population of judgments, decisions, games, and markets experiments, the results are not without some irony. On the home turf of economists—'game and market' studies—incentives may matter less than it is traditionally assumed. In contrast, on the home turf of psychologists—'judgment and decision' studies—incentives may matter more. While the former conclusion (about the game and market studies) conflicts with Smith and Walker's (1993), the latter (about the judgment and decision studies) is in line with the results observed in our nonopportunistic sample of studies drawn from the *Journal of Behavioral Decision Making* (Hertwig and Ortmann, 2001).

5. FINANCIAL INCENTIVES: WHERE TO GO FROM HERE?

The picture that emerges from these results can be summarized as follows: First, financial incentives matter more in some areas than in others (Camerer and Hogarth, 1999). Second, in the area of behavioral decision-making they matter more often than not (see Camerer and Hogarth, 1999; Hertwig and Ortmann, 2001), while the evidence for game and market experiments is contradictory (Camerer and Hogarth, 1999, vs. Smith and Walker, 1993). Third, if beneficial effects are obtained, they seem to be twofold: While financial incentives do not guarantee optimal decisions, in many cases they bring decisions closer to the predictions of the normative models. Equally important, they seem to reduce error variance substantially. Fourth, all these conclusions are based on relatively small (and partly opportunistic) samples of empirical studies and, thus, may not be the last word.

This state of affairs suggests the following policy recommendation. We propose that in research areas in which performance criteria are available and in which researchers seek and intend to make inferences about maximal performance, psychologists and economists ought to make a decision about appropriate incentives. In our view, this decision should be informed by the empirical evidence available. If there is evidence in the past research that incentives affect behavior meaningfully in a task identical to or similar to the one under consideration, then financial (or possibly other) incentives should be employed. If previous studies consistently show that financial incentives do not matter, then not employing incentives can be justified on the basis of this evidence. In cases where there is no or only mixed evidence, we propose that researchers employ a simple 'do-it-both-ways' rule (Hertwig and Ortmann, 2001)—that financial incentives (or, for that matter, other key variables of experimental design) be accorded the status of independent variables in experiments. This practice would rapidly give rise to a database that would eventually enable experimenters from both fields to make data-driven decisions about how to realize the key variables of experimental design. In addition, such a procedure would distribute the effort of studying the impact of design variables among many researchers in the scientific community, thus also increasing the credibility of the obtained evidence.

In our view, a 'do-it-both-ways' policy also takes into account psychologists' concerns that obligatory financial incentives unduly stress monetary motivators at the expense of others. The systematic comparison of incentive (be they monetary or of any other nature) and non-incentive conditions would allow researchers to explore systematically the impact of different motives, for every experiment that employs financial incentives also implicitly suggests something about other motivators (e.g., altruism, trust, reciprocity, or fairness). If, for example, in the Prisoner's Dilemma games (or public good, trust, ultimatum, or dictator games), the behavior of participants does not correspond to the game-theoretic predictions—if they show more altruism (trust, reciprocity, or fairness) than the theory predicts—then these findings also reveal information about the other non-monetary motivators (assuming that the demand effects are carefully controlled, and the experiments successfully implement the game-theoretic model).

We agree with the argument that the implementation of financial incentives has its own ethical risks. But there are ways to reduce them. It is important, for example, that payments are given privately, as is the standard practice in economics experiments. We also agree that 'asking purely hypothetical questions is inexpensive, fast and convenient' (Thaler, 1987, p. 120). However, we conclude by suggesting that the benefits of being able to run many studies do not outweigh the costs of generating results of questionable reliability (see also Beattie and Loomes, 1997, p. 166).

6. DECEPTION: TO WHAT EXTENT DO ECONOMISTS' AND PSYCHOLOGISTS' EXPERIMENTAL PRACTICES DIVERGE, AND WHY?

Deceiving participants is generally taboo among experimental economists (Davis and Holt, 1993, p. 24); indeed, economics studies that the use of deception can probably be counted on two hands. Table 13.1 lists the statements of various prominent experimental economists who oppose deception (for a rare dissenting view in economics, see Bonetti, 1998; but see also Hey, 1998; McDaniel and

Table 13.1. *Economists' rationales for prohibiting deception*

Hey (1991, pp. 21, 119, 173, 225). I feel that it is crucially important that economics experiments actually do what they say they do and that subjects believe this. I would not like to see experiments in economics degenerate to the state witnessed in some areas of experimental psychology where it is common knowledge that the experimenters say one thing and do another. (Subjects) believing what the experimenters tells them . . . seems to me to be of paramount importance: once subjects start to distrust the experimenter, then the tight control that is needed is lost.

Davis and Holt (1993, pp. 23–24). The researcher should . . . be careful to avoid deceiving participants. Most economists are very concerned about developing and maintaining a reputation among the student population for honesty in order to ensure that subject actions are motivated by the induced monetary rewards rather than by psychological reactions to suspected manipulation. Subjects may suspect deception if it is present. Moreover, even if subjects fail to detect deception within a session, it may jeopardize future experiments if the subjects ever find out that they were deceived and report this information to their friends.

Ledyard (1995, p. 134). It is believed by many undergraduates that psychologists are intentionally deceptive in most experiments. If undergraduates believe the same about economics, we have lost control. It is for this reason that modern experimental economists have been carefully nurturing a reputation for absolute honesty in *all* their experiments.

Starmer, 1998). What commonly underlies economists' opposition to deception is the fear that participants' expectations of being deceived produces suspicion and second-guessing, and that these reactions rather than the experimental scenario, instructions, and incentives guide, motivate, and ultimately distort experimental behavior.

Two mechanisms are assumed to induce suspicion and second-guessing. The first mechanism is *firsthand* experience with deception gained by participating and being debriefed in deception experiments. The second mechanism is *vicarious* experience with deception gained via communication channels such as campus scuttlebutt, media coverage of psychological research, and under-graduate teaching. Economists do assume that vicarious experiences suffice to engender the contamination of the participant pool. Therefore, they consider participants' expectation that they will not be deceived (i.e., honesty on the part of the experimenter) a common good of sorts (such as air or water) that would be depleted (contaminated), quickly even, if only a few of their tribe practiced deception.

Unlike economists, psychologists use deception. To estimate the frequency of deception, we focused on the high-ranked *Journal of Personality and Social Psychology (JPSP)* (and its predecessor, the *Journal of Abnormal and Social Psychology*), because in this journal the most comprehensive and recent figures are available. After a sharp upswing during the 1960s when the percentage of deception studies tripled from 16 percent in 1961 to 47 percent in 1971, the use of deception maintained a high level throughout the 1970s, reaching a height of

59 percent in 1979, before it dropped to 50 percent in 1983 (Adair et al., 1985). Since then it has fluctuated between 31 percent and 47 percent (1986: 32 percent; 1992: 47 percent; 1994: 31 percent; 1996: 42 percent; as reported in Adair et al., 1985; Sieber et al., 1995; Nicks et al., 1997; and Epley and Huff, 1998). Some of the fluctuations may reflect substantial changes in the applied methods (e.g., the initial upswing in the 1960s), ethical standards, and the federal regulation of research; others may reflect the different definitions of what constitutes deception (e.g., compare the more inclusive criteria employed by Sieber et al. with the criteria used by Nicks et al.).

Although the use of deception has declined since its heyday in the late 1960s and 1970s, the absolute level is still high: A conservative estimate is that every third study published in *JPSP* in the 1990s employed it (compared to 4.7 percent 1921–48). In a few other social psychology journals, such as the *Journal of Experimental Social Psychology*, the proportion of deception studies appears to be even higher than in *JPSP* (e.g., Gross and Flemming, 1982; Nicks et al., 1997). Moreover, deception is not confined to research practices in social psychology— it is, for instance, also used in marketing and consumer research (see Toy et al., 1989), in personality research (see Nicks et al., 1997), and in research on behavioral decision-making (Hertwig and Ortmann, 2001).

Why do psychologists use deception? The primary motive seems to rest on two methodological arguments: First, if participants were aware of the true purpose of a study—especially when it concerns 'sensitive' issues (e.g., conformity, prejudices, anti-social behavior)—they might respond strategically and not reveal their true preferences, opinions, attitudes, etc.; and the investigator might lose experimental control. For instance, one might expect participants to alter their behavior in order to prove how accepting they are of members of other races if they know that they are participating in a study of racial prejudices. Therefore, so the argument goes, investigators sometimes need to camouflage the purpose of the experiment to achieve experimental control—according to Herrera (1997), this is the standard justification for using deception (see also Kelman, 1967, p. 6). Second, deception can be used to produce situations of special interest that are unlikely to arise otherwise—for instance, an emergency situation in which bystander effects can be studied. For other arguments in the support of deception, see the recent debate in the *American Psychologist* (Bröder, 1998; Kimmel, 1998; Korn, 1998; Ortmann and Hertwig, 1997, 1998).

Although the frequent use of deception appears to imply a widespread consensus among psychologists that it is a methodological necessity, there has been a longstanding and persistent concern among some psychologists regarding its long-term consequences. Table 13.2 compiles some statements from the 1960s (but similar concerns have persisted over the years, see, e.g., Wallsten, 1982). It is striking how much psychologists' statements from the 1960s mirror economists' statements from the 1990s. Similar to the later concerns of economists, psychologists worried that firsthand (Seeman, 1969, in Table 13.2) but also vicarious experience with deception (e.g., Adelson, 1969 and Orne, 1962, in Table 13.2)

Table 13.2. *A sample of conclusions from psychologists regarding the negative effects of deception*

Orne (1962, pp. 778–79). (The use of deception) on the part of psychologists is so widely known in the college population that even if a psychologist is honest with the subject, more often than not he will be distrusted. As one subject pithily put it, "Psychologists always lie!" This bit of paranoia has some support in reality.

Ring (1967, p. 118). What is the perceptive student to think, finally, of a field where the most renowned researchers apparently get their kicks from practicing sometimes unnecessary and frequently crass deceptions on their unsuspecting subjects? . . .
The short-run gains may be considerable, but it does not appear chimerical to suggest that the ultimate price of deception experiments may be the creation of extremely mistrustful and hostile subject pools. It would be ironic indeed if, by their very style of research, social psychologists were to put themselves out of business.

Kelman (1967, p. 6). How long, however, will it be possible for us to find naïve subjects? Among college students, it is already very difficult. They may not know the exact purpose of the particular experiment in which they are participating, but at least they know, typically, that it is *not* what the experimenter says it is. . . . If he resents the experimenter's attempt to deceive him, he may try to throw a monkey wrench into the works; I would not be surprised if this kind of Schweikian game among subjects became a fairly well-established part of the culture of sophisticated campuses.

Argyris (1968, p. 187). Many experiments have been reported where it was crucial to deceive the students. . . . One result that has occurred is that students now come to experiments expecting to be tricked. The initial romance and challenge of being subjects has left them and they are now beginning to behave like lower level employees in companies. Their big challenge is to guess the deception (beat the management). If one likes the experimenter, then he cooperates. If he does not, he may enjoy botching the works with such great skill that the experimenter is not aware of this behavior.

Adelson (1969, p. 220). . . . when the campus population learns, as it can hardly fail to do, about the common tendency of psychologists to deceive, so that all kinds of unanticipated, unknown expectations enter the experimental situation, the subject aiming to 'psych' the experimenter's 'psyching' of him, subject and experimenter entangled in a web of mutual suspicion, mutual deception.

Seeman (1969, pp. 1025–6). When a subject has once participated in a study using deception he is no longer a naïve subject but a sophisticated subject who brings to subsequent studies a variety of personal theories and hypotheses that guide the behavior of the subject quite as decisively as theories and hypotheses guide the behavior of an experimenter. In view of the frequency with which deception is used in research we may soon be reaching a point where we no longer have naïve subjects, but only naïve experimenters. It is an ironic fact that the use of deception, which is intended to control the experimental environment, may serve only to contaminate it.

---

would create the expectation among participants that they will be tricked in experiments, making them distrustful or even hostile. A discipline encumbered with the reputation of using deception, it was argued, would compromise the very asset deception was meant to secure—experimental control (see e.g., Ring, 1967, and Seeman, 1969, in Table 13.2).

7. DECEPTION: WHAT ARE THE CONSEQUENCES OF ITS USE?

Is there evidence that firsthand, or even just vicarious, experiences with deception destroys experimental control? Moreover, is there any evidence that participants' suspicion—through whatever experiences it is brought about—has negative consequences? Drawing on our analyses (Hertwig and Ortmann, 2002; Ortmann and Hertwig, in press), we report some of the major empirical findings. We begin with the second question.

7.1. Is Suspicion an Inconsequential Side Effect of Deception?

Could suspicion *per se* ultimately be inconsequential because the experimental situation is real—or innocuous—enough? There are at least three ways to examine this question. One way is to record the participants' suspicion post-experimentally (before debriefing them) and then analyze people's performance as a function of it. A second way is to take the bull by the horn, engendering participants' suspicion from the outset and studying their subsequent performance as a function of it. Yet another approach considers psychologists' institutional arrangements and their evolution over time as an indication of their regard toward suspicion and its potentially damaging influence on experiments (see Ortmann and Hertwig, in press).

7.1.1. *Post-Experimental Identification of Suspicion*
To find relevant studies, we (Hertwig and Ortmann, 2002) searched the PsycINFO database using the keyword 'deception' in combination with 'suspicion'. Our search turned up 14 studies that examined experimental performance as a function of suspicion. In toto, this collection can be taken as a case study of the effects of suspicion and distrust on a dependent variable under consideration. All of these studies were concerned with conformity behavior—a research topic that arose out of Solomon Asch's remarkable finding that people with a normal vision would ignore what they had seen, in order to agree publicly with an obviously inaccurate group judgment.

In Asch's paradigm, participants are recruited to participate in a visual discrimination task. They are asked to announce publicly which one of three comparison lines matched a standard length. Although seven to nine people typically participate in each session, only one is a naïve participant: The others are instructed to answer correctly on the first two trials, then incorrectly but unanimously on the remaining trials (see Cialdini and Trost, 1998).

Do participants who suspect whether experimenter is speaking the truth—not fully at least—exhibit the same kind of conformity behavior as non-suspicious participants? Among the 14 studies we analyzed (Hertwig and Ortmann, 2002), we found the following: In ten studies (71 percent), suspicious participants conformed less than non-suspicious participants. In nine of these, enough information was given to calculate the effect size eta (see Cohen, 1988), the reduction in conformity due to suspicion was of a medium to large effect size (for details see table 3 in Hertwig and Ortmann, 2002). In the remaining four studies, suspicion did not significantly change the amount of conformity behavior. Albeit limited to the conformity paradigm, these results demonstrate that participants' suspicion *can* systematically alter the very behavior the experimenter intends to measure.

A final remark on conformity studies: In an extensive search of the conformity literature, Stang (1976) identified 21 studies that reported the percentage of participants who were classified as suspicious. Interestingly, he found that participants' suspicion has risen through the decades, with particularly steep increases in the second half of the 1960s (which corresponds closely to the dramatic increase of deception experiments during that period).

7.1.2. *Ex-Ante Manipulation of Suspicion*

A small group of studies actively planted suspicion in order to examine its effects (e.g., participants were given detailed tip-offs about the true purpose of the experiment). Some studies found no effect from this manipulation, and others a good deal. Nevertheless a trend is discernable (for detailed results see table 4 in Hertwig and Ortmann, 2002). When participants receive specific, definite information about deception, experimental performance is indeed altered. However, if the information is vague and deception is merely a possibility, performance is not likely to change (in comparison to a control group).

Is this reason enough to call off the alarm? Not according to Finney (1987, p. 45), who argued that being informed about the possibility of deception 'merely reaffirms subjects' prior belief that deception may occur in an experiment and, therefore, causes no change in their anticipation' (in comparison to participants in the control group who share the same prior belief).

7.1.3. *Psychologists' Institutional Arrangements*

If psychologists believed suspicion to be inconsequential, they probably would not bother to take any measures against it. But they appear to do so—both on an individual and collective level. For instance, a colleague of ours who attended the *CEPR* conference on psychology and economics told us that at his laboratory, in which deception is used and in which students are eligible to participate in multiple experiments, the experimenter routinely probes for suspicion at the end of the studies. In addition, the experimenter asks the participants to list the previous studies they have participated in. If the experimenter needs naïve participants, she can discount all data from participants who have previously participated in a deception study. Or she might choose to analyze those data separately and estimate the effects of experience with prior deceptions. As far as we know, this kind of arrangement is not institutionalized throughout psychological laboratories but are left to the discretion of the individual researcher (and is thus likely to be contingent on his or her access to participants as well as financial resources).[2]

Beyond the obvious ways to deal with the possible consequence of participants' suspicion, there also appear to be more subtle arrangements. Consider, for instance, the salient changes in the selection and composition of psychology's subject pool. Sieber and Saks (1989) reported the responses of 326 psychology departments with subject pools (see also Vitelli, 1988). They found that of the 74 percent that reported having a participant pool, 93 percent recruited from introductory courses. In contrast, in his summary of human participant sources in three journals of the American Psychological Association, Schultz (1969, table 1, p. 217) found, on average, that fewer than 40 percent of human participants were recruited from introductory psychology courses. While the data are not completely comparable, they suggest that during the two decades between Schultz (1969) and Sieber and Saks (1989), the percentage of participants from introductory courses has roughly doubled.

One speculation is that the peculiar institutional arrangements in psychology (namely, the widespread use of participants from introductory courses) result from an evolutionary process: psychology departments have increased their attempts to minimize participants' suspicion by relying on participants who are less likely to have a firsthand experience with deception. In other words, one way to read the two snapshots presented in Schultz (1969) and Sieber and Saks (1989) is that psychologists took the advice of Silverman et al. (1970, p. 211) 'that the practice of using the same subjects repeatedly be curtailed, and whenever administratively possible, subjects who have been deceived and debriefed be excluded from further participation.'

In our view, the available evidence suggests that suspicion is not simply an inconsequential side effect of deception but has the potential to alter the very behavior the experimenter intends to measure. Judging from the evolution of various institutional arrangements, psychologists seem to assume it does. How is participants' suspicion caused in the first place? Does it require firsthand experience (which was present in the above mentioned studies on the impact of suspicion on conformity behavior or on the impact of planted suspicion) or does vicarious experience suffice?

---

[2] The failure to standardize such arrangements may have the unfortunate, and paradoxical, consequence that researchers who do not use deception are more likely to become a victim of its potentially distorting effects: they might be less inclined to probe their participants for suspicion and, thus, be less able to control for the effect of prior experience with deception.

7.2. Is Vicarious Experience as Consequential as Firsthand Experience?

Unfortunately, there is scant empirical evidence to answer this question. We have found very few attempts to quantify participants' vicarious experience. The little evidence available (summarized in Hertwig and Ortmann, 2002) is mostly concerned with the effect of undergraduate teaching. According to Rubin and Moore (1971), undergraduate training, specifically the teaching of classic social psychological experiments (e.g., Milgram experiments, conformity experiments), can serve to develop students' expectation of what experimenters do. They observed that the number of psychology courses which students had completed—not the number of deception experiments in which participants recall having taken part—correlated with the participants' level of suspicion. In line with this result, Higbee (1978) observed that students rated psychologists as being less truthful at the end of the semester than at the beginning (eta = 0.51), and students who had taken at least five psychology courses rated psychologists as less truthful than students without any course experience (eta = 0.43).

Higbee concluded 'if psychologists expect the subjects to believe them, perhaps they should get the subjects at the beginning of the semester' (Higbee, 1978, p. 133; a refinement of the advice given by Silverman et al., 1970). The widespread use of students from introductory courses (described above) could be an attempt to approximate this advice.

8. DECEPTION: WHERE TO GO FROM HERE?

The methodological costs of deception are neither well explored nor well understood. The little we know, however, does help us to evaluate both the present experimental practices and calls to change them. We believe that the available evidence is not sufficient to convince researchers in psychology to abandon a widely used and powerful research tool. In particular, the lack of research regarding the effects of vicarious experience does not allow substantiation of the reputational spillover effects predicted by various researchers (see Tables 13.1 and 13.2). We caution, however, that such a lack may be the result of institutional responses to the very problem. That said, the evidence regarding the consequences of firsthand experience with deception counsels us to treat deception as a last-resort strategy, thus minimizing the number of participants with firsthand experience. This is in fact the policy currently recommended in the guidelines of the American Psychological Association (APA).[3]

---

[3] According to the APA rules of conduct, 'psychologists do not conduct a study involving deception unless they have determined that the use of deceptive techniques is justified by the study's prospective scientific, educational, or applied value and that equally effective alternative procedures that do not use deception are not feasible' (APA, 1992, p. 1609). In other words, the APA rules allow that deception may be indispensable under certain circumstances but treat it as a last-resort strategy, to be used only if its benefits justify its use *and* there are no feasible alternatives.

Even a cursory glance at contemporary deception studies, however, reveals that deception is not treated as a last resort. Consider the following study—recently published in a social psychological journal—which had participants play, among others, an ultimatum game. Participants were falsely told that they would be paired with one of the other participants, that on the basis of a chance procedure they alone were assigned the role of the allocator (who had to divide a certain amount of money), and that their income would be contingent on the allocator's and/or responder's decisions. In addition, the participants were told that the experimenter would hand the allocator's decision to the recipient (involving a rather complicated procedure) and thus decisions would remain anonymous. At the end of the experiment, participants were debriefed, discovering that all participants were allocators and that all received the same amount of money.

This study is not an example of dramatic deception. In fact, the lies were rather mild. This study, however, is a good example of the use of deception where it is completely unnecessary (as witnessed by the many economic studies researching ultimatum games without deception). In the present case, deception was probably used to increase the number of players who are allocators. Sometimes, deception and the lack of financial incentives provide the same benefits: Both practices are inexpensive, fast, and convenient. Deception, however, is only inexpensive if there will be no costs for future experiments. Indeed, why would these participants, who ultimately found out that their decisions and monetary rewards were not contingent, believe the promises of performance-dependent monetary rewards in future experiments? Mistrust of such a promise in future experiments has the clear potential to affect their experimental performance.

This study demonstrates, along with evidence of its widespread use in psychology, that deception is an accepted way of doing business rather than a strategy of last resort, as recommended by the APA. Although the APA rules of conduct are considerably stricter now than in the 1960s (and indeed seem to have successfully reduced the severity of deceptive techniques), they have not changed (some) psychologists' somewhat cavalier approach to deception.

The question is, why—even after the very public debates of the 1970s—are the APA rules of conduct not effective in enforcing deception as a last-resort strategy? Elsewhere we have argued that the main problem is that the key decision whether deception is justified by its anticipated utility is left to those that stand to benefit from its use (Ortmann and Hertwig, 1997, 1998). Notwithstanding the mediating role of institutional review boards (which tend to focus on the ethical rather than the methodological consequences of deception), this practice leaves the assessment of private benefits (e.g., relatively quick publication, see Adelson, 1969) and public costs (contamination of the participant pool) to the interested party (the experimenter)—a classic moral-hazard problem with a solution that is currently not incentive-compatible.

We have suggested a pragmatic solution that we believe is significantly more incentive-compatible (Hertwig and Ortmann, 2002). Specifically, we have proposed that experimenters about to perform deception studies post their experimental designs on an APA website for a specified time period, thus giving those opposed to deception a chance to suggest workable alternatives. Such a procedure might spur a spirited case-by-case debate about deception's necessity, and might ultimately lead to methodological innovation. Over time, such a website would offer successful alternatives, with examples of experiments in which they were used, so that experimenters considering deception could easily 'browse' through them.

We are aware that the evidence and the conclusions expressed in this chapter are not undisputed. In either field there are researchers who disagree with our views, while others are more favorable. For an extensive sample of opinions see the comments on our target article in the *Behavioral and Brain Sciences* (Hertwig and Ortmann, 2001).

9. EPILOGUE

To look at methodological practices across disciplinary borders can be extremely useful, as it allows us to put our daily routines, habits, and beliefs into perspective and to reflect on their costs and benefits. Economics and psychology—two related disciplines—have surprisingly different conceptions of good experimentation even in highly overlapping areas such as research on behavioral decision-making. We believe that both disciplines should use their pronounced differences as an opportunity to more closely and systematically evaluate their methodological preferences. We hope that this chapter will contribute to a spirited discussion of the costs and benefits of those preferences.

REFERENCES

Adair, J.G., Dushenko, T.W., and Lindsay, R.C. L. (1985). Ethical regulations and their impact on research practice. *American Psychologist, 40,* 59–72.

Adelson, J. (1969). Personality. *Annual Review of Psychology, 20,* 217–52.

American Psychological Association (1992). Ethical principles of psychologists and code of conduct. *American Psychologist, 47,* 1597–611.

Argyris, C. (1968). Some unintended consequences of rigorous research. *Psychological Bulletin, 70,* 185–97.

Beattie, J. and Loomes, G. (1997). The impact of incentives upon risky choice experiments. *Journal of Risk and Uncertainty, 14,* 155–68.

Bonetti, S. (1998). Experimental economics and deception. *Journal of Economic Psychology, 19,* 377–95.

Bröder, A. (1998). Deception can be acceptable. *American Psychologist, 53,* 805–6.

Camerer, C.F. (1990). Do markets correct biases in probability judgment? Evidence from market experiments. In L. Green and J. Kagel (Eds.), *Advances in behavioral economics* (pp. 125–72). Northwood, NJ: Ablex Publisher.

——— (1995). Individual decision-making. In J.H. Kagel and A.E. Roth (Eds.), *Handbook of experimental economics* (pp. 587–703). Princeton: Princeton University Press.

—— and Hogarth, R.M. (1999). The effects of financial incentives in experiments: A review and capital–labor–production framework. *Journal of Risk and Uncertainty, 19*, 7–42.

Chu, Y.-P. and Chu, R.-L. (1990). The subsidence of preference reversals in simplified and marketlike experimental settings: A note. *American Economic Review, 80*, 902–11.

Cialdini, R.B. and Trost, M.R. (1998). Social influence: Social norms, conformity, and compliance. In D.T. Gilbert, S.T. Fiske and G. Lindzey (Eds.), *The handbook of social psychology* (Vol. 1, 4th ed.). Boston: Mcgraw-Hill.

Cohen, J. (1988). *Statistical power analysis for the behavioral sciences* (2nd ed.). Mahwah, NJ: Erlbaum.

Davis, D.D. and Holt, C.A. (1993). *Experimental economics.* Princeton: Princeton University Press.

Dawes, R.M. (1996). The purpose of experiments: Ecological validity versus comparing hypotheses. *Behavioral and Brain Sciences, 19*, 20.

—— (1999). Experimental demand, clear incentives, both, or neither? In D. V. Budescu, I. Erev, and R. Zwick (Eds.), *Games and human behavior: Essays in honor of Amnon Rapoport* (pp. 21–8). Mahwah, NJ: Erlbaum.

Deci, E.L., Koestner, R., and Ryan, R.M. (1999). A meta-analytic review of experiments examining the effects of extrinsic rewards on intrinsic motivation. *Psychological Bulletin, 125*, 627–68.

Eisenberger, R. and Cameron, J. (1996). Detrimental effects of reward. Reality or myth? *American Psychologist, 51*, 1153–66.

Epley, N. and Huff, C. (1998). Suspicion, affective response, and educational benefit as a result of deception in psychology research. *Personality and Social Psychology Bulletin, 24*, 759–68.

Finney, P.D. (1987). When consent information refers to risk and deception: Implications for social research. *Journal of Social Behavior and Personality, 2*, 37–48.

Grether, D.M. (1978). Recent psychological studies of behavior under uncertainty. *American Economic Review, 68*, 70–4.

—— and Plott, C.R. (1979). Economic theory of choice and the preference reversal phenomenon. *American Economic Review, 69*, 623–38.

Gross, A.E. and Fleming, I. (1982). Twenty years of deception in social psychology. *Personality and Social Psychology Bulletin, 8*, 402–8.

Harrison, G.W. (1989). Theory and misbehavior of first-price auctions. *American Economic Review, 79*, 749–62.

—— (1992). Theory and misbehavior of first-price auctions: Reply. *American Economic Review, 82*, 1426–43.

—— (1994). Expected utility theory and the experimentalists. *Empirical Economics, 19*, 223–53.

Herrera, C.D. (1997). A historical interpretation of deceptive experiments in American psychology. *History of the Human Sciences, 10*, 23–36.

Hertwig, R. and Ortmann, A. (2001). Experimental practices in economics: A methodological challenge for psychologists? *Behavioral and Brain Sciences, 24*, 383–451.

—— and —— (2002). Does deception destroy experimental control? A Review of the evidence. Manuscript submitted for publication.

Hey, J.D. (1991). *Experiments in economics.* Oxford: Basil Blackwell.

—— (1998). Experimental economics and deception: A comment. *Journal of Economic Psychology, 19*, 397–401.

Higbee, K.L. (1978). How credible are psychological researchers to college students? *The Journal of Psychology, 99,* 129–33.

Hogarth, R.M. and Reder, M.W. (Eds.) (1987). *Rational choice: The contrast between economics and psychology.* Chicago: University of Chicago Press.

Jenkins, Jr., G.D., Mitra, A., Gupta, N., and Shaw, J.D. (1998). Are financial incentives related to performance? A meta-analytic review of empirical research. *Journal of Applied Psychology, 83,* 777–87.

Kelman, H.C. (1967). Human use of human subjects: The problem of deception in social psychological experiments. *Psychological Bulletin, 67,* 1–11.

Kimmel, A.J. (1998). In defense of deception. *American Psychologist, 53,* 803–5.

Koehler, J.J. (1996). The base rate fallacy reconsidered: Descriptive, normative, and methodological challenges. *Behavioral and Brain Sciences, 19,* 1–53.

Korn, J.H. (1998). The reality of deception. *American Psychologist, 53,* 805.

Ledyard, J.O. (1995). Public goods: A survey of experimental research. In J.H. Kagel and A.E. Roth (Eds.), *Handbook of Experimental Economics* (pp. 111–94). Princeton: Princeton University Press.

McDaniel, T. and Starmer, C. (1998). Experimental economics and deception: A comment. *Journal of Economic Psychology, 19,* 403–9.

Nicks, S.D., Korn, J.H., and Mainieri, T. (1997). The rise and fall of deception in social psychology and personality research, 1921 to 1994. *Ethics and Behavior, 7,* 69–77.

Orne, M.T. (1962). On the social psychology of the psychological experiment: With particular reference to demand characteristics and their implications. *American Psychologist, 17,* 776–83.

Ortmann, A. and Hertwig, R. (1997). Is deception acceptable? *American Psychologist, 52,* 746–7.

—— and —— (1998). The question remains: Is deception acceptable? *American Psychologist, 53,* 806–7.

—— and —— (in press). The costs of deception: Evidence from psychology. *Experimental Economics.*

Prendergast, C. (1999). The provision of incentives in firms. *Journal of Economic Literature, 37,* 7–63.

Rabin, M. (1998). Psychology and economics. *Journal of Economic Literature, 36,* 11–46.

Ring, K. (1967). Experimental social psychology: Some sober questions about some frivolous values. *Journal of Experimental Social Psychology, 3,* 113–23.

Rubin, Z. and Moore, Jr., J.C. (1971). Assessment of subjects' suspicions. *Journal of Personality and Social Psychology, 17,* 163–70.

Schultz, D.P. (1969). The human subject in psychological research. *Psychological Bulletin, 72,* 214–28.

Seeman, J. (1969). Deception in psychological research. *American Psychologist, 24,* 1025–8.

Sieber, J.E., Iannuzzo, R., and Rodriguez, B. (1995). Deception methods in psychology: Have they changed in 23 years? *Ethics and Behavior, 5,* 67–85.

—— and Saks, M.J. (1989). A census of subject pool characteristics and policies. *American Psychologist, 44,* 1053–61.

Silverman, I., Shulman, A.D., and Wiesenthal, D.L. (1970). Effects of deceiving and debriefing psychological subjects on performance in later experiments. *Journal of Personality and Social Psychology, 14,* 203–12.

Smith, V.L. (1976). Experimental economics: Induced value theory. *American Economic Review, 66,* 274–9.

—— (1982). Microeconomic systems as an experimental science. *American Economic Review, 72,* 923–55.

Smith, V.L. (1991). Rational choice: The contrast between economics and psychology. *Journal of Political Economy, 99,* 877–97.

—— and Walker, J.M. (1993). Monetary rewards and decision costs in experimental economics. *Economic Inquiry, 31,* 245–61.

Stang, D.J. (1976). Ineffective deception in conformity research: Some causes and consequences. *European Journal of Social Psychology, 6,* 353–67.

Thaler, R. (1987). The psychology of choice and the assumptions of economics. In A. E. Roth (Ed.), *Laboratory experimentation in economics: Six points of view* (pp. 99–130). Cambridge: Cambridge University Press.

Toy, D., Olsen, J., and Wright, L. (1989). Effects of debriefing in marketing research involving 'mild' deceptions. *Psychology & Marketing, 6,* 69–85.

Tversky, A. and Kahneman, D. (1987). Rational choice and the framing of decisions. In R. M. Hogarth and M.W. Reder (Eds.), *Rational choice: The contrast between economics and psychology* (pp. 67–94). Chicago: University of Chicago Press.

Vitelli, R. (1988). The crisis issue assessed: An empirical analysis. *Basic and Applied Social Psychology, 9,* 301–9.

Wallsten, T.S. (1982). *Research through deception* (Letter to the editor). New York Times Magazine, October.

14

Psychology and the Financial Markets: Applications to Understanding and Remedying Irrational Decision-Making

'Everyone complains about his memory, and no-one complains about his judgement.' La Rochefoucauld

The origin of this chapter lies in a report that I wrote for a financial think-tank in the City of London, in which my brief was to identify ways in which psychology-driven applications could help banks make even more money (Hilton, 1999). The way I went about this was to identify some individual and collective biases in decision-making that are well-known to psychologists (e.g. Bazerman, 1998; Hogarth, 1987; Lopes, 1994; Russo and Schoemaker, 1991), and then seek empirical evidence that these biases influence real financial behavior. The evidence that exists would seem to me to confirm the view that finance professionals are very prone to the kinds of biases that experimental psychologists have studied in controlled settings, often using students participating for minor or non-existent financial incentives. At the very least, the studies I review in this chapter should go some way to allaying concerns that cognitive biases studied in psychological experiments will fail to generalise to real economic activity (e.g. Hertwig and Ortmann, in press).

Having identified and substantiated the existence of such biases in financial decision-making, I go on to identify some economic applications of such knowledge. In this I have a slightly different focus to economists who seek either to refine economic theories with behavioral components (e.g., Rabin, 1998), or to

This chapter is a revised and updated version of the paper *Psychology and the financial markets: Applications to trading, dealing and investment analysis*, published in *Journal of Psychology and the Financial Markets*, Lawrence Erlbaum Associates, Inc, forthcoming, whose origin in turn was the report *Psychology and the City: Applications to trading, dealing and investment analysis* published by the Centre for the Study of Financial Innovation (publication no. 38), London, 1999 (material reproduced with permission). I thank Juan Carrillo, Andrew Hilton, and Daniel Kahneman for comments on earlier drafts, and Bruno Biais and Philip Hemmings for much helpful discussion.

recommend optimal financial strategies to rational agents operating in a world of irrational agents, such as banks lending to overoptimistic entrepreneurs (e.g., Manove and Padilla, 1999). Nor is my major focus that of marketing (of financial or other products), where psychology may be used to facilitate maximal client satisfaction or simply a quick sale. Rather, I focus mostly on ways in which psychology could be used to remove irrationality from investors and institutions such as banks, through debiasing strategies based on identifying the causes of irrationality and suggesting remedies.

Paradoxically, a successful application of this last debiasing strategy in human resource management (selection, training, decision-aiding, and control) should make markets more efficient and investors less irrational, thus removing or reducing the need for the first two applications. However, as we shall see below, the existence of collective rationality in a market does not imply that all the individuals in the market are rational, only that some of them are. This point is important, since it implies that even if markets are efficient, individuals will still have a lot to gain from debiasing. This implies that psychology has much to contribute to improving an *individual's* economic performance even if the market is rational, as market rationality does not imply rationality in all the individual participants.

1. INDIVIDUAL IRRATIONALITY AND COLLECTIVE RATIONALITY IN AN EXPERIMENTAL MARKET: IMPLICATIONS FOR ECONOMICS AND PSYCHOLOGY

Work on experimental markets demonstrates that markets can be highly rational even if a majority of the individual participants in the market are irrational. Forsythe et al. (1992), created and tracked a political stock market in which traders dealt in shares in Bush and Dukakis through a computerised system prior to the 1988 US presidential election. Most profits went to a small minority of 'marginal traders' who succeeded in buying low and selling high. These traders seemed to be able to resist 'confirmation bias' by interpreting 'news' dispassionately. For example, after each of the three televised debates, the marginal traders adjusted their holdings in the candidates appropriately, regardless of whether they were themselves a Bush or a Dukakis supporter. Other traders were more likely to see the result of each of these televised debates as favouring their own preferred candidate. In addition, the successful marginal traders were free of the *false consensus* bias, a tendency to overestimate the number of other people who share your preferences.

This experimental market was remarkably efficient, in that the prices of shares in Bush and Dukakis predicted the vote share on election day better (through a simple conversion formula) than all the major public opinion polls. This result was replicated in the 1992 US election (Lopes, 1994), as well as in seven out of eight other political stock markets. It therefore substantiates the *Hayek hypothesis*, namely that a market can be efficient even if most of its participants are not fully rational. What this study adds, of course, is the finding that the profits of arbitrage go to those who are free of judgmental biases. It seems to illustrate Soros's (1998, p. 25) claim that a Popperian 'disconfirmation bias' is (i) rational, (ii) rare, and (iii) profitable.

Forsythe et al.'s (1992) study opens up intriguing perspectives for economists and psychologists. It suggests that even if a market price is fully rational, this does not imply that the individuals who participate in the market are themselves rational. Indeed, these individuals may be systematically, predictably, and insistently irrational, despite having relevant expertise on the asset in question, and clear market incentives to behave rationally. It also implies that a psychological analyses of judgmental biases can identify ways in which individual decision-making can be improved, with consequent implications for improved performance in financial markets. In Section 2, I review several well-known sources of judgmental bias and the evidence that they can impact on financial decision-making. I begin by considering some well-known cognitive biases, and then move on to consider some social factors that can exacerbate (or attenuate) these tendencies to bias and error. As we shall see, many of these biases can be found in experts, and in decision-makers with high incentives to make a rational decision. Likewise, many of these biases and errors can be attenuated or removed by factors other than financial incentives.

2. THE COGNITIVE SOURCES OF BIAS AND ERROR IN FINANCIAL JUDGMENT

2.1. Illusion of Control

The *illusion of control* refers to individuals' tendency to overestimate the control they have over outcomes. It can be induced by cues that suggest that the individual's skill and ability can make a difference to the outcome, even when these are irrelevant. A classic demonstration of this was given by Langer (1975). Participants receive lottery tickets either through drawing them themselves (illusion of control) or through the lottery proprietor (no illusion of control). When asked for selling prices, those who had drawn the tickets themselves wanted approximately twice as much, presumably reflecting their greater belief in the probability of winning. Fenton O'Creevy et al. (1998) found that traders who suffer from an illusion of control (as measured by the perceived ability to influence the movement of a point on a screen) were *less* likely to show a successful performance, based on both the self-report and supervisor assessments of contribution to the overall desk profits (see Figure 14.1).

Further evidence that illusion of control hurts trading performance comes from the studies of individual investors. A cognate of illusion of control is comparative optimism, which may include optimism in comparison to the outcomes of others, to the expectations of others or to what people expect for others (Harris and Middleton, 1994), as well as optimism in comparison to reality (see also Section 2.2). Excessive optimism about one's chances of success compared to

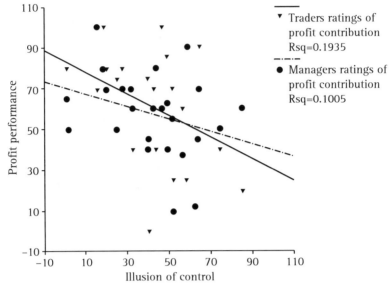

Lines are 'least squares' regression lines'

Figure 14.1. *The relations between measured overconfidence and perceived earnings of traders (rated by the traders themselves and their supervisors). Adapted from Fenton O'Creevy et al. (1998)*

others may incite people to trade more often, perhaps because they believe that they are reading the market better than other players. Consistent with this, Barber and Odean (2000) found that there was an average of 75 percent turnover per year in portfolios held at a discount brokerage, which is highly suggestive of an excessive optimism in trading. However, the problem with this kind of self-belief is that it can simply lead people to trade more often without a compensating increase in earnings. Barber and Odean compared high- and low-frequency traders in their sample, and found that high-frequency traders did *not* make higher gross profits (see Figure 14.2), but simply incurred greater trading costs (the average round-trip transaction costs of a trade due to commission and bid-ask spread is about 6 percent).

Barber and Odean's findings clearly run counter to the predictions of a rational analysis of trading behavior, which would expect trades to occur only when expected profits outweigh transaction costs; but the findings fit a model of trading behavior where traders are unrealistically overconfident about their abilities. One kind of investor that seems particularly likely to be overconfident in this way is the male: survey research indicates that, compared to women, men spend more time and money on security analysis, rely less on their brokers, trade more actively, believe that returns are more highly predictable, and anticipate higher returns than do women. Consistent with their argument that men are more likely

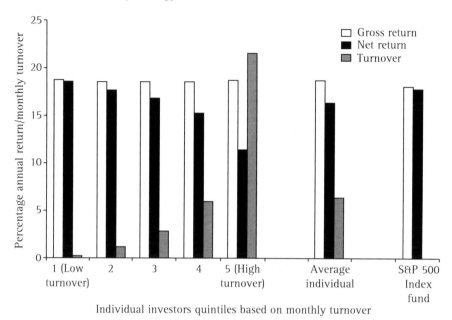

Figure 14.2. *The monthly turnover and annual performance of individual investors. Adapted from Barber and Odean (unpublished)*

to be overly optimistic about their financial acumen, Barber and Odean's (2000b) analysis of discount brokerage accounts found that men take riskier positions than women. More significantly, they also found that men trade more often than women, and as a consequence incur less net returns. This difference between the sexes is especially marked when single men are contrasted to single women!

2.2. Overconfidence in Predictions

Expert predictions are often quite inaccurate in many domains. For example, a review by Russo and Schoemaker (1991; see also Camerer, 1981) of domains such as medicine, psychological analysis, stock price forecasting and financial analysis, showed that while predictions made by experts in these fields on the basis of case information correlated on an average of 0.33 with the actual results, the simple linear models correlated on an average of 0.64 with the actual results. These simple linear models were created by taking the first half of a set of cases (e.g., stock profiles with financial results) in order to create a linear model through regression analysis, and then running the linear model on the remainder of cases to check its predictive ability. For example, in the case of stock analysis, the linear model was able to correlate at 0.80 with the actual stock performance, whereas the predictions of the professional stock analysts used in the sample only correlated at 0.23 with the actual stock performance.

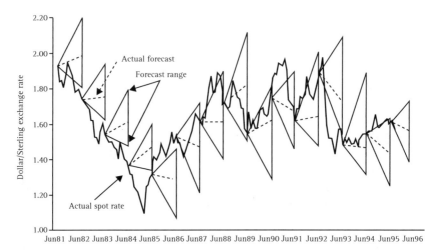

Figure 14.3. *Forecasts of the US$/£ spot rate at a twelve-month horizon from forty top foreign exchange forecasters during 1981–96 (courtesy of Record Treasury Management). Every June Euromoney magazine surveys the top 40 professional foreign exchange forecasters for their forecasts of the $/£ spot rate at a twelve-month horizon. The triangles on the chart illustrate the range of forecasts, the dotted line the resulting average forecast, and the thick black line the spot rate.*

A comprehensive illustration of the pervasive inaccuracy of expert prediction in finance comes from data collected by *Euromoney* and Record Treasury Management on financial experts' and corporate treasurers' predictions about £/US$ and £/DM rates over a period of twenty years (see Figures 14.3 and 14.4). A simple inspection of the data reveals that the actual exchange rate rarely falls in the middle of the range created by taking the highest and lowest prediction made by 40 experts, and indeed very frequently falls *outside* this range. A related finding is that Wilkie-Thompson et al. (1998) found that a panel of financial experts actually did worse than the fourth year students of mathematical finance at making predictions from a simulated series.

Some economists have argued that investment managers may have an incentive to 'follow the herd' even if their private information indicates otherwise (e.g., Scharfstein and Stein, 1990) and professional forecasters may likewise seek to make interesting forecasts, rather than accurate ones, in order to get noticed and build reputation. If this were the only explanation for inaccuracy in expert forecasts, one might expect considerably more accuracy when psychologists come in to test professionals' predictions in their area of expertise, on the assumption that the experts would consider that the rational response to a psychological testing situation should be to demonstrate their forecasting ability. However, as we see below, not only are experts less accurate than might be hoped in such tests, they are often likely to be unaware of their inaccuracy because they overestimate the quality of their judgments.

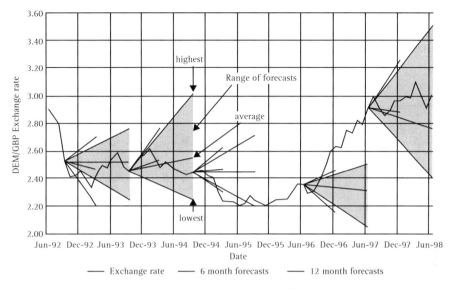

Figure 14.4. *Six-month and one-year forecasts of US$/£ rates by the UK corporate treasurers in 1990–98 (courtesy of Record Treasury Management)*

This overconfidence effect in expert judgment is well-known to psychologists (Russo and Schoemaker, 1991), and can be assessed and corrected. A common way of assessing the faulty calibration of predictions is to ask people to make a range prediction such that they are 90 percent sure that the actual value will fall within the range specified. For example, a money manager asked to make a prediction about the £/Euro exchange rate in six months time could say that he is 90 percent sure that the exchange rate will be between 0.64 and 0.74 pounds. If the manager is well-calibrated, nine out of ten currency values should fall within the predicted range ('hits') and he should thus expect only one out of ten 'misses' due to predictions falling outside the predicted range. Using this procedure with 36 foreign exchange traders in a globally operating bank, Stephan (1998) found strong evidence of a faulty calibration, with high miss-rates not only on exchange-rate predictions (71.1 percent), but also on the stock price questions (83.3 percent) and general knowledge questions (78.6 percent). Such over-confidence may be costly: in a simulated experimental market, Biais et al. (2000) found that participants who were overconfident (as measured by the mis-calibration of the accuracy of their responses to questions in a trivia test) were more likely to lose money in trading.

It is timely to reflect at this point on the role of information in today's markets. Information is a double-edged sword—while its presence should help us make accurate predictions and rational decisions, it can also make us unduly overconfident in our predictions and decisions. This is especially likely to happen when the human decision-maker has more information than he can effectively

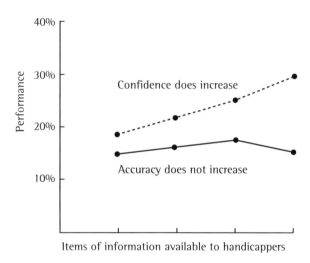

Figure 14.5. *The relationship between number of items of information available to horse-race handicappers, confidence in and accuracy of odds given. (adapted from Russo and Schoemaker, 1991)*

handle—as is often the case in today's financial markets. The point is made by an unpublished study on horse-race handicapping by Slovic and Corrigan, reported by Russo and Schoemaker (1991). The eight handicappers who participated in this study were allowed to select five, ten, twenty, and then forty pieces of information from 'past performance charts', which give nearly one hundred pieces of information on each horse and its history. At each point they were asked to make a prediction. Overall, accuracy did *not* increase (see Figure 14.5). This flat curve is due to three handicappers decreasing in accuracy, two improving, and three staying about the same. However, the handicappers' confidence in their predictions *did* increase with further information, such that they became even more overconfident with forty items of information than they were with five.

Finally, 'star performers' may appear who seem to make better-than-average predictions. However, it needs to be remembered that in any sample of market some traders will inevitably appear to be better than average (for a while) simply through chance. If they are genuinely skilful, then they should show consistently superior performance. Hartzmark (1991) tested this hypothesis through an analysis of traders' positions in the US future markets in commodities, T-bonds, and T-bills in 1977–81. He found strong support for the view that predictions in these markets were randomly generated. 'Stars' from the first two-year period showed regression to the mean in the second period, and initial underperformers also showed a tendency to 'improve'. Hartzmark concluded that luck, rather than forecast ability, was the best explanation for their superior forecast performance.

The failure of financial decision-makers to learn from the feedback and calibrate predictions accurately is especially intriguing given that markets are supposed to correct inaccurate expectations: one would expect that people playing the market every day would get corrective (and expensive) feedback— for 'experience is a dear teacher' (Benjamin Franklin). There seem to be several plausible reasons for this. Humans have a horror of accepting randomness and seek causal explanations even where behavior is random (Heider and Simmel, 1944; Oatley and Yuill, 1985). *Hindsight bias* (Fischhoff, 1982*b*) means that post-hoc explanations are always easy to invent after the fact, making events such as the allied victory in the Gulf War in 1991, the pound's departure from the ERM in 1992, and LIFFE's collapse in 1998 seem inevitable in retrospect, thus making the world seem more predictable than it is. Financial markets seem especially prone to rewriting history with the benefit of outcome information. As Baruch Fischhoff (1982*b*) put it, when discussing examples of hindsight bias: 'One of my favourite contrasts is that when the market rises following good economic news, it is said to be responding to the news; if it falls, that is explained by saying that the good news had already been discounted'.

Feedback in financial markets may be inherently difficult to recognise due to the high level of noise in markets. Failure to learn action–outcome relations may be accentuated by self-serving attributions for success and failure (taking credit for successes and laying blame on external factors). Feedback may be asymmetrical in that corporate treasurers and pension fund managers may invoke procedures to limit losses but not gains. Hedge fund managers may be symmetrical in terms of feedback, leading to a short half-life due to the greater probability of having to leave one's position if the fund underperforms. However, those that survive three years in a row and get good 'reputations' for persistently performing 'above average' may do so only through chance.

2.3. Mistaken Beliefs: Illusory and Invisible Correlations

For the rational expectations theory to work as a model of market behavior, market participants must be able to form accurate beliefs about the correlations between characteristics; that higher price does indeed correlate with better quality, spending money on advertising will increase market share, and so on. Otherwise, rational agents pay unnecessarily high prices for products, or waste time and money on pointless advertising campaigns. Likewise, a rational agent should not fail to notice relationships that are predictive of product quality, market share, and so on.

However, research suggests that the business world is rife with *illusory correlations*—beliefs which inaccurately suppose that there is a relation between a certain type of action and an effect, such as the belief that unstructured interviews enable accurate assessments of people's personality (Dawes, 1994). The world of finance appears to be no exception: in a recent article in the *Journal of Applied Corporate Finance*, Albéric Braas and Charles N. Bralver argue that managers typically overattribute trader profits to speculative positioning and fail to take into account 'the value of the turn'—that is, profits that accrue from being able to keep the bid-offer spread. Their analysis suggest that the reality is that players with a stronger market-making capacity get to keep the lion's share of the spread, and these firms generate the majority of their profits this way. They cite a head fixed-income trader for a New York powerhouse who told them 'Any trader I put in the 5- to 7-year chair makes a lot of money for us; each of them thinks that he is making the money with his smart calls. But it's really the chair that makes the money'. Failure to recognise this is a classic example of a particular kind of illusory correlation known as the *fundamental attribution error*—overattributing performance to the person and underattributing it to the situation.

Conversely, an *invisible correlation* may be said to exist if a correlation that is 'out there' is not spotted by a relevant community of experts. An example of this is the correlation between smoking and cancer, which was not spotted by doctors for three centuries. Some recent research at the Max Planck Institute's Center for Adaptive Behavior and Cognition (Gigerenzer et al., 1999) suggests that the finance community may also have failed to spot some interesting correlations. As part of their research program on 'simple but smart' heuristics, researchers at the MPI used the fame of German companies to predict share performance. They asked German lay people if they recognised a list of firms or not, and invested in firms that were recognised by over 90 percent or respondents in their survey. A similar procedure was used in America with the US firms and American lay people. Over six months, the portfolios constructed this way had an overall better performance than the market, and outperformed both the Dax30 and Dow30 indices, as well as the German Hypobank and Fidelity Growth funds, which were used as benchmarks. While this finding may not reflect a universal advantage for the recognition heuristic, but simply a tendency for large capitalization companies to do well during the period of the test, the fact that the investment strategy prompted by the recognition heuristic outperformed the stockmarket indices and the professionally managed funds suggests that these funds were slow in picking up a clearly identifiable pattern.

2.4. Loss Aversion, the 'Disposition Effect', and the Framing of Investment Choices

Kahneman and Tversky (1979) have convincingly demonstrated loss aversion using simulated gambles. Do financial decision-makers show irrational and/or systematic loss aversion? Some recent research indicates that this may be the case. One does not have to look far to see the importance of this principle for financial markets. It predicts the 'disposition effect' (Shefrin and Statman, 1985)—the tendency to sell winners too early and ride losers too long due to loss aversion. For example, Odean's (1998) study of individual investors' accounts with a discount brokerage in the US shows that investors tend to buy the same number of winners and losers, but to sell more winners than losers, except in December when there are tax incentives to sell losers. Investors also sell both winners and losers too early—the securities they buy underperform the ones they sell over a one-year time period, although losers tend to recover in the second year.

The disposition effect is also liable to affect professional traders and investors. Thus, Shapira and Venezia (2000) report market data suggesting that the Israeli fund managers show the disposition effect. Although the fund managers showed a less strong disposition effect than private investors, this effect could not be explained by the tax incentives as profits are not taxed in Israel. In a study on corporate investors, Steil (1993) found that the corporate treasurers showed a clear loss aversion in their responses to a survey in which they were presented with problems involving a foreign exchange risk. He concluded that their behavior in these realistic problems could not be explained by rational (Bayesian) models.

Finally, Kahneman and Tversky's (1979) research shows that when, what is objectively, the same gamble is reframed as involving losses rather than gains, people become risk-seeking rather than risk-averse. Another in-depth study was conducted on ten traders at one of Wall Street's ten largest investment banking firms, Shapira (1999) found ample evidence that professional traders' behavior is indeed affected by framing: specifically, whether they are showing a profit or a loss for the day's trading. As Kahneman and Tversky's model would predict, even for professional traders, the losses loom larger than gains, and they are more likely to take risks if they are losing with respect to their reference point. Shapira tracked the trades of twenty Government bond traders, and was able to show that the greater the profit or loss (P&L) account from the previous day, the more traders bought and sold the following day. Traders also took riskier positions the following day if they ended the previous day with a loss rather than a profit. Finally, this tendency to risk seeking after losses also manifested itself within the day's trading; traders showed a tendency to take 'long shots' in the last hour or two of trading at the end of the day if they were in a loss at 3 o'clock. None of this behavior can be predicted by the rational models of choice, and seems unlikely to contribute to the overall efficiency of a trading desk's performance.[1]

2.5. Underuse of Information and Lack of Insight in Decision-Making

Numerous studies of professional decision-making show that expert judges seem to: (i) use few cues to make decisions, (ii) have little insight as to which cues actually influence their decisions, and (iii) use cues different from those used by other experts, leading to little inter-expert consistency. Doctors, thus, use fewer clinical signs than they think to make decisions, have little insight into which

---

[1] Taking 'long shots' at the end of a period could be viewed as rational if it is more important to attain a threshold (e.g., an earnings target) than to avoid losses, however large. This might be the case with end-of-the-year behaviour by traders who take long shots in order to reach their earnings objectives in order to avoid being sacked. However, this kind of argument seems much more difficult to apply to Shapira's data, which shows that such risky 'long shots' are practiced on a *daily basis*. This strategy seems to be self-defeating as it should lead traders to make more bad trades during the period used by their desk chiefs to evaluate them (usually monthly, quarterly, or yearly).

clinical signs have most impact on their diagnoses, and show little agreement with other doctors presented with the same cases. Financial decision-makers are not likely to be very different: for example, Cornelli and Goldreich (2000) report that an investment bank's 'decision policy' for pricing initial public offerings can be modelled by two cues alone (average limit price of bids and oversubscription).

Slovic (1969) reports a 'policy capturing' study in which two stockbrokers were presented with 128 hypothetical companies, which varied systematically in terms of eleven investment indices such as yield, near-term prospects, earnings quarterly trend etc. The results yielded some surprises. Although the first judge had aided in the creation of the investment scenarios and the definition of the eleven dimensions of evaluation for stocks, an analysis of his judgment patterns revealed that he was only influenced by eight of them. The second judge used seven of these factors, and overall only five of the eleven factors were used by both judges, and even these five were often weighted quite differently. This latter finding helps explain why there was only 32 percent agreement between the two experts, although it is interesting to note that the second stockbroker was recruited because it was thought that he had a similar investment policy to the first. Finally, the two stockbrokers were asked to say how much importance they accorded to each factor; whereas the first judge had considerable insight into his own judgment policy, the second judge had very little insight. A follow-up study on 13 stockbrokers revealed that the longer an investment broker had been in the business, the less insight he had into his weighting policy (Slovic, 1972).

One reason that people may not have an insight into the reasons for their financial choices is that they have positive 'feelings' about financial products that are not based on relevant information. For example, they may have a positive 'image' of a market sector such as 'major pharmeceuticals' because this sector is associated with 'healing', 'beauty products', 'cleanness', and so on, whereas another sector such as 'railroads' may be associated with negative features such as 'dirty', 'old', 'used by poor people', and so on. In May 1995, MacGregor et al. (2000) tested this hypothesis by asking 57 business students to write the first three images that came to mind for forty industry groupings, and then to rate how positive these evaluations were on a 7-point scale. They were then asked to say how well these sectors had done in 1994 and how well they would do in 1995, and indicate their own willingness to buy shares in these sectors. Their judgments of how well these industry groupings had done in 1994 and would do in 1995, and their willingness to buy were quite well predicted by how positive their images were of these sectors. However, these judgments of sector performance, as well as the willingness to buy in these sectors, were only weakly related to the indicators of actual performance.

These results suggest a mechanism for overconfidence: based on the subconscious retrieval of positive (or negative) associations, people may 'feel good' (or bad) about an industry sector and therefore predict successful (or unsuccessful) performance in that sector. Ganzach (in press) presents a study of business school finance majors that suggests that the analysts' judgments of the attractiveness of an asset are, particularly, likely to be based on an overall affective evaluation when the familiarity of the asset being evaluated is low. In such cases, the judges are likely to rate either the risk to be low *and* return high or the risk high and the return low (see Finucane et al., in press, for similar results in evaluating non-financial risks). The trouble is, of course, that these automatic and subconscious judgments may be based on information that is irrelevant to predicting actual financial performance. With the increasing participation of private individuals who are untrained in financial analysis in the financial markets, market behaviour may be increasingly driven by the 'emotional value' of securities rather than by the objective financial criteria.

3. SOCIAL ORIGINS OF BIAS AND ERROR IN FINANCIAL JUDGMENT

3.1. The Aggregate Mind and Market Confidence: Bears, Bulls, and Overreaction

Keynes compared markets to beauty contests, in which judges not only had to take into account their own preferences about the prettiest face, but also the preferences of other judges. Finance professionals may, therefore, see it as part of their job to talk to other players and, thus, be influenced by others' opinions in picking stocks. What they may be less aware of is the potential influence of such information on their own mood and behavior.

Consider the difference in the likely state of mind of an investor in stable and unstable markets. Investors in a long-term stable bull market, such as the US stock market in 1949–60, which rose almost continually during this period by over 600 percent, are likely to feel self-confident; they will feel that their investment strategies are working as they are making money. Investors in a long-term unstable market, such as the US stock market in 1966–82, which went down overall 9 percent after wild fluctuations, are less likely to feel sure of themselves. Social psychological research shows that people who feel sure of themselves and their judgments are likely to pay little attention to the opinions of others in forming their judgments, unlike people that are unsure of themselves (Crutchfield, 1955).

Following this reasoning, Schachter and his colleagues (1985) reasoned that investors in the stable bull market in 1949–60 would think more independently than those of the unstable market in 1966–82. Independently thinking investors should be less likely to be shaken from their strategies by 'news' due to external events impinging on the market. Schachter and his colleagues obtained corroboration of this reasoning. For example, the markets reacted rather less to the results of the US Presidential elections during 1949–60 than 1966–82, the volume of post-election day trading going up to an average of only 9.2 percent in 1949–60, but 47.3 percent in 1966–82. In another analysis, they showed that the 1949–60 market reacted less than the 1966–82 one to airline disasters; trading in the shares of the airline and/or manufacturer affected went up to 29.6 percent during 1949-60, but 166.7 percent during 1966-82. A more focused analysis of bull and bear runs within these time periods painted the same picture; the investors reacted more to external news and tips during bear runs than bull runs.

3.1. Herding and Bubbles: Rational Calculation or Mental Contagion?

Schachter et al.'s results are consistent with much laboratory research, which shows that individuals with low self-esteem are more susceptible to having their opinions influenced by others. It is perhaps possible to give a 'rational' explanation of such behavior if the higher reactivity to news is a more rational strategy in a volatile market.[2] Even if this were shown to be the case, Schachter's analysis shows that such behavior may not necessarily be the product of a cold rational analysis, but rather the product of general social psychological processes that influence an individual's confidence in his judgments. Such social processes would clearly seem to be implicated in the production of financial bubbles such as the Dutch tulip craze (Mackay, 1841/1932) and dot.com stocks (Dreman, 1999).

3.2. Aggregation of Information in Groups: A First Approximation

A simple-minded initial approach to understanding how a group forms an opinion is to assume that individual preferences and beliefs are simply aggregated to come out with some kind of overall or average group judgment or preference. This assumes that individual opinions are independent, in the same sense that the reading given by each group of thermometers, which measure heat in a room, is not influenced by the readings given by the other thermometers. Of course, groups in the real world *communicate* (either implicitly or explicitly) with each other; and the two principal kinds of communication are observation and discussion.

Economists interested in psychology have begun to explore how the observation of others' actions and imitation may produce a herding behavior in markets. For example, Bikhchandani et al. (1998) have argued that it is rational in the sense of payoff maximizing not to listen to private information and, rather, do what the other people are doing and that such strategies lead with some probability to informational cascades in which all people do the wrong thing forever. In some recent empirical research, Kraemer et al. (2000) examine a situation where market participants can infer the price of a security through observing the behavior of other participants in the market, of whom some have private information, or by buying information themselves. Interestingly, they find that the participants systematically overestimate the private signal value. This result that many participants undervalue the information obtainable by observing others, seems to run counter to many findings in social psychology that suggest that people are overly influenced by others and underestimate the impact of

---

[2] I am grateful to Juan Carrillo for pointing this out.

situational influences on their judgment. One possible explanation is that the subjects in these experiments did not *communicate* directly with each other, rather, they simply observed the behavior of computer-generated participants.

It is this possibility of communicating directly with others that typically distinguishes small groups such as work teams from larger aggregates such as the markets. As we shall see in Section 3.3, such communication with others is a part and parcel of business life, and can have important and unexpected effects on decisions. Consequently, in my discussion of the implications of social psychological research on small group decision-making for financial behavior, I will focus on its potential implication for managing work *teams* (e.g., an investment analysis group of five to six members, a trading desk) who share the same goals and communicate with each other, rather than for understanding and predicting the behavior of *aggregates* (e.g., markets) where participants do not share the same goals and learn about how others are thinking through observation.

3.3. Groupthink and Risky Shift in Small Group Decision-Making

Mintzberg (1973) has estimated that the average manager spends over two-thirds of his time in talking to colleagues, workers, and anybody else he chances to come across during the day. These meetings and conversations, whether formal or informal, enable a manager to get an enormous number of decisions made. Financial decison-making would seem to fit this general pattern: traders generally work on desks with eight to twelve other colleagues, and investment managers are unlikely to take major decisions without having called a meeting with partners, analysts, and researchers. In addition, both the traders and the investment managers seem to spend a lot of time on the telephone or in bars and restaurants, discussing the market news with their colleagues and contacts. Consequently, it behoves us to understand how decision-making is affected through the interaction with others.

In general, experimental research supports the belief that group decision-making will generally be better than individual decision-making, as knowledge and information will be pooled, enabling better decisions to be made (Einhorn et al., 1977; Hinsz et al., 1997). However, this is not always the case. One well-known phenomenon in group decision-making is groupthink—a process whereby a group of individuals mutually reinforce each other into believing that their collective point of view is right (Janis, 1982). Research on groupthink grew out of the identification of the group polarization phenomenon, which began with the discovery of the *risky shift* in group decision-making by Stoner (1968). When presented with risky choices to make, students at the School of Industrial Management at the Massachusetts Institute of Technology were often likely to prefer riskier options after group discussion. Thus, Stoner found that twelve of the thirteen groups he studied showed a significant collective shift towards greater risk after the discussion, compared to the average of each individual's position before discussion. Moreover, the subjects were asked to record their own private opinion before and after the discussion, and appeared to have genuinely changed their minds as a result of the discussion. The risky shift effect has proved to be very robust, having been replicated in more than a 100 studies conducted in over a dozen countries.

With certain kinds of topics, the group discussion tends to lead to greater caution, an effect known as *cautious shift*. The cautious shift typically occurs, for example, after the discussion of risky decisions involving health or human life. Social psychologists thus prefer to talk about *group polarization*—the intensification of shared attitude positions (to anything ranging from risky decisions to politicians) through group discussion. Explanations for this include information sharing (through discussion each individual may hear of new reasons to support his initial position, leading him or her to become more confident), and diffusion of responsibility (the individual's neck is no longer on the line if the group takes a risky decision and it goes wrong).

The groupthink phenomenon shows that group decision-making does not always lead to efficient information integration. These cases may be more frequent than people think: for example, research on brainstorming suggests that it is a *less* productive method of generating ideas than having the same people work individually on generating ideas (Wilke and van Knippenberg, 1996). While some of the productivity loss of ideas generated in teams may (at least in Western individualist cultures) be due to social loafing (the tendency to let others in a group do the work; cf. the moral hazard problem of teams analysed by Holmstrom, 1982), research also shows that group discussion is more likely to improve the decision quality if it is conducted in ways that facilitate information pooling and objective and complete analysis of options (e.g., Hall and Watson, 1970). It therefore seems plausible that certain kinds of group discussion styles are likely to lead to better financial decisions (as measured by some objective criterion), independently of the private incentives of each of the participants in a team. A rational manager may, thus, be more likely to further *her* goals of effective use of participants' time if she uses the right techniques to structure group discussion.

4. POTENTIAL APPLICATIONS OF PSYCHOLOGY FOR FINANCE

In this section, I review some potential applications of psychology to economics and finance. There are three main areas, financial strategy, marketing of financial products and human resource management. Of these three areas, I shall have most to say about the last, with specific reference to the selection and training of traders and dealers, and to investment decision-making.

4.1. Behavioral Economics: The Psychology of Markets and Financial Strategy

The first application of psychology to economic behavior is indirect and mediated by its influence on economics, and in particular by helping economists specify ways in which the human behavior departs systematically from the predictions of the efficient markets hypothesis. Thus, the new field of behavioral finance (Lifson and Geist, 1999; Shefrin, 1999; Statman, 1995; Thaler, 1993), argues that markets are composed of imperfectly rational players in imperfect markets (de Bondt, 1998), and which seeks to identify and explain anomalies in economic behavior, such as underreaction, overreaction, and calendar effects in security prices (Thaler, 1992). These in turn suggest investment strategies of various kinds (De Bondt, 1998; Dreman, 1999), such as *momentum strategies* (going with the trend) for short-term investments (6–12 months) and *contrarian strategies* (going against the trend) for longer-term investments (3–5 years).

More generally, through enabling a better understanding of phenomena such as price stickiness and temporal discounting, psychology can help economists make better predictions about how markets will respond to interventions such as changes in the prices and interest rates, and thus influence economists' recommendations about how to manage such interventions. This *behavioral economics* perspective is advocated by economists such as Rabin (1998), and readers are referred to his excellent review for further details.

4.2. The Psychology of the Client and Marketing of Financial Products

Psychology has long influenced marketing in general, and it should therefore be no surprise that psychology can be relevant to financial products marketing Shefrin and Statman (1993). One can imagine that psychology can be applied in three main areas:

4.2.1. *The Design of Financial Products*
Portfolio managers have to satisfy their clients, which means having to take the client's 'psychology' into account. For most investors, risk means the chance of a loss rather than the swings in the value of an investment, although the latter definition of risk corresponds to that used in classical economics (Fortuna, 1998). Because clients think about risk in this way, and are highly averse to losses, financial products such as 'click funds', which reduce downside risk, are likely to prove very attractive (Smid and Tempelaar, 1997).

4.2.2. *The Presentation of Financial Products*
Benartzi and Thaler's (1998) research shows that very minor changes in the presentations of portfolios can lead to substantial changes in client preferences. They argue that when choosing pension funds, investors tend to use a 'diversification' heuristic of dividing their investments equally between the kinds of investments offered. Thus, if offered a bond fund and a stock fund, people will tend to split their contributions equally. However, if offered two bond funds and one stock fund they will tend to put a third into each. Their attitude to risk seems,

therefore, to be very contingent to what kind of choices are presented to them. These kinds of findings are consistent with a wide range of research on the construction of preferences in psychology and marketing (Hilton, 1997), which has yet to be applied to financial products. This would seem to be an obvious area for further research.

4.2.3. *Communication, Client Satisfaction, and Loyalty*

Psychology has long contributed theories and methods to marketing research, and can therefore be used in financial marketing. Thus, psychological research can be used to develop theories about how best to present and explain complex financial products to clients, such that the one they select corresponds the closest to their needs. Mental framing strategies can be used to 'teach' clients how to think appropriately about risk, and to avoid nasty surprises later on. Measures such as these should ensure greater client satisfaction and fidelity. At the present stage of knowledge, more research on communication and framing strategies for financial products seems to be needed.

4.3. The Psychology of Financial Decision-Makers: Human Resource Management

4.3.1. *Psychological Profiles of Successful Traders and Dealers*

It is clear that modern traders, investment managers, and investment analysts are bombarded with information from all round the world. Increasingly, a competitive advantage is to be gained through being able to cope better with this avalanche of information, to separate the signal from the noise. Traders who are better at this should make more money. Thus, in a study of the 'geography of information', Hau (2000) has shown that being a German-language trader (whether based in Frankfurt, Vienna, or Zurich) predicts a successful performance on the Frankfurt stock exchange, presumably because being a linguistic and cultural insider enables these traders to interpret market information better. Similar research needs to be done to identify the psychological characteristics of successful traders and dealers. The relevant psychological characteristics can be divided into four types: *cognitive, personality, ability and knowledge,* and *sociometric.* Establishment of these profiles could be used to aid selection and training. These and other questions (Hilton, 1999) seem eminently researchable, and to have clear implications for the bottom line.

4.3.1.1. Decision training and debiasing. Research has indicated that it is not always easy to debias decision-makers (Fischhoff, 1982a). Nevertheless, it can be done and it sometimes leads to success. Russo and Schoemaker (1991) report that Shell has used calibration techniques to debias its geologists' forecasts of where to drill for oil, with corresponding savings for the corporation. Bolger and Onkal-Ontay (1998) report that calibration and feedback led to substantial improvement of management students' predictions of equity prices. Research should therefore be conducted to see whether calibration and feedback techniques are effective in reducing biases in financial decision-making.

4.3.1.2. Decision-aiding. The technological revolution has made the problem of information overload ever more pressing for financial decision-makers. Current research on screen design endeavours to use psychological research on perception and information-processing to present information in the way that is the most 'user-friendly'. Nevertheless, it is not difficult to envisage how decision-making research could lead to the development of screens that provide an active role in decision-aiding. This could be done through the development of 'smart screens' which offer decision-aiding facilities. For example, screens could be programmed to solicit explicit probability judgments for predictions, to store them, and then to retrieve them for calibration exercises. These 'automatic auditing' functions should aid financial decision-making performance. As another example of how structuring screens could affect financial behavior, if the kind of profit and loss (P&L) account on traders' screens does indeed affect their risk taking behavior, desk managers should choose to show P&L information (e.g., indexed to the last day vs. the whole year) which is most likely to influence traders' behavior in the desired way.

4.3.2. Financial Expert Systems
Research has shown that experts are regularly outperformed by simple regression equations based on the experts' own 'theories' about the relationships between variables (Camerer, 1981; Russo and Schoemaker, 1991). This phenomenon—known as *bootstrapping*—explains why computers can even outperform super-experts whose knowledge was used to create them. For example, Christine Downton, the chief investment officer of fund manager Pareto Partners, London, contributed her knowledge of investment decision-making to the creation of an expert system that manages bond portfolios in 12 major markets. The program uses rules that relate investment decisions to fundamental economic indicators. Back-testing suggests that the model has 'a potential to outperform the index by 4–5 percent. Although Downton checks the model's predictions, she never alters its recommendations. She explains that 'we implement exactly what it says, we don't second-guess it. Usually, if I second guess it, I'm wrong. And that's probably because I got out of bed on the wrong side'. Her philosophy of the market is that the winners are those with consistent long-term views, whereas the losers are those who have no views and change their minds on the basis of recent data. 'Most research into cognitive bias' says Downton 'suggests that investors tend to overweight recent information'.

4.3.3. Management Control Systems and Trading Desks
The introduction of screen-based trading has made management control and record-keeping much easier. Desk managers may use their own screens to examine what their traders and dealers are doing at any moment. The new

technology has made new forms of management control and compensation possible. There is considerable theory and research in economics and organisational behavior on team management and compensation practices (e.g., Gibbon and Murphy, 1992; Holmstrom, 1982). However, there seems to be plenty of scope for using psychological research to enrich the kinds of questions asked in research on how to manage, say, trading desks. Should desk managers be directive or democratic in managing their teams? Should they give regular feedback to traders and dealers on their performance? Should traders regularly account to their managers? More trickily, should compensation be individual, collective or a mixture of the two?

4.4. Conclusion: From Behavioral Economics to the Psychology of Financial Decision-Making

In reviewing this area I was struck by how little empirical work has actually been done on the psychological processes underlying trading, dealing, and investment decision-making. This observation is made all the more striking when one reads Slovic's (1972) review of the field, which makes innumerable suggestions for studies that still remain to be carried out. These include studies of policy capturing, how information acquisition may lead to overconfidence, how market players may learn illusory correlations, etc.

What *has* happened since Slovic's (1972) review is that economics has rediscovered psychology (Lewin, 1996), and this has spawned the new discipline of behavioral economics (Thaler, 1992). Although inspired by laboratory experiments in psychology (usually done on psychology students), the typical level of analysis of behavioral economics nevertheless remains that of the market behavior. Behavioral economists typically use psychological findings on judgmental heuristics such as availability or overconfidence in judgments, to infer explanations for observed market behavior as indexed by price movements or volume of trading. The continuing stream of publications in behavioral economics attests to the success of this strategy in explaining market irrationalities, which conventional economic models have difficulty explaining.

Nevertheless, the behavioral economics approach has the weakness of not being able to test hypothesised causal relationships by manipulating them. The proponents of behavioral economics (or behavioral finance) take known anomalies in real-life economic behavior such as saving, market overreaction, or gender differences in trading, and seek to explain them in terms of psychological constructs such as mental accounting, availability or overconfidence (Barber and Odean, 2000*b*; Thaler, 1992). However, *post-hoc* explanations clearly carry the risk that the hypothesised psychological constructs are not the real causes of behavior. On the other hand, experimental studies are clearly better able to establish causality. For example, in studies on experimental trading games, Biais et al. (2000) were able to replicate Barber and Odean's (2001) real-world finding that men trade more often than women; however, they found no support for

Barber and Odean's suggestion that this difference is mediated by men's greater confidence. They did this through measuring the participants' susceptibility to cognitive biases, and correlating these measures with the trading performance. The merit of the experimental approach is, therefore, that intervening cognitive variables are measured or manipulated, thus enabling causal relationships to be established.

I thus hope that I have made the case for applying the theories and methods of experimental psychology directly to the study of financial judgments and biases, rather than just indirectly through its impact on economic theorizing and modelling. Experimental psychology, which aims at understanding the mental processes that produce an individual's judgments and decisions, produces models whose causal nature suggest different applications to economic life than those of traditional economics, with its characteristic focus on mathematical models that enable the predictions of collective behavior (e.g., the prices at which assets are negotiated). Because they seek to test their models through manipulating the mechanisms that *produce* these effects, experimental psychologists are scientific realists (Hacking, 1983). They are, thus, able to suggest techniques that will enable an individual to reduce overconfidence, to attenuate risk aversion, change discounting rates, and so on, and thus improve his or her own decision-making behavior. This improvement may be self-initiated (e.g., by a trader, dealer, or investor wishing to improve her performance) or other-initiated (e.g., by a manager wishing to set incentives or design office systems that will improve performance). If adopted successfully, the Hayek hypothesis will become a thing of the past, as there will be no irrational players left in the financial markets!

REFERENCES

Barber, B. and Odean, T. (2000). Trading is hazardous to your wealth: The common stock investment performance of individual investors. *Journal of Finance, 55,* 773–806.

—— and —— (2001). Boys will be boys: Gender, overconfidence and common stocks investments. *Quarterly Journal of Economics, 116,* 261–92.

Bazerman, M. (1998). *Judgement in managerial decision-making* (4th ed.). London: Wiley.

Benartzi, S. and Thaler, R.H. (1998). *Naïve diversification strategies in defined contribution saving plans.* Unpublished paper, UCLA.

Biais, B., Hilton, D.J., Mazurier, K., and Pouget, S. (2000). Psychological traits and trading strategies. Paper presented at the Conference on Economics and Psychology, Brussels, June.

Bikhchandani, S., Hirshleifer, D., and Welch, I. (1998). Learning from the behavior of others: Conformity, fads, and informational cascades. *Journal of Economic Perspectives, 12*(3), 151–70.

Bolger, F. and Onkal-Atay, D. (1998). The effects of feedback on judgemental probability forecasts from time series. *Conference on judgemental inputs to the forecasting process,* University College, London, November.

Camerer, C.F. (1981). General conditions for the success of bootstrapping models. *Organizational Behavior and Human Performance, 27,* 411–22.

Cornelli, F. and Goldreich, D. (2000). Bookbuilding: How informative is the order book? Paper presented at *European Summer Symposium in Financial Markets.* Studienzentrum Gerzensee, Switzerland, July.

Crutchfield, R.S. (1955). Conformity and character. *American Psychologist, 10,* 191–8.

Davies, R.M. (1994). *House of cards: Psychology and psychotherapy built on myth.* Glencoe: Free Press.

De Bondt, W. (1998). The psychology of under- and overreaction in world equity markets. IIR seminar on *Behavioral Finance: The psychology of investment decision-making,* London, November 1998.

Dreman, D. (1999). Investor overreaction. In L.E. Lifson and R.A. Geist (Eds.), *The psychology of investing.* New York: Wiley.

Einhorn, H.J., Hogarth, R.M., and Klempner, E. (1977). Quality of group judgement. *Psychological Bulletin, 84,* 158–72.

Fenton O'Creevy, M. Nicholson, N., Soane, E., and Willman, P. (1998). Individual and contextual influences on the market behavior of finance professionals. ESRC Conference Paper.

Finucane, M.L., Alhakami, A., Slovic, P., and Johnson, S.M. (in press). The affect heuristic in judgements of risks and benefits. *Journal of Behavioral Decision-Making.*

Fischhoff, B. (1982a). Debiasing. In D.E. Kahneman, P. Slovic, and A. Tversky (Eds.), *Judgement under uncertainty: Heuristics and biases.* Cambridge: Cambridge University Press.

—— (1982b). For those condemned to study the past: Heuristics and biases in hindsight. In D.E. Kahneman, P. Slovic, and A. Tversky (Eds.), *Judgement under uncertainty: Heuristics and biases.* Cambridge: Cambridge University Press.

Forsythe, R., Nelson, F., Neumann, G.R., and Wright, J. (1992). Anatomy of an Experimental Stock Market. *American Economic Review, 82,* 1142–61.

Fortuna, P. (1998). The downside of alternative risk measures—An implementation case study. *IIR Seminar on Behavioral Finance: The psychology of investment decision-making,* London, November, 1998.

Ganzach, Y. (in press). Judging risk and return of financial assets. *Organizational Behavior and Human Decision Processes.*

Gibbon, R. and Murphy, K.J. (1992). Optimal incentive contracts in the presence of career concerns: Theory and evidence. *Journal of Political Economy, 100,* 468–505.

Gigerenzer, G., Todd, P.M., and the ABC research group (1999). *Simple but smart Heuristics.* Oxford: Oxford University Press.

Hacking, I. (1983). *Representing and intervening: Introductory topics in the philosophy of science.* Cambridge: Cambridge University Press.

Hall, J. and Watson, W.H. (1970). The effects of a normative intervention on group decision-making performance. *Human Relations, 23,* 299–317.

Harris, P. and Middleton, W. (1994). The illusion of control and optimism about health: On being less at risk but no more in control than others. *British Journal of Social Psychology, 33,* 369–86.

Hartzmark, M.L. (1991). Luck versus forecast ability: Determinants of trader performance in futures markets. *Journal of Business, 64,* 49–74.

Hau, H. (2000). Information and geography: Evidence from the German stock market. Paper presented at the CEPR/FMG workshop on *New Approaches to Modelling Financial Transactions,* LSE, February 2000.

Heider, F. and Simmel, M. (1944). An experimental study of apparent behavior. *American Journal of Psychology, 57,* 243–69.

Hilton, D.J. (1997). Constructive processes in attitudes, judgement and decision-making: Implications for psychology and marketing. *Swiss Journal of Psychology,* 56, 112–26. (Special issue on *Context and biases,* F. Butera, P. Legrenzi, and M. Oswald Eds.)

—— (1999). *Psychology and the city: Applications to trading, dealing and investment analysis,* publication no. 38 of the Centre for the Study of Financial Innovation

Hinsz, V.B., Tindale, R.S., and Vollrath, D.A. (1997). The emerging conceptualization of groups as information processors. *Psychological Bulletin, 121,* 43–64.

Hogarth, R.M. (1987). *Judgement and choice* (2nd ed.). Chichester: Wiley.

Holmstrom, B. (1982). Moral hazard in teams. *Bell Journal of Economics,* 324–40.

Janis, I. (1982). *Groupthink* (2nd ed.). Boston, MA: Houghton-Mifflin.

Kahneman, D.E. and Tversky, A. (1979). Prospect theory: An analysis of decision under risk. *Econometrica, 47,* 263–91.

Kraemer, C., Nöth, M., and Weber, M. (2000). Information aggregation with costly information and random ordering: Experimental evidence paper presented at *European Summer Symposium in Financial Markets,* Studienzentrum Gerzensee, Switzerland, July.

Langer, E. (1975). The illusion of control. *Journal of Personality and Social Psychology, 32,* 311–28.

Lewin, S.B. (1996). Economics and Psychology: Lessons for our own day from the early Twentieth Century. *Journal of Economic Literature, 34,* 1293–323.

Lifson, L.E. and Geist, R.A. (1999). *The psychology of investing.* New York: Wiley.

Lopes, L.L. (1994). Psychology and economics: Perspectives on risk, co-operation and the marketplace. *Annual Review of Psychology, 45,* 197–227.

MacGregor, D.G., Slovic, P., Dreman, D., and Berry, M. (2000). Imagery, affect and financial judgement. *Psychology and the financial markets, 1,* 104–10.

Mackay, C. (1841). *Extraordinary popular delusions and the madness of crowds.* London: Office of the National Illustrated Library. (Reprinted by L.C. Page and Co., Boston, 1932.)

Manove, M. and Padilla A.J. (1999). Banking conservatively with optimists. *RAND Journal of Economics, 30,* 324–50.

Mintzberg, H. (1973). *The nature of managerial work.* New York: Harper and Row.

Oatley, K. and Yuill, N. (1985). Perception of personal and interpersonal action in a cartoon film. *British Journal of Social Psychology, 24,* 115–24.

Odean, T. (1998). Volume, volatility and profit when all traders are above average. *Journal of Finance,* 1887–934.

Rabin, M. (1998). Psychology and economics. *Journal of Economic Literature, 36,* 11–46.

Russo, J. and Schoemaker, P.J.H. (1991). *Confident decision-making: How to make the right decision every time.* London: Piatkus.

Schachter, S., Hood, D.C., Gerin, W., Andreassen, P., and Rennert, M. (1985). III: Some causes and consequences of dependence and independence in the stock market. *Journal of Economic Behavior and Organization, 6,* 339–57.

Scharfstein, D.S. and Stein, J.C. (1990). Herd behavior and investment. *American Economic Review, 80,* 465–79.

Shapira, Z. (1999). Aspiration levels and risk taking: A theoretical model and empirical study on the behavior of government bond traders. Unpublished manuscript, New York University.

—— and Venezia, I. (2000). Patterns of behavior in professionally managed and independent investors. Unpublished manuscript, New York University.

Shefrin, H. (1999). *Beyond greed and fear: Understanding behavioral finance and the psychology of investing.* Boston: Harvard University Press.

—— and Statman, M. (1985). The disposition to sell winners too early and ride losers too long: Theory and evidence. *Journal of Finance, 40,* 777–90.

—— and —— (1993). Behavioral aspects of the design and marketing of financial products. *Financial Management,* 123–34.

Slovic, P. (1969). Analyzing the expert judge: A descriptive study of a stockbroker's decision processes. *Journal of Applied Psychology, 53,* 253–63.

—— (1972). Psychological study of human judgement: Implications for investment decision-making. *Journal of Finance, 27,* 779–99.

Smid, P.P.M. and Tempelaar, F.M. (1997). Click funds in the Netherlands: The how and why of an index-linked financial innovation. University of Groningen, Faculty of Economics, research report 98C14 (SOM).

Soros, G. (1998). *The crisis of global capitalism: Open society endangered.* London: Little Brown.

Statman, M. (1995). Behavioral finance versus standard finance. In A. Wood (Ed.), *Behavioral finance and decision theory in investment management.* Charlottesville, VA: Association for Investment Management and Research.

Steil, B. (1993). Corporate foreign exchange risk management: A study in decision-making under uncertainty. *Journal of Behavioral Decision-Making, 6,* 1–31.

Stephan, E. (1998). Anchoring and adjustment in economic forecasts: The role of incentives, ability and expertise. *Conference on Judgemental Inputs to the Forecasting Process,* University College, London, November.

Stoner, J.A.F. (1968). Risky and cautious shifts in group decisions: The influence of widely held values. *Journal of Experimental Social Psychology, 4,* 442–59.

Thaler, R.H. (1992). *The winner's curse: Paradoxes and anomalies of economic life.* New York: Free Press.

Wilke, H. and van Knippenberg, A. (1996). Group performance. In M. Hewstone, W. Stroebe, and G.M. Stephenson (Eds.), *Introduction to Social Psychology* (2nd Ed.). Oxford: Blackwell.

Wilkie-Thompson, M.E., Onkal-Atay, Pollock, A.C., and Macaulay, A. (1998). The influence of trend strength on directional probabilistic currency predictions. *Conference on Judgemental Inputs to the Forecasting Process.* University College, London, November.

15

What Causes Nominal Inertia? Insights from Experimental Economics

ERNST FEHR AND JEAN-ROBERT TYRAN

1. INTRODUCTION

In this chapter we examine, among other things, the conditions under which *individual*-level money illusion causes nominal prices to be sticky at the *aggregate* level. The relation between micro-motives and macro-behavior is at the heart of the differences in opinions between economists and psychologists. Many disagreements between economists and psychologists can be interpreted as disputes about how important individual-level deviations from the assumptions of the rational choice paradigm are for aggregate-level phenomena (Hogarth and Reder, 1987, p. 9). It seems that psychologists tend to extrapolate evidence from individual-level 'anomalies' to the aggregate level, whereas economists often believe that the feedback and the arbitrage opportunities provided by market interactions somehow mitigate these anomalies.[1] Although psychologists have provided considerable evidence that a substantial fraction of the people violate the economic model of rational and selfish *individual* decision-making, most economists have so far been reluctant to take this evidence into account.

From an economic viewpoint a crucial question is to what extent individual-level deviations from the economic model cause significant deviations from, or inhibit adjustment to, the predicted *equilibrium* in an environment with strategically interacting individuals. For example, to what extent does the presence of people who violate the axioms of expected utility theory change the functioning of insurance and asset markets? To what extent does the presence of fair-minded and honest actors change the functioning of contracts, firms, organizations, and labor markets? Or, to refer to the question we are going to address: How important is individual-level money illusion for the response of aggregate nominal prices to changes in monetary policy? These are not just rhetorical questions because there

---

[1] The disagreements between economists and psychologists may stem from different modes of scientific investigation in the two disciplines. Psychology is inductive, starting from a detailed individual-level observation to construct a multiplicity of low-level theories. In contrast, standard economics is deductive, starting from a few individual-level assumptions to build a relatively uniform body of theory (see Hogarth and Reder, 1987, for a discussion).

is also considerable evidence from many experimental markets indicating that the aggregate predictions of the economic model are often accurate (see e.g., Davis and Holt, 1993). Thus, there are relevant situations in which individual-level deviations from the rational choice paradigm do not matter, in the sense that they do not lead to deviations from the aggregate predictions of the standard economic model.

The question then is: Under which conditions do individual-level anomalies cause systematic and large deviations from the aggregate predictions of the rational choice paradigm and when are these individual-level anomalies irrelevant or only of minor importance for aggregate phenomena? To answer this question we need good theories and good data. In our view, an important ingredient of a good theory in this realm is the assumption that people are heterogeneous. The evidence from many experiments in psychology and in experimental economics, that a non-negligible fraction of the people violate the assumptions of the standard economic model of individual decision-making, has to be taken into account. However, in our view, a good theory will also have to allow for the presence of people who obey the assumptions of the standard model because this kind of individual heterogeneity is also a basic fact (see e.g., Hey and Orme, 1994). Moreover, it has been shown theoretically that the heterogeneity of people interacts in important ways with the economic environment (Haltiwanger and Waldmann, 1985, 1989; Fehr and Schmidt, 1999; Shleifer 2000). In Fehr and Schmidt it has, for example, been shown that there are conditions in which even a large majority of fair-minded actors have no or only a minor impact on the aggregate outcome. Yet, there are also other relevant conditions in which even a minority of fair-minded actors can induce large and systematic deviations from the equilibrium predictions of the standard economic model (Sansgruber and Tyran, 2002).

While there has been some progress at the theoretical level, there has been less progress at the empirical level. For example, despite the huge literature that documents the violations of the axioms of the expected utility theory we know very little about the empirical conditions under which these individual-level violations also cause aggregate deviations from the standard economic model. However, in principle the methods of experimental economics are well suited to better understand such issues because economic experiments provide simultaneous observations of individual and aggregate activity.

In this chapter we discuss how experimental methods can be used to investigate whether money illusion causes aggregate-level nominal inertia. We argue that experimental methods provide insights into this potential cause of nominal inertia, which cannot be gained by the empirical approaches traditionally used by economists (e.g., regressions with aggregate-level field data). In addition, experimental methods may have important advantages over modes of investigation regularly used in psychology (e.g., questionnaires). We show empirically that, under conditions of strategic complementarity, money illusion can have massive aggregate-level effects, even if money illusion is almost absent at the individual level. However, in the absence of strategic complementarity the economists' standard assumption of illusion-free individuals provides very accurate predictions of aggregate-level behavior.

We proceed as follows. Section 2 explains why economists have been interested in nominal inertia and discusses the particular strengths of the experimental approach. Section 3 reports evidence from questionnaire studies suggesting that money illusion is an important phenomenon at the individual level, and explains under which conditions these individual-level effects may translate to the aggregate level. Section 4 briefly describes our experimental design and reports the main findings. Section 5 concludes the paper.

2. NOMINAL INERTIA AND EXPERIMENTAL ECONOMICS

Nominal inertia refers to a tendency of *nominal* prices and wages to adjust slowly to nominal shocks. One of the reasons why economists ever since the writings of David Hume (1752) have been interested in nominal inertia is that nominal inertia implies monetary non-neutrality. That is, nominal inertia implies that changes in monetary policy affect real macroeconomic variables like output or employment. In principle, money illusion could provide an explanation for the inertia of nominal prices and wages. However, the notion of money illusion seems to be thoroughly discredited in mainstream economics. Tobin (1972, p. 3), for example, described the negative attitude of most economic theorists towards money illusion as follows: 'An economic theorist can, of course, commit no greater crime than to assume money illusion.' The reason for this negative attitude is that money illusion contradicts basic rationality assumptions and does not nicely fit into the equilibrium mould of economics. As a consequence, economists have sought for explanations of nominal inertia that are based on the assumption of fully rational agents holding rational expectations. For example, factors like informational frictions (Lucas, 1972), staggering of contracts (e.g., Fischer, 1977; Taylor, 1979), and costs of price adjustment (Mankiw, 1985) have been invoked to explain nominal inertia in a fully rational framework.

The inertia of nominal prices and wages has been claimed to be an important phenomenon (see e.g., Akerlof et al., 1996; Kahn, 1997). However, despite the vast amount of empirical and theoretical literature on nominal inertia, very little is known about the *causes* of nominal inertia. One of the reasons for this lack of knowledge is that the empirical research strategies applied so far were inept to isolate the causes of nominal inertia. For example, Alan Blinder and his colleagues (1998, p. 3) ask: 'Why are wages and prices so 'sticky'? The abject failure of standard research methodology to make headway on this critical issue in the micro-foundations of macroeconomics motivated the unorthodox approach of the present study.' The 'unorthodox' approach chosen by Blinder and his colleagues is to ask managers about how and why they change prices. The unorthodox approach we choose is to conduct economic laboratory experiments. We argue that experimental methods allow to shed new light on this old and important issue. We develop an experimental framework to investigate whether money illusion causes nominal inertia. In particular, we investigate the adjustment of nominal prices after an anticipated monetary shock, in an environment in which firms face no exogenous obstacles to price adjustment whatsoever. Therefore, none of the rationality-based explanations for nominal inertia mentioned above applies. As a consequence, our investigation does not intend to question the potential relevance of these rationality-based explanations. However, our results do demonstrate the importance of money illusion, expectation formation, and strategic complementarity in understanding the causes of nominal inertia. The results suggest, in particular, that money illusion has prematurely been dismissed as a candidate explanation of nominal inertia.

2.1. Why Use Experimental Methods to Investigate Nominal Inertia?

In laboratory experiments, we observe the behavior of real people who are exposed to real economic incentives in a controlled environment. In what respect do experimental investigations have advantages over empirical investigations with field data? An obvious first advantage is the *correct measurement* of endogenous variables like prices and real economic activity. In contrast, the conclusions drawn from field studies investigating the real effects of monetary shocks appear to be extremely non-robust with respect to measurement problems (e.g., Belongia, 1996). Second, data that are crucial for many economic theories can be gathered in the laboratory but cannot be directly observed in the field. In our context *expectation data* are especially valuable. The third and most important advantage of the experimental method is *control over the environment and the information conditions*. The ability to control the environment has several implications. For example, truly *exogenous* monetary shocks can be implemented in the laboratory. In contrast, macroeconomic field studies are plagued by notorious causality problems. In the laboratory, the theoretical equilibrium values of the economy under study are known. Therefore, the observing experimentalist can distinguish between the equilibrium and out-of-equilibrium realizations of endogenous variables. This is a crucial advantage since nominal inertia is a disequilibrium phenomenon. In addition, we control information conditions, that is, we control what economic agents know about their economic environment and what they know about the information of other agents. As will be explained in Section 3, this allows us to implement an anticipated monetary shock.

Finally, *causal relations* can be established in an experiment through controlled *ceteris paribus* variations of the decision environment. The causes of nominal inertia can be isolated by changing only one aspect of the environment and by comparing nominal price adjustment in the respective treatments. Our main objective is to investigate whether money illusion is a cause of nominal inertia. As will be explained in the next section in more detail, money illusion means that behavior depends on whether the same objective situation is framed in nominal or in real terms. A particularly transparent example of money illusion arises if people behave differently when they receive payoff information in real or in nominal terms. Unfortunately, business life does not seem to provide examples in which the same objective situation is sometimes represented in nominal terms and sometimes in real terms. In fact, almost all business transactions involve nominal payoff information. Therefore, a major advantage of the experimental approach to the causes of nominal inertia is that the 'frame' is under the control of the experimenter. In particular, we implemented a treatment condition in which payoffs were represented in nominal terms, and a control condition in which payoffs were represented in real terms.

The above arguments show that experimental methods can be very useful for the examination of nominal inertia. We also would like to stress, however, that these methods are not a substitute for the analysis of field data. Laboratory experiments are, in our view, complements to the standard econometric techniques of the analysis of field data. Both methods should be used to increase our knowledge. Yet, due to the relative lack of experimental investigations so far, the marginal return from this method is likely to be high.[2]

3. MONEY ILLUSION AS AN EXPLANATION OF NOMINAL INERTIA

Section 3.1 discusses evidence from questionnaire studies on money illusion at the individual level. Section B explains under which conditions individual-level money illusion may have aggregate-level effects.

3.1. Money Illusion at the Individual Level

The term 'money illusion' has been used differently by various authors although the intuition on which the term is based seems to be rather similar.[3] The basic intuition says that if the *real* incentive structure, that is, the *objective* situation an individual faces, remains unchanged, the *real* decisions of an illusion-free individual do not change either. This intuition builds on two crucial assumptions: First, the objective function of the individual does not depend on nominal but only on real magnitudes. Second, people perceive that purely nominal changes do not affect their opportunity set. For example, people have to understand that an equiproportionate change in all nominal magnitudes leaves the real constraints unaffected. Some economists suspected that these assumptions do not always hold. For example, Irving Fisher (1928, p. 4) was convinced that ordinary people, in general, fail 'to perceive that the dollar, or any other unit of money expands or shrinks in value' after a monetary shock.

However, whether people are indeed able to 'pierce the veil of money' is an empirical question. Shafir, Diamond and Tversky (henceforth SDT, 1997) conducted questionnaire studies which indicate that frequently one or both

---

[2] We believe that the application of questionnaire methods can be very useful for a similar reason.
[3] For the different definitions of money illusion see Howitt (1989).

preconditions for the absence of money illusion are violated. Their results suggest that people's preferences as well as their perceptions of the constraints are affected by nominal values. Moreover, many people do not seem to be prone only to money illusion; they also expect that other people's preferences and decisions be affected by money illusion. Problem 1 of SDT's questionnaire study neatly illustrates these claims. SDT presented the following hypothetical scenario to two groups of respondents:

Consider two individuals, Ann and Barbara, who graduated from the same college a year apart. Upon graduation, both took similar jobs with publishing firms. Ann started with a yearly salary of $ 30 000. During her first year on the job there was no inflation, and in her second year Ann received a 2% ($ 600) raise in salary. Barbara also started with a yearly salary of $ 30 000. During her first year on the job there was 4% inflation, and in her second year Barbara received a 5% ($ 1500) raise in salary.

The respondents of group 1 were then asked the happiness question: '*As Ann and Barbara entered their second year on the job, who do you think was happier?*' Thirty-six percent thought that Ann was happier while 64 percent believed that Barbara was happier. This indicates that most subjects believed that preferences are affected by nominal variables because in real terms Ann does better of course.[4] The respondents of group 2 were asked the following question: '*As they entered their second year on the job, each received a job offer from another firm. Who do you think was more likely to leave the present position for another job?*' In line with the response to the happiness question, 65 percent believed that Ann, who is doing better in economic terms, is more likely to leave the present job. Thus, a majority believed that other people's decisions are affected by money illusion.

Since the absence of money illusion means that an individual's preferences, perceptions and, hence, choices of real magnitudes are not affected by purely nominal changes it is natural to view *money illusion as a framing effect*. From this viewpoint, an individual exhibits money illusion if the preferences or the perception of the constraints and the associated decisions depend on whether the same environment is represented in nominal or real terms. SDT's analysis is based on a large body of research in cognitive psychology that shows that alternative representations of the same situation may well lead to systematically different responses (Tversky and Kahneman, 1981, 1986). Representation effects seem to arise because people tend to adopt the particular frame that is presented and evaluate the options within this frame. Because some options loom larger in one representation than in another, an alternative framing of the same options can give rise to different choices.

SDT argue that people tend to have multiple representations but that the nominal representation is often *simpler and more salient*. They suggest that

---

[4] There was a third group of respondents who was asked whether Ann or Barbara is doing better in economic terms. Seventy-one percent answered that Ann is in fact doing better in economic terms.

people are generally aware of the difference between nominal and real values, but because money is a salient and *natural unit*, people often think of transactions predominantly in nominal terms.

Economists tend to question the relevance of results from questionnaire studies on two grounds. First, economists suspect that there may be considerable differences between what people say they would do in a hypothetical scenario and what they actually do when exposed to economic incentives. Second, from an economic viewpoint, it is not sufficient to show that money illusion prevails at the individual level, to conclude that money illusion will be of any importance at the aggregate level. For example, the individual-level effects of money illusion may cancel out with interaction and may therefore be irrelevant at the aggregate level. Experimental methods enable the researcher to address these objections. In experimental investigations the interaction between economic agents, which are exposed to economic incentives, can be studied.

3.2. Aggregate-Level Effects of Money Illusion and Strategic Complementarity

To understand why money illusion may have important aggregate-level effects, we need to introduce the concept of strategic complementarity. Strategic complementarity means that if other agents change the value of their action variable (e.g., prices), it is optimal for a rational agent to change the value of his action variable (e.g., his price) in the same direction. Technically speaking, strategic complementarity implies a positive slope of the reaction function. The intuition behind the concept is that rational agents have an incentive to 'follow the crowd'. It has been argued that strategic complementarity is an important characteristic of macroeconomic relations (Cooper and Haltiwanger, 1996), and it certainly is a natural property of price competition.

A standard theoretical result of the macroeconomic literature is that there is no nominal inertia if common knowledge of rationality prevails, if the monetary shock is anticipated and if price setters are free to change nominal prices at any time and at no cost. However, if one of these assumptions is relaxed, nominal inertia may prevail. For example, given strategic complementarity, a *small* group of non-rational price setters can have *large* effects on the adjustment process to equilibrium (Haltiwanger and Waldman, 1989). The intuition behind this theoretical result is that, because of strategic complementarity the rational agents partially imitate the behavior of the non-rational agents and thereby magnify the effects of the latter on the aggregate price level. However, this model relaxes the rationality assumption in a special manner. On the one hand, there are non-rational agents who do not optimally adjust their nominal prices to the monetary shock (for some unexplained reason). On the other hand, the rational agents in fact are assumed to be 'super-rational'. These agents are assumed to know how many non-rational agents there are and how these agents react to the shock. In addition, the super-rational agents are assumed to know how the other super-rational agents react to everybody else's pricing decisions. Note that being able to predict what everybody else does is a very difficult task. It requires, for example, being able to predict other peoples' predictions about what everybody else does. Therefore, the rationality requirements are still very high in this model.

Suppose that human decision-makers are only rational (but not super-rational). That is, human decision-makers may be able to choose a rational action given that they know what everybody else does, but they may not be able to perfectly predict what everybody else does. That is, strategic uncertainty may prevail. In particular, human decision-makers may be unable to perfectly predict how other human decision-makers adjust nominal prices to a monetary shock or how these other decision-makers predict again others to adjust prices. They may not be completely sure, for example, whether other agents suffer from money illusion. Therefore, they may assume with positive probability that some others suffer from money illusion and, as a result, they assume that others do not adjust fully to the shock. This belief, in turn, then induces the rational agents to adjust only imperfectly to a shock. An interesting aspect of this idea is that a mere belief about others' money illusion may cause nominal inertia even if not a single individual is, in fact, prone to money illusion. That is, given strategic complementarity, there may be important aggregate-level effects of money illusion even if individual-level money illusion is very small or non-existent.

4. EXPERIMENTAL INVESTIGATION

Section 4.1 provides a brief description of the basic design, and Section 4.2 explains the hypotheses. Section 4.3 presents the main results.

4.1. Design

In our experiment, $n = 4$ subjects are in the role of firms and simultaneously choose nominal prices in each of T consecutive periods. The firms are free to change nominal prices at no (menu) cost in every period. Price competition is characterized by strategic complementarity, that is, if an agent believes that his competitors increase their prices, it is optimal for the agent to increase his price, too. After the simultaneous pricing decision, each firm receives information about the aggregate price level (resulting from other firms' choices) and their own payoff. Firms take their decisions in a fully stationary environment, that is, there is no exogenous uncertainty whatsoever. The experiment has a pre-shock and a post-shock phase with a length of $T/2$ periods each. The pre-shock phase mainly serves to equilibrate the system. The post-shock phase serves to observe how inertial nominal prices adjust to the monetary shock in various treatment conditions (for details see Fehr and Tyran, 2001).

The real payoff of player i, π_i, depends on his own nominal price p_i, on the *average* price chosen by competing firms p_{-i} (i.e., the price level, excluding the choice of i), and on a nominal shift variable (the quantity of money M) in the following way: $\pi_i = \pi_i(p_i/p_{-i}, M/p_{-i})$. Thus, the real payoff remains unchanged if all prices and M change by the same percentage. Information about payoffs is given to subjects in payoff tables (payoff matrices). This is possible because for a given level of M the payoff depends only on p_i and p_{-i}. The payoff table shows the nominal or the real payoffs of a player for all feasible p_i-p_{-i}-combinations. Whether the payoff table shows the nominal or the real payoff depends on the treatment condition (see below). All players are fully informed about their own payoff table and the payoff tables of the other $n-1$ players in the group. The monetary shock is implemented by distributing new payoff tables, which are based on a smaller quantity of money. In particular, at the end of period $t = T/2$ it is publicly announced that all n firms receive new payoff tables. Again each player is informed about his own new payoff table and the new payoff table of the other $n-1$ players. By this procedure, we implement an *anticipated* monetary shock because the firms get the new tables (with sufficient time to study) before they have to take their decisions in $T/2 + 1$, they know the new payoff tables of the other firms and they know that others know this, etc. We implement a *negative* monetary shock because the new payoff tables are based on a quantity of money M_1 that is smaller than the previous quantity M_0 ($M_1 = M_0/3$). Finally, we implement an *exogenous* monetary shock because the firms get the new tables in $t = T/2$ irrespective of previous decisions. The parameters of the experiment imply a unique money-neutral equilibrium. Since the quantity of money falls by two-thirds, the equilibrium price level also falls by two-thirds. In particular, the average price taken over by all n firms falls from 18 (in the pre-shock equilibrium) to 6 (in the post-shock equilibrium).

To investigate whether money illusion is a cause of nominal inertia, we chose the following design (see Table 15.1). The first variation concerns the variation of the *representation of payoffs*. In the real representation, the payoff tables show *real* payoffs. That is, the numbers in the payoff table show how much the subjects will be paid at the end of a period for any feasible p_i-p_{-i}-combination. In the nominal representation, the payoff tables show nominal payoffs. To know what the corresponding real payoffs are, subjects must deflate nominal payoffs. That is, they must divide the nominal payoff shown in the table by the prevailing level of p_{-i}. Note that, with one exception, the payoff tables are completely identical in the two representations. In the nominal representation, all real payoffs are multiplied by the relevant average price p_{-i}, while in the real representation this is not the case. Before the beginning of the experiment we also instructed the subjects who participated in the nominal treatment how to calculate real payoffs from nominal payoffs. Subjects had to solve several control questions to make sure that they know how to perform these computations. In addition, subjects received a pocket calculator to facilitate such computations. All subjects solved all exercises successfully.

The second variation concerns *whether subjects have to form expectations* about the price choices of other firms (i.e., whether there is strategic uncertainty). In the 'human opponents' treatments, subjects know that they interact with $n-1$

Table 15.1. *Treatment conditions*

		Strategic uncertainty	
		Yes (Human opponents)	No (Computerized opponents)
Representation of payoffs	Nominal	NH ($N=44$ subjects in 11 groups)	NC ($N=24$ human subjects)
	Real	RH ($N=40$ subjects in 10 groups)	RC ($N=22$ human subjects)

other human subjects (see Table 15.1). Subjects participating in these treatment conditions have to indicate their expectations about the price level p_{-i} in each period. In the 'computerized opponents' treatments, subjects know that they play against $n-1$ computers, and they know how these computers are programmed. In particular, the computers are programmed to simulate 'superrational opponents.' Thus, each subject i knows for sure, that if i chooses price x, then the $n-1$ computers are going to choose prices that result in a price level p_{-i} of y. This means that there is no need for subjects to form expectations in the computerized treatments. A subject's task is reduced to an individual optimization problem.[5] The experimental parameters are such that if subject i knows where the equilibrium is, he or she has no incentive whatsoever not to choose the equilibrium.

4.2. Hypotheses

If one neglects disequilibrium play, as it is routinely done in rational expectations equilibrium models, there should be no nominal inertia in all four cells of Table 15.1. The reason is that these models assume money illusion and strategic uncertainty to be irrelevant since the full rationality of all agents is assumed to be common knowledge. Therefore, nominal prices should instantaneously and equiproportionately adjust to the anticipated monetary shock. As a consequence, the anticipated monetary shock should be perfectly 'neutral' (i.e., have no effect on the efficiency of the experimental economy) in all four treatments.

The deviation of post-shock nominal prices from equilibrium prices in the real representation with computerized opponents (RC) is a measure of individual-level irrationality that is unrelated to money illusion. For example, some subjects may be inattentive or be confused by the monetary shock. In this case, nominal prices will not instantaneously adjust to the nominal shock in cell RC.

---

[5] The rationality requirements are much higher to attain an equilibrium than for individual maximization as pointed out, e.g., by Arrow (1987). To attain the equilibrium involves 'an informational burden of an entirely different magnitude than simply optimizing at known prices.' (1987, p. 201).

The effect of strategic uncertainty is measured by the difference in adjustment speed between RH and RC. In both treatments, payoffs are represented in real terms. In RH, subjects have to form expectations about the effect of the monetary shock on other subjects' pricing decisions, whereas they don't have to do so in RC. If nominal prices are more inertial in RH than in RC, it must be because some subjects expected other subjects not to fully adjust nominal prices or because the presence of strategic uncertainty confuses some subjects.

The effect of individual-level money illusion is measured by the difference in adjustment speed between NC and RC. In both cases, subjects do not have to form expectations about the decisions of other firms. The only difference between these two treatments is the nominal vs. the real representation of payoffs. Therefore, the difference in adjustment speed between NC and RC measures how money illusion affects individual behavior, that is, it measures only individual-level money illusion. Any indirect effects of money illusion, that are due to the interaction of subjects with money illusion, or the interaction of rational subjects with subjects who suffer from money illusion, are ruled out in the NC condition.

The most interesting comparison is between NH and RH. In both treatments subjects have to form expectations about the pricing decisions of the other human subjects. The only difference between these treatments is the nominal vs. real representation of payoffs. In particular, the difference in adjustment speed between NH and RH measures the direct and indirect effects of money illusion.

4.3. Results

The main results are summarized in Figure 15.1. This figure shows average nominal prices in the four treatments. The data shown have been generated by the decisions of 130 subjects that earned $28 on an average. Each subject only participated in one of the four treatments. The first thing to notice is that prices equilibrated quite nicely to the pre-shock equilibrium level of 18 in all four treatments.

In the real representation with computerized opponents (RC), *100 percent of the subjects* (22 out of 22) *instantaneously and perfectly adjust* prices to the shock. Therefore, observed behavior is perfectly in line with the prediction of standard (macro-)economic theory. As a consequence of this perfect price adjustment, the anticipated monetary shock does not have any real economic impact effects, that is, anticipated money is perfectly 'neutral' in this case. We conclude, from this observation, that there is no noticeable confusion of subjects by the shock itself. However, it should be noted that the laboratory environment we implement is rather simple and easy to understand for subjects.

In the real representation with human opponents (RH), only 35 percent of the subjects (14 out of 40) instantaneously and perfectly adjust nominal prices to the shock, but most initial post-shock price choices are close to the equilibrium. The comparison of RC and RH shows that nominal prices are significantly more inertial if subjects have to form expectations than when they don't (see

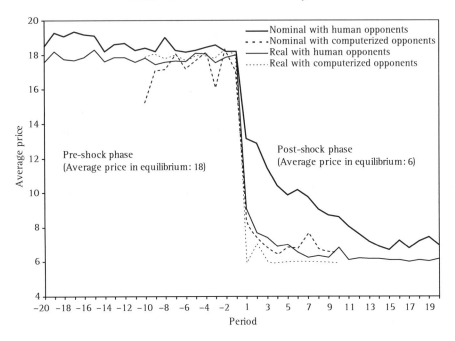

Figure 15.1. *The evolution of average prices*

Figure 15.1). A regression analysis shows that average prices in RH are significantly different from the equilibrium price level for two periods. We conclude
that our human subjects are not able to perfectly solve the problem of coordi-
nating expectations on the equilibrium. Put differently, the assumption of
common knowledge of rationality does not seem to hold.

In the nominal representation with computerized opponents (NC), 79 percent of
the subjects (19 out of 24) instantaneously and perfectly adjust prices to the
shock. Taken together, the results from the treatments with computerized
opponents indicate that there is only a small amount of money illusion at the
individual level, but that there is no individual-level irrationality beyond that.
Since price adjustment is only slightly slower in the NC than in the RC, we
conclude that individual-level money illusion does not cause pronounced
nominal inertia (compare the two dotted lines in Figure 15.1).

In the nominal representation with human opponents (NH) *nominal prices
adjust very inertially* to the monetary shock (see heavy and solid line in
Figure 15.1). In particular, in the first post-shock period, only 11 percent of the
subjects (5 out of 44) fully adjust nominal prices to the equilibrium level, and, as
a consequence, the nominal price level falls by less than half of the predicted
amount. According to our regression analysis, it takes 12 periods for full price
adjustment in NH, whereas nominal prices equilibrate already after two periods in
RH. The observed differences in adjustment speed in NH and RH also translate

into the different real effects of the monetary shock in the two treatments. For example, the average income loss is roughly twice as large in the NH as in the RH over the first ten post-shock periods. Since the adjustment of nominal prices is much more inertial in the NH than in the RH, we conclude that the direct and indirect effects of money illusion are an important cause of nominal inertia (compare the two solid lines in Figure 15.1). As a consequence, the anticipated monetary shock is far from being neutral in this environment.

A closer look at the expectations data reveals that the reason why nominal prices were much more sticky in the nominal representation (NH) than in the real representation (RH) is that expectations were much more sticky in NH than in RH. That is, subjects expected other subjects to choose high prices in the nominal representation. Because subjects act in an individually rational manner (more than 80 percent of subjects choose best replies to their expectations in NH and RH) and because of strategic complementarity, sticky expectations translate into sticky price choices.

4.3.1. *Asymmetric Effects of Positive and Negative Monetary Shocks*
So far, the results have shown that money illusion, in fact, causes nominal inertia and that the reason why it does is that price expectations were much stickier in the nominal than the real representation. But why were price expectations much stickier in the nominal representation? Since we implement a *negative* monetary shock, the equilibrium price level must fall. By definition, the high nominal payoffs prevail at high price levels. If subjects believed that the high nominal payoffs 'look attractive' to other subjects and if they believe that this causes other subjects to choose high prices in the post-shock phase, they rationally respond by choosing high prices in the post-shock phase. To test for this hypothesis, we implemented a *positive* monetary shock with human opponents (NH, RH). If our hypothesis about the cause of the stickiness of expectations is correct, prices should adjust much more quickly after the positive than after the negative shock. The reason is that with a positive shock, equilibrium price levels have to rise and therefore subjects have to adjust their price choices in the direction of high 'attractive' nominal payoffs. The experiments were run with additional 96 subjects and strongly confirm this hypothesis (see Fehr and Tyran, 2001, for details). We observe a pronounced *asymmetry* in nominal inertia, that is, a much quicker convergence to the equilibrium after a positive shock than after a negative shock in the NH. This finding also suggests that money illusion may provide a microfoundation for the apparently observed asymmetrical real economic effects of positive and negative monetary shocks (e.g., Cover, 1992; Peltzman, 2000).

4.3.2. *Does Strategic Complementarity Cause Nominal Inertia?*
The explanation provided above for why money illusion causes nominal inertia is based on the idea that money illusion systematically affects price expectations and the decision-makers react rationally to these expectations. Sticky expectations after the negative shock in NH translates into sticky price choices because of

strategic complementarity. According to this reasoning, strategic complementarity plays a key role in determining whether sticky expectations translate into aggregate-level effects of money illusion. To test for the role of strategic properties, we implemented a negative shock with a nominal representation (NH) and either strategic complements (a positive slope of the reaction function) or strategic substitutes (a negative slope of the reaction function). Rational agents expecting under-adjustment by illusion-prone agents tend to imitate the behavior of illusion-prone agents if strategic complements prevail, but to compensate for their behavior if strategic substitutes prevail. Therefore, subjects prone to money illusion should have a disproportionately large effect on the aggregate price level if strategic complements prevail but a disproportionately small effect if strategic substitutes prevail. Our results strongly support this hypothesis. We find that there is no nominal inertia and that the anticipated monetary shock is almost neutral if subjects' actions are strategic substitutes (see Fehr and Tyran, 2002, for the details).

5. SUMMARY AND CONCLUSION

In principle, money illusion is a candidate explanation of nominal inertia and, as a consequence, of the non-neutrality of money. However, mainstream economists have dismissed this 'psychological' explanation for two reasons. First, money illusion is rejected on a priori grounds, simply because it contradicts basic rationality assumptions of economics. Second, there was no convincing evidence for the existence and relevance of money illusion. Recently, however, Shafir et al. (1997) provided evidence from questionnaire studies suggesting that money illusion is an important phenomenon at the individual level. However, some economists tend to argue that the evidence from such questionnaire studies, for the existence of money illusion, is weak and irrelevant. It is weak because people have no real incentive to think about their decisions, and it is irrelevant because individual-level effects may wash out with interaction. Experimental methods allow addressing these criticisms. In experimental studies, the actual behavior of real people is observed under controlled conditions and these people are motivated by economic incentives. We developed an appropriate experimental design to investigate whether money illusion is a cause of nominal inertia. In particular, our design clearly isolates the aggregate-level behavioral effects of money illusion. Our results show that under conditions of strategic complementarity money illusion can have massive aggregate-level effects even if individual-level money illusion is small.

Strategic complementarity prevails if agents have an incentive 'to follow the crowd'. Strategic complementarity has been found to be characteristic of many macroeconomic relations, and it certainly is a natural property of price-setting decisions. Given strategic complementarity, rational agents have an incentive not to fully adjust nominal prices if they expect other agents not to (fully) adjust nominal prices after a monetary shock. Our results suggest that following a negative monetary shock, money illusion induces expectations of inertial price adjustment and that these 'sticky' price expectations translate into inertial pricing decisions if strategic complementarity prevails. Furthermore, the results indicate that money illusion induces asymmetric effects of positive and negative nominal shocks. In particular, price adjustment is much faster and real effects are much less pronounced after a positive than after a negative nominal shock. Finally, it is shown that strategic complementarity is a key element in understanding the causes of nominal inertia. In particular, we show that nominal inertia is much more pronounced if strategic complementarity prevails than if strategic substitutability prevails.

We believe that these results constitute important insights into the causes of nominal inertia, insights that seem almost impossible to achieve without controlled laboratory experiments. This method makes it possible to precisely identify those conditions under which standard equilibrium models are correct, and those conditions under which they fail to capture important economic forces and facts. Since strategic complementarity seems to be an important feature of reality (Cooper and Haltiwanger, 1996), we believe that those conditions, under which rational expectations equilibrium models provide the wrong guide for short- and medium-run price adjustment, should be taken seriously.

REFERENCES

Akerlof, G.A., Dickens, W.T., and Perry, G.L. (1996). The macroeconomics of low inflation. *Brookings Papers on Economic Activity, 1*, 1–76.

Arrow, K.J. (1987). Rationality of self and others in an economic system. In R.M. Hogarth and M.W. Reder (Eds.), *Rational choice: The contrast between economics and psychology* (pp. 201–15). Chicago: University of Chicago Press.

Belongia, M.T. (1996). Measurement matters: Recent results from monetary economics reexamined. *Journal of Political Economy, 104*(5), 1065–83.

Blinder, A.S., Canetti, E.D., Lebow, D.E., and Rudd, J.B. (1998). *Asking about prices. A new approach to understanding price stickiness.* New York: Russell Sage Foundation.

Cooper, R. and Haltiwanger, J. (1996). Evidence on macroeconomic complementarities. *Review of Economics and Statistics, 78*(1), 78–93.

Cover, J.P. (1992). Asymmetric effects of positive and negative money-supply shocks. *Quarterly Journal of Economics, 107*(4), 1261–82.

Davis, D.D. and Holt, C.A. (1993). *Experimental Economics.* Princeton: Princeton University Press.

Fehr, E. and Schmidt, K. (1999). A theory of fairness, competition and cooperation. *Quarterly Journal of Economics, 114*(3), 817–68.

—— and Tyran, J.-R. (2001). Does money illusion matter? *American Economic Review, 91*(5), 1239–62.

—— and —— (2002). *Does strategic complementarity cause nominal inertia?*, mimeo, Institute for Empirical Research in Economics, University of Zürich.

Fischer, S. (1977). Long-term contracts, rational expectations, and the optimal money supply rule. *Journal of Political Economy, 85*(1), 191–205.

Fisher, I. (1928). *The money illusion.* Toronto: Longmans.

Haltiwanger, J.C. and Waldmann, M. (1985). Rational expectations and the limits of rationality: An analysis of heterogeneity. *American Economic Review, 75*(3), 326–40.

—— and —— (1989). Rational expectations and strategic complements: The implications for macroeconomics. *Quarterly Journal of Economics, 104*(3), 463–84.

Hey, J.D. and Orme, C.D. (1994). Investigating generalizations of expected utility theory using experimental data. *Econometrica, 62*(6), 1291–326.

Hogarth, R.M. and Reder, M.W. (1987). Introduction. Perspectives from economics and psychology. In R.M. Hogarth and M.W. Reder (Eds.), *Rational choice: The contrast between economics and psychology* (pp. 1–23). Chicago: University of Chicago Press.

Howitt, P. (1989). Money illusion. In J. Eatwell, M. Milgate, and P. Newman (Eds.), *Money* (pp. 244–7). New York, London: W.W. Norton.

Hume, D. (1752). Of money; Of interest. Reprinted in E. Rotwein (Ed.) (1970), *Writings on Economics.* Madison: University of Wisconsin Press.

Kahn, S. (1997). Evidence of nominal wage stickiness. *American Economic Review, 88*(5), 993–1008.

Lucas, Jr., R.E. (1972). Expectations and the neutrality of money. *Journal of Economic Theory, 4*(2), 103–24.

Mankiw, N.G. (1985). Small menu costs and large business cycles: A macroeconomic model of monopoly. *Quarterly Journal of Economics, 100*(2), 529–37.

Peltzman, S. (2000). Prices rise faster than they fall. *Journal of Political Economy, 108*(3), 466–502.

Sansgruber, R. and Tyran, J.-R. (2002). A little fairness may induce a lot of redistribution in democracy. Mimeo, University of St. Gallen.

Shafir, E., Diamond, P.A., and Tversky, A. (1997). On money illusion. *Quarterly Journal of Economics, 112*(2), 341–74.

Shleifer, A. (2000). *Inefficient markets.* Oxford: Oxford University Press.

Taylor, J.B. (1979). Staggered wage setting in a macro model. *American Economic Review, 69*(2), 108–13.

Tobin, J. (1972). Inflation and unemployment. *American Economic Review, 62*(1), 1–18.

Tversky, A. and Kahneman, D. (1981). The framing of decisions and the psychology of choice. *Science, 211*, 453–8.

—— and —— (1986). Rational choice and the framing of decisions. *Journal of Business, 49*(4), 251–78.

Index